Popular Musicians

Popular Musicians

Volume 4
Sonny and Cher - ZZ Top
Indexes

Editor

Steve Hochman

Project Editor

McCrea Adams

SALEM PRESS
Pasadena, California   Hackensack, New Jersey

Managing Editor: Christina J. Moose
Project Editor: McCrea Adams
Acquisitions Editor: Mark Rehn
Research Supervisor: Jeffry Jensen
Production Editor: Yasmine A. Cordoba
Photograph Editor: Karrie Hyatt
Copy Editors: Lauren M. D'Andrea; Douglas Long
Research Assistant: Jun Ohnuki
Design and Layout: James Hutson

Library of Congress Cataloging-in-Publication Data

Popular Musicians / consulting editor, Steve Hochman ; project editor, McCrea Adams.
　　p.　cm.
　　Includes discographical references and index.
　　ISBN 0-89356-986-0 (set : alk. paper). — ISBN 0-89356-987-9 (vol. 1 : alk. paper). — ISBN 0-89356-988-7 (vol. 2 : alk. paper). — ISBN 0-89356-989-5 (vol. 3 : alk. paper). — ISBN 0-89356-990-9 (vol. 4 : alk. paper).
　　1. Musicians — Biography — Dictionaries.　　2. Musical groups — Dictionaries.
　I. Hochman, Steve,　1956-

ML105.P66　　1999
781.64'092'2—dc21　　　　　　　　　　　　　　　　　　　　　　　　　　　　99-11658
[B]　　　　　　　　　　　　　　　　　　　　　　　　　　　　　　　　　　　　　CIP

First Printing

Contents

Popular Musicians

Popular Musicians

Sonny and Cher / Cher

Sonny and Cher

MEMBERS: Sonny Bono (Salvatore Bono, 1935-1998), Cher (Cherilyn Sarkasian LaPier, b. 1946)
FIRST SINGLE RELEASE: "I Got You Babe," 1965

Cher

BORN: El Centro, California; May 20, 1946
FIRST SINGLE RELEASE: "All I Really Want to Do," 1965
MUSICAL STYLES: Rock and roll, pop

A married singing duo, Sonny and Cher enjoyed more enduring success than most pop acts and carved their own special niche in pop music history. In addition to the hit songs they recorded together, Sonny's many songs recorded by other acts, and their popular television show, Sonny and Cher are remembered for their fun-loving and unconventional but wholesome image during the so-called hippie era. After divorcing at the height of their popularity, they went on to unexpected successes in other fields. While Cher continued to record as a solo vocalist, she also won respect as a serious dramatic actress. Sonny meanwhile was embarked on a promising political career when his life was cut short by an accident.

Origins. With an actress mother who groomed her for the stage, Cher grew up in Southern California performing in musical events and plays, while dreaming of becoming a celebrity. Sonny—born in Detroit a decade earlier—moved to Southern California with his family and aspired to become a singer. He started writing songs at twelve and at twenty-two got a writing and producing job for a Los Angeles record company. A few years later he became an assistant to Phil Spector, then on the threshold of fame as a rock producer. His duties included hiring musicians and backup singers for recording sessions.

Accounts of how Sonny and Cher met differ, but by the early 1960's they were working together at recording sessions, in which Cher sang backup with such artists as the Ronettes, Crystals, and Righteous Brothers. Her first attempt at a single, "Ringo, I Love You" (under the name "Bonnie Jo Mason") flopped. In another solo recording session she asked Sonny to join her; together they cut Sonny's song "Baby Don't Go." It so impressed Spector that he bought into its publishing rights.

In 1963 Sonny and Cher tried to capitalize on the notoriety of the blockbuster film *Cleopatra* by performing as "Caesar and Cleo." After getting married in Tijuana, Mexico, on October 27, 1964, they reverted to their real names and signed with Atlantic Records' Atco subsidiary. Release of their single "I Got You Babe," which reached the number 1 position on *Billboard*'s singles chart in August, 1965, lifted them to stardom. They also had solid hits with "The Beat Goes On," "But You're Mine," "What Now My Love," "Little Man," and other songs, most of which were written by Sonny. Meanwhile, Cher never ceased to record as a solo act. In 1966 she had her own hit with "Bang Bang (My Baby Shot Me Down)."

Stardom. Sonny and Cher enjoyed about five years of rock stardom before their teenage audience began to erode. Several successful guest appearances on television variety shows in the late 1960's introduced them to an older audience, opening the way for them to headline on the adult nightclub circuit. Changing their act to project a more mature image, they continued to sing many of their old hits, adding witty repartee built around Cher's hip sarcasm and Sonny's self-deprecating humor.

After they hosted a successful late-summer variety show on CBS-TV in 1971, the network signed them to a regular series. In late December, *The Sonny and Cher Show* debuted. A hit from the start, *The Sonny and Cher Show* was broadly similar to CBS's cancelled *Smothers Brothers Comedy Hour*—most of whose production team it inherited. It mixed musical numbers (scored by Billy Barnes), skits, and stand-up comedy. Its sketches typically spoofed other shows, giving Cher scope to stretch her singing and acting skills. Using new video technology, the show often superimposed video images, allowing Sonny and Cher to play multiple parts simultaneously. Like the earlier Smothers Brothers' show, much of the new show's humor emerged from the good-natured repartee be-

Sonny and Cher, 1966 (AP/Wide World Photos)

ers, and regular performers. With a different female guest star appearing each week in Cher's old place, *The Sonny Comedy Review* lasted only thirteen weeks.

Meanwhile, CBS signed Cher to her own show. *Cher* debuted in February, 1975, six weeks after Sonny's show ended. Each episode began with Cher singing low from the shadows of a darkened stage; as the tempo rose, she was gradually revealed to the audience, always attracting attention in outfits that exposed her navel—a television first. *Cher* did well enough to be renewed but was cancelled the following January.

Never comfortable working alone, Cher announced that she would again team up with Sonny, although by then she was married to Gregg Allman of the Allman Brothers. In February, 1976, the new *Sonny and Cher Show* debuted on CBS—the first show ever to star a divorced couple. The first episode captured a large audience but later episodes gradually lost viewers. Lacking most of the routines and performers from Sonny and Cher's original show, it presented an obviously pregnant Cher forced to wear more modest outfits. Worse still, after delivering her second child Cher divorced Allman before the fall season began. The fun-loving chemistry of the old Sonny and Cher act was gone.

Solo Careers. Cancellation of *The Sonny and Cher Show* in August, 1977, forever ended Sonny and Cher's partnership. Sonny turned his attention to other kinds of entertainment work, including occasional acting roles, and opened successful restaurants in Los Angeles and in Palm Springs, where he was elected mayor in 1988. A few years later he was publicly ridiculed for making a bid for

tween its stars. Every episode ended with the couple singing "I Got You Babe."

Throughout those years, Sonny and Cher's growing television audiences helped their record sales, as both solo and duet acts. During their show's first season, their *Sonny & Cher Live* album went gold, and Cher's single "Gypsys, Tramps, and Thieves" topped the *Billboard* chart. Cher also scored number 1 hits in 1973 with "Half-Breed" and in 1974 with "Dark Lady."

In early 1974, several days before taping the last episode of *The Sonny and Cher Show*, Sonny filed for divorce. Despite the couple's marital problems, their show finished the season ranked number 8 overall. Shortly afterward, ABC signed Sonny to his own show, importing *The Sonny and Cher Show*'s format and most of its writers, produc-

the Republican nomination for U.S. senator, but he was elected to the House of Representatives in 1994. Just as he was winning respect for his work during his second term in Congress, he was killed in a skiing accident. His third wife, Mary Bono, was appointed to his vacated seat in Congress.

Meanwhile, Cher continued recording and performing in concerts with growing success. In 1979 another of her singles, "Take Me Home," hit number 1 on *Billboard*. The following year she toured with Black Rose and recorded an album with the band, *Black Rose*. She also launched new careers as a physical fitness expert and as a dramatic actress. Public interest in her music diminished somewhat during the 1980's, but her acting career gathered momentum. She was nominated for an Academy Award for her supporting role in the film *Silkwood* (1983) and won a Best Actress Academy Award for her lead role in *Moonstruck* (1987). Afterward, her musical career began reviving. Her 1987 album, *Cher*, went gold, and "I Found Someone" made the singles chart in 1988.

—*R. Kent Rasmussen*

SELECT DISCOGRAPHY

Sonny and Cher

■ SINGLES

"I Got You Babe," 1965
"Laugh at Me," 1965 (Sonny solo)
"Baby Don't Go," 1965
"The Beat Goes On," 1967
"All I Ever Need Is You," 1971

■ ALBUMS

Look at Us, 1965
Baby Don't Go, 1965
In Case You're in Love, 1967
Sonny and Cher Live, 1971
All I Ever Need Is You, 1972
Mama Was a Rock and Roll Singer, Papa Used to Write All Her Songs, 1973

Cher

■ SINGLES

"All I Really Wanna Do," 1965
"Bang Bang (My Baby Shot Me Down)," 1966
"You Better Sit Down Kids," 1967
"Gypsies, Tramps, and Thieves," 1971
"Half-Breed," 1973

"Dark Lady," 1974
"I Found Someone," 1988
"After All," 1989 (with Peter Cetera)
"If I Could Turn Back Time," 1989

■ ALBUMS

All I Really Want to Do, 1965
Cher, 1966
With Love, Cher, 1967
Backstage, 1968
3614 Jackson Highway, 1969
Cher, 1971
Foxy Lady, 1972
Half-Breed, 1973
I'd Rather Believe in You, 1976
Cherished, 1977
Take Me Home, 1979
Prisoner, 1979
Cher, 1987
Love Hurts, 1991
It's a Man's World, 1996

SELECT AWARDS

Academy Award for Best Actress for *Moonstruck*, 1988 (Cher)

SEE ALSO: Allman Brothers Band, The; Righteous Brothers, The; Ronettes, The.

For the Record

After recording "I Got You Babe" with Cher, Sonny eagerly sent the tape to Atlantic Records. Confident that the song would become a hit, he was stunned when a company official was more interested in the B-side tune, "It's Gonna Rain." To prevent Atlantic from putting "I Got You Babe" on the B-side, Sonny persuaded a Los Angeles disk jockey to play it repeatedly until it was proved it could be a smash.

§

In 1965 Sonny and Cher had five top-twenty songs on the *Billboard* chart at once, a feat duplicated only by Elvis Presley and the Beatles.

Soundgarden

ORIGINAL MEMBERS: Kim Thayil (b. 1960), Hiro Yamamoto (b. 1961), Chris Cornell (b. 1964)
OTHER MEMBERS: Scott Sundquist, Hunter "Ben" Shepherd (b. 1968), Matt Cameron (b. 1962), Jason Everman (b. 1967)
FIRST ALBUM RELEASE: *Screaming Life*, 1987 (EP)
MUSICAL STYLES: Alternative, punk rock, heavy metal

The Seattle music scene went through a transformation during the mid-1980's when bands began incorporating various musical styles and genres into their songs. Disregarding stereotypical definitions of heavy metal and punk rock, Soundgarden absorbed elements of many genres of music and created their own unique sound.

The Beginning. Kim Thayil (guitar) and Hiro Yamamoto (bass) founded Soundgarden in Seattle in 1984 after moving from Chicago. Thayil

Soundgarden (Paul Natkin)

acquired a degree in philosophy from the University of Washington while playing in the band. His musical interests began developing very early, and he started playing guitar at eight. Chris Cornell, a Seattle native, played drums in the early days of Soundgarden before becoming the vocalist for the group. Drummer Scott Sundquist was replaced in 1987 with Matt Cameron, a native of San Diego, California, whose credits include the song "Puberty Love" from the 1978 motion picture *Attack of the Killer Tomatoes.*

In 1986, Soundgarden contributed three songs to *Deep Six*, a recording that collected the works of six prominent Seattle bands: Soundgarden, Green River, SkinYard, the Melvins, Malfunkshun, and U-Men. Rereleased in 1994 as a classic from the postpunk era, the original effort worked to garner attention and respect for the Seattle music scene, which had taken a distinctly alternative turn. These bands were known as the "Deep Six" because of the underground nature of the changing Seattle scene. Soundgarden tracks on the album are "All Your Lies," "Tears to Forget," and "Heretic."

Early Success. Cornell's girlfriend, Susan Silver, became the band's manager in 1987. Two EPs were released during 1987 and 1988: *Screaming Life* on SST Records and *Fopp* on the Sub Pop label. The band's first single, "Hunted Down," attracted attention on a large scale. Soundgarden released the album *Ultramega OK* in November of 1988 on the SST label. Within months, A&M Records had signed the band. In 1990, Soundgarden released *Louder than Love*, which had a tremendous impact on pop music for the next several years.

Jason Everman, formerly of Nirvana, replaced Yamamoto in 1990 after Yamamoto decided to pursue graduate studies (he

For the Record

The name of this Seattle group has a peculiarly local origin. It is named after an outdoor metal sculpture in Seattle called the "Soundgarden" because of the sounds made by wind blowing through its metal parts.

later joined the Seattle band Truly, who recorded two albums for Capitol Records). Before the end of the year, Everman quit and was replaced by bass guitarist Ben Shepherd, who had left the Seattle punk rock band March of Crimes. By this point, Soundgarden had created a niche for itself on the local scene unmatched by any other band.

The 1990's. After touring with Guns n' Roses in 1991, Soundgarden began to gain more national and international followers. The album *Badmotorfinger* hit the charts in 1992 and went platinum in 1993. In 1994, Soundgarden released its third major effort on A&M Records, *Superunknown*, which debuted on the U.S. charts at number 1. Before the end of the year, the album had sold over three million copies. Accolades and awards continued to accumulate for the band as Soundgarden picked up Grammys for their songs "Black Hole Sun" and "Spoonman."

Down on the Upside was produced by the band members themselves and was released on A&M Records in 1996, only to be followed by an announcement in early 1997 that the band was dissolving after thirteen years of hard work. In direct contrast to most band breakups, Soundgarden opted out of the music scene at the top of their careers. Drummer Cameron went back on the road almost immediately in the summer of 1998 with the band Pearl Jam.

Notwithstanding the demise of the band, A&M Records released *A-Sides* in November of 1997. This album chronicled the evolution of Soundgarden. By including early releases and later hits, *A-Sides* provided a ready reference of Soundgarden's musical history. —*Donna Addkison Simmons*

SELECT DISCOGRAPHY
■ ALBUMS
Screaming Life, 1987 (EP)
Fopp, 1988 (EP)
Ultramega OK, 1988
Louder than Love, 1989
Badmotorfinger, 1991
Superunknown, 1994
Down on the Upside, 1996
A-Sides, 1997

SELECT AWARDS
MTV Video Music Awards Best Metal/Hard Rock Video for "Black Hole Sun," 1994
Grammy Awards for Best Hard Rock Performance for "Black Hole Sun" and for Best Metal Performance for "Spoonman," 1994

SEE ALSO: Guns n' Roses; Nirvana; Pearl Jam.

The Specials

ORIGINAL MEMBERS: John "J. B." "Brad" Bradbury, Jerry Dammers (b. 1954), "Sir" Horace "Gentleman" Panter, Lynval Golding (b. 1951), Terry Hall (b. 1959), Roddy "Radiation" Byers, Neville Staple
OTHER MEMBERS: Mark Adams, Adam Birch, Silverton Hutchinson, Aitch Hyatt, others
FIRST ALBUM RELEASE: *The Specials*, 1979
MUSICAL STYLES: Rock and roll, ska

The Specials helped establish the ongoing fascination in Britain with a fusion of Jamaican ska of the 1960's (a proudly working-class dance music) with punk and other urban British styles. The Specials were always loosely organized, enjoying only a very brief period (1979-1981) of cohesion as a recognizable band. The Specials underwent numerous changes in name and drastic changes in personnel (most notably the substitution of John Bradbury for Silverton Hutchinson on drums and later the defection of Lynval Golding, Neville Staple, and Terry Hall). During the late 1970's and early 1980's, the band was an influential voice in British music through their distinctive sound, the formation of the 2-Tone Records label, and their heroic efforts to promote racial harmony in England and abroad.

Forming the Band. The band eventually known as the Specials formed in Coventry, England, in 1978. The band's membership has always been interracial. The first incarnation was called the Automatics. After learning that another band of that name was starting to make records, they went through a host other names. In 1979, Hutchinson was replaced by Bradbury as the band's drummer (although Hutchinson can be heard on a few tracks released later on *Dawning of a New Era*), and Staple joined as a second vocalist. At this time, the band gained considerable attention opening on tour for the Clash.

Following the tour, the band settled at last on the name the Specials. They formed their own record label called 2-Tone Records. The name refers to the interracial nature of the band and its commitment to promoting harmonious race relations. They recorded their first single, "Gangsters," in July, 1979. It was a tremendous hit and reached number 6 on the British charts. With this success, 2-Tone Records signed with Chrysalis Records, forming a prosperous partnership. The small label was used to sign other ska bands, including the English Beat, Madness, and the Selector.

Second-Wave Ska. With the release of their first album, *The Specials* (produced by Elvis Costello), the band took a central role in an international revival of interest in Jamaican ska. Historians of the style referred to this revival as ska's second wave. The album contained the hit single "Gangsters" along with fourteen new songs, two of which also became hits as singles. "A Message to You Rudy" reached number 10 on the British charts, and "Too Much Too Young," a song with a pointed procontraception message, reached number 1. "Concrete Jungle" also offered a direct social message by calling attention to racially motivated crime in England's inner cities. In an appealing and plaintive tone, lead singer Hall gave voice to the kind of uncertainty and frustration stemming from the racially motivated violence that plagued England's younger generations living in working-class neighbor-

For the Record

The Specials may hold a record for having recorded or toured under more names than any other group. Their names have included the Automatics, the Jaywalkers, the Hybrids, the Coventry Automatics, the Special AKA the Automatics, the Special AKA, and the Specials.

hoods. The song opened with these lyrics: "I'm going out tonight/ Don't know if I'll be all right/ Everyone wants to hurt me/ There's heavy danger in the city/ Concrete jungle: The animals are after me/ Concrete jungle: It ain't safe on the streets." While social messages permeated the Specials's songs, the general tone of the band was upbeat. Even the most despairing social commentaries, such as "Concrete Jungle," were presented in the form of lively dance songs.

The distinctive sound achieved not only by the Specials but also by other ska bands depends on characteristic rhythmic and metric features. The meter is always divisible into four beat units, and the tempo of their songs is usually rather fast. The drums and bass generally stay off the odd-numbered beats, creating a weak downbeat and strong offbeats. Lynval Golding and Roddy "Radiation" Byers (the Specials's guitar players) do a superb job of emphasizing only the afterbeats by creating a feeling of always being a little late. Taken together, these rhythmic and metric elements give the Specials a sound that virtually demands dancing. Skanking, a vigorous dance characterized by bent elbows and knees, remains the preferred dance associated with ska. Ska bands usually feature a horn section. On their first album, the Specials employed Rico Rodriguez on trombone and Dick Cuthell on coronet. Rodriguez distinguished himself with several superb solos.

Their second album, *More Specials* (1979), lacked the tight and upbeat punch that made *The Specials* one of the most influential debut albums of the late 1970's. Nevertheless, it contained three hit songs that soared on the British charts: "Do Nothing" reached number 4, "Rat Race" reached number 5, and "Stereotypes" reached number 6 in 1981. On this album, Rodriguez and Cuthell returned on horns and were complemented by Lee "Kix" Thompson's and Paul Heskatt's blistering saxophone playing.

Some of the band's best songs never found their way onto albums. The Specials's most commercially successful song, "Ghost Town," offers a fine case in point. Released in 1981, "Ghost Town" became a number 1 hit in England and was backed by a superb video. At the time, terrible economic depression gripped England's large cities. To a haunting accompaniment, Staple intoned: "This town is coming like a ghost town/ All the clubs are being closed down." Earlier, the band's anti-Margaret Thatcher song "Maggie's Farm" had reached number 4 in the United Kingdom and established the band's unmistakable working-class sensibility.

Fragmentation. Just as the band was attaining international success, it effectively broke up. Golding, Hall, and Staple splintered to form the band Fun Boy Three. Jerry Dammers tried to keep the Specials functioning under the name the Special AKA. He scored two hits with his highly politicized songs "Racist Friend" and "Nelson Mandela." The latter was featured at Mandela's Seventieth Birthday Party concert held at London's Wembley Stadium 1988.

During the 1990's, ska enjoyed its third wave of popularity. The Specials were by no means central to this revival. Their first return to recording was a collaboration with Desmond Dekker on the album *King of Kings*. In 1996, the band reformed to record *Today's Specials*, an album revealing more soul influences and a softening of the band's ska roots in favor of reggae. This album saw the reunion of Golding, Staple, and Byers. The band was rounded out by three newcomers. —*Michael Lee*

SELECT DISCOGRAPHY
■ SINGLES
"Gangsters," 1979
"Maggie's Farm," 1981
"Ghost Town," 1981

■ ALBUMS
The Specials, 1979
More Specials, 1980
In the Studio, 1984 (as the Special AKA)
King of Kings, 1993 (with Desmond Dekker)
Today's Specials, 1996

SEE ALSO: English Beat, The.

The Spice Girls

ORIGINAL MEMBERS: Melanie "Scary Spice" Brown (b. 1975), Geri "Ginger Spice" Halliwell (b. Geraldine Sjovik, 1972), Melanie "Sporty Spice" Chisholm (b. 1974), Victoria "Posh Spice" Addams (b. 1974), Emma "Baby Spice" Bunton (b. 1976)
FIRST ALBUM RELEASE: *Spice,* 1996
MUSICAL STYLE: Pop

Taking their name from the expression Variety Is the Spice of Life, the Spice Girls began their careers espousing three themes: the importance of imperfect individuality, the motto of Girl Power, and the presentation of a personable song-and-dance act aimed at young female fans. In early interviews, the members defined Girl Power as being true to oneself, having fun, and having a positive attitude. These attributes, combined with infectious recordings, humorous videos, and light-hearted harmonies, made the Spice Girls the most successful British pop band since the Beatles.

Getting Together. The original Spice Girls— Brown, Chisholm, Addams, and Halliwell—came together in 1994 after answering an advertisement by Trinity Studios seeking actors and singers. After passing the auditions, the girls were placed under the guidance of manager Chris Herbert and producer Ian Lee. Originally called Touch after the expression You Can Look but You Can't Touch, songwriter Tim Hawes allegedly created the name Spice Girls after crafting the song "Sugar and Spice." After rehearsals, the group put on shows at Knaphill Studios for local politicians.

In March of 1995, the girls reportedly stormed out of Trinity without explanation and lived together in a house in Maidenhead, Bercanshire, England. Becoming a quintet after recruiting Emma Bunton, the group set about organizing their image and synthesizing their various tastes and personalities. To avoid imitating previous girl groups, they stressed individuality by not dressing alike and not dancing in tandem. They created the gimmick of sharing the Spice surname with appropriate first names. Former commercial model Halliwell became Ginger Spice, emphasizing her sex appeal, and Brown was dubbed Scary Spice for her outspokenness. The stylish Addams became Posh Spice for her interest in glamour, and ballet-trained soccer fan Melanie Chisholm became Sporty Spice. A professional entertainer for most of her life and a trained karate expert, Bunton, the youngest of the group, was dubbed Baby Spice.

Fast Success. In May, 1995, the act began seeking attention from record companies after signing with manager Simon Fuller. After some competition among record companies, Virgin Records signed the group later that year and issued their first single, "Wannabe." Accompanied by their tongue-in-cheek video for the record, the song had immediate success in thirty-two countries, despite being banned for overt sexuality in various Southeast Asian countries. This success led to numerous media comparisons between the girls and British band the Beatles, who had previously been the most successful musical phenomenon in history.

"Wannabe" entered U.S. *Billboard* charts at number 11, tying a record for highest debut position by a new act. The band immediately flew to Hollywood, California, and began filming their second video, "Say You'll Be There," in California's Mojave Desert.

Derision. After the release of their first album, *Spice* (1996), critics began to mock and criticize

The Spice Girls (Reuters/Jerry Lampen/Archive Photos)

the group extensively, comparing them unfavorably with previous female bands such as Wilson Phillips. Reviewers noted that the group's music was clearly derivative of American popular music and complained that the singers' English accents were only apparent in interviews and spoken word sections of their shows. However, while being compared to such juvenile acts as the Teenage Ninja Mutant Turtles, the Spice Girls' success led to one of the most lucrative merchandising campaigns in music history, as the Spice Girls marketed their names with magazines, potato chips, body fragrances, and action figures.

Setting Records. On April 12, 1997, the Spice Girls made their U.S. television debut on *Saturday Night Live* and the subsequent month flew to Cannes, France, to announce plans for their forthcoming film before appearing in South Africa with South African president Nelson Mandela. In November, they issued their second album, *Spiceworld*, which yielded their sixth hit video in two years, "Spice Up Your Life." By year's end, the group was the globe's number 1 recording act, *Spiceworld* had sold over twenty million copies, and the group had the best-selling debut album in history. With their single "Too Much," the Spice Girls became the first act to ever have six consecutive number 1 songs in England. In December, 1997, *Billboard* magazine named them Best New Artists of the Year and named *Spiceworld* Best Album.

In January, 1998, the *Spiceworld* film was released. Critics quickly complained the group stole scenes from other films and claimed the motion picture was more a variety show than a film. Other problems followed, including the group being booed off the stage at galas in Barcelona and Madrid, Spain. In May, 1998, the Spice Girls toured Norway as a quartet shortly before Halliwell announced she was leaving the group.

—*Wesley Britton*

SELECT DISCOGRAPHY
■ ALBUMS
Spice, 1996
Spiceworld, 1997

SEE ALSO: En Vogue; Go-Go's, The; Monkees, The; Supremes, The; Village People, The.

The Spinners

ORIGINAL MEMBERS: Bobby Smith (b. 1946), Pervis Jackson (b. 1938), Henry Fambrough (b. 1935), Billy Henderson (b. 1939), George W. Dixon (1909-1994)
OTHER MEMBERS: Edgar "Chico" Edwards, G. C. Cameron, Philippe Wynne (1941-1984), John Edwards
FIRST ALBUM RELEASE: *Party: My Pad! After Surfin*, 1963
MUSICAL STYLES: Rhythm and blues, pop

Pervis Jackson, Billy Henderson, and Henry Fambrough began singing together while still in elementary school in the early 1950's. In 1955, while at Ferndale High School (Detroit, Michigan), they were joined by George Dixon and became the Domingoes. One of the first groups to incorporate dance routines into their musical performances, they were discovered by producer Harvey Fuqua around 1961. The renamed Spinners had one hit with Tri-Phi records ("That's What Girls Are Made For," 1961) but languished when the label merged with Motown. Although the Spinners had a number of rhythm-and-blues Top-20 hits between 1965 and 1970, they were never considered a major act at Motown and were therefore underproduced.

A New Label. The Spinners came into their own with a move to Atlantic Records in 1972. Always considered a secondary act by a Motown label that had a full stable of stars, the Spinners were courted by Stax and Avco before taking Aretha Franklin's advice to sign with her label, Atlantic. The first single, "I'll Be Around," quickly jumped to number 3 on the pop charts. Producer Thom Bell and lead singer Philippe Wynne helped create a distinctive pop, rhythm-and-blues sound that produced eight Top-20 singles, including their only number 1 pop hit, "Then Came You" (1974), with Dionne Warwick.

At the peak of their popularity, between 1972 and 1976, the Spinners produced five gold albums and five Top-10 pop hits, including "Then Came You," "I'll Be Around" (number 3, 1972), "Could It Be I'm Falling in Love," (number 4,

For the Record

The Spinners were extremely popular in the United Kingdom, where they were known as the Detroit Spinners in order to distinguish them from the British group the Spinners. "Working My Way Back to You" (1979), their first hit after John Edwards became lead singer, went to number 1 in the United Kingdom.

1972), "They Just Can't Stop It (the Games People Play)" (number 5, 1975), and "The Rubberband Man" (number 2, 1976). *New and Improved Spinners* (1974) and *Pick of the Litter* (1975) both hit the Top 10.

New Vocalist. After Wynne's departure for a solo career in 1977, John Edwards fronted the band. They produced two Top-10 pop singles ("Working My Way Back to You," 1979, and "Cupid/I've Loved You for a Long Time," 1980). Although they continued to produce records throughout the 1980's and into the 1990's, they never managed to recapture the popular magic of the Wynne years. The Spinners briefly returned to the charts in 1995 when rapper Rappin' 4-Tay used the Spinners' original music and chorus for his own version of "I'll Be Around."

—*John Powell*

SELECT DISCOGRAPHY

■ ALBUMS
Spinners, 1973
Mighty Love, 1974
Spinners Live! 1975
Yesterday, Today and Tomorrow, 1977
Spinners 8, 1977
The Best of the Spinners, 1978 (compilation)
Dancin' and Lovin', 1979
Labor of Love, 1981
Grand Slam, 1983
Down to Business, 1989
The Very Best of the Spinners, 1993 (compilation)

SEE ALSO: Warwick, Dionne.

Bruce Springsteen

BORN: Freehold, New Jersey; September 23, 1949
FIRST ALBUM RELEASE: *Greetings from Asbury Park, N.J.*, 1973
MUSICAL STYLES: Rock and roll, pop, folk

One of the most acclaimed performers in rock-and-roll history, Bruce Springsteen is the American hometown boy made good. Hailed in the mid-1970's as rock's savior, by the mid-1980's he had become widely recognized as its most distinguished practitioner. With a series of consistently brilliant albums and countless inspiring live performances, Springsteen helped to revitalize the rock genre and earned a place in its pantheon.

Jersey Boy. Born in 1949 in Freehold, New Jersey (a region that would figure in many of his songs), Springsteen experienced a fairly typical childhood and home life; however, his relations with his father, Douglas Springsteen, were often strained. An average student, Springsteen enrolled in a vocational school but soon dropped out. His musical drive and abilities were readily apparent at an early age. Usually shy and a loner, Springsteen's way of opening up and gaining the self-confidence he lacked was through music. "Miami" Steve Van Zandt (guitar) and Clarence Clemons (saxophone) were some of his early bandmates and would later become vital parts of Springsteen's E Street Band.

By the early 1970's Springsteen had decided to make his living with his music. This disappointed and frustrated his father, who did not believe that such a thing was possible. Springsteen hired manager Mike Appel to represent him. (Springsteen did not realize at the time that, in the deal, he was giving up rights to his songs and allowing Appel to collect a hefty part of his royalties.) Appel got him an audition with John Hammond, Sr., of Columbia Records. Hammond was a legendary talent scout who had previously signed, among others, Bob Dylan, Aretha Franklin, and Pete Seeger. Springsteen, acoustic guitar in hand, played for Hammond and walked out of the office with a record contract. Springsteen released his first album, *Greetings from Asbury Park, N.J.*, in 1973.

While it was not commercially successful, it caught the attention of critics, who immediately began comparing Springsteen to other respected folk-rockers and singer-songwriters such as John Prine and even Bob Dylan. (The album's first track, "Blinded by the Light," would become a hit for the Manfred Mann Earth Band three years later.)

The Wild, the Innocent, and the E Street Shuffle, released in November of 1973, was the first album to feature the E Street Band. For this album it was composed of Gary Tallent, Clarence Clemons, Danny Federici, David Sancious, and Vini "Mad Dog" Lopez. The wistful "4th of July, Asbury Park (Sandy)" was perhaps the song that shared the closest kinship with his debut album, while "The E Street Shuffle," with its use of horns, somewhat resembles the sound of the group Chicago. By far the album's most well-known track is "Rosalita (Come Out Tonight)," a rollicking street scene painted in song that epitomizes the energy for which Springsteen would become famous. It is one of Springsteen's most enduring songs, and for many years he used it as the closer for his live shows.

Neither of his first two albums sold very well, and it is said that Columbia considered dropping him from their roster. Changes occurred in the band between the second and third albums, with Sancious leaving and both original drummer Lopez and then replacement drummer Ernest "Boom" Carter leaving as well. Springsteen's live shows, however, were becoming well-known in the Northeast for their excitement. A respected rock critic, Jon Landau, came to see a Springsteen show in early 1974 and was dazzled; in Boston's *Real Paper*, he wrote the oft-quoted line, "I have seen rock & roll future and its name is Bruce Springsteen."

Born to Run. Interest in Springsteen began to grow, and he prepared to record his next album. More personnel changes had occurred in the band: Springsteen brought in old friend Van Zandt on guitar and hired a proficient new pianist, Roy Bittan, and a solid, steady drummer, Max Weinberg. Bittan, Weinberg, Tallent, and Clemons formed the core of the E Street Band that would remain with Springsteen for the next ten years.

While critical acclaim and recognition for his energetic live shows was increasing, he still was not widely known beyond New Jersey, New York, Philadelphia, and Boston. The third album would be a critical one for Springsteen in many ways.

Springsteen wanted a heavily produced, densely packed sound reminiscent of producer Phil Spector, but in the studio things were not coming together. He eventually sought assistance from Landau, with whom he had become friendly since Landau's glowing review. Landau was brought on board to assist with the production of *Born to Run*, a situation which quickly caused Appel, who had produced the first two albums, to feel that he was being superseded by Landau. Landau tightened up song arrangements and kept work in the recording studio moving along. Springsteen had intended to make a guitar-heavy album, but it proved to feature Bittan's piano work prominently. When *Born to Run* was released in October of 1975, Springsteen appeared simultaneously on the covers of *Time* and *Newsweek*, and the album received rave reviews. Opening with "Thunder Road" and closing with "Jungleland," the album was a celebration of rock and roll, with lyrics by turns jubilant and reflective. He and the band embarked on a U.S. tour, buoyed by their newfound fame.

Dark Times Coming. Before he could capitalize further on his new success, however, Springsteen learned that Appel was planning to prevent Landau's involvement with his next album. Springsteen filed a massive lawsuit against Appel in July, 1976, charging him with fraud and breach of trust. The lawsuit kept Springsteen out of the studio and off the road at a critical time in his career. The only songs he could bring himself to finish were for other people, most notably "Because the Night" for Patti Smith.

Springsteen testified in court that the emotional stress had so impaired him that no amount of money could compensate for the loss he would sustain if he were not allowed to work with Landau. According to Springsteen, Landau was the only one who could take the jumbles that Springsteen furiously produced and turn them into usable songs. The lawsuit finally ended in 1977 in

Springsteen's favor. He, Landau, and the band quickly returned to the studio, releasing *Darkness on the Edge of Town* in 1978.

Darkness on the Edge of Town showed evidence that the lawsuit had affected Springsteen's music. Where his early albums had told stories of summer love and boardwalks, *Darkness on the Edge of Town* dealt with such subjects as the hardships of the working life and father-son conflicts. The relationship between Springsteen and his father was a common theme of his songs, and Springsteen often freely discussed it during his concerts. Springsteen would comment ironically that his father still suggested it "wasn't too late to take classes at community college" and make something of himself. "Adam Raised a Cain" explored these volatile times with an angry passion, while "Factory" was a tribute to his father and his blue-collar working life. Springsteen's touring during this time cemented his reputation as one of rock's greatest live acts. It would be two years before Springsteen would release another album or tour again. His energy would be devoted to a project that eventually encompassed a double album, *The River.*

The River (1980) paired songs against each other, exploring the landscapes of working people's lives. Though it contained uptempo songs such as "Cadillac Ranch," the album had a darker side, reflecting on life's injustices. The album ended with "Wreck on the Highway," a song in which a man wrestles with his own mortality and the fear of leaving a loved one behind after witnessing a deadly car wreck.

Springsteen toured again, drawing his biggest audiences ever, and began performing benefit concerts for factory workers losing their jobs. He also participated in the famous *No Nukes* antinuclear protest concerts of 1979. Always working, Springsteen soon began recording tracks for his next album. Recording at home, playing an acoustic guitar into a tape deck, Springsteen created what many consider to be one of rock's masterpieces.

The 1982 album *Nebraska* painted a haunting, stark landscape of an America that Springsteen could not ignore. It is hard to imagine another commercial artist who would have dared to release a decidedly noncommercial album while poised on the edge of superstardom, but

Bruce Springsteen (Lissa Wales)

For the Record

Springsteen spent weeks debating whether to release *Nebraska* based on his original recordings, and carried the master cassette tape in his back pocket, unprotected. Because of this, mastering *Nebraska* was so difficult that it was nearly released on cassette only.

Springsteen believed in following his instincts. One of rock's most naked albums, the songs tell the story of mass murderer Charles Starkweather (from Starkweather's point of view) and other dark stories.

Glory Days. After an acoustic tour, Springsteen and the E Street Band returned to the studio and recorded what would be the biggest album of their career, 1984's *Born in the U.S.A.* While some of the songs dated from the *Nebraska* sessions, the rest of the album was new. At Landau's suggestion, the songs were made more pop-sounding and radio friendly through the use of a more polished sound—including Springsteen's first use of synthesizers. The technique worked, launching Springsteen into huge stadium tours for the first time. He also appeared in videos for the first time. The album also thrust Springsteen into the political spotlight via President Ronald Reagan. Reagan decide to espouse Springsteen as an example of the conservative, patriotic American. Reagan had no idea that the song "Born in the U.S.A.," far from being jingoistic, was an angry protest over the way veterans had been treated during and after the Vietnam War.

Yet despite the angry tone of the title track, *Born in the U.S.A.* was essentially a sketchbook of the American dream and way of life, both good and bad. The *Born in the U.S.A.* tour lasted for fifteen months and pushed Springsteen into the forefront of rock and roll. Springsteen also married during this time, settling down with actress Julianne Phillips in Rumson, New Jersey. Eventually, *Born in the U.S.A.* sold over fifteen million copies and become one of the best-selling albums of all time.

During the band's break from touring and recording, Springsteen's workaholic nature got the best of him, and he began planning the release of a live album. By Christmas, 1986, Springsteen had released what fans had requested most: a massive five-album live set covering ten years' worth of touring. It achieved what many fans saw as impossible by capturing the power of Springsteen's live performances. (A few critics complained that it did not contain enough of the covers Springsteen was famous for performing in concert.) Lasting nearly three and a half hours—roughly the length of an actual Springsteen concert—*Bruce Springsteen and the E Street Band Live: 1975-1985* was an excellent testament to the power of Springsteen's live shows.

By 1987's release of *Tunnel of Love*, it seemed that married life had mellowed Springsteen. The album was softer and more intimate than his previous albums, with Springsteen looking at love from various angles and analyzing the perils of love and commitment. Ironically, the happiness that should have been there was rarely found. "Brilliant Disguise," for example, spoke of two lovers who had drifted apart by hiding their true selves from each other. "Walk Like a Man," a tribute to his father, reflected the reconciled relationship he and his father now shared. *Tunnel of Love* probably reflected Springsteen's personal life more than he would have liked; he and Phillips had drifted apart. While they were separated, a tabloid photo showed Springsteen and Patti Scialfa, a backup singer hired during the *Born in the U.S.A.* tour, sharing an intimate moment beside a pool in Rome. Springsteen's marriage ended in divorce in 1989, and soon afterward Scialfa gave birth to the first of their three children. She and Springsteen were married June 8, 1991.

Springsteen's divorce, remarriage, and fatherhood were only the beginning of the drastic changes he would undergo. He and his family moved into a fourteen-million-dollar mansion in Los Angeles, far away from the blue-collar roots he so espoused in his songs. Most devastating to fans, however, was the news that he was disbanding the E Street Band (who had not played together fully since the *Born in the U.S.A.* tour), saying that he wanted to seek new musical directions with other musicians. Fans and critics waited nervously to see what his next move would be.

He returned to the record stores in 1992 with *Human Touch* and *Lucky Town*. Released simultaneously, they presented two different aspects of a maturing musician. *Human Touch* shared a kinship with *Tunnel of Love*, reflecting the newer, more introspective Springsteen interested in relationships and family, while *Lucky Town* was rock and roll similar to his earlier albums. Springsteen worked with Jon Landau and E Street keyboardist Roy Bittan on the albums, which kept them from straying far into new territory. If anything, the albums pointed to the fact that he was not as driven as he once was. He told *Rolling Stone* in 1992 that he had entered therapy to deal with being a workaholic, which had manifested itself largely in the four-hour concerts he had performed every night for over ten years.

While *Lucky Town* and *Human Touch* might not have set the recording world on fire, his next single, "Streets of Philadelphia," earned him four Grammy Awards and an Academy Award. A haunting song about AIDS and its victims, Springsteen contributed it to the 1993 film *Philadelphia*. In March of 1995 he released a greatest hits album that featured a brief reunion of the E Street Band on four new tracks including "Murder Incorporated," a leftover from the *Born in the U.S.A.* sessions.

By November, 1995, Springsteen had surprised critics once more with the release of *The Ghost of Tom Joad*, named after the central character in John Steinbeck's *The Grapes of Wrath*. Springsteen had again widened his vision of America, this time to include California and the migrant worker community. The album, supported by a solo acoustic tour by Springsteen, won a Grammy Award for best folk album. Though dealing with the death of his father in 1998, Springsteen finished preparing a boxed set of previously unreleased songs. The four-disc set, *Bruce Springsteen: Tracks*, was released later that year. It contains fifty-six songs recorded between 1972 and 1998. The set includes his first demo recordings, over-seen by John Hammond, album outtakes, alternate versions, and B sides of singles. As one of rock's strongest voices, Springsteen's work will continue to be one of the standards by which other rock writers and musicians are judged.

—*Kelly Rothenberg*

SELECT DISCOGRAPHY
■ ALBUMS
Greetings from Asbury Park, N.J., 1973
The Wild, the Innocent, and the E Street Shuffle, 1973
Born to Run, 1975
Darkness on the Edge of Town, 1978
The River, 1980
Nebraska, 1982
Born in the U.S.A., 1984
Live 1975-1985, 1986
Tunnel of Love, 1987
Human Touch, 1992
Lucky Town, 1992
The Ghost of Tom Joad, 1995
Bruce Springsteen: Tracks, 1998

SELECT AWARDS
Grammy Award for Best Rock Vocal Performance, Male, for "Dancing in the Dark," 1984
Grammy Award for Best Rock Vocal Performance, Solo, for *Tunnel of Love*, 1987
Academy Award for Best Original Song for "Streets of Philadelphia," 1993
Grammy Awards for Song of the Year, Best Rock Song, Best Rock Vocal Performance, Male, and Best Song Written Specifically for a Motion Picture or for Television for "Streets of Philadelphia," 1994
Grammy Award for Best Contemporary Folk Album for *The Ghost of Tom Joad*, 1996
Rock and Roll Hall of Fame, inducted 1999

SEE ALSO: Cash, Johnny; Dylan, Bob; Petty, Tom, and the Heartbreakers; Seger, Bob; Smith, Patti.

Squeeze

ORIGINAL MEMBERS: Glenn Tilbrook (b. 1957), Chris Difford (b. 1954), Julian "Jools" Holland (b. 1958), Gilson Lavis (b. 1951)

OTHER MEMBERS: Keith Wilkinson (b. 1954), John Savannah, Paul Carrack (b. 1951), Andy Metcalfe

FIRST RELEASE: *Packet of Three*, 1977 (extended-play single)

MUSICAL STYLES: Pop, new wave, punk

Squeeze was formed in 1974 as one of the crop of new bands seeking to push the frontiers of popular music, which were currently ruled by disco. In the two decades that followed, Squeeze released thirteen albums of original music. Much more melodious and literate than many of the new-wave bands of the era, the group blended predictable yet catchy melodies with narrative-style lyrics. From their first few albums, Squeeze achieved a Top-40 hit, earned critical praise, and developed a devoted following.

Emergence and Early Success. At its essential core, Squeeze is the songwriting team of Chris Difford (lyrics) and Glenn Tilbrook (music). Tilford Difbrook, as the two have sometimes called themselves, began by experimenting in the nebulous punk genre in the mid-1970's. Their first record, a 1977 extended-play single entitled *Packet of Three*, revealed the team's cleverness and innovation. Even while working in a genre that sought to ridicule and destroy conventions, Difford and Tilbrook created music that drew upon classic elements of rock, soul, honky-tonk, and rhythm and blues. Compared to their later work, however, their early compositions were somewhat rough and sloppy. Difford and Tilbrook were still experimenting with experimentation. In this and other ways, the two would frequently be compared to the Beatles's John Lennon and Paul McCartney.

In 1978 Squeeze released its first full-length album. Typically considered the group's real debut album, the album was entitled simply *Squeeze* in Britain. In the United States, however, the album was entitled *U.K. Squeeze* in order to distinguish the group from a Philadelphia band that called itself Tight Squeeze. The album was well received by critics for its unusually skillful and witty treatment of a marginally punk sound.

In each of the next four years Squeeze would release a new album. Difford and Tilbrook soon developed a distinctive, recognizable style that almost entirely abandoned the punk sounds of *U.K. Squeeze*. Their new tracks were generally upbeat and bouncy, with strategically placed hooks and an occasional unexpected chord change. The lyrics continued in a narrative style, salted with double entendres and abstruse references. The distinctive tenor voice of lead singer Tilbrook exuded youth and confidence, while at the same time hinting at worldly experience that might make more cynical men bitter.

The group gained plaudits from many music critics as well as increased commercial success. The title track on *Cool for Cats* (1979) quickly rose to number 2 on the British charts. Although never as popular across the Atlantic Ocean, Squeeze acquired a loyal following in the United States. *Argybargy's* (1980) "Pulling Mussels (from a Shell)" and "Another Nail for My Heart," for example, received considerable airplay in the United States.

It was *East Side Story* (1981), however, that established Squeeze as an influential force in American and British pop music. More polished and with catchier melodies and witty, engaging lyrics, *East Side Story* was one of 1981's most notable albums. Keyboardist Julian Holland was now gone, but Difford and Tilbrook continued to serve as the group's soul. Indeed, Squeeze would eventually undergo so many personnel changes that only the nucleus of Difford and Tilbrook would remain constant. *East Side Story's* "Tempted" became a sort of theme song of the group, so quintessentially was it Squeeze. The group was frequently compared with new-wave giant Elvis Costello—a linkage made more explicit by Costello's coproducing of *East Side Story* and his appearance on "Tempted."

For the Record

Squeeze is said to have taken its name from the Velvet Underground album of the same name.

The following year Squeeze released *Sweets from a Stranger*. The new album included "Black Coffee in Bed," a song that rivaled "Tempted" in its wide appeal (and which, like "Tempted," included an appearance by Elvis Costello). *Sweets from a Stranger* made the Top-40 charts, and Squeeze's presence in the public eye was at its peak. A collection of their greatist hits was released in 1982, and eventually went gold. The group also was appearing on the late-night talk show circuit. It came as something of a surprise, therefore, when the group announced it was disbanding in 1982.

Reunion and a Second Life. In 1985 the group's members reassembled for a charity performance. Apparently rejuvenated after a three-year hiatus, Difford and Tilbrook took the group into a recording studio to produce *Cosi Fan Tutti Frutti* (1985). The tracks were clearly recognizable as Squeeze, with Tilbrook's vocals ensuring the trademark sound. The music relied more heavily on electronics than the group's earlier albums, but it contained Squeeze's familiar bright, catchy melodies with unexpected and unusual hooks. If anything, the music in Squeeze's second life seized the defining characteristics of the group's earlier incarnation and emphasized them. This was especially evident in the lyrics. Difford and Tilbrook were more intentially artistic, making extensive use of their natural skills as word- and tunesmiths.

Subsequent albums provided Difford and Tilbrook new opportunities to push their trademark artistry and narrative lyrics to ever greater heights while still containing the music within the confines of the Squeeze sound. Squeeze eventually was recognized as a major musical presence of the 1980's. *Babylon and On* (1987) included two Top-40 hits ("Hourglass" and "853-5937"), and the album itself made the Top 40. Yet the band was never able to achieve the celebrity it had achieved in the early 1980's. Instead, Squeeze was known as an institution—a continuing endeavor by Difford and Tilbrook to showcase their cleverness, their musical talents, and the semi-narrative style that they virtually owned.

By the late 1980's, however, critics began to complain that the group had run out of new ideas. Although concept albums such as *Play* (1991), whose songs were loosely connected in the format of a stage play, showed that Difford and Tilbrook were still experimenting, their work contained few musical surprises. Though steadfast fans continued to loyally purchase each new release, the group's later albums were not commercially successful in the United States. Their reception in Great Britain generally remained better, with the single "This Summer" reaching the Top 40 in 1995.

—Steve D. Boilard

SELECT DISCOGRAPHY
■ ALBUMS
U.K. Squeeze, 1978
Cool for Cats, 1979
Argybargy, 1980
East Side Story, 1981
Sweets from a Stranger, 1982
Singles—45's and Under, 1982 (compilation)
Cosi Fan Tutti Frutti, 1985
Babylon and On, 1987
frank, 1989
A Round and a Bout, 1990
Play, 1991
Some Fantastic Place, 1993
Ridiculous, 1995

SEE ALSO: Costello, Elvis.

The Staple Singers

ORIGINAL MEMBERS: Roebuck "Pops" Staples (b. 1915), Cleotha Staples (b. 1934), Yvonne Staples (b. 1939), Mavis Staples (b. 1940)
OTHER MEMBERS: Pervis Staples (b. 1935)
FIRST SINGLE RELEASE: "These Are They," 1953
MUSICAL STYLES: Gospel, folk, soul

From their beginnings in Chicago-area churches in the late 1940's through their chart-topping successes in the 1970's and beyond, this family group has been defined by the soulful singing of Mavis Staples and the distinctive blues guitar playing of Pops Staples. (The group has been known both as the Staple Singers and simply as the Staples.) As important as their sound, though, is their ongoing commitment to the idea that music can do more than entertain—it can also spread a powerful message of equality and justice.

The Beginnings. Pops Staples grew up hearing a cappella gospel singing in the churches of Mississippi. As a teenager, though, he also became interested in the blues. He sang with a gospel quartet before moving to Chicago in 1936 with his wife Oceola and their young family. Eventually he bought a second-hand guitar, which he used to accompany his family's singing in the evenings.

One day in 1948, the family was invited to sing at church by Pops Staples's sister Katie. Their informal one-song performance was so successful that they were soon singing in churches throughout the Chicago area. Their 1956 recording "Uncloudy Day" was their first hit record and is considered a gospel classic.

Through their early years of growing popularity, Pops kept a steady job and refused to take the group on tour. He believed that a stable home life for his

The Staple Singers (Archive Photos/Frank Driggs Collection)

family was more important than any money or fame they might have earned by touring. When his youngest daughter Mavis graduated from high school in 1957, though, Pops left his job at a steel mill and took the family on tour. They soon gained a national following among gospel audiences, supported by a series of albums recorded for the labels Vee Jay (1955-1962), Riverside (1962-1963), and Epic (1964-1968).

Music with a Message. The Staple Singers' recordings had always been characterized by strong religious and moral content, but in 1964 they recorded the first of many protest songs, Bob Dylan's "Masters of War." They were inspired by Dr. Martin Luther King, Jr., to support the Civil Rights movement of the 1950's and 1960's with

their music. The song "Why (Am I Treated So Bad?)" was a response to an incident the family had witnessed in which black children were barred from boarding a school bus. The song laments a political climate that forces schoolchildren to be victims of racial prejudice. "Marching up Jesus' Highway," about the famous 1965 march from Selma to Montgomery, Alabama, became a classic song of the Civil Rights movement.

Throughout the 1960's the group acted as a musical conscience in the United States, releasing a series of albums protesting racial and social inequality in the country. This period culminated with the release of *Soul Folk in Action* (1968), a collection of protest songs that was also their debut album with Stax Records.

The Stax Years. From 1968 to 1974, the Staple Singers recorded for Stax Records. The albums from this period, mostly produced by Al Bell, were the most popular of their career, as the group moved from the relatively small world of gospel to the broader audience of mainstream pop and soul music. The song "I'll Take You There" was a number 1 single on both the pop and rhythm-and-blues charts, earning a Grammy Award nomination in 1972. Other Top-40 hits from the early 1970's include "Respect Yourself," "Heavy Makes You Happy," "This World," "Touch a Hand, Make a Friend," and "If You're Ready (Come Go with Me)."

The sound the group displays on the Stax recordings is their trademark style. On most of the recordings, Pops's blues guitar is the backbone of the sound, with Mavis' intense, gospel-style singing taking the lead. Cleotha and Yvonne punctuated the vocal lines in call-and-response style, often with the support of a horn section. An important innovation of these recordings was the use of reggae ("I'll Take You There") and calypso ("Touch a Hand, Make a Friend") rhythms.

When Stax began to fall apart due to financial problems, the group took the opportunity to move to Curtis Mayfield's Curtom label, where they had their biggest hit single, "Let's Do It Again." The song, written for the 1975 film of the same name, was a departure for the group, since the suggestive title seemed to indicate a move away from their gospel roots. The sexual content was more suggestive than overt, though, and the Staple Singers were able to convince their fans that they were still true to the gospel message despite their brush with the secular music world.

Though they moved to Warner Bros. and changed their name to the Staples, the group would not recapture the level of mainstream popularity that they enjoyed during the years at Stax, although they would continue to perform. The 1990's found Mavis and Pops recording as solo artists in addition to singing with the group. Mavis recorded the albums *Time Waits for No One* (1989) and *The Voice* (1993) for Prince's Paisley Park label. Pops recorded his first solo albums, *Peace to the Neighborhood* (1992) and *Father Father*

For the Record

When the Staple Singers were asked to record the song "Let's Do It Again" for the sound track of the Bill Cosby-Sidney Poitier comedy of the same name, Pops did not want to accept the offer because he believed the song was too suggestive. His daughters talked him into it, and the song went on to be their biggest hit.

(1994). The first album was nominated for a Grammy Award, and in a fitting tribute to his long career, *Father Father* won the Grammy for Best Contemporary Blues Album. In the same year, he was honored as a positive parental role model in the first annual National Parents' Day ceremony in Washington, D.C.

Musical Style. The song "Why (Am I Treated So Bad?)" from 1966 illustrates the Staple Singers' style perfectly. It begins with a simple blues riff on guitar, joined immediately by soft bass and drum lines. Over this bluesy texture, Pops preaches an introduction before singing the chorus. The song features backup singing that alternates between the moaning and shouting styles typical of African American gospel music, along with hand clapping from the Pentecostal tradition. It ends with a return to the solo guitar line that opened the song. The ingredient that makes the sound distinctive is a country twang that has roots both in Pops's Mississippi upbringing and the group's association with country-western producer Billy Sherrill during their years with Epic. The lyrics are not overtly religious, but their strong moral message shows their gospel roots.

The Staple Singers proved that a gospel group could attain mainstream popularity without being corrupted by it. The connection between gospel and soul is obvious in the music of Al Green, Aretha Franklin, and many other popular singers of the 1970's, but few were able to strike such a successful balance between the two as the Staple Singers.
—*E. Douglas Bomberger*

SELECT DISCOGRAPHY

■ ALBUMS

Hammer and Nails, 1962
The Twenty-Fifth of December, 1962
This Little Light, 1966
Why, 1966
For What It's Worth, 1967
Soul Folk in Action, 1968
I Had a Dream, 1970
Heavy Makes You Happy, 1971
The Staples Swingers, 1971
Beatitude: Respect Yourself, 1972
City in the Sky, 1974
Let's Do It Again, 1975
Family Tree, 1977
Unlock Your Mind, 1978
The Staple Singers, 1985
Respect Yourself: The Best of the Staple Singers, 1988
   (compilation)

SELECT AWARDS

Grammy Award for Best Contemporary Blues Album for *Father Father*, 1994 (Pops Staples)
Rock and Roll Hall of Fame, inducted 1999

SEE ALSO: Franklin, Aretha; Green, Al; Mayfield, Curtis; Prince.

Starship. *See* Jefferson Airplane / Jefferson Starship

Steely Dan

ORIGINAL MEMBERS: Donald Fagen (b. 1948), Walter Becker (b. 1950), Denny Dias, Jeff Baxter (b. 1948), Jim Hodder (d. 1990), David Palmer (b. 1961)
OTHER MEMBERS: Michael McDonald (b. 1952), other sidemen
FIRST ALBUM RELEASE: *Can't Buy a Thrill*, 1972
MUSICAL STYLES: Rock, jazz

Steely Dan's seven original albums included some of the most critically acclaimed music of the 1970's. Collectively, the albums represent virtually a genre unto itself within the broad landscape of popular music. In its nine-year existence, Steely Dan underwent a number of personnel changes. Steely Dan was less a "band" and more a number of extensively mixed albums of material written by Donald Fagen and Walter Becker and performed by them along with studio musicians. At the same time, Steely Dan was far more than the talents of Fagen and Becker: It was a decade-long mission to master and conquer the recording technology of the era. Most of their wide and devout following believed that they succeeded.

The Team Is Formed. Donald Fagen and Walter Becker met as students at Bard College in Annandale-on-Hudson, New York. In a series of developments loosely referenced in Steely Dan's "My Old School," Fagen and Becker came to write songs together and play in local bands. Highly literate, creative, and driven, the two moved to Los Angeles, California, at the behest of producer Gary Katz. They assembled a group of musicians that included Denny Dias on guitar, Jim Hodder on drums, and David Palmer on vocals, with Becker on bass and Fagen on keyboards and vocals. Steely Dan released their first album in 1972. The album, *Can't Buy a Thrill*, was quite successful. "Do It Again" and "Reelin' in the Years" quickly rose into the Top 40.

Judged by their work on *Can't Buy a Thrill*, Steely Dan were a somewhat mainstream early 1970's rock band. The instrumentation, arrangements, and harmonies were not exotic; rather, the electric guitar riffs, keyboard fills, and background vocals were typical of that period. The rhythms were unadorned, with the notable exception of the rhythm guitar and percussion on "Do It Again." The tempos were perhaps a bit slower than much of the other rock music of the era, and the vocals—particularly those performed by Palmer—were straightforward. What made *Can't Buy a Thrill* distinctive was not so much the melodies (composed by Becker) or the musicianship (good as it was), but rather the record's studied production and Fagen's lyrics, which combined unusual metaphors, evocative imagery, and abstruse references. It was in the realm of production engineering that Steely Dan was most focused. *Can't Buy a*

Thrill was a carefully produced record for its day. Subsequent Steely Dan albums were not so much recorded as crafted, meticulously assembled from segments of solos, background vocals, and other song elements.

Steely Dan's distinctive characteristics became even more pronounced on their next two albums. *Countdown to Ecstasy* (1973) and *Pretzel Logic* (1974) contained several hits, including "Rikki Don't Lose That Number." The band was also gaining plaudits from music critics and a solid, devoted following of fans. With each album, Steely Dan were pushing the limits of recording and mixing technologies, with the tracks ever more refined and perfected. Becker's musical composition began to range somewhat wider, from the almost rockabilly drive of "Bodhisattva" to the relentless rhythms of "Boston Rag," the jaunty clip of "With a Gun," the jazz influences of "Parker's Band" and "Barrytown," and the sentimental ballad "Pearl of the Quarter." Stylistically, the music was sophisticated and intricate, and identifiably Steely Dan. Fagen, for his part, wrote increasingly abstruse lyrics, as exemplified in "Your Gold Teeth." Fagen also provided all the lead vocals for all of Steely Dan's songs after the first album. His uniquely nasal, East Coast-accented voice became a defining feature of the group.

Endings and New Beginnings. Steely Dan broke up after their third album, owing to a number of problems. Most trying was touring. The band, and especially Fagen and Becker, were exasperated by their inability to capture Steely Dan's studio sound in live performances. Becker and Fagen continued to write material and soon

Steely Dan—Donald Fagen and Walter Becker—in 1979 (Deborah Feingold/Archive Photos)

returned to the studio. Assembling the necessary studio musicians, they recorded a new album. *Katy Lied* (1975) continued the now-familiar eclecticism of Steely Dan's music while at the same time maintaining a fairly consistent feel of jazz-informed rock. ("Chain Lightning" and "Daddy Don't Live in That New York City" were quintessential examples.) In the following year, Fagen and Becker released their fifth Steely Dan album: *The Royal Scam*. Filled with historical references and dark imagery, *The Royal Scam* represented a maturing of the Steely Dan genre. It was as if Fagen was trying to be as cryptic as possible while still leaving tantalizing clues to what he was thinking. *The Royal Scam* was Steely Dan's most musically cohesive album to date, infused with synthesizers, driving and relentless rhythms, and haunting melodies. Yet the production was again the star of the album.

Aja (1977) represented the height of Steely Dan's popularity and artistic achievement. With no fewer than four Top-40 singles ("Aja," "Deacon Blues," "Peg," and "Josie"), the album made Steely Dan one of the most talked-about musical forces at the time. The addition of the Doobie Brothers' Michael McDonald in *Aja*'s backing vocals gave the album a musical recognizability and mass appeal. The album earned a Grammy Award for Best Engineered Non-Classical Album.

Gaucho (1980) was Steely Dan's last studio album. Although the album was commercially successful ("Hey Nineteen" and "Babylon Sisters" made the Top 40), the quest for technical perfection may have robbed the music of its soul. The album's instrumentation and music were detailed virtually to the last note. More than three dozen musicians were employed, including Dire Straits' Mark Knopfler, jazz guitarist Larry Carlton, and singer Patti Austin. The result was a sparkling triumph of engineering with a somewhat astringent quality. Some critics were beginning to feel that Steely Dan had run their course. Indeed, no new Steely Dan albums would be recorded. The group's cult following, however, remained as loyal as ever.

Post-Steely Dan Developments. Steely Dan's seven studio albums continued to attract fans even in the 1980's and 1990's. The music seemed to transcend the 1970's and represented important milestones in the development of pop music. In 1993, *Aja* achieved double-platinum status. In that same year, "Can't Buy a Thrill," "Katy Lied," "Pretzel Logic," and "The Royal Scam" were all certified platinum.

Although no Steely Dan albums were made after 1980, Becker and Fagen continued to work in music, albeit separately for the most part. In 1981, Fagen recorded a solo album, *The Nightfly*, which many regarded as the logical extension of Steely Dan. Amid constant rumors about an imminent resurrection of Steely Dan, Becker and Fagen helped to produce (and perform on) an album by newcomer Rosie Vela in the mid-1980's. Fagen's second solo album, *Kamakiriad* (1993), was actually a collaboration with Becker and might rightly be regarded as a Steely Dan album. Critic Stephen Thomas Erlewine called it "Aja recorded with 1990's technology." Becker and Fagen even assembled a group of musicians and toured together, playing a mix of cuts from *Kamakiriad* and Steely Dan classics. The act was billed as "An Evening with Steely Dan," and the 1994-1995 concert cuts were compiled as *Alive in America* (1995).   —*Steve D. Boilard*

SELECT DISCOGRAPHY
■ ALBUMS
Steely Dan
Can't Buy a Thrill, 1972
Countdown to Ecstasy, 1973
Pretzel Logic, 1974
Katy Lied, 1975
The Royal Scam, 1976
Aja, 1977
Gaucho, 1980
Donald Fagen solo
The Nightfly, 1982
Kamakiriad, 1993

SELECT AWARDS
Grammy Award for Best Engineered Album (Non-Classical) for *Aja*, 1977

SEE ALSO: Doobie Brothers, The / Michael McDonald.

Steppenwolf

ORIGINAL MEMBERS: John Kay (b. Joachim Krau-
ledat, 1944), Jerry Edmonton (b. Jerry McCro-
han, 1946-1993), Goldy McJohn (b. John
Goadsby, 1945), Rushton Moreve (1948-1981),
Michael Monarch (b. 1950)

OTHER MEMBERS: Nick St. Nicholas (b. Klaus Karl
Kassbaum, 1943), George Biondi (b. 1945),
Larry Byrom (b. 1948), Kent Henry, Bobby
Cochran, Andy Chapin (d. 1985), Michael
Wilk, Ron Hurst, Danny Johnson, Rocket
Ritchotte, Brett Tuggle, Wayne Cook, Michael
Palmer, Steve Palmer, Chad Perry, Gary Link

FIRST ALBUM RELEASE: *Steppenwolf*, 1968

MUSICAL STYLE: Rock and roll

John Kay (lead vocals, guitar, harmonica) was
born in Tilsit, East Prussia, Germany. At age six,
he escaped to West Germany. By age thirteen,
declared legally blind, he was being awed by the
rock and roll he heard on Armed Forces Radio
and determined to make music his career. In
1959, he moved to Toronto, Canada, where he
learned English. After performing on amateur
radio shows, he roamed the North American con-
tinent performing acoustic blues in coffeehouses
and bars. In 1965, he joined a Canadian band the
Sparrows, which included Dennis Edmonton,
Jerry Edmonton, Rushton Moreve, and Goldy
McJohn. After migrating to New York and then
the West Coast, the band broke up in 1967 after
several failed recordings for Columbia Records.

Magic Carpet Ride. In 1968, Kay and most
Sparrow bandmates formed Steppenwolf, naming the band after the 1927 Hermann Hesse
novel. Mike Monarch replaced Dennis Edmonton, who had changed his name to Mars Bonfire.
While working on Steppenwolf's first Dunhill album in late 1967, Bonfire presented the band his
song "Born to Be Wild." The following year, the
song reached number 2 on the *Billboard* charts,
became an immediate rock anthem, and gained a
second life when actor Dennis Hopper chose it as
the theme for the 1969 film *Easy Rider.*

From 1968 through 1969, Steppenwolf issued
three best-selling albums, *Steppenwolf, Second,* and
At Your Birthday Party, each demonstrating the
group's interest in topical issues, psychedelic lifestyles, and resistance to the Vietnam War. Kay's
gritty vocals, hard-rock delivery, and strongly
worded lyrics distinguished the band in a crowded
market, which led to a series of hits including
Bonfire's "Magic Carpet Ride," Hoyt Axton's "The
Pusher," and "Rock Me," from the 1968 film
Candy. After the third album, personnel changes
became frequent. Nick St. Nicholas was an on-
and-off member, his erratic behavior and inconsistent playing resulting in his replacement by
George Biondi. Conflicting with Kay, Monarch
departed, to be succeeded by Larry Byrom, who
cowrote the hits "Hey Lawdy Mama" and "Who
Needs Ya." *Monster* (1969) was the group's last
major statement, followed by more straight-ahead
rock and roll on *Steppenwolf 7* (1970) and *For Ladies
Only* (1971) with new guitarist Kent Henry. From
these last albums, the band continued to issue
singles, including "Move Over" and Hoyt Axton's
"Snow Blind Friend," an early country-flavored
comment on cocaine. Feeling the band had run
its course, Kay disbanded the group on Valentine's Day, 1972, in San Francisco.

Reborn. Kay then issued solo albums until
St. Nicholas and McJohn toured illegally using the
Steppenwolf name. After legal battles, Kay and
Edmonton became joint owners of the name with
Steppenwolf Incorporated. Kay, Edmonton,
McJohn, and Biondi formed John Kay and Steppenwolf in 1974 with guitarist Bobby Cochran,
nephew of 1950's hitmaker Eddie Cochran. After
releasing three lackluster albums for CBS, Kay
reorganized the group without Edmonton, who
retired to pursue photography.

From 1984, the group maintained a steady
lineup including Michael Wilk (keyboards, bass,
vocals), Rocket Ritchotte (guitar), and drummer-
vocalist Ron Hurst. Since reestablishing the name,
John Kay and Steppenwolf released six albums
and toured annually on a worldwide basis. After
1987's disappointing *Rock & Roll Rebels*, the group
released the noteworthy 1990 *Rise and Shine*,
which featured "Rock and Roll War," the group's
most successful song since 1971. The album also
included "The Wall," Kay's personal reflections

on the 1989 tearing down of the Berlin Wall.

In 1994, Kay returned to play concerts in the former East Germany, where he was reunited with friends and relatives. Kay's autobiography, *Magic Carpet Ride*, written with John Einarson, also appeared in 1994. That year the group also released their silver anniversary set, *Live at 25*. While recording 1996's *Feed the Fire*, guitarist Danny Johnson (formerly with Rick Derringer's group) joined the band. In 1998, Kay reported thirty-seven Steppenwolf songs had been licensed for films and thirty-six television programs.

—*Wesley Britton*

SELECT DISCOGRAPHY
■ ALBUMS
Steppenwolf, 1968
The Second, 1968
At Your Birthday Party, 1969
Monster, 1969
Rise and Shine, 1990
Feed the Fire, 1996 (as John Kay and Steppenwolf)

SELECT AWARDS
Canadian Academy of Recording Arts and Sciences (CARAS) Hall of Fame, inducted 1996 (John Kay)

SEE ALSO: Animals, The / Eric Burdon.

Cat Stevens

(Steven Demetri Georgiou)
BORN: London, England; July 21, 1947
FIRST ALBUM RELEASE: *Matthew & Son*, 1967
MUSICAL STYLES: Folk rock, pop

Englishman Cat Stevens reigned as one of the most popular singer-songwriters of the 1970's. A number of his gentle, folk-rock songs, including "Wild World" and "Moonshadow," sold well as singles, but he enjoyed greater success as an album artist. Stevens turned his back on his career and music itself in the latter part of the 1970's after converting to Islam and changing his name to Yusuf Islam. His distinctive voice remained silent through the 1980's, but he made something

of a comeback in the 1990's with religiously oriented albums.

Young Star. Stevens was born Steven Demetri Georgiou, the child of a Greek father and Swedish mother. Musically precocious, he began writing songs while a student at Hammersmith College of Art in his native London. A producer from Decca heard a demo tape and signed the teenager to the company's Deram label. By the end of 1967, the seventeen-year-old had placed two pop tunes on the British charts, "I Love My Dog" and "Matthew and Son." The Tremolos also earned a hit with a third Stevens song, "Here Comes My Baby." The future looked bright indeed for the young singer-songwriter. Then tragedy struck.

In 1968, Stevens nearly died from tuberculosis.

Cat Stevens in 1973 (AP/Wide World Photos)

He blamed the disease on stage fright and the high living that came with success: "In order to get on stage, I used to have to drink. To get drunk. To be out of my mind. That kind of life—drinking, staying up late, smoking and going to parties and everything—had its effect." The malady and his long convalescence from it changed Stevens. He started asking fundamental questions about life and seeking answers for them through a spiritual quest that altered the course of his existence.

Stevens made a musical comeback in 1970 with *Mona Bone Jakon,* revealing a more mature, gentler artist with an acoustic, folk-like sound. It sold well, with the single "Lady D'Arbanville" reaching the British Top 10. International success came with the A&M release of *Tea for the Tillerman* later in 1970. It went gold in the United States, largely due to the hit "Wild World." While the song was clearly a statement of advice, few knew to whom it was directed. Stevens has explained, "I was writing to myself saying that I knew that I was going to turn into what I was before, a pop star. Only this time I knew what that was."

Teaser & the Firecat appeared in 1971 and featured the memorable "Peace Train" and "Morning Has Broken." Such hits helped establish Stevens as a folk-rock singer-songwriter of the first order, alongside such contemporaries as James Taylor, Harry Chapin, and Jim Croce. His career received a further boost when several songs were used in the 1971 film *Harold and Maude.* Stevens's next few albums did not generate big hit singles, but they still sold very well. *Catch Bull at Four* (1972) reached the top of the charts and *Foreigner* (1973) placed in the Top 3. A final hit single came in 1974 with "Oh Very Young" from the album *Buddha and the Chocolate Box.*

Lyrics. While his fans found significant meaning in his lyrics, Stevens discouraged reading too much into them, saying his songs had no point. Perhaps, but sometimes Stevens's lyrics did contain opaque meanings. For example, "Longer Boats" actually refers to unidentified flying objects (UFO's)—a fact the singer-songwriter made more clear by later adding a more obvious verse. Stevens's interest in extraterrestrials is worth consideration. He claimed that it stemmed from an actual occurrence, where he was "sucked" into a flying saucer above him. On the other hand, Stevens also let on that there was something more to his belief: "My whole interest in them [aliens] is something to occupy my thoughts." In the same interview, he explained that he was afraid of going crazy, of becoming a prisoner of his own mind. Despite commercial success, Stevens still appeared to be a troubled soul.

Matters came to a head for him while swimming on a California beach in 1973. Alone, Stevens found himself being pulled from shore by a strong current. He called out to God and promised to work in his behalf in exchange for life. Stevens recalled a wave then pushing him toward shore. Soon after, his brother returned from a trip to Jerusalem bearing a gift. It was a copy of the Muslim holy book, the Qur'an. Upon reading it, Stevens concluded that Islam was the world's true religion and soon made his own journey to Jerusalem.

Conversion. Back in London, Stevens continued to delve into the religion and finally converted in 1977, taking the Muslim name Yusuf Islam. This, however, was just the beginning. The Muslim faith holds a deep disregard for music. Religious sound arts do exist within Islam, but they are never called "music." Moreover, chanting is favored over instrumental music, which tends to have secular connotations. Within this overall context, it is not surprising that the former Cat Stevens turned his back on music, especially his own, in becoming Yusuf Islam.

Most Stevens fans were taken aback by his conversion. *Rolling Stone* called it "bizarre." Rumors swirled about, one even claiming that Stevens had

For the Record

When asked during a public lecture if he sometimes listens to his old songs, Yusuf Islam quickly answered "no." He then paused, started laughing, and said, "Um, yes I do."

become a monk. To the contrary, he continued to live in London, helping raise his children and taking an active role in the city's Muslim community. He simply was not making music anymore. Then fate dealt him a difficult hand.

In 1989, Iran's Ayatollah Ruhollah Khomeini called for the death of Salman Rushdie for his controversial 1988 novel *The Satanic Verses*. People wanted to know what Yusuf Islam, as a Muslim, thought about the matter. The news reported that he was for Khomeini's indictment, but Yusuf Islam claimed that his response was misinterpreted. He did find Rushdie's book blasphemous and noted the Qur'an's clear punishment for blasphemy, but he stopped far short of joining the call for the author's death. Be this as it may, many fans found it hard to reconcile the old Cat Stevens, gentle singer of "Tea for the Tillerman" and "Peace Train," with the new, seemingly fanatical Yusuf Islam.

Islam began to reemerge as a recording artist during the latter part of the 1990's. In 1995, he made *The Life of the Last Prophet*, but it mainly consisted of spoken-word text with a few added hymns. In 1998, he released *I Have No Cannons That Roar*. A moving tribute to the victims of the war in Bosnia, it contains reworked folk songs and two new numbers by the former Cat Stevens, "Mother, Father, Sister, Brother" and "The Little Ones." It is unclear whether this marked the return of the singer-songwriter to recording or was merely a special situation inspired by his concern for fellow Muslims in Bosnia. —*David Lee Fish*

SELECT DISCOGRAPHY

■ ALBUMS

Matthew & Son, 1967
World of Cat Stevens, 1970
Tea for the Tillerman, 1970
Teaser & the Firecat, 1971
Catch Bull at Four, 1972
Foreigner, 1973
Buddha & the Chocolate Box, 1974
The Life of the Last Prophet, 1995
I Have No Cannons That Roar, 1998

SEE ALSO: Chapin, Harry; Croce, Jim; Taylor, James.

Rod Stewart

BORN: London, England; January 10, 1945
FIRST ALBUM RELEASE: *Truth*, 1968 (with the Jeff Beck Group)
FIRST SOLO ALBUM RELEASE: *The Rod Stewart Album*, 1969
MUSICAL STYLES: Rock and roll, pop, folk rock, soul, blues

Blessed with the perfect gravelly voice for singing rock and roll, Rod Stewart established himself as one of rock music's premier stylists in the 1970's. While Stewart's swagger, rooster haircut, and tongue-in-cheek humor added to his early stature as a rock icon, by the late 1970's he had squandered his vocal talents with poor creative choices. During the 1990's, he attempted to recapture some credibility with mixed success.

The Beginnings. Roderick David Stewart was the youngest of five children. His parents, Robert and Elsie Stewart, had moved from Scotland to Highgate, North London, in 1939, where they opened a store. Although Rod was the only Stewart child not to be born in Scotland, he considered himself a Scot throughout his adulthood. He attended William Grimshaw School with Ray Davies and Dave Davies (brothers who would later form the Kinks). Stewart played guitar in a school band known as the Kool Kats. After leaving school, Stewart earned money digging graves, erecting fences, performing other odd jobs. His first love, however, was soccer, and he signed on as an apprentice with the Brentford Football Club in 1961. He became frustrated with having to spend most of his time on the bench and eventually quit the club.

Stewart then spent time as a street singer in Europe. According to some accounts, Stewart traveled around Europe with folksinger Wizz Jones, a claim that Jones has denied. Deported from Spain for vagrancy, Stewart returned to England and eventually joined a rhythm-and-blues band, Jimmy Powell and the Five Dimensions, as a vocalist and harmonica player. In 1964, Long John Baldry heard Stewart singing in the Twickenham train station and asked Stewart to join his

Rod Stewart (Paul Natkin)

band, the Hoochie Coochie Men. After the group broke up, Stewart joined Steampacket, in which he shared vocals with Baldry and Julie Driscoll. Other members of Steampacket included Brian Auger (keyboards), Rick Brown (bass), and Mickey Waller (drums). The group disbanded in 1966, and Stewart teamed up with Peter Green (guitar), Mick Fleetwood (drums), Dave Ambrose (bass), Peter Bardens (keyboards), and Beryl Marsden (vocals) to form the blues rock band Shotgun Express, which released one single before falling apart.

Stardom Just Around the Corner. In December, 1966, Stewart joined the Jeff Beck Group. Beck was already famous for the guitar work he had done as a member of the Yardbirds. In addition to Stewart on vocals and Beck on lead guitar, the band featured Ron Wood on bass and Ray Cook on drums. Cook was eventually fired and replaced by Aynsley Dunbar. Possessing a pound-

ing blues-rock sound, the band released its first album, *Truth,* in 1968. The album rose to number 8 on the British pop charts and number 15 on the U.S. pop charts. Working off Beck's lead guitar, Stewart's sandpaper vocals on such songs as "You Shook Me" and "Let Me Love You" showed that he was maturing into a brilliant rock stylist.

In 1969, the Jeff Beck Group released its second album, *Beck-Ola,* which was popular on both sides of the Atlantic Ocean. While the albums were solid efforts and both Stewart and Beck possessed the charisma to excite concert crowds, the personal and professional differences within the band doomed it to failure. Before the end of 1969, the Jeff Beck Group disbanded. Stewart went on to sign a recording contract with Phonogram Records as a solo artist. He and Wood also teamed up with the remaining members of the Small Faces to form the Faces. The Small Faces had been led by Steve Marriott, but he left the band in order to form Humble Pie with Peter Frampton. In addition to Stewart and Wood, the Faces included Ronnie Lane (bass), Ian McLagan (keyboards), and Kenney Jones (drums).

In late 1969, Stewart released his first solo album, *The Rod Stewart Album* (released in England as *An Old Raincoat Won't Ever Let You Down*). Unfortunately, the album did not make it onto the British pop charts and only reached number 139 on the U.S. pop charts. Stewart experimented with various music styles including blues, folk ballads, and funk on the album. While his interpretative skills hit the mark in original and ambitious ways with such songs as Mike D'Abo's "Handbags and Gladrags," the Rolling Stones' "Street Fighting Man," and Ewan MacColl's "Dirty Old Town," Stewart's own songs, including "Cindy's Lament," "An Old Raincoat Won't Ever Let You Down," and "Man of Constant Sorrow," revealed a powerful songwriter in the making.

The Faces' first album, *First Step,* was released in the spring of 1970. Although it was a very uneven record, *First Step* foreshadowed the good-natured bar-band approach that highlighted the band's live shows and its future classic albums. Not about to slow down at this point, Stewart put the finishing touches on his next solo album, *Gasoline*

Alley. Released in late 1970, the album showed how much more focused Stewart had become as a solo artist when compared to the playful sloppiness that surrounded all Faces projects. For *Gasoline Alley,* Stewart recorded excellent cover versions of Bob Dylan's "Only a Hobo" and Elton John's "Country Comfort." The title song for the album was written by Stewart and Wood and was one of the best songs they ever wrote together. *Gasoline Alley* climbed to number 27 on the U.S. pop charts and led to a tour of the United States.

The next year was a watershed year for Stewart. Early in 1971, the Faces released its second album, *Long Player.* The album did relatively well, but it was Stewart's next solo album that made him a bonafide rock star. *Every Picture Tells a Story* (1971) contained the perfect mix of cover songs and original compositions. Showing that he was one of the best interpretive singers around, Stewart took such songs as Tim Hardin's "Reason to Believe," Dylan's "Tomorrow Is a Long Time," and the Temptations' "(I Know) I'm Losing You" and made them his own. The real surprises on the album, however, were Stewart's own songs. "Maggie May," "Mandolin Wind," and "Every Picture Tells a Story" were authentic songs that became instant classics. *Every Picture Tells a Story* went to number 1 on both the U.S. and British pop charts. Although "Maggie May" had begun as the B-side of a single ("Reason to Believe" was the A-side), it

For the Record

"Maggie May" helped to make Rod Stewart a star, but he almost took it off his album after a friend told him it did not have anything melodic to offer. Stewart was inclined to agree with him but decided it was too late to remove the song. "When it came out on a single, it was a B-side . . . and it was a disc jockey in Cleveland, I believe, that turned it over. Otherwise, I wouldn't be here today. I'd still be digging graves in the cemetery."

was soon switched to the A-side thanks to a radio disc jockey in Cleveland. "Maggie May" went on to reach number 1 on the pop charts and stayed there for five weeks. For one week, Stewart had both the number 1 album and the number 1 single in England and the United States.

To finish off the year, the Faces released the rowdy good-time album *A Nod Is as Good as a Wink . . . to a Blind Horse.* The album reached the Top 10 on both the U.S. and British pop charts and included the Faces' only American Top-40 single, "Stay with Me." In 1972, Stewart released the solo album *Never a Dull Moment,* which went to number 2 on the U.S. pop charts and included the hit single "You Wear It Well." After the Faces' album *Ooh La La* (1973), the dissension within the group came to a head, causing Lane to quit. In 1975, Wood joined the Rolling Stones as the replacement for guitarist Mick Taylor, who had recently quit. With the breakup of the Faces, Stewart turned his attention to reveling in his position as a rock star.

Success Can Be a Killer. While Stewart continued to release popular albums during the late 1970's—including *Atlantic Crossing* (1975) and *A Night on the Town* (1976)—he was criticized heavily for becoming no more than a parody of his former self. Stewart also seemed to have a weakness for women with blonde hair and had a well-publicized relationship with the actress Britt Ekland. In 1979, Stewart married Alana Hamilton, the former wife of actor George Hamilton. They would separate in 1984. Some of Stewart's most notable and notorious singles of this period were "Tonight's the Night (Gonna Be Alright)," "Hot Legs," "You're in My Heart (the Final Acclaim)," and "Da Ya Think I'm Sexy?" During the 1980's, Stewart continued to confound critics and fans alike. He could still produce platinum albums, but most of what he was doing seemed to be no more than mere posturing.

Always a generous individual, Stewart was active in a number of charity causes. One of the high points of the 1980's was his collaboration with his old friend Jeff Beck on a remake of the Impressions' "People Get Ready" for Beck's 1985 album *Flash.* Stewart joined the other members of the

Faces at a London benefit in 1986 to perform for Ronnie Lane, who was suffering with multiple sclerosis. While Stewart's mid-1980's recordings failed to chart as consistently as earlier recordings, his 1988 album *Out of Order* showed signs that Stewart was not completely washed up yet. In 1989, the definitive box set *Storyteller* was released. It included a cover version of Tom Waits' "Downtown Train," which reached number 3 on the U.S. pop singles charts.

In 1990, Stewart married twenty-one-year-old New Zealand supermodel Rachel Hunter in Beverly Hills, California. Although she was much younger than Stewart, she seemed to bring stability and focus to his life. During the 1990's, Stewart reclaimed some of his stature as a recording star with such albums as *Vagabond Heart* (1991), *Unplugged . . . and Seated* (1993), and *A Spanner in the Works* (1995). In 1998, he released his strongest album in many years, *When We Were the New Boys*, which included a number of cover versions of songs written by a younger generation of musicians, including Oasis' "Cigarettes and Alcohol," Ron Sexsmith's "Secret Heart," and Primal Scream's "Rocks." Stewart also included a cover of the Lane song "Ooh La La" out of respect for his former Faces mate Ronnie Lane, who had died from complications related to his multiple sclerosis in 1997.

— *Jeffry Jensen*

SELECT DISCOGRAPHY
■ ALBUMS
the Jeff Beck Group
Truth, 1968
Beck-Ola, 1969
the Faces
Long Player, 1971
A Nod Is as Good as a Wink . . . to a Blind Horse, 1971
Ooh La La, 1973
Rod Stewart solo
The Rod Stewart Album, 1969
Gasoline Alley, 1970
Every Picture Tells a Story, 1971
Never a Dull Moment, 1972
Atlantic Crossing, 1975
A Night on the Town, 1976

Foot Loose and Fancy Free, 1977
Blondes Have More Fun, 1978
Tonight I'm Yours, 1981
Camouflage, 1984
Out of Order, 1988
Storyteller: The Complete Anthology, 1964-1990, 1989 (box set)
Vagabond Heart, 1991
Unplugged . . . and Seated, 1993 (live)
A Spanner in the Works, 1995
When We Were the New Boys, 1998

SELECT AWARDS
Rock and Roll Hall of Fame, inducted 1994

SEE ALSO: Bad Company; Brown, James; Cooke, Sam; Dylan, Bob; Hall and Oates; John, Elton; Palmer, Robert; Redding, Otis; Rolling Stones, The; Seger, Bob.

Sting

(Gordon Matthew Sumner)
BORN: Newcastle, England; October 2, 1951
FIRST ALBUM RELEASE: *The Dream of the Blue Turtles*, 1985 (first solo release)
MUSICAL STYLES: Rock and roll, pop, reggae, fusion

Starting with his rise to stardom with the Police and continuing through his successful solo career, Sting made a name for himself that few others have equaled in 1980's and 1990's pop music. Sting possesses a unique voice in addition to his impressive songwriting and arranging talents

Beginnings. Born Gordon Matthew Sumner, Sting grew up in the shipbuilding town of Newcastle, England, a city whose dreary working-class environs motivated him to rise to something better. Music gave him a focus; though he played guitar from a young age, his instrument of choice became the electric bass. Although as a teenager he saw performances by such bands as the Jimi Hendrix Experience and Cream, he was drawn not to rock but to the local Newcastle jazz scene. An industrial town, Newcastle was also a university city, and the resulting intellectual undercurrent of its musical community gave Sting the chance to learn and play with jazz musicians, an experience that gave him a strong foundation in chart-reading and music theory.

As he grew older, Sting drifted through jobs that included stints as a ditch digger, factory worker, and bus driver, but at twenty-two he found a direction for himself in teaching. However, music remained a large part of his life, and he and several friends started a fusion jazz band called Last Exit. After working in the classroom for several years, Sting realized that he could chart his future—rising through the ranks to become headmaster—and the image made him come to a decision. Turning his back on a safe, settled life as a teacher, he decided to try for something more.

Moving to London with his family in order to take Last Exit to better, larger venues, Sting found himself without a band or career when two of the four members of the band went back on their pledge to make the move. As a result Sting, then twenty-six years old, found himself teaming with drummer Stewart Copeland and (after a brief search) veteran guitarist Andy Summers to form the Police.

Their first album, *Outlandos D'Amour* (1977), was chiefly driven by the energy of founding member Stewart Copeland, but the strongest singles, such as "Roxanne" and "Can't Stand Losing You," came from Sting. Though the Police received little recognition at first, after a series of brutal tours—and brilliant publicity and marketing stunts hatched largely by the band's manager, Miles Copeland (Stewart's brother)—the band rocketed to stardom. It soon became clear that Sting's songs were the group's strongest material, and he generated all the Police's singles after the first album.

Starting off with a sound that was largely taken from reggae-influenced rhythm and bass lines, the band's compositions grew increasingly sophisticated with each album. The songs provided a framework within which the three musicians could create a tapestry of swirling rhythms and washes of sound. Despite the significant contributions of all three band members, Sting—with his unique vocal sound and striking looks—became,

Sting in 1996 (AP/Wide World Photos)

to the public, the focus of the band. As their fame rose, so did tensions among Sting, Copeland, and Summers, but with a common drive to succeed and make music the tension seemed to work in their favor.

Over the course of the Police's five studio albums, Sting continued to grow as a musician. The third album, *Zenyatta Mondatta*, saw him playing fretless upright bass as well as saxophone on a number of tracks. On that album he also began to explore the use of vocal overdubs. Another marked influence in his development as a writer came from the band's extensive world tours, which exposed him to larger concerns that were reflected in his music. With the release of their fifth album, *Synchronicity*, the Police were for a time the world's most successful band, a status achieved in part as a result of their world tours. Singles penned by Sting such as "Every Breath You Take" and "King of Pain" climbed the charts. *Sychronicity*, however, proved to be the band's last album and tour: Having reached the pinnacle of success within the structure of a band, Sting was ready to move on.

Solo Career. In 1985 Sting's first solo project, an album entitled *The Dream of the Blue Turtles*, found him gathering some of the world's top session musicians to record an album whose sound was quite new. Pushing beyond the reggae influences from which he had borrowed while with the Police (and also dropping the bass in favor of guitar), Sting returned to his roots in jazz to create an album that fused the musicianship and spontaneity of jazz with the solid power and energy of rock. The result was a fusion album, and such songs as "Love Is the Seventh Wave," "If You Love Someone Set Them Free" (which reached number 3 on the pop charts), and "Fortress Around Your Heart" (number 8) launched Sting's career as a solo artist. After his first solo tour, he released a live album, *Bring on the Night*, which showed off both his own and his superstar band's virtuosity and energy as live performers.

Having established a new sound for himself that was a step away from the Police, Sting decided to reinvent his sound yet again. His second studio album, *Nothing Like the Sun*, was a lush, richly produced and overdubbed album that pulled back from the high energy of *The Dream of the Blue Turtles*. The change in direction led to a battle with his record company to release the album. Sting's willingness to take risks proved sound, and as he toured the world with his band, such songs as "We'll Be Together" (a number 7 hit) and "Lazareth Heart" drove the album to number 9 on the charts. With a second successful album and a new level of sophistication in his lyrics and arranging, the album established Sting as a solo artist.

Mature Style. Sting's third studio album was slow in coming. Grappling with the death of both of his parents, he found that he had severe writer's block. When at last he dealt with the pain of his loss, his block dissolved, and in the course of a matter of weeks he wrote what many consider to

For the Record

It was while gigging with a jazz band in the early 1970's that Gordon Sumner earned his distinctive nickname. He showed up at a gig wearing a yellow-and-black striped sweater and was dubbed "Sting" by the other musicians in the band, giving him the moniker which he has used as his professional and personal name ever since.

be his finest album, *The Soul Cages* (1991). A collaboration with producer/engineer Hugh Padgham (who had produced the Police's last two albums), the album is full of poignant, recurring symbols that echo Sting's relationship with his father and his own decisions to liberate himself from his upbringing via music. The imagery of ships and the sea as well as the redemption of fathers and sons reflects not only Sting's Newcastle childhood but also his ability to turn his personal experiences into powerful art. The title single won a Grammy Award, and it and "All This Time" (a number 5 hit) propelled the album to a number 2 position. In the following tour, Sting abandoned the large band of his two previous solo tours and picked up the bass on stage once more. Sting attacked the tour circuit with newfound energy and determination. It was, except for the addition of a keyboardist, the return to a lean "fighting unit" band much like the beginning years of the Police.

Riding on the energy of the *Soul Cages* tour, in 1993 Sting returned to studio with his live band and quickly cut *Ten Summoner's Tales*, an album that has the spontaneous energy of a live concert (several of its songs were, in fact, born from jams on the preceding tour). The album's two strong singles "If I Ever Lose My Faith in You" (a number 17 hit that earned Sting his sixteenth Grammy) and "Fields of Gold" (a number 23 hit), as well as the infectious crafting of such songs as "Seven Days," "It's Probably Me," and "Epilogue: Don't

Know Nothing About Me," propelled the album to double-platinum status. That same year, a single for the film *The Three Musketeers* performed by Sting, Bryan Adams, and Rod Stewart rode up the charts to number 1. In 1994, Sting also released a greatest hits collection that included remixes of several of his earlier songs by Hugh Padgham as well as two new songs, "When We Dance" and "This Cowboy Song."

In 1997 Sting released his fifth studio album, *Mercury Falling*, a work whose mature, restrained style showcases his meticulous song craft and production values more than his pop sensibilities. Though the single "Let Your Soul Be Your Pilot" received limited airplay, the overall lack of the accessible pop tunes that usually drove Sting's albums caused a dropoff in sales for the first time in his career. That said, *Mercury Falling* remains an interesting work with engaging songs and clever, thought-provoking lyrics. Like *The Soul Cages*, the album contains multiple reflections on a few recurring images, the foremost of which is the cycle of seasons. Though many songs seem to reflect the move from spring to winter, there is always present the sense that growth and new life lie just beyond in the cycle. As he sings in the final track, "Lithium Sunset," "I've been scattered, I've been shattered/ I've been knocked out of the race/ But I'll get better/ I'll feel your light upon my face/ Heal my soul oh lithium sunset/ And I'll ride the turning world/ Into another night."

Over the course of his varied career, Sting has proven himself to be a risk taker. Though his detractors have sometimes labeled Sting's music "pretentious," his supporters assert that his work simply assumes that listeners are intelligent enough to follow his lead.   —*Todd A. Elhart*

SELECT DISCOGRAPHY
■ ALBUMS
The Dream of the Blue Turtles, 1985
Bring on the Night, 1986
Nothing Like the Sun, 1987
The Soul Cages, 1991
Ten Summoner's Tales, 1993
Fields of Gold, 1994 (compilation)
Mercury Falling, 1997

SELECT AWARDS
Grammy Award for Song of the Year for "Every Breath You Take," 1983
Grammy Award for Best Pop Vocal Performance, Male, for *Bring on the Night*, 1987
Grammy Award for Best Rock Song for "Soul Cages," 1991
Grammy Award for Best Pop Vocal Performance, Male, for "If I Ever Lose My Faith in You," 1993

SEE ALSO: Police, The.

The Stone Temple Pilots

ORIGINAL MEMBERS: Scott Weiland (b. 1967), Robert DeLeo (b. 1966), Dean DeLeo (b. 1961), Eric Kretz (b. 1966)
FIRST ALBUM RELEASE: *Core*, 1992
MUSICAL STYLE: Rock and roll

Critics tend to cluster San Diego band the Stone Temple Pilots with their contemporaries, Seattle-based grunge bands such as Pearl Jam, Nirvana, and Alice in Chains. Though there are vocal similarities, the Stone Temple Pilots' sound places more emphasis on an amalgam of early 1970's hard rock and late 1970's British punk.

Going to California. Robert DeLeo left New Jersey for Southern California after his high school graduation. Though he had played bass in a bar band with his brother Dean, he had not considered a career in music. Vocalist Scott Weiland moved to Southern California from Cleveland, Ohio, at age fifteen. He met DeLeo at a Black Flag concert when they discovered they were both dating the same woman. The two also discovered that they were musically compatible and became songwriting partners. Drummer Eric Kretz was spotted while playing in a club, and the threesome moved to Los Angeles. When they were ready to record demos, Robert convinced his guitarist brother to move from New Jersey and join them. The quartet became Mighty Joe Young, debuting at the Whiskey a-Go-Go on the Sunset Strip in 1990.

In Flight. On April 1, 1992, the band was signed to Atlantic Records. One month later, while they were recording their debut album, they were informed that a blues singer already owned the name Mighty Joe Young. After two weeks of deliberation, Stone Temple Pilots, or STP, emerged. The name derived from Weiland's memory of the STP motor oil logo stickered to his boyhood bicycle seat. After experimenting with word combinations, the band just liked the way the words Stone Temple Pilots sounded together.

Core, released in September, 1992, was an immediate hit, especially after MTV put the first single, the anti-date-rape song "Sex Type Thing," into heavy rotation. The song has an aggressive riff, vocals that insinuate violence, first-person narrative, told from a male's perspective. This caused many to misconstrue the lyrics and de-

The Stone Temple Pilots' Scott Weiland (Scott Harrison/Archive Photos)

nounce the band for advocating, even inviting, rape. Lyricist Weiland, who has been an outspoken proponent of women's rights, vigorously fought to clarify his position. The band's most loved single, "Plush," helped propel Stone Temple Pilots toward a win at each of the major 1993 music awards shows.

In November of 1993, the band taped a critically acclaimed segment of *MTV Unplugged*. Then, they returned to the studio and recorded their second album, *Purple*, in only three weeks. Released in June, 1994, *Purple* (which never mentions the album's title on the cover) entered the *Billboard* Top 200 at number 1 and yielded three hit singles, "Vasoline," "Interstate Love Song," and "Big Empty." The album went triple platinum. STP also contributed a semiacoustic version of "Dancing Days" to 1995's *Encomium: A Tribute to Led Zeppelin*.

Offshoot Projects. In February of 1995, Weiland organized a side band called the Magnificent Bastards. The group recorded only one song, "Mockingbird Girl," which appeared on the *Tank Girl* film sound track. In May, 1995, Weiland was arrested for cocaine and heroin possession. After initial resistance, he finally succumbed to rehabilitation.

Recruiting singer Dave Coutts, the rest of the group formed a secondary band, Talk Show. In June, 1995, Weiland returned and STP managed to record a third album, 1996's *Tiny Music: Songs from the Vatican Gift Shop*. However, the accompanying tour had to be aborted so that Weiland could return to rehabilitation. The free time allowed Talk Show the chance to record their self-titled, self-produced debut from 1997. The band's sound drew comparisons to Aerosmith and other hard-rock acts, but the album was not well received. Vocalist Coutts was fired in May of 1998.

Weiland declared himself drug-free at the end of 1996 and immediately immersed himself in a solo career (though insisting that STP was still together). His first project was two tracks for the 1997 film *Great Expectations*. "Lady Your Roof Brings Me Down" was on the sound track, while "Desperation No. 5" was featured in the film. In 1998, Weiland released a much maligned solo album, *12 Bar Blues*, once more promising that next would come a Stone Temple Pilots project. However, in June while on tour supporting his solo album, Weiland was arrested for heroin possession in New York, and the band's future was again in question. —*Deirdre Rockmaker*

SELECT DISCOGRAPHY
■ ALBUMS
Core, 1992
Purple, 1994
Tiny Music: Songs from the Vatican Gift Shop, 1996

SELECT AWARDS
Grammy Award for Best Hard Rock Performance with Vocal for "Plush," 1993
American Music Award for Best Rock Artist, 1993
Billboard, named Best New Artist and Best Rock Artist, 1993
MTV Video Music Award for Best New Artist, 1993
Billboard, named Best Rock Artist, 1995

SEE ALSO: Alice in Chains; Nirvana; Pearl Jam.

George Strait

BORN: Pearsall, Texas; May 18, 1952
FIRST ALBUM RELEASE: *Strait Country*, 1981
MUSICAL STYLES: Country, western swing

Every one of George Strait's albums has received gold certification and nineteen have platinum or multi-platinum certification. *Pure Country*, the sound track from his 1992 film, sold five million copies. His quadruple-platinum boxed set, *Strait out of the Box*, is the best-selling country boxed set of all time. Every MCA single has made the charts and thirty-two have made it to number 1. Strait has garnered the most important awards from both the Country Music Association and the Academy of Country Music, including Entertainer of the Year (in 1989 and 1990).

Beginnings. George Strait was born May 18, 1952, in Pearsall, Texas, the second of three children of a high school math teacher. During his teenage years, he, like most teenagers of the 1960's, gravitated to rock and roll. After high school, he enrolled at Southwest Texas State University, but he dropped out, married his high school sweetheart, Norma, and enlisted in the Army. Strait spent most of his military service in Hawaii, in the payroll and disbursement division. It was during this time, in the early 1970's, that he taught himself guitar. In 1973, Strait auditioned for the lead-singer position in an Army-sponsored country-and-western band. He won the job and spent his last year in the service singing. After his Army stint, Strait returned to San Marcos, Texas, where he joined the Ace in the Hole band, which played classic western-swing music to the dance-hall patrons in that area of western Texas. After several recordings for regional labels and three unsuccessful trips to Nashville in pursuit of a major recording contract, he finished his degree in agriculture at Southwest Texas State University. Just as he was on the verge of giving up on music and accepting a job with a cattle pen company in Uvalde, Texas, his wife convinced him that he should give his music career one more try.

Erv Woolsey had owned a San Marcos club called the Prairie Rose, where Strait and his band had performed. Even after he sold the club, Woolsey kept in touch with Strait. In 1980, Woolsey, who had also formerly worked in MCA promotions, helped Strait get a recording session at MCA. Recorded on his second demo session, "Unwound" excited MCA executives. The released song rose to number 4 on the country charts and MCA quickly signed Strait to a contract in February, 1981. Woolsey became his manager and Blake Mevis became his producer.

Number One. Strait was offered the opportunity to sing "Fool Hearted Memory" during a barroom brawl scene in the Universal Pictures film *The Soldier* (1982). Even though few people saw the film, the song earned Strait his first number 1 single in August, 1982. His next chart topper came more than one year later (September, 1983) with "A Fire I Can't Put Out," which came from his second album, *Strait from the Heart* (1983). From there followed a string of five consecutive number 1 singles.

The urban-cowboy fad of the early 1980's had pressured several country artists to change their performing style to pop country. Strait resisted the temptation and remained faithful to his country-swing roots. Instead of changing his style, he changed producers for his third album, *Right or Wrong* (1983).

For his next recording project, *Does Fort Worth Ever Cross Your Mind* (1984), Strait once again changed producers. This time he turned to Jimmy Bowen, who had produced albums for such artists as Dean Martin and Frank Sinatra. Bowen allowed Strait to coproduce for the first time. Both the Country Music Association (CMA) and the Academy of Country Music (ACM) selected the project as Album of the Year.

MCA gathered hits from Strait's first four years into his first greatest-hits collection in 1985. Later that year, the *Something Special* album was released. Just before Christmas, 1985, "The Chair" became Strait's seventh number 1.

In June, 1986, Strait's teenage daughter, Jenifer, was killed in a car accident. When Strait won the CMA Male Vocalist of the Year Award, he dedicated the trophy to his daughter's memory.

For the first time in the history of *Billboard*'s country album chart, a new release entered the chart in the number 1 position. It was Strait's *Ocean Front Property* (1987), which was certified double platinum in 1997. The album produced three number 1 hits: the title cut, "Am I Blue," and "All My Ex's Live in Texas," which brought Strait his first Grammy Award nomination.

The Hits Keep Coming. Strait's eleventh album, *If You Ain't Lovin' (You Ain't Livin')* (1988), produced three more number 1 songs, including "Famous Last Words of a Fool," "Baby Blue," and the title cut, which was written in 1953 by Tommy Collins. Strait was now the top-grossing country performer with concert-ticket sales of more than $10 million. After five straight nominations for the CMA Entertainer of the Year Award, he finally won in 1989. He won the same honor at the Academy of Country Music Awards ceremony.

Beyond the Blue Neon, released in 1989, became the seventh Strait album to top the country chart. From it came "Baby's Gotten Good at Goodbye,"

George Strait (MCA/Mike Rutherford)

"What's Going On in Your World," and "Ace in the Hole," completing a run of eleven consecutive number 1 albums dating back to 1986. During the Grammy Awards ceremony, a new commercial for Budweiser beer debuted, which featured Strait performing "Ace in the Hole."

Strait's first album of the new decade was *Livin' It Up* (1990), which sold one million copies and not only was a number 1 country album but also rose to number 35 on the pop album chart. "Love Without End, Amen," Strait's first single of the 1990's, was the first single in thirteen years to spend five consecutive weeks in the number 1 position on the *Billboard* country singles chart. This song was Strait's biggest single. "I've Come to Expect It from You," another cut from the album, also spent five weeks at the top of the chart.

Diversity. George Strait came to film screens all over the country in 1992, when his *Pure Country* motion picture was released. The film introduced Strait to millions of filmgoers who until then had never heard of him or knew very little about him. The immensely successful sound track became Strait's first quintuple-platinum album. The album would go on to become one of the twenty best-selling country albums in history.

Lead On, Strait's 1994 album, debuted at number 1 on the charts and, like most of his other efforts, earned platinum certification. *Lead On* yielded "The Big One," which spent five weeks at number 1, making it another of Strait's best chart performers.

In 1995, MCA released Strait's most ambitious recording project: *Strait out of the Box,* the seventy-two-song, four-compact-disc boxed set that became one of the biggest-selling boxed sets in all genres of music. Its contents ranged from his previous number 1 singles to obscure recordings from his early years. The boxed set also produced another number 1 song: "Check Yes or No." The song won numerous honors, including CMA, ACM, and The Nashville Network/Music City News (TNN/MCN) Single of the Year Awards. It was also voted the Video of the Year by TNN/MCN.

Blue Clear Sky, Strait's 1996 album, entered *Billboard*'s country album chart at number 1 and sold two million copies. The title cut lasted two weeks at number 1, while "Carried Away" collected three weeks there.

Strait's 1997 MCA album, *Carrying Your Love with Me*, debuted at number 1 and yielded two number 1 hits: "One Night at a Time," which spent five weeks at number 1, and the title cut, which stayed on top for four weeks.

All but two of Strait's albums are certified platinum or better, and he has sold more than thirty-nine million albums. He also matches his success as a recording artist in his live performances. In the 1990's, his concerts, which have always sold out, set records for how quickly they sold out. Strait has three of the four biggest songs of the 1990's.

George Strait's greatest ambition, to become a member of the Country Music Hall of Fame, seems very well within his grasp. This soft-spoken, privacy-loving Texan has been unequaled for persistent high quality, consistency of sales, and influence on country music since his 1981 debut.

—*Don Tyler*

SELECT DISCOGRAPHY

■ ALBUMS

Strait Country, 1981
Strait from the Heart, 1983
Right or Wrong, 1983
Does Fort Worth Ever Cross Your Mind, 1984
Greatest Hits, 1985 (compilation)
Something Special, 1985
Ocean Front Property, 1987
Greatest Hits, Volume 2, 1987 (compilation)
If You Ain't Lovin' (You Ain't Livin'), 1988
Beyond the Blue Neon, 1989
Livin' It Up, 1990
Pure Country, 1992 (sound track)
Easy Come, Easy Go, 1993
Lead On, 1994
Strait out of the Box, 1995 (four-CD boxed set, compilation)
Blue Clear Sky, 1996
Carrying Your Love with Me, 1997

SELECT AWARDS

Academy of Country Music Male Vocalist of the Year Award, 1985
Country Music Association Album of the Year and Male Vocalist of the Year Awards for *Does Fort Worth Ever Cross Your Mind*, 1985
Academy of Country Music Album of the Year and Male Vocalist of the Year Awards, 1986
Country Music Association Male Vocalist of the Year Award, 1986
Academy of Country Music Male Vocalist of the Year Award, 1989
Country Music Association Entertainer of the Year Award, 1989, 1990
Academy of Country Music Entertainer of the Year Award, 1990
Academy of Country Music Single Record of the Year Award for "Check Yes or No," 1996

For the Record

There is only one personal goal that George Strait has not achieved: He has not won the team roping competition at the annual Kingsville, Texas, rodeo event that he sponsors.

Country Music Association Album of the Year for *Strait Out of the Box*, Single of the Year for "Check Yes or No," and Male Vocalist of the Year Awards, 1996

Country Music Association Male Vocalist of the Year Award, 1998

SEE ALSO: Brooks, Garth; Gill, Vince; Sinatra, Frank; Travis, Randy.

The Stray Cats / Brian Setzer

The Stray Cats

ORIGINAL MEMBERS: Brian Setzer (b. 1969), Slim Jim Phantom (b. Jim McDonnell, 1961), Lee Rocker (b. Lee Drucker, 1961)

FIRST ALBUM RELEASE: *Stray Cats*, 1981

Brian Setzer

BORN: New York, New York; April 10, 1959

FIRST ALBUM RELEASE: *The Knife Feels Like Justice*, 1986

MUSICAL STYLES: Rockabilly, rock and roll, big band

Formed in Long Island, New York, in 1979, the Stray Cats helped to fuel a resurgence of interest in rockabilly music on both sides of the Atlantic Ocean. Although this trio's meteoric rise to worldwide stardom in 1982 was followed by an equally swift decline in popularity, the Stray Cats produced some very memorable music in a brief period of time and made a lasting mark on pop music with some of the biggest selling rockabilly tunes ever recorded.

The Beginnings. While much of the early 1980's popular music scene revolved around the synthetic sounds of new wave, the Stray Cats burst onto the musical stage with straight-ahead guitar, bass, and drums rock and roll. Rockabilly music is a type of rock and roll that was born in the southern United States. Most heavily influenced by country music, rockabilly features basic guitar and bass (often acoustic) with driving, snappy rhythms. Rockbilly's heyday was in the mid-to late 1950's, and the Stray Cats' style harked back to the sounds of Buddy Holly, Elvis Presley, Ricky Nelson, Roy Orbison, and Carl Perkins.

Although the group started out in the late 1970's in New York, it was not until they relocated to London, England—where rockabilly was more popular—that the Stray Cats established themselves. There they teamed up with rockabilly guitarist Dave Edmunds, whose reputation as a producer surpassed his popularity as a solo artist and member of Rockpile. Edmunds produced the Stray Cats' first two breakthrough albums in the United Kingdom.

Stardom. In November, 1980, the Stray Cats' single "Runaway Boys" landed in the British Top 10. With Brian Setzer's smooth vocals and a clean, rowdy, fast-paced sound, the Stray Cats offered music that felt lively and new. Their U.S. debut, *Built for Speed* (1982), contained songs from their first two British releases. *Built for Speed* included their big hits, "Rock This Town" and "Stray Cat Strut." Most of their best-known music is found on this album. *Rant n' Rave with the Stray Cats* (1983) was less successful than their U.S. debut, but it did result in another Top-10 single in "Sexy + 17."

Swift Decline. The band broke up in 1983, as band members pursued solo interests. In 1986 they reunited to produce *Rock Therapy*, an album that did not result in a hoped-for comeback. Setzer, meanwhile, contributed to Robert Plant's *Honeydrippers* and portrayed early rocker Eddie Cochran in the 1987 film about Ritchie Valens, *La Bamba*.

Their 1989 release, *Blast Off*, reunited the Stray Cats with producer Dave Edmunds. It also represented a return to the vitality and energy of the early days. By this time, however, the public showed little interest in the Stray Cats' driving rockabilly sound.

Setzer Solo. Of the members of the Stray Cats, Setzer has remained the most visible and commercially viable. In the mid-1980's his bandmates, Lee Rocker and Slim Jim Phantom, joined forces with former David Bowie guitarist Earl Slick to form Phantom, Rocker, and Slick. Rocker has also performed with the traditional rockabilly group Big Blue.

Setzer's mid-1980's solo offerings include 1986's *The Knife Feels Like Justice* and 1988's *Live*

Brian Setzer (Lissa Wales)

SEE ALSO: Orbison, Roy; Presley, Elvis.

Barbra Streisand

BORN: Brooklyn, New York; April 24, 1942
FIRST ALBUM RELEASE: *The Barbra Streisand Album*,
    1963
MUSICAL STYLES: Pop, easy listening

Nude Guitars, the latter featuring much of the same musical intensity that defined the early Stray Cats recordings. A creative and imaginative musician, Setzer reignited his career in 1994 with the release of *The Brian Setzer Orchestra*. This unorthodox rock-and-roll outfit combined Setzer's driving rockabilly guitar with a sixteen-piece big-band orchestra. A few old Stray Cats hits were included in a varied repertoire consisting of blues, romantic standards, and big-band numbers. The Brian Setzer Orchestra has received critical acclaim and by 1998 was enjoying a significant following.

—*Benjamin Pensiero*

Barbra Streisand, the self-termed "actress who sings," has built her nearly forty-year career, which has produced an overwhelming fifty-four albums, on exceptional talent, personal eccentricity, and a driving ambition to be the greatest entertainer of her generation. With thirty-nine gold albums, she is third on the all-time record sales charts, with only Elvis Presley and the Beatles ahead of her. Not only have more than three dozen of her albums become gold, but twenty-five have reached platinum status, and the Recording Industry Association of America recently noted that she is the only female artist to have collected twelve multiplatinum albums.

The Beginnings. Born Barbara Joan Streisand to Jewish parents in Brooklyn, New York, Streisand began life in a small, poor family. Less than a year after her birth, Streisand's father, a highly respected teacher, died suddenly of a brain aneurysm. Streisand spent her early childhood in a cramped and loveless environment with her mother and older brother Sheldon. She started yeshiva, Jewish school where both religious and secular subjects are taught, in 1947. Concerned that her daughter was too thin, Streisand's mother sent her to a health camp that summer to gain weight. Streisand disliked the health camp so much that she developed psychosomatic asthma while there. Since that summer, she has been a hypochondriac.

Complicating the already tumultuous state of Streisand's emotional life, her mother, Diana Streisand, remarried in 1950. A few days after the wedding, Streisand's half sister Rosalynd was born. Streisand's stepfather, Louis Kind, moved the five of them into a one bedroom apartment and withdrew Streisand and her brother from yeshiva, one act of many that contributed to Streisand's lack of love for Kind. Even as a young girl, Streisand demonstrated her desire to perform. Her mother and stepfather worked to squelch her enthusiasm for performing by constantly telling her that she was too unattractive to be entertaining. Streisand's reaction to such pronouncements was characteristically rebellious, and she became all the more determined to succeed.

Early Career. While in high school, Streisand excelled at academics and joined the chorus, but was socially distant from her peers. After her mother and stepfather divorced in 1956, she secretly took acting lessons with money set aside for her college education. Streisand's talent grew rapidly and, after lying about her age, the sixteen-year-old girl won her first stage part in *The Desk Set*. While still performing in *The Desk Set*, Streisand graduated from high school in January, 1959. Though she was fourth in her class, Streisand refused to go to college and instead moved to Manhattan to pursue her acting career. It was while living in Manhattan that Streisand met Marty Erlichman, her lifelong manager.

In 1962, Streisand's first Broadway performance, *I Can Get It for You Wholesale*, was tremen-

For the Record

Barbra Streisand is the only performer to have had a number 1 album in the 1960's, 1970's, 1980's, and 1990's. She won a Grammy for her first album, an Emmy for her first television special, and an Academy Award for her first film. She is also the only person to have won Academy Awards for both acting and songwriting.

dously successful. During this production, she established her reputation as being very difficult to work with. She was late for rehearsals, demanding, argumentative, and inconsistent. Despite the trouble backstage, the production was so successful that Streisand signed a musical contract with Columbia Records to record her own album, *The Barbra Streisand Album*. While recording this album, Streisand married Elliot Gould, her costar in *I Can Get It for You Wholesale*, on September 13, 1963. The album made Streisand nationally known. Listeners marveled at her singing, with its combination of emotion, power, and control. The proof of Streisand's burgeoning success and popularity came when, early in 1964, she won two 1963 Grammy Awards for *The Barbra Streisand Album*. She was only twenty-one years old.

In 1964, her role as Fanny Brice in *Funny Girl* took Broadway by storm. That year she also had a major hit with the song "People" from the show. In 1965 and 1966, Streisand continued to win major industry awards, and she appeared on *The Ed Sullivan Show*, *The Judy Garland Show*, and *The Tonight Show*. Her photographs made the cover of *Time* and *Life* magazines; women all over America imitated her hairstyle, makeup, and clothing. Despite all her success, Streisand's self-image was often jeopardized by her mother's negative comments.

Motherhood, Career Moves, Divorce. Streisand gave birth to her son Jason Gould on December 29, 1966. Of motherhood she said, "It is the height of creativity for any woman." Streisand stayed home with her son briefly before going to

Hollywood to fulfill her life's dream of being a film star.

Once in California, Streisand began demonstrating a fear of public appearances and live performances that would become legendary. At her first Hollywood party, she hid from the other guests, many of whom were influential and could have greatly helped her film career. After ruining a second chance to meet Hollywood's most powerful people, Streisand told the press that the Hollywood locals were boring and self-centered. Despite such affronts to the filmmaking establishment, Streisand starred in the film version of *Funny Girl* (1968). The filming of *Funny Girl* caused an international furor by pairing the Jewish Streisand with an Egyptian actor, Omar Sharif, at the time Israel and Egypt were fighting the Six Day War. To further incite matters, Streisand had a highly publicized affair with Sharif, which contributed to her separation from Elliot Gould in 1969. She would date other famous actors, athletes, journalists, and businessmen before finally marrying actor James Brolin in mid-1998.

In the 1970's Streisand continued her interwoven film and recording careers. In 1973 she starred with Robert Redford in *The Way We Were* and had a number 1 hit with its title song. In 1977 she repeated the feat with the film *A Star Is Born* (this time starring with Kris Kristofferson) and its love theme, "Evergreen." The single "Woman in Love" went to number 1 in 1980. She also recorded hit duets, including the number 1 "You Don't Bring Me Flowers" with Neil Diamond (1978), "No More Tears (Enough Is Enough)" with Donna Summer (1979), and "Guilty" with the Bee Gees' Barry Gibb (1980).

Other Interests. As Streisand's career progressed and she met with continued success as an actress and singer, her interests branched into other aspects of the entertainment industry. While in her thirties, she became active in politics and social issues other than Jewish issues and support for Israel, causes to which she had always been a partisan. Streisand established the Barbra Streisand Foundation to support liberal political causes, and she has supported gay and women's rights and environmentalism. The progress of the feminist movement in the 1960's and 1970's encouraged Streisand to found First Artists Production Company. This company gave her and its other members more control over the final forms of their films. *Up the Sandbox* (1972), released by First Artists, was Streisand's first effort as the producer and star of a film, but met with very little success. She began directing films in 1983 with *Yentl*, which was also her first effort as director, producer, and star.

—*Melissa R. Grimm*

Barbra Streisand (Columbia/Randee St. Nicholas)

SELECT DISCOGRAPHY

■ SINGLES

"People," 1964
"Stoney End," 1970
"The Way We Were," 1973
"Love Theme from *A Star Is Born* (Evergreen)," 1977
"You Don't Bring Me Flowers," 1978 (with Neil Diamond)
"No More Tears (Enough Is Enough)," 1979 (with Donna Summer)
"Woman in Love," 1980
"Guilty," 1980 (with Barry Gibb)

■ ALBUMS

The Barbra Streisand Album, 1963
Funny Girl, 1964 (sound track)
People, 1964
My Name Is Barbra, 1965
Hello, Dolly!, 1969 (sound track)
On a Clear Day You Can See Forever, 1970 (sound track)
The Owl and the Pussycat, 1970 (sound track)
Barbra Joan Streisand, 1971
The Way We Were, 1974 (sound track)
Funny Lady, 1975 (sound track)
A Star Is Born, 1976 (sound track)
Yentl, 1983 (sound track)
One Voice, 1987
Just for the Record, 1991 (4-CD boxed set)
Barbra: The Concert, 1994
Higher Ground, 1997

SELECT AWARDS

Grammy Awards for Album of the Year and Best Vocal Performance, Female, for *The Barbra Streisand Album*, 1963
Grammy Award for Best Vocal Performance, Female, for "People," 1964
Grammy Award for Best Vocal Performance, Female, for *My Name Is Barbra*, 1965
Emmy Awards for Outstanding Individual Achievement and Outstanding Program Achievement for *My Name Is Barbra*, 1965
Tony Star of the Decade Award, 1970
Academy Award for Best Song for "Love Theme from *A Star Is Born* (Evergreen)," from *A Star Is Born*, 1976 (with Paul Williams)
Grammy Awards for Song of the Year (wr. with Paul Williams) and Best Vocal Performance, Female, for "Love Theme from *A Star Is Born* (Evergreen)," 1977
Grammy Award for Best Pop Performance by a Duo or Group with Vocal for "Guilty," 1980 (with Barry Gibb)
Grammy Award for Best Pop Vocal Performance, Female, for *The Broadway Album*, 1986
Grammy Living Legend Award, 1992
Grammy Award for Lifetime Achievement, 1995

Styx

ORIGINAL MEMBERS: Dennis DeYoung (b. 1947), Chuck Panozzo (b. 1948), John Panozzo (1948-1996), John Curulewski (d. 1988), James Young (b. 1949)
OTHER MEMBERS: Tommy Shaw (b. 1953), Todd Sucherman
FIRST ALBUM RELEASE: *Styx*, 1972
MUSICAL STYLE: Rock and roll

Along with Foreigner, Styx was one of the most successful art-rock bands of the 1970's, producing rock ballads with over-arranged instruments and mammoth guitar solos that defined what came to be known as "pomp" rock. Their conceptual approach to albums worked well with their theatrical approach to live performance, and although the band was initially slow to gain popularity, in the late 1970's Styx recorded four triple-platinum albums in a row.

The Tradewinds. Styx came together on the South Side of Chicago in the 1960's, when Chuck and John Panozzo, practicing their music in the basement of their house after school, invited an accordian-playing Dennis DeYoung to join them. Eventually they were joined by other aspiring musicians, including guitarist John Curulewski, and the group soon played local clubs and high school dances as the Tradewinds and, later, TW4.

When the group lost a guitar player, DeYoung recruited another area musician, James Young, to join as one of their principal singers. Before long the band had cultivated a strong regional following, prompting Wooden Nickel Records to offer them a recording contract in 1972, contingent upon changing their name. Styx's first few albums received little airtime, until listeners began to bombard Chicago station WLS with requests for "Lady," DeYoung's tribute to his wife, Suzanne. In 1975, two years after its initial release, the song became a Top-10 hit, elevating the album *Styx II* (1973) to belated gold status.

In 1975 the band released *Equinox*, their first album for A&M Records; it featured DeYoung's "Suite Madame Blue," an extended allegory for the moral decline of the United States. Just as Styx was about to embark on their next concert tour, however, Curulewski left the band. He was replaced by twenty-three-year-old Alabama musician Tommy Shaw, who ended up writing four of the songs on the group's next album, *Crystal Ball* (1976).

String of Success. Their seventh album, *The Grand Illusion*, was released on July 7, 1977. It was the first of four triple-platinum albums in a row, one each year for the rest of the decade. DeYoung's "Come Sail Away," with its slow, melodic opening and frantically energetic finish, was a Top-10 hit for the group. *Pieces of Eight* (1978) featured Shaw's hard-hitting "Renegade" and "Blue Collar Man." On *Cornerstone* (1979) Shaw demonstrated a different side of his talent with the exotic "Boat on the River," while DeYoung gave the group their first number 1 hit, "Babe." The band's masterpiece, however, was the concept album *Paradise Theater* (1980), which used the metaphor of Chicago's famous film theater to express the U.S. national sense of disillusionment.

The ambitious *Kilroy Was Here* (1983) carried the concept album one step further, telling the story of a dystopian future in which rock music has been banned. The tour performances incorporated multiple sets, costumes, scripted dialogue, and even an eleven-minute film. The album produced two Top-10 hits, "Mr. Roboto" and "Don't Let It End," but it failed to meet the high mark set by the previous four. After releasing an uninspired live album, *Caught in the Act* (1984), the group disbanded until 1990, when all the

---

For the Record

After the 1991 Styx reunion tour, the theatrical Dennis DeYoung found a place for himself in the musical theater, playing the part of Pontius Pilate in the national company of the Andrew Lloyd Webber and Tim Rice musical *Jesus Christ Superstar*.

---

band members but Shaw reunited for *Edge of the Century* and the Gulf War hit "Show Me the Way."

The death of John Panozzo in 1996 was a blow to his former bandmates, but a few weeks later the remaining members of the group, including Shaw, came together once again to record new versions of their old hits for *Return to Paradise* (1997). They also recorded several new songs for the album, including "Dear John," written by Shaw in memory of Panozzo.   —Ed McKnight

SELECT DISCOGRAPHY
■ ALBUMS
Styx, 1972
Styx II, 1973
The Serpent Is Rising, 1973
Man of Miracles, 1974
Equinox, 1975
Crystal Ball, 1976
The Grand Illusion, 1977
Pieces of Eight, 1978
Cornerstone, 1979
Paradise Theater, 1980
Kilroy Was Here, 1983
Caught in the Act, 1984
Edge of the Century, 1990
Return to Paradise, 1997

SEE ALSO: Foreigner.

Sublime

ORIGINAL MEMBERS: Brad Nowell (1968-1996), Eric Wilson, Floyd "Bud" Gaugh
FIRST ALBUM RELEASE: *40 oz. to Freedom*, 1992

MUSICAL STYLES: Punk rock, alternative, ska, reggae, psychedelic rock, hip-hop

Formed in Long Beach, California, in 1988, Sublime started as a below-average garage-punk band that ultimately escalated into a considerable musical entity. The trio—consisting of singer-songwriter and guitarist Brad Nowell, bassist Eric Wilson, and drummer Bud Gaugh—grew to fame in the mid-1990's in the wake of the California punk explosion engendered by bands such as Green Day and the Offspring. Though punk influenced, Sublime prided themselves on not fitting into any musical category. Their sound has been described as a blending of an aggressive punk influence with ska, reggae, and psychedelic rock. Sublime was gaining momentum in the mid-1990's, and a long-term career seemed promising, when Nowell died of a heroin overdose in 1996. In the wake of Nowell's death, Sublime became more popular than ever, with their third album becoming one of the best-selling rock albums of 1997.

The Making of a Cult Classic. Started in 1988, Sublime worked its way up from being a favorite band to have at local parties to the focus of fanatical regional support among the surfing and skateboarding crowd in Long Beach. Sublime played its first show on July 4, 1988, at a Long Beach club. Their performance helped set off the infamous "Peninsula Riot" of Long Beach. The group began touring aggressively after this and continued to

For the Record

Like De La Soul and other artists who have experimented with using sampled sounds in their music, Sublime have been forced to pay royalties to original artists they have sampled or else remove the samples from their albums. In fact, "Get Out," a signature Sublime song that exemplifies the band's creative use of sampling, had to be cut from the *40 oz. to Freedom* album.

build its fan base among the culture of Southern California's beach cities.

In 1992, Nowell teamed up with long-time Sublime producer Michael "Miguel" Happoldt and founded Skunk Record, which released Sublime's first album, *40 oz. to Freedom* (1992). Nowell had to pawn all the band's equipment to establish Skunk Records, but the risk paid off. As Sublime toured around playing live shows, they sold the album out of the back of their van. Two years, three vans, and five tours later, the album had sold in excess of forty thousand copies despite never having had a distributor.

The album itself was an aggressive blend of thrashing punk rock and ska rhythms, but it also took significant cues from the reggae of Bob Marley. In making the album, Sublime also made extensive use of sampling—everything from old Minutemen records to hip-hop music to conversations with homeless people—creating in their music a collage of modern sound that would come to be recognized as a trademark of the band.

Remarkably, *40 oz. to Freedom* was on the *Billboard* Alternative New Artist Albums chart for fifty weeks in 1992 and 1993, spending the last thirty of these in the Top 20. The album also broke into *Billboard*'s Heatseeker (Top 50 new artists) chart, while the band spent five weeks as the top-selling new artist in *Billboard*'s Pacific region. In 1997, the album enjoyed a resurgence, selling ten thousand copies weekly and achieving the status of a cult classic.

On the strength of Sublime's airplay on alternative rock radio stations, MCA Records signed the band. In 1994, MCA Records released Sublime's second album, *Robbin the Hood*, which continued to reflect the experimental ethic that had emerged in Sublime's first album. In contrast to the well-tuned, highly produced sound of the California punk revival, Sublime's sound, as exemplified in their second album, was more cut-and-paste and raw. Though *40 oz. to Freedom* and *Robbin the Hood* each contained more than twenty tracks, each was produced for less than ten thousand dollars.

Success, Collapse, and Legacy. *Robbin the Hood* set the stage for the breakout of Sublime's self-titled third album in 1996. Just two months before its release, however, Nowell was found dead from a heroin overdose in a San Francisco apartment. Although the band collapsed in the wake of Nowell's death, the album *Sublime* went on to become a success. The song "What I Got" was a hit on alternative radio stations and, by the end of 1996, the album went gold. Even though the band's surviving members decided not to promote the album by touring under the Sublime name, it became one of 1997's best-selling rock records.

Produced by the legendary Paul Leary of the Butthole Surfers, the album *Sublime* reflected the band's wide range of musical influences. Songs on the album variously reflected reggae and ska sounds, Jimi Hendrix-influenced psychedelic rock, and early hardcore punk of the 1980's. Once again, extensive samples ranging from episodes in Southern California living rooms to the rantings of a science fiction writer punctuated the album's songs. Though the band's life ended with Nowell's death, Sublime's unique sound made its mark on a sea of fans as well as other Southern California bands of the era such as No Doubt. After Nowell's death, MCA Records released *Second Hand Smoke*, an album of unreleased tracks, remixes, and demos. —*Amanda Walzer Scott*

SELECT DISCOGRAPHY

■ ALBUMS
40 oz. to Freedom, 1992
Robbin the Hood, 1994
Sublime, 1996
Second Hand Smoke, 1997
Acoustic: Bradley Nowell and Friends, 1998

SEE ALSO: Green Day; Hendrix, Jimi; Marley, Bob; No Doubt.

Sublime (MCA/John Dunne)

The Sugarcubes. *See* Björk / The Sugarcubes

Donna Summer

(Donna Gaines)

BORN: Boston, Massachusetts; December 31, 1948
FIRST ALBUM RELEASE: *Love to Love You*, 1975
MUSICAL STYLES: Disco, soul, rhythm and blues, pop

One of the biggest stars of the late 1970's, Donna Summer helped usher in the disco era with a string of racy dance-oriented hits. The Boston-born singer was one of the few disco performers to parlay her initial success into a full-fledged pop career. Later a born-again Christian, she was the subject of controversy for allegedly making anti-gay remarks, an act she has consistently denied.

Donna Summer (AP/Wide World Photos)

The Beginnings. Summer sang in churches in her native Boston and made her professional debut at Beantown's Psychedelic Supper in 1967. She then moved to New York, and later to Europe, where she secured her first professional job as a member of the Munich, Germany, cast of Gerome Ragni, James Rado, and Galt MacDermott's musical *Hair.* At this time, she also married Austrian actor Helmut Sommer; although she later divorced him, she kept his surname, anglicizing it to Summer. During her European years, Summer appeared in Dubose Heyward and Ira and George Gershwin's *Porgy and Bess,* staged by the Vienna Folk Opera, and as a backup singer at Munich's Musicland Studios. The latter stint brought her to the attention of producers Giorgio Moroder and

Pete Bellotte, who fashioned a series of European hits for the Oasis label.

A Disco Diva Is Born. In 1975, Summer returned to the United States on the wings of her first hit, "Love to Love You Baby," a seventeen-minute song with sexually explicit lyrics. The song (number 2, pop; number 3, rhythm and blues) established the fledgling Casablanca Records as a major force and proved to be the first of nearly two dozen Top-40 hits for Summer.

Summer's early successes included "I Feel Love" (number 6, pop; number 9, R &B), "MacArthur Park" (her first number 1 pop hit), and the Grammy Award- and Academy Award-winning "Last Dance," from the 1978 film *Thank God It's Friday.* Her 1979 release, *Bad Girls,* fueled by the hit singles "Hot Stuff" (number 1, pop; number 20, rhythm and blues) and the title track (number 1, pop and rhythm and blues), broadened her audience to include disco, pop, and even rock fans. Other hits of this period included "No More Tears (Enough Is Enough)," a number 1 pop duet with Barbra Streisand, "Heaven Knows," (number 4, pop; number 10, rhythm and blues), and "Dim All the Lights" (number 2, pop; number 13, rhythm and blues).

New Record Deal. In 1980, Summer sued her manager, Joyce Bogart, and Bogart's husband, Neil (president of Casablanca Records), for ten million dollars, for allegedly mismanaging her career. Summer ended her contract with Casablanca and switched to the Geffen label. Her first release on the new label, *The Wanderer* (1980), featured the number 3 pop title single but did not sell as well as anticipated. Also, in 1980, Summer married Bruce Sudano, the lead singer of Brooklyn Dreams and her singing partner on "Heaven Knows."

Around this time, Summer was rumored to have made the comment that the burgeoning acquired immunodeficiency syndrome (AIDS) epidemic was God's revenge on homosexuals. The born-again Christian singer, who had included a Christian song on *The Wanderer,* denied these remarks, but she lost much of her gay fan base as a result—although in the 1990's, she would make overtures to the gay community.

The Hits Slow Down. Although she would continue to record successful hits, Summer's last Top-10 album was 1983's *She Works Hard for the Money*, which featured the number 3 title track and a popular video on MTV. Summer returned to the Top 10 in 1989 with the single "This Time I Know It's for Real" (number 7), from her album *Another Place, Another Time.*

In the 1990's, Summer continued to expand her musical horizons. She released *Mistaken Identity*, a soulful but less dance-oriented album; recorded "Does He Love You," a duet with Liza Minnelli on the latter's *Gently* album; wrote the title track for Reba McEntire's 1996 album, *Starting Over*; and has been collaborating on a Broadway musical with her husband, pop producer Michael Omartian, and two-time Academy Award winner Al Kasha. —*Robert DiGiacomo*

SELECT DISCOGRAPHY
■ ALBUMS
Love to Love You, 1975
A Love Trilogy, 1976
The Four Seasons of Love, 1976
I Remember Yesterday, 1977
Once upon a Time, 1977
Bad Girls, 1979
On the Radio: Greatest Hits, 1979 (compilation)
The Wanderer, 1980
Walk Away—Collector's Edition, 1980
Donna Summer, 1982
She Works Hard for the Money, 1983

For the Record

"I'm not a person who runs after success, per se," Donna Summer has said. "Whatever happens, happens. So many times you gear yourself up for something and think, 'Oh, this is it. This is the big one.' And it fizzles . . . and you sit there disappointed. So you adjust yourself. You wait until things happen, then you get excited. That's my modus operandi."

Cats Without Claws, 1984
All Systems Go, 1987
Another Place and Time, 1989
Mistaken Identity, 1991
Anthology, 1993 (compilation)

SELECT AWARDS
Grammy Award for Best R&B Vocal Performance, Female, for "Last Dance," 1978
Grammy Award for Best Rock Vocal Performance, Female, for "Hot Stuff," 1979
Grammy Award for Best Inspirational Performance for "He's a Rebel," 1983
Grammy Award for Best Inspirational Performance for "Forgive Me," 1984

SEE ALSO: Bee Gees, The; KC and the Sunshine Band; Village People, The.

Supertramp

ORIGINAL MEMBERS: Roger Hodgson (b. 1950), Richard Davies (b. 1944), Dave Winthrop (b. 1948), Richard Palmer, Bob Miller
OTHER MEMBERS: Frank Farrell, Kevin Currie, John Anthony Helliwell (b. 1945), Dougie Thomson (b. 1951), Bob C. Benberg
FIRST ALBUM RELEASE: *Supertramp*, 1970
MUSICAL STYLES: Pop, progressive rock, blues

Supertramp began, oddly enough, when singer Richard Davies met a young Dutch millionaire by the name of Stanley August Miesegaes in 1969. At the time, Davies was in a band called the Joint, which happened to be playing in Munich, Germany, when Miesegaes took Davies aside. He said that he would sponsor a band of Davies' choosing, so Davies placed advertisements in London newspapers for new band members. Offered a genuine opportunity to play in a rock band, four musicians answered the ad for the group Daddy, which was quickly renamed Supertramp.

Early Failures. Despite Miesegaes's support and a contract with A&M Records, their first album, *Supertramp*, failed to chart in 1970. Undefeated, Supertramp released a second album in 1971, *Indelibly Stamped*, but again the album failed and a tour taken to promote the album was a disaster. Everyone except the songwriting-singing team Hodgson and Davies departed, including Miesegaes, although he generously took responsibility for their debts, which ran to several thousand U.S. dollars. Hodgson and Davies recruited more members and appointed Dougie Thomson to handle the group's business affairs in 1973.

A Logical Break. Secluded in a seventeenth-century farmhouse called Southcombe in Somerset county, England, Supertramp produced another album in 1974. In England, *Crime of the Century* was highly promoted and climbed the charts. It even had minor success in the United States. Supertramp toured both the United Kingdom and the United States before releasing a few more albums that were minor hits. *Even in the Quietest Moments . . .* garnered Supertramp a Top-20 hit in the United States, "Give a Little Bit," in 1977.

Supertramp's unique sound was the result of electric piano rhythm-based tracks and dual vocalists Hodgson and Thomson. By 1979 this music was finally appreciated in Supertramp's native country as well as in the United States. *Breakfast in America* was a huge hit at number 3 in England and number 1 in the United States for six weeks,

eventually selling more than eighteen million copies. "The Logical Song" and "Take the Long Way Home" made it into the Top 10, and "Goodbye Stranger" made it into the Top 20. In 1980, Supertramp recorded a live album, *Paris*, which included all of their previous hits. It also reached the Top 10 and went gold. The live version of "Dreamer" made it to the Top 20, and the live "Breakfast in America" became a minor hit in the United States.

Another Dreamer. After the huge success of *Breakfast in America*, Supertramp returned to putting out a succession of minor hit albums, even experimenting with the blues in 1985 with *Brother Where You Bound?* A surprise, "I'm Begging You" made the U.S. dance charts in 1987. Lead singer Hodgson left the band in 1984 to find limited success as a solo artist, though he briefly reunited with Supertramp in 1986 to promote a greatest-hits album. His only hit of the 1980's, "Had a Dream (Sleeping with the Enemy)" (1984) did not make the Top 40.   —*Rose Secrest*

SELECT DISCOGRAPHY

■ ALBUMS

Supertramp, 1970
Indelibly Stamped, 1971
Crime of the Century, 1974
Crisis? What Crisis? 1975
Even in the Quietest Moments . . . , 1977
Breakfast in America, 1979
Paris, 1980
In the Eye of the Storm, 1984 (Roger Hodgson solo)
Brother Where You Bound? 1985
Free as a Bird, 1987
Hai Hai, 1987 (Roger Hodgson solo)
Some Things Never Change, 1997

SEE ALSO: Cheap Trick; Moody Blues, The; Queen; Styx; Yes.

For the Record

In 1975, Supertramp toured the United States for the first time. The singles from their then-current album *Crime of the Century*, "Dreamer" and "Bloody Well Right," had barely made it into the Top 40. A&M Records found themselves giving away most of the tickets.

§

The name "Supertramp" is taken from the 1907 book *The Autobiography of a Super-Tramp*, written by the British poet William Henry Davies (1871-1940). He called himself a "super-tramp" because of his extensive travels in the United States as a hobo.

The Supremes

ORIGINAL MEMBERS: Florence Ballard (1943-1976), Barbara Martin, Diana Ross (b. 1944), Mary Wilson (b. 1944)

OTHER MEMBERS: Cindy Birdsong (b. 1939), Jean
  Terrell (b. 1944), Lynda Laurence, Scherrie
  Payne (b. 1944), Susaye Greene
FIRST ALBUM RELEASE: *Meet the Supremes*, 1963
MUSICAL STYLES: Pop, rhythm and blues, soul

In the late 1950's and 1960's, girl groups such as
the Chantels, the Marvelettes, Martha and the
Vandellas, the Ronettes, the Shangri-Las, and the
Shirelles were popular recording artists. However,
the most successful girl group of the 1960's was
the Supremes. Indeed, in terms of number of hit
records, the Supremes became the most successful girl group of the twentieth century.

From Primettes to Supremes. In Detroit in the
1950's and 1960's, many teenagers belonged to
singing groups, and a popular group at that time
was the Primes, whom Motown would later make
famous worldwide as the Temptations. One of the
Primes, Paul Williams, talked to Florence Ballard
about forming the Primettes which would be the
Primes' sister group. Three other girls were recruited: Betty McGlown, Diana Ross, and Mary
Wilson. The female quartet, formed in 1959, sang
at social functions in the Detroit area, and each
Primette took turns singing lead. During the girls'
first year together, they won the Detroit/Windsor
Freedom Festival's amateur talent contest and
recorded two songs on the Lupine label: "Tears of
Sorrow," with Ross singing lead, and "Pretty Baby,"
with Wilson singing lead. However the record did
not succeed due to distribution problems, and the
Primettes became interested in Motown, a new
record company.

Motown was founded by Berry Gordy, Jr., a
songwriter and record producer. Envisioning his
company as "the sound of young America," Gordy
aimed to create music that people of all races
would enjoy and that would abolish barriers between black and white popular music. Smokey
Robinson and his group, the Miracles, had recorded several hits by the time Ross, a friend of
Robinson's niece, asked Robinson to introduce
the Primettes to Gordy. Robinson agreed, and the
Primettes auditioned at Motown. Gordy liked the
group but did not offer a recording contract. He
told the girls to contact him after they graduated

from high school. Soon after, McGlown announced that she was getting married and leaving
the group. Barbara Martin replaced her.

Before offering the group a recording contract
in 1961, Gordy encouraged the quartet to change
its name. The group considered several names
before agreeing on Ballard's choice—the Supremes. The group began recording at Motown, and
the girls soon earned the nickname of the "no-hit
Supremes" because, beginning with "I Want a
Guy" in 1961 and ending with "A Breathtaking
Guy" in 1963, the Supremes released six records
that failed to generate impressive sales. During
this period, other Motown acts such as the Con-
tours, Marvin Gaye, Martha and the Vandellas,
the Marvelettes, the Miracles, and Mary Wells had hit
records. In 1962 Martin, who was pregnant, left
the Supremes; this time the group did not seek a
replacement. The quartet was transformed into a
trio. Another major change occurred in 1963:
Gordy assigned the highly talented team of Brian
Holland, Lamont Dozier, and Eddie Holland to
write for and produce the Supremes.

Extraordinary Success. Beginning with
"When the Lovelight Starts Shining Through His
Eyes" (1963) and ending with "Forever Came Today" (1968), Holland, Dozier, and Holland were
the Supremes' main songwriters who created seventeen hit records, including ten number 1 songs
(and gold records) for the group. "When the
Lovelight Starts Shining Through His Eyes"
reached as high as the twenty-third position on
the *Billboard* charts. In 1964 the Supremes toured
with "Dick Clark's Caravan of Stars." Initially the
Supremes were the opening act, yet by the end of
the tour, the Supremes had the number 1 record
in the United States with the group's tenth single,
"Where Did Our Love Go." The Supremes finished
the tour as the show's headliners. "Where Did Our
Love Go" (1964), which sold more than two million records, was the third Motown song to reach
number 1 and the first Motown single to remain
on the *Billboard* charts for more than one year.
After the success of "Where Did Our Love Go,"
Gordy decided that Ross would be the lead vocalist. Gordy believed that Ross's voice had the most
commercial appeal and that she was the trio's most

The Supremes: Mary Wilson, Diana Ross, Cindy Birdsong (Archive Photos/Frank Driggs Collection)

engaging performer. After the release of the group's next five singles, "Baby Love" (1964), "Come See About Me" (1964), "Stop! In the Name of Love" (1965), "Back in My Arms Again" (1965), and "I Hear a Symphony" (1965), the Supremes became the first singing group to have six consecutive million sellers in one year. The Supremes enjoyed the status of international celebrities. *Billboard* magazine cited the Supremes as the third biggest act of the 1960's; only the Beatles and Elvis Presley ranked higher. The Supremes headlined at top U.S. nightclubs including New York's Copacabana and Las Vegas showrooms as well as concert halls such as the Lincoln Center in New York. They made national and international promotional tours, including tours to Europe and the Far East. With increased frequency, the group appeared on television shows including *The Ed Sullivan Show, Hullabaloo, Shindig, American Bandstand, The Tonight Show,* and *The Hollywood Palace.*

Changes. As a trio, Ballard, Ross, and Wilson were at the pinnacle of the entertainment world, but the media and the public began focusing more attention on the group's lead singer. In 1967 the name of the group was changed to Diana Ross and the Supremes to reflect Ross's growing popularity. Also in 1967, Ballard, who had become increasingly dissatisfied over the years with her role as a backup singer, left the group. Ballard was replaced by Cindy Birdsong. Another major change for the Supremes was the departure of Holland, Dozier, and Holland from Motown, yet the Supremes had two more number 1 singles: "Love Child" (1968) and "Someday We'll Be Together" (1969), a song on which neither Wilson nor Birdsong performed. Session vocalists substituted for them on the last single released by Diana Ross and the Supremes. In 1970 Ross left the Supremes and began her successful solo career.

Ross's replacement in the Supremes was Jean Terrell, and the group had several modest hits including "Up the Ladder to the Roof" (1970), "Stoned Love" (1970), "Nathan Jones" (1971), and "Floy Joy" (1972). The Supremes continued to release albums, including two with another Motown group, the Four Tops: *The Magnificent Seven* (1970) and *The Return of The Magnificent Seven* (1971). Wilson kept the Supremes together with various singers until 1977, when the group disbanded.

Legacy. Although there were nine women active in the various versions of the Supremes, when the public thinks of the legendary Motown group they invariably think of Diana Ross, Florence Ballard, and Mary Wilson. The trio outdistanced all other 1960's recording acts (except for the Beatles and Elvis Presley) and set standards for the female groups that followed.

Supremes fans worldwide hoped for a special reunion performance featuring Ross, Ballard, and Wilson, but it never occurred. Ballard, who was unsuccessful in her efforts as a solo artist, died in 1976. Wilson began a solo career and later published two autobiographies: *Dreamgirl: My Life as a Supreme* (1986) and *Supreme Faith: Someday We'll Be Together* (1990). Ross also published her autobiography, *Secrets of a Sparrow: Memoirs* (1993). The story of the Supremes lives on in autobiographies, biographies, and most important, their music.

—*Linda M. Carter*

For the Record

Michael Bennett's production of the Tom Eyen and Henry Krieger musical *Dreamgirls*, which opened on Broadway in 1981, was inspired by the story of the Supremes' rise to fame.

SELECT DISCOGRAPHY
■ SINGLES
"When the Lovelight Starts Shining Through His Eyes," 1963
"Where Did Our Love Go," 1964
"Baby Love," 1964
"Come See About Me," 1964
"Stop! In the Name of Love," 1965
"Back in My Arms Again," 1965
"I Hear a Symphony," 1965
"Love Is Like an Itching in My Heart," 1966
"You Can't Hurry Love," 1966
"You Keep Me Hangin' On," 1966
"Love Is Here and Now You're Gone," 1967
"The Happening," 1967
"Reflections," 1967
"Love Child," 1968
"Someday We'll Be Together," 1969
"Up the Ladder to the Roof," 1970
"Stoned Love," 1970
"Nathan Jones," 1971
"Floy Joy," 1972

SELECT AWARDS
Rock and Roll Hall of Fame, inducted 1988

SEE ALSO: Reeves, Martha, and the Vandellas; Ronettes, The; Ross, Diana.

Keith Sweat

BORN: New York, New York; July 22, 1961
FIRST ALBUM RELEASE: *Make It Last Forever*, 1987
MUSICAL STYLES: Rhythm and blues, pop

With his good looks and aching voice, Keith Sweat was the first star of Teddy Riley's late 1980's "new jack swing" movement, fusing hip-hop street music and traditional rhythm and blues. Unlike many of the early proponents of the "new jack swing" sound, however, Sweat was both versatile and business-savvy. As "new jack swing" began to fragment in the early 1990's, Sweat evolved his own smoldering soul sound and remained one of the most consistent rhythm-and-blues artists of the 1990's.

Early Life. Sweat grew up in the Grant projects in Harlem, New York, not far from the famed

Apollo Theatre. After seeing a Jacksons concert at the age of fourteen, he knew that he wanted to be a performer, and he joined his first group the following year. While attending City College in New York, Sweat became the front man for Jamilah, a funk band that opened for artists including Teddy Pendergrass, the Whispers, and the Delfonics. Wanting to chart his own direction, however, Sweat quit the band and continued to work toward his degree in communications. After graduation he went to work on Wall Street as a commodities broker.

Though a successful businessman by day, Sweat continued to write songs, record demos, and search for a recording contract by night. His big break came while working on a project at the Power Play studio in Queens, New York. There he ran into Teddy Riley, a young musician and producer he had met while with Jamilah. Riley offered Sweat an early version of "I Want Her" (1987), and together they worked it into the number 1 rhythm-and-blues hit (number 5, pop). "I Want Her" paved the way for all the "new jack swing" artists who followed and enabled Sweat to quit his job on Wall Street. It was also the first of four hit singles from the number 1 rhythm-and-blues album *Make It Last Forever* (1987), including "Something Just Ain't Right" (number 3, rhythm and blues), "Make It Last Forever" (number 2, rhythm and blues) and "Don't Stop Your Love" (number 9, rhythm and blues).

Second Success. After a worldwide tour of sold-out shows, Sweat followed the triple-platinum *Make It Last Forever* with his second number 1 rhythm-and-blues album, *I'll Give All My Love to You* (1990). Though geared to a more mature audience, it still contained plenty of edgy pop, including the smash crossover hit "Make You Sweat" (number 1, rhythm and blues; number 14, pop). Sweat produced and wrote or cowrote all the songs on *I'll Give All My Love to You*, which sold more than one million copies in less than two months and eventually went multiplatinum. His third album, *Keep It Comin'* (1991), also went platinum, with both the album and the title track quickly going to number 1 on the rhythm-and-blues charts.

Keith Sweat (Ken Settle)

In 1992 Sweat kept up a relentless work schedule. He supported the *Keep It Comin'* album on the "Triple Threat Tour" with Bell Biv DeVoe and Johnny Gill, then toured on his own. He also formed his own label, Keia Records, and began producing artists such as Silk, Kut Klose, Triflin' Pack, and About Face from his Sweat Shop studio in Atlanta, Georgia.

Going Strong. Sweat's fourth album, *Get up on It* (1994), was another big crossover hit, reaching number 8 on the pop charts and going platinum, though he lost some of the urban singles crowd in the process. He regained much of the momentum with "Twisted" (number 4, pop) and a self-titled fifth album (1996) that broke into the pop Top 20. In 1997 he joined with rhythm-and-blues stars Gerald Levert and Johnny Gill to record *Levert-Sweat-Gill*, which went to number 2 on the rhythm-and-blues charts in 1998.　　　*—John Powell*

SELECT DISCOGRAPHY
■ ALBUMS
Make It Last Forever, 1987
I'll Give All My Love to You, 1990
Keep It Comin', 1991
Get up on It, 1994
Keith Sweat, 1996
Just a Touch, 1997
Levert-Sweat-Gill, 1997 (with Gerald Levert and Johnny Gill)
Still in the Game, 1998

SEE ALSO: New Edition.

T

Taj Mahal
(Henry Saint Clair Fredericks)

BORN: Springfield, Massachusetts; May 17, 1942
FIRST ALBUM RELEASE: *Taj Mahal*, 1967
MUSICAL STYLES: Blues, jazz, rock and roll, gospel, folk

One of nine children, Henry Saint Clair Fredericks grew up in Springfield, Massachusetts, in a home filled with music. His father, an enthusiastic fan of jazz, was a Jamaican composer and arranger. His mother, who loved to sing gospel, was a schoolteacher. From his father's shortwave radio set he listened to music from London, Rio de Janeiro, Havana, Kingston, Moscow, and different regions of the United States. As a teenager, he became an avid fan of American musical pioneers Jimmy Reed, Howlin' Wolf, Chuck Berry, Bo Diddley, Big Mama Thornton, and Sonny Terry.

From 1961 to 1963, Fredericks performed with his group called Taj Mahal and the Elektras. In 1964, he received his B.A. degree in agriculture and animal husbandry from the University of Massachusetts. The year following his graduation, he became known simply as Taj Mahal and emerged professionally as a cofounder, with guitarist Ry Cooder, of the Rising Sons. Within three years, he signed a recording contract as a solo artist and released his first three albums, *Taj Mahal* (1967), *The Natch'l Blues* (1968), and *Giant Step/De Ole Folx at Home* (1969).

Taj Mahal, an enthusiastic reader of philosophy who is also fluent in five languages, was self-taught and plays more than twenty instruments. Perhaps equally impressive is his voice. Listeners will note that he has a wide vocal range which can be smooth and gliding or gruff and gravelly. As a result of his early international musical influences, his skill on a variety of instruments, and his vocal talent, the music of Taj Mahal is rich, soulful, and textured. His music has been described as a seasoned gumbo, with influences that originate in the Caribbean, West Africa, and the southern states and inner cities of the United States.

Since 1968, Taj Mahal has toured, recorded, or performed with some of the greatest names in music, including Eric Clapton, Bonnie Raitt, B. B. King, John Lee Hooker, Miles Davis, Jimi Hendrix, Bob Dylan, Bob Marley, the Pointer Sisters, the Neville Brothers, John Lennon, George Harrison, Jethro Tull, the Who, and the Rolling Stones. Beyond his work in contemporary music, Taj Mahal has worked with distinction in the motion picture industry as an actor and as a composer of musical scores in eight films. In addition, Taj Mahal has received Grammy Award nominations for his albums for children and for his musical score written for the Broadway production *Mule Bone*, which was based on a play by Langston Hughes and Zora Neale Hurston.

Recording Classics. Throughout his musical career, Taj Mahal has remained one of the premier troubadours of the United States. The soul stirring African American musical traditions of blues, folk, rhythm and blues, zyedeco, gospel, and jazz have been revealed and expanded upon throughout his thirty-six albums and hundreds of concert performances. In particular, one album stands out as the platform from which Taj Mahal's music launched an entirely new sound. In the album *The Real Thing*, released in 1971 by Columbia Records, Taj Mahal played the blues like no other musician had before.

His unique approach to the blues is demonstrated in the song "Ain't Gwine to Whistle Dixie (Any Mo')," which was cowritten by Taj Mahal, Jesse Davis, Gary Gilmore, and Chuck Blackwell. In the arrangement of this song, Taj Mahal took the traditional blues instruments and added an array of horns and woodwinds that had not been heard in this musical genre. The song begins with the melody being whistled by Taj Mahal and accompanied softly by a conga and an electric piano.

As the melody builds, French horns enter as counterpoint, and a tuba anchors the bass line. Trumpets, flute, saxophone, fluegelhorn, electric guitar, and maracas provide a wall of bold harmony as they play triumphantly together and then slowly disappear and make way, one more time, for whistling accompanied by maracas and a soft guitar that slowly disappears.

The song ends in a tremendous ovation from the live audience at Bill Graham's Fillmore East in New York as they realized that they had been witness to the birth of a new sound. This addition of horns and woodwinds to blues was bold, new, and daring. Decades later, this blues song with its outstanding arrangement would still stand as one of the major breakthroughs in the history of American music.

Legacy. The career of Taj Mahal could have been based solely on his breakthrough song, "Ain't Gwine to Whistle Dixie (Any Mo')." He could have collected a lifetime of accolades for his innovation and creativity and rested on this one, huge, shining success. However, this was not to be the case. Taj Mahal went on to release three dozen albums that continued to address his love and advocacy of world music.

In 1996, he experimented again with the blues genre and recorded with two superb Indian musicians. In this recording Taj Mahal teamed with Vishwa Mohan Bhatt, who played a twenty-one-stringed lute, and Narasimhan Ravikiran, who played a modified slide guitar. The Indian instruments provided bent-note melodic phrases and scales and rhythms, making the improvised sound colorful, entrancing, exotic, sensual, even poetic. The trio interpreted two rhythm-and-blues standards, "Come On in My Kitchen" and "Stand by Me," with great emotion. One critic wrote, "The blues, in accord with Hindustani and Karnatak music, is made miraculously new." The legacy of Taj Mahal is that he continues to seek new horizons, and in doing so he inspires his listeners to seek their own.

—*Albert Valencia*

Taj Mahal (Archive Photos/Fotos International)

SELECT DISCOGRAPHY
■ ALBUMS
Taj Mahal, 1967
The Natch'l Blues, 1968
Giant Step/De Ole Folx at Home, 1969
Brothers, 1971
The Real Thing, 1971
Happy Just to Be Like I Am, 1971
Recycling the Blues and Other Related Stuff, 1972
Oooh So Good 'n Blues, 1973
Mo' Roots, 1974
Music Keeps Me Together, 1975
Music Fuh Ya' (Musica para Tu), 1977
Evolution (The Most Recent), 1978
Best of Taj Mahal, Volume 1, 1981
World Music, 1993
Dancing the Blues, 1993
Mumtaz Mahal, 1995

An Evening of Acoustic Music, 1995
Phantom Blues, 1996
Señor Blues, 1997
Taj Mahal and the Hula Blues, 1997

SELECT AWARDS
Grammy Award for Best Contemporary Blues Album for *Señor Blues*, 1997

SEE ALSO: Clapton, Eric; Davis, Miles; Dylan, Bob; Hendrix, Jimi; Hooker, John Lee; King, B. B.; Lennon, John; Marley, Bob; Neville Brothers, The / Aaron Neville; Pointer Sisters, The; Raitt, Bonnie; Rolling Stones, The; Who, The.

Talking Heads / David Byrne

Talking Heads

ORIGINAL MEMBERS: David Byrne (b. 1952), Chris Frantz (b. 1951), Tina Weymouth (b. 1950), Jerry Harrison (b. 1949)
FIRST ALBUM RELEASE: *Talking Heads: 77*, 1977

David Byrne

BORN: Dumbarton, Scotland; May 14, 1952
FIRST ALBUM RELEASE: *My Life in the Bush of Ghosts*, 1981 (with Brian Eno)
MUSICAL STYLES: Punk rock, new wave, disco, funk, Cajun, country

Formed at a time when punk rock and disco represented two extremes of the rock music continuum, Talking Heads successfully fused these two disparate styles—as well as a number of others—into a unique sound, one which had significant appeal to the college crowd and the art scene. Because of this postmodern blend of influences, Talking Heads has both attracted and defied labels ranging from new wave icons to minimalist preppies. From its beginnings, David Byrne represented the somewhat unsettling, surrealistic embodiment of Talking Heads not only through his clever, absurd, often nihilistic lyrics, but also through his clean, spare guitar playing, elastic voice, and nervous stage presence. However, upon inspection of the individual members' work outside of Talking Heads, it is apparent that the group's success was the result of a true synergy of creative efforts.

The Early Days. In the early 1970's, David Byrne, Chris Frantz, and Tina Weymouth were fellow art students at the Rhode Island School of Design (RISD). Weymouth and Frantz specialized in painting, while Byrne's interests were more conceptually oriented, incorporating photography, video, painting, and poetry. While at RISD, singer-guitarist Byrne and drummer Frantz formed the Artistics, which was primarily a cover band, although Byrne contributed a few original songs to their repertoire. The Artistics broke up in the spring of 1974, at which time Byrne, Frantz, and Weymouth moved to New York City, sharing a loft in the Lower East Side. Byrne and Frantz were interested in forming a new band, and encouraged Weymouth, whose primary musical experience was as a singer and guitarist, to learn the bass. The trio began working together in January of 1975, building upon the repertoire of the Artistics by combining Byrne's original songs with an ironic mix of 1960's "bubblegum" tunes and punk covers. In June of 1975, the group adopted the name Talking Heads (the television term for a head-and-shoulders camera shot of a speaking figure) and presented their first public performance, opening for the Ramones at CBGB's, one of the leading punk-rock venues in lower Manhattan.

And Then There Were Four. The trio made its first demos in early 1976, and in November of that year signed with Sire Records, recording their first single, "Love Goes to Building on Fire," the following month. During this period, the group was in search of a fourth member to cover keyboards and rhythm guitar. Jerry Harrison was an art student at Harvard University, studying painting as an undergraduate and playing keyboards (and later guitar) in a number of bands. The most successful of these, the Modern Lovers, lasted until March of 1974, at which time the original members disbanded and Harrison returned to Harvard, continuing graduate studies in architecture. Harrison left school to join the Talking Heads in late 1976, and the band recorded its first album between April and July of 1977. (Inciden-

Talking Heads in 1983: David Byrne, Jerry Harrison, Tina Weymouth, Chris Frantz (Deborah Feingold/Archive Photos)

tally, it was also at this time that Frantz and Weymouth were married.) *Talking Heads: 77* was released the following September and proved to be an auspicious debut, establishing the group's reputation through such works as "Psycho Killer," with its schizophrenic bilingual monologue and its eerie, quasi-dadaistic refrains.

New Directions. The next three studio albums chronicled the group's artistic blossoming—including an augmentation of the band's personnel and the exploration of African rhythms in its continuing foray into funk music—and exhibit the influence of former Roxy Music keyboardist Brian Eno as coproducer (on *More Songs About Buildings and Food,* 1978, and *Fear of Music,* 1979) and as producer and co-lyricist (on *Remain in Light,* 1980). Over hypnotic grooves supplied by the enlarged band (which included such distinc-

tive personalities as King Crimson guitarists Robert Fripp and Adrian Belew), Byrne's paranoid, stream-of-consciousness monologues provided a starkly surreal counterpoint in songs such as "Born Under Punches" and "Once in a Lifetime," while in "Life During Wartime," Byrne admonishes "This ain't no party, this ain't no disco,/ This ain't no fooling around."

The next two albums, 1982's *The Name of This Band Is Talking Heads* (a double-album collection of greatest hits culled from live performances between 1977 and 1981) and *Speaking in Tongues* (1983), were released following solo ventures by Byrne, Harrison, and the Tom Tom Club (Frantz and Weymouth's project), amid rumors that the band was breaking up. *Speaking in Tongues,* however, dispelled such rumors, selling more than one million copies in the United States with its more direct rock-and-roll sound, evidenced in such hit singles as "Burning Down the House" and "Girlfriend Is Better." The "Speaking in Tongues" tour was the subject of Jonathan Demme's 1984 film *Stop Making Sense*, and the image of lanky David Byrne twitching marionette-like in a grotesquely oversized suit remains one of the most memorable icons of 1980's popular music.

The next two albums represent further explorations into popular music idioms, with a dilution of the band's hard edged aesthetic of its early years as a natural consequence. *Little Creatures* (1985) marked a return to the leaner sound of the early quartet's recordings, though they incorporated elements of folk, country, and Cajun music with the addition of steel guitar and accordian. Byrne's eccentric persona was perhaps alluded to in a line from "Creatures of Love" ("Doctor, doctor, tell me what I am/ Am I one of those human beings"), while "Road to Nowhere" delights in an ironically joyous existentialism. *True Stories* (1986) was a collection of songs from Byrne's 1986 feature film of the same name and included such popular singles as the playfully raucous "Wild Wild Life" and the nostalgic "City of Dreams."

Released in 1988, *Naked* was to be the final Talking Heads album, although the group did not officially break up until the end of 1991. Recorded in Paris with an international lineup of musicians, including a full horn section, this album presented yet another side of Talking Heads, with influences of salsa and Caribbean music evidenced in such songs as "Blind" and the unabashedly extroverted "Mr. Jones." Four songs recorded by the group following the release of *Naked* were included in the double-album compilation *Popular Favorites 1976-1992: Sand in the Vaseline*, released in 1992.

Independent Ventures. Arguably the creative impetus behind the group, David Byrne had perhaps the most varied and successful solo career of all of the members of Talking Heads. Beginning in 1981 with *My Life in the Bush of Ghosts*, a joint venture with Brian Eno, Byrne has collaborated with some of the most influential artists of his generation, including choreographer Twyla Tharp (*The Catherine Wheel*, 1981), stage director

Robert Wilson ("Knee Plays," 1985), minimalist composer Philip Glass (*Songs from Liquid Days*, 1986), and film director Bernardo Bertolucci (*The Last Emperor*, 1987). Byrne established his recording company, Luaka Bop, to promote the music of Brazilian, Cuban, and Asian artists, in addition to his own solo releases, including *Rei Momo* (1989) and *Uh-Oh* (1992).

In an effort to establish some creative independence from Talking Heads, Chris Frantz and Tina Weymouth formed Tom Tom Club in the early 1980's, releasing their self-titled debut album in 1981. The group toured as the opening act for the Talking Heads' 1982 tour, and in 1989 staged a solo tour to promote their third album *Boom Boom Chi Boom Boom*. Jerry Harrison has been a frequent collaborator as both performer and producer, working with such renowned artists as the BoDeans, Fine Young Cannibals, Violent Femmes, and Crash Test Dummies. He has also pursued a solo career with such albums as *The Red and the Black* (1981) and *Casual Gods* (1988).

Following the breakup of Talking Heads, Frantz, Weymouth, and Harrison formed the Heads, releasing their debut album *No Talking Just Heads* (a not-so-veiled reference to the conspicuously absent David Byrne) in October of 1996. To substitute for the lack of a regular lead singer, the Heads' first project included a variety of singer-songwriters (including Andy Partridge of XTC and Deborah Harry of Blondie), each of whom contributed original material to the album.

—*Joseph Klein*

James Taylor

BORN: Boston, Massachusetts; March 12, 1948
FIRST ALBUM RELEASE: *James Taylor*, 1968
MUSICAL STYLES: Pop, rock, folk, blues

James Vernon Taylor was born to a wealthy southern family living in Boston while his father was an intern at Massachusetts General Hospital. Encouraged by their mother, a soprano who had studied voice at the New England Conservatory of Music, the Taylor children learned to play several instruments. James studied the cello as a child, but soon lost interest in the instrument, favoring the guitar instead. At age twelve his parents gave him his first guitar as a gift. The family often played and sang together at gatherings when the children were in high school.

Getting Started. At age fifteen, Taylor and one of his close friends, Danny Kortchmar, won a local hootenanny contest. When Taylor and Kortchmar performed, they alternated on vocals, with Taylor playing guitar and Kortchmar playing harmonica.

Their interest in folk music was eventually eclipsed by a love for rock music. At age sixteen, Taylor left high school to join a rock band, known as the Fabulous Corsairs, with his older brother Alex. Taylor eventually returned to the boarding school he had previously attended, but at age seventeen became increasingly despondent and suicidal. In 1965, he spent nine months in the McLean Hospital, a mental institution, located in Belmont, Massachusetts. Soon after, Taylor graduated from high school and left for New York to join Kortchmar in a new band. Known as the Flying Machine, the band traveled throughout the New York area playing low-paying shows.

Taylor's first big break in the music industry came in 1968, when he left New York for London. Frustrated by his situation and consumed by a drug habit, he saw the move to London as an opportunity to straighten out his life and escape his heroin addiction. His involvement with drugs did not diminish, however, as Taylor was introduced to acid by his friends in London. Determined to break into the music business, Taylor rented a studio and recorded some demo tapes of his material. Like so many aspiring musicians, he distributed the tapes to several record companies. Apple Record Company producer Peter Asher liked Taylor's musical style and offered him a three-year contract. His first album, *James Taylor*, was released in 1968 but sold poorly, in spite of high praise from critics. Paul McCartney was so impressed by Taylor that he played bass background for part of the album. One single from the album, "Carolina on My Mind," did become a Top-40 hit. Taylor's successful break into the music industry did little, however, to rid him of his all-consuming drug habit. In December of 1968 he was admitted to another mental hospital, Austin Riggs of Stockbridge, Massachusetts, for drug-addiction treatment.

The Big Break. By mid-1969, Apple Records was in financial difficulty, and Taylor managed to acquire a new contract with Warner Bros. His 1970 debut album with the label, *Sweet Baby James*, sold more than two million copies. The platinum album, and its top-selling single, "Fire and Rain," were nominated for five Grammy Awards. His first album became increasingly popular as well and has since become a cult item. Recordings from his early days playing with Kortchmar and the Flying Machine, titled *James Taylor and the Flying Machine—1967*, were also released by Euphoria in early 1971. Almost overnight, Taylor became a national celebrity. *Mud Slide Slim and the Blue Horizon*, Taylor's third album, was released in 1971 by Warner Bros. and became an immediate commercial success. It contained the number 1 hit single "You've Got a Friend," written by Carole King. His twenty-seven-city tour in the spring of 1971 drew huge crowds.

Taylor's 1972 *One Man Dog* album did not achieve the acclaim of his two previous albums, nor did his 1974 album, *Walking Man*. The slump was short-lived, however, and many credit his improved private life for his comeback, which began in the mid-1970's. His marriage to singer-songwriter Carly Simon in 1972 was a major turning point in his life. Many believed Simon's influence had a tremendous impact on Taylor's new confidence and emotional stability. He appeared more relaxed onstage and achieved a much better rapport with his audiences. The couple's 1974 duet single "Mockingbird," a remake of Inez Foxx's 1963 recording, became a popular hit. Taylor's 1975 gold album, *Gorilla*, was his best work since the early 1970's, according to some critics. *Gorilla* was followed one year later by *Greatest Hits* and *In the Pocket*, his last release for Warner Bros.

In 1977 his new label, Columbia Records, released *JT*, which quickly went platinum and included the Top-10 single "Handy Man." By the close of the decade, Taylor was at the height of his career. *Flag* (1979) and *Dad Loves His Work* (1981), both released by Columbia Records, went gold. A champion of the antinuclear movement, he performed at numerous nuclear disarmament rallies in 1979 and 1980 with Bruce Springsteen, Linda Ronstadt, Joan Baez, and others. The largest of the disarmament rallies, held in New York's Central Park, attracted a gathering of more than one million people. He also participated with other artists in recording an album entitled *No Nukes* that was released on Asylum in 1979.

Activist. Taylor's career began to experience difficulties in the early 1980's, as did his personal life. In 1982, with their marriage in shambles, Simon filed for a divorce. Taylor continued to perform concerts that were well attended by his vast following, but he failed to produce another album until late 1985. Haunted by addictions to heroin and alcohol, he managed to finally overcome his problem with substance abuse by 1985, the year he married his second wife, actress Kathryn Walker. *That's Why I'm Here*, his 1985 album, was not as well received as some of his previous works. Taylor did continue to tour and spent several months in Australia, Europe, and Brazil in 1985 and 1986. He began appearing regularly at special benefit performances for political and social causes by the late 1980's. Taylor took part in the Amnesty International celebration of Human Rights Day held in Washington, D.C., late in 1987. He also joined Bruce Springsteen, Paul Simon, and Billy Joel for a concert at New York's Madison Square Garden that raised funds for medical relief for the homeless. His *Never Die Young* album, released in early 1988, was much more subdued than any of his previous works, indicative of the changes taking place in his music career. He continued to work, however, and began to appear more frequently as a guest on the television talk circuit.

During the period between 1991 and 1997, Taylor produced four albums. His 1997 album, *Hourglass*, peaked at number 9 on the charts and sold seventy thousand copies the first week of its release. As Taylor's seventeenth original album, the one that put his total record sales at more than twenty-nine million, it has proven a real testament to his ability to survive and adapt in the ever-changing music industry. Despite the death of his father in 1996, the end of his marriage to Walker, and the death of his best friend, Don Grolnick,

For the Record

In February of 1994, James Taylor appeared as himself on the popular animated television show *The Simpsons*.

Taylor remained active on the tour circuit and has appeared regularly on television. He appeared on *The Tonight Show* four times in the early to mid-1990's, once on *Late Night with David Letterman*, and twice on *Saturday Night Live*. He has also appeared several times on the public television network show *Sesame Street*. His soft lyrics and sweet melodies remain popular and seem to transcend generational boundaries.   —*Donald C. Simmons, Jr.*

SELECT DISCOGRAPHY
■ ALBUMS
James Taylor, 1968
Sweet Baby James, 1970
James Taylor and the Flying Machine—1967, 1971
Mud Slide Slim and the Blue Horizon, 1971
One Man Dog, 1972
Walking Man, 1974
Gorilla, 1975
In the Pocket, 1976
Greatest Hits, 1976 (compilation)
JT, 1977
Flag, 1979
Dad Loves His Work, 1981
That's Why I'm Here, 1985
Never Die Young, 1988
New Moon Shine, 1991
James Taylor (LIVE), 1993
Hourglass, 1997

SELECT AWARDS
Grammy Award for Best Pop Vocal Performance, Male, for "You've Got a Friend," 1971
Grammy Award for Best Pop Vocal Performance, Male, for "Handy Man," 1977

SEE ALSO: Baez, Joan; King, Carole; McCartney, Paul; Mitchell, Joni; Ronstadt, Linda; Simon, Carly; Springsteen, Bruce.

Tears for Fears

ORIGINAL MEMBERS: Roland Orzabal (b. 1961), Curt Smith (b. 1961)
OTHER MEMBERS: Manny Elias, Ian Stanley, Nicky Holland , Oleta Adams, Gail Ann Dorsey, Andy Davis, Jeffrey Trott, Jebin Bruni, Brian MacCleod

FIRST ALBUM RELEASE: *The Hurting*, 1983
MUSICAL STYLES: Rock and roll, alternative

Roland Orzabal was immersed in music from childhood, due to the influence of his French father who ran a small music business from his home. In his early years, Orzabal, born Raoul Jaime Orzabal de la Quintana, preferred to study mathematics, but his musical talents emerged, and he set out to develop his performing career. In 1974, he overheard Curt Smith singing and decided to collaborate on songwriting and performance with him. This was the focus that Smith needed to leave off his mildly criminal behaviors, and the duet was begun.

The Early Years. Orzabal and Smith, who had each been in several other bands in the Bath, England, area teamed with John Baker, Andy Marsden, and Steve Buck to form a group known as the Graduate which produced only one album, *Acting My Age* (1980), which was released only in the United Kingdom and never rose above number 106. When the band members parted ways the next year, Orzabal and Smith formed Tears for Fears, which took its name from an Arthur Janov book's first line. Having studied psychology, Orzabal set the tone for the introspective and often mysterious lyrical songs of Tears for Fears. This tone was already evident in the first album, *The Hurting* (1983). Both Orzabal and Smith seemed comfortable with the psychological lyrics, and while the music evolved to a more mellow guitar-based tone later, the early songs of Tears for Fears featured an often hectic tone reminiscent of the Beatles, evidenced on the hits "Shout" and "I Believe" from the 1985 album *Songs from the Big Chair*.

The album *Songs from the Big Chair* took its title from the 1977 film *Sybil*, which featured a woman with multiple personalities who referred to sitting in the psychiatrist's "big chair" during treatment sessions. From the mid-1980's, however, Orzabal's style and musical vision dominated the duo and at times overshadowed Smith's contributions. After prolonged artistic differences, Smith left the band, and Orzabal retained the name. The parting was not a happy or easy one, and though the band had been successful touring after the albums *Songs from the Big Chair* and its 1989 follow-up, *The Seeds of Love*, the conflicts were exhausting. After leaving Tears for Fears, Smith went on to produce his own solo album, *Soul on Board* (1993), and form a new group, Mayfield, which in May of 1997 released its first album, *Mayfield*.

After the Breakup. Orzabal took some time after the 1989 separation from Smith and helped to produce *Tears Roll Down—Greatest Hits '82-'92* (1992). In 1993 Tears for Fears released the hit album *Elemental*, which seemed, as Orzabal stated, to embody at least in part the "resentment and negative feelings" of the split. Several songs from the album, such as "Elemental" and "Cold," convey Orzabal's uneasiness concerning his new direction and his old wounds. *Elemental* was successful, and the subsequent tour focused the new band's energies and creativity.

Now in total artistic control and excited and inspired by the successful "Elemental" tour, Orzabal, with Tim Palmer and Alan Griffiths, began to produce the deeply personal *Raoul and the Kings of Spain* (1995), which resurrected the title originally considered for *The Seeds of Love*. Where *Elemental* had been about Orzabal's anger and introspection, *Raoul* was about families and how to survive them. The album was not a concept album, but a psychological exploration of the hereditary chain and the breaking of its cycle. With his own son in mind and his own intense interest in psychoanalysis, Raoul (Roland) searches for familial ties and even spiritual roots. For Orzabal, music was therapeutic as well as artistic; he said it "is really about releasing something that is inside of you, something that you can't quite define. . . . You allow it to exist separately from you. At that point, you are freed."

All five of the band's Top-10 hits came from the Orzabal-Smith era. They were "Shout," "Everybody Wants to Rule the World," and "Head Over Heels" from *Songs from the Big Chair* and "Sowing the Seeds of Love" and "Woman in Chains" from *The Seeds of Love*. Though Orzabal's solo albums have not yielded any Top-10 hits, he has attributed this to a shrinking audience, a natural phenomenon of an artist exploring more inwardly his own artistic values.

After the moderately successful *Raoul*, Orzabal produced the collection of B-sides known as *Saturnine Martial & Lunatic* (1996), which included several musical oddities such as "Johnny Panic and the Bible of Dreams," the title of which is taken from poet Sylvia Plath's short story but has no apparent thematic connection to it. Orzabal has produced albums for vocalists Nicky Holland and Oleta Adams, in an effort to help their careers. He formed Bread and Buddha Productions to gain even more control over how and what he produces with his own band and with others. Although Tears for Fears would continue making music, Orzabal has been reluctant to predict the band's future direction.   —*Marc E. Waddell*

SELECT DISCOGRAPHY
■ ALBUMS
The Hurting, 1983
Songs from the Big Chair, 1985
The Seeds of Love, 1989
Tears Roll Down—Greatest Hits '82-'92, 1992
Elemental, 1993
Raoul and the Kings of Spain, 1995
Saturnine Martial & Lunatic, 1996

The Temptations

ORIGINAL MEMBERS: Elbridge Bryant, Melvin Franklin (b. David English, 1942-1995), Eddie Kendricks (1939-1992), Otis Williams (b. Otis Miles, 1941), Paul Williams (1939-1973)
OTHER MEMBERS: David Ruffin (1941-1991), Dennis Edwards (b. 1943), Damon Harris (b. 1950), Glenn Leonard, Richard Street (b. 1942), Ron Tyson (b. 1948), Ali Ollie Woodson, Theo Peoples
FIRST ALBUM RELEASE: *Meet the Temptations*, 1964
MUSICAL STYLES: Rhythm and blues, soul, pop

The Temptations outdistanced all competition and became the most successful male rhythm-and-blues group of the 1960's and early 1970's. The Temptations mesmerized national and international audiences with energetic harmonies and smooth choreography. Music critics and fans worldwide proclaimed that the Temptations out-sang and outdanced all other groups. As a result, the Temptations attained legendary status.

Original Temptations. The Distants and the Primes were popular groups in Detroit, Michigan, in the late 1950's, although neither group had a hit record. In 1960, after several members left the groups, the remaining Distants (Elbridge Bryant, Melvin Franklin, and Otis Williams) merged with the remaining Primes (Eddie Kendricks and Paul Williams) to form the Temptations. The group signed a recording contract in 1961 with Berry Gordy, Jr.'s Motown Records. From 1961 to 1963, the Temptations released fourteen songs with Paul Williams singing lead on most of the recordings and Kendricks singing lead on the remainder. "Dream Come True," a tune featuring Kendricks on lead, was the only song during this period that reached the rhythm-and-blues charts (number 22).

Classic Temptations. In December, 1963, Bryant left the Temptations, and in January, 1964, he was replaced by David Ruffin, who had sung with the Dixie Nightingales, toured with the Staple Singers, and recorded several songs as a solo artist. Ruffin's raspy tenor blended smoothly with Franklin's bass, Kendricks's high tenor, Otis Williams's second tenor and baritone, and Paul Williams's baritone. From 1964 to 1968, the Temptations recorded multiple hits beginning with "The Way You Do the Things You Do"; many of the group's songs during the four-year period were written by legendary Motown songwriter and entertainer William "Smokey" Robinson.

The Temptations' repertoire, whether up-tempo songs or ballads, included rhythm and blues, soul, pop, and Broadway show tunes. The Temptations' voices place them among the most commanding and memorable singers in rhythm and blues, soul, and pop music. While other 1960's groups typically featured one lead vocalist, each Temptation could sing lead. Franklin and Otis Williams seldom sang lead, yet "Ol' Man River," with Franklin singing lead, and "Don't Send Me Away," with Otis Williams singing lead, are stellar recordings. After Ruffin joined the group, Paul Williams was no longer the principal vocalist. His signature leads included "Don't Look Back" and "For Once in My Life."

Most leads alternated between Kendricks and Ruffin, the group's most charismatic and dynamic vocalists. Among the Temptations' classics with Kendricks as lead are "The Way You Do the Things

The Temptations (Archive Photos)

You Do," "The Girl's Alright with Me," "Girl (Why You Wanna Make Me Blue)," "Get Ready," and "Please Return Your Love to Me." Classic Temptations songs with Ruffin singing lead include "My Girl," the group's first number 1 record; "It's Growing"; "Since I Lost My Baby"; "Ain't Too Proud to Beg"; "Beauty Is Only Skin Deep"; "(I Know) I'm Losing You"; "All I Need"; "(Loneliness Made Me Realize) It's You That I Need"; "I Wish It Would Rain"; and "I Could Never Love Another (After Loving You)." Kendricks and Ruffin shared the lead on the hit "You're My Everything." Each new Temptations single and album was eagerly awaited by a generation of fans, black and white; indeed the Temptations helped Gordy make Motown Records the "voice of young America."

During Ruffin's years with the Temptations, they recorded thirteen albums. The first album, *Meet the Temptations*, featured the five young men on the cover. During this period, record companies frequently substituted photographs of Caucasians or cartoons for images of African Americans in order to appeal to the mass market. Gordy's decision to showcase the Temptations on the album cover sent a bold message to the record-buying public that the group's talent could overcome racial opposition. The Temptations, along with other Motown superstars, helped to tear down racial barriers in the recording industry and in society. Other memorable Temptations al-

For the Record

Otis Williams recalls how the group got its name. They were "throwing around names when off the top of my head I blurted out, 'Temptations' . . . Bill [Mitchell] said he really liked it. But when he asked the other four their opinions, we all took one look at ourselves in our raggedy, long winter coats and cracked up. We knew we were unlikely to tempt anyone or anything, but what the hell, it was as good a name as any."

bums of this period are *Temptations Sing Smokey* (1965), a collection of songs written by Smokey Robinson; and *In a Mellow Mood* (1967), a collection of show tunes.

Fans of the Temptations flocked to see the group in concert during national and international tours and relished the Temptations' appearances on various television shows. In 1968 the group starred in the television special, *The Temptations Show*, and an album by the same name was also released. Also in 1968 the Temptations co-starred with the Supremes in the television special *TCB*. (In 1970 the two groups had a second special, *On Broadway*.) They also recorded several albums with the Supremes. The television specials and recordings with the Supremes paired Motown's premier male and female groups.

The Temptations possessed an electrifying stage presence that was enhanced by Paul Williams's dazzling choreography. The quintet executed impressive dance moves. When Williams choreographed steps known as the "Temptation walk" for the song "Don't Look Back," he created a dance craze. Famed dancer Cholly Atkins later choreographed their stage routines.

Additional Temptations. Ruffin and Kendricks left the group in order to pursue solo careers. Ruffin left in 1968, and Kendricks left in 1971, the year he sang lead on the hit, "Just My Imagination (Running Away with Me)." Also in 1971, ill health forced Paul Williams to leave the group; he died two years later.

Since the legendary grouping of Franklin, Kendricks, Ruffin, Otis Williams, and Paul Williams, more than ten new Temptations have sung the classic hits as well as new songs. Dennis Edwards, Ruffin's replacement, sang principle lead on such memorable hits as "Cloud Nine," "I Can't Get Next to You," and "Papa Was a Rollin' Stone." Richard Street, former Distants member, was Paul Williams's replacement and sang with the group for more than two decades before his departure in the early 1990's. One of his best leads was on "Hey Girl (I Like Your Style)." Ron Tyson, Kendricks's fourth replacement, debuted with the group singing lead on the ballad "Sail Away" and has been a Temptation since 1983. Ali Ollie Woodson, who replaced Edwards, reinvigorated the Temptations with an energy reminiscent of Ruffin's. Woodson sang lead on such 1980's hits as "Treat Her Like a Lady" and "Lady Soul."

In 1982 Ruffin and Kendricks toured with Franklin, Otis Williams, Edwards, Glenn Leonard (Kendricks's third replacement), and Street. The successful reunion tour led to the "Standing on the Top" single and *Reunion* album. Ruffin and Kendricks left after the tour. In 1989 the Temptations (Franklin, Kendricks, Ruffin, Otis Williams, Paul Williams, and Edwards) were inducted into the Rock and Roll Hall of Fame. By 1995 death claimed three more Temptations: Ruffin (drug overdose), Kendricks (lung cancer), and Franklin (brain seizure).

The Temptations would continue to record and appear in concert for fans of all generations, although Otis Williams, author of the group's biography, *Temptations* (1988), would be the only original group member. Since 1964, the Temptations have released more than fifty albums. *For Lovers Only* (1995), a noteworthy example, is a collection of well-known love songs ranging from rhythm and blues to Broadway tunes; one of the highlights is "Some Enchanted Evening."

Legacy. Most male rhythm-and-blues groups and a number of male pop groups that began recording after the 1960's have acknowledged the influence of the Temptations. Solo artists such as Michael Jackson have been influenced by the quintet. Timeless music, soul-penetrating voices, flawless harmony, and expert dancing can be summarized in two words: the Temptations

—*Linda M. Carter*

SELECT DISCOGRAPHY
■ SINGLES
"The Way You Do the Things You Do," 1964
"My Girl," 1964
"Since I Lost My Baby," 1965
"Get Ready," 1966
"Ain't Too Proud to Beg," 1966
"Beauty Is Only Skin Deep," 1966
"(I Know) I'm Losing You," 1966
"All I Need," 1967
"You're My Everything," 1967

"I Wish It Would Rain," 1967
"I Could Never Love Another (After Loving You)," 1968
"Cloud Nine," 1968
"Runaway Child, Running Wild," 1969
"I Can't Get Next to You," 1969
"Psychedelic Shack," 1969
"Ball of Confusion (That's What the World Is Today)," 1970
"Just My Imagination (Running Away with Me)," 1971
"Papa Was a Rollin' Stone," 1972
"Masterpiece," 1973
■ ALBUMS
Temptations Live! 1967
Together, 1969 (with the Supremes)
Anthology, 1973 (compilation)
Reunion, 1982
The Temptations' 25th Anniversary, 1986
Emperors of Soul, 1994

SELECT AWARDS
Grammy Award for Best R&B Performance by a Duo or Group, Vocal or Instrumental, for "Cloud Nine," 1968
Grammy Awards for Best R&B Vocal Performance by a Duo, Group, or Chorus and Best R&B Instrumental Performance for "Papa Was a Rollin' Stone," 1972
American Music Award for Best Vocal Group, 1974
Rock and Roll Hall of Fame, inducted 1989

SEE ALSO: Robinson, Smokey; Supremes, The.

10,000 Maniacs / Natalie Merchant

10,000 Maniacs

ORIGINAL MEMBERS: Natalie Merchant (b. 1963), Robert Buck (b. 1958), Dennis Drew (b. 1957), Steven Gustafson (b. 1957), Jerome Augustyniak (b. 1958), John Lombardo (b. 1952)
OTHER MEMBERS: Mary Ramsey
FIRST RELEASE: *Human Conflict Number Five*, 1982 (extended-play single)
MUSICAL STYLES: Pop, rock and roll, folk pop

Natalie Merchant

BORN: Jamestown, New York; October 26, 1963
FIRST ALBUM RELEASE: *Tigerlily*, 1995
MUSICAL STYLES: Pop, folk rock

In its original incarnation, with Natalie Merchant as vocalist, 10,000 Maniacs was one of the most innovative and talented acts to emerge in the 1980's. The band maintained high standards with its socially conscious lyrics.

During its heyday, 10,000 Maniacs was something of a study in contradictions. While their moniker made those unfamiliar with their music think of heavy metal or punk, the band created lilting, melodic pop and folk rock. On the other hand, as bright-sounding as their music often was, their lyrics were often dark and challenging, leaning toward socially relevant dissertations on a world in chaos.

The Beginnings. The band's original members—guitarist Robert Buck, keyboardist Dennis Drew, and bass player Steven Gustafson—met through the college scene at Jamestown Community College and the State University of New York (SUNY) at Fredonia. "In Jamestown," Drew was once quoted as saying, "there was never any music community for us to become part of or be influenced by . . . so we were able to develop in a vacuum and come out sounding like ourselves."

The three played as a trio, taking the name 10,000 Maniacs, which was a misreading of a B-movie cult film, *2000 Maniacs*. Merchant, a student at Jamestown Community College, became friendly with Drew and Gustafson because they worked at the student radio station. She often attended their shows, and after it was discovered that she could sing, Merchant stepped up to the microphone. The band's first two records—*Human Conflict Number Five* and *Secrets of the I Ching*—were recorded at SUNY through the school's sound-engineering program. (Years later, in 1990, their record label released *Hope Chest*, a compilation of songs from those first two recordings.)

Success. In 1985 10,000 Maniacs signed a contract with Elektra Records and that same year released *The Wishing Chair*, a critical success but

Natalie Merchant (Ken Settle)

commercial failure. Lombardo quit the band after its first major tour, linking up with singer Mary Ramsey to perform as a duo.

Peter Asher whose work as a producer with James Taylor and Linda Rondstat was well-known, was recruited to produce the band's next album, 1987's *In My Tribe*. A word-of-mouth success that stayed on the charts for years, *In My Tribe* (which hit number 37) is considered by most critics to be the pinnacle of 10,000 Maniacs' career. The band's musical hunger and creativity was never more evident than on this album, polished to perfection by Asher.

From the opening strains of "What's the Matter Here?"—a tale of child abuse told by an observer who swings between indignant outrage and fear of getting involved—the album showed a new-found confidence, both musically and in Merchant's plaintive, compelling vocals. Between her singing style and her unusual whirling-dervish stage presence, Merchant was an immediate standout, and the band's profile rose higher when they opened for R.E.M. during their 1988 U.S. tour. (R.E.M. lead singer Michael Stipe and Merchant became close friends—there were even rumors of a romance—and he dueted with her on "A Campfire Song").

In My Tribe dealt with an array of social issues, including child abuse, illiteracy ("Cherry Tree"), and alcoholism ("Don't Talk"). Other songs were equally challenging: "Hey Jack Kerouac" used real-life Beat-movement figures—Kerouac, Allen Ginsburg, and William Burroughs—as a springboard for Merchant's keen observations: "You chose your words from mouths of/ Babes got lost in the woods/ The hip flask slinging madmen/ Steaming cafe flirts/ In Chinatown/ Howling at night." *In My Tribe* also featured the band's cover of Cat Stevens's "Peace Train." The band dropped the song from later pressings and from their concert repertoire, however, after Stevens—who had left music and become a devout Muslim—voiced support for the bounty placed on the life of author Salman Rushdie by Ayatollah Khomeini after he condemned Rushdie's novel *The Satanic Verses* as blasphemous.

The Rise Continues. By the time *Blind Man's Zoo* was released in 1989, the Maniacs—most notably Merchant—were becoming big stars. That album quickly reached gold status and placed

higher on the charts than *In My Tribe*—reaching number 13—despite the fact that musically it was no match for the previous album. Again, Merchant and company dealt with social concerns, but this time their songs seemed to many critics to be more concerned with editorializing than entertaining. Ironically, the CD's most popular track was its gentlest: "Trouble Me," which Merchant had written for and about her father when he was ill.

In 1992 the band released *Our Time in Eden*, switching producers from Asher to Paul Fox. *Our Time in Eden* again touched on serious themes but seemed more musically grounded than *Blind Man's Zoo*. It also showed a broader sound for the band, including horns on songs such as "Few and Far Between" and "Candy Everybody Wants." One single, "These Are Days" became a minor hit.

A Change of Singers. The band's increasing popularity was obvious when they were asked to perform at the MTV Inaugural Ball for President Bill Clinton in January of 1993. That summer, however, Merchant—citing a "desire for change and a need for growth"—announced that she would leave the band following its tour to pursue a solo career. The band appeared on MTV's *Unplugged* series just before she left, and it released their *MTV Unplugged* CD just afterward. (The record also featured Lombardo, who had rejoined the band, and his singing partner, Mary Ramsey, who would replace Merchant in the regrouped 10,000 Maniacs.)

The new incarnation of the band—with all the original members backing Ramsey—released its debut CD, *Love Among the Ruins* in the summer of 1997. One single from the album, a cover of Roxy Music's "More than This," hit the airwaves but did not cause much of a stir on the charts. As of 1998, the band's future was uncertain.

Merchant's Solo Career. Merchant released her first solo album, *Tigerlily*, in 1995. The album proved that she could easily go it alone, and it reached triple platinum status on the strength of singles such as "Carnival" and "Jealousy."

In May, 1998, Merchant's long-awaited sophomore solo effort, *Ophelia*, was released. It featured guest appearances by an array of artists, including

For the Record

Merchant was still a teenager when she joined 10,000 Maniacs, and her mother strongly disapproved. Sneaking out of the house to sing with the band, Merchant allegedly was tracked down at the band's local gigs by her mom, who occasionally pulled her offstage and took her home.

jazz musician Chris Botti, vocalist Karen Peris of the Innocence Mission, Tibetan devotional singer Yunchen Llhamo, and Zaire superstar Lokua Kanza. Merchant also announced plans to perform that summer as coheadliner in Sarah McLachlan's Lilith Fair all-female concert tour.

—*Nicole Pensiero*

SELECT DISCOGRAPHY
10,000 Maniacs
■ SINGLES
Human Conflict Number Five, 1982
   (extended-play single)
■ ALBUMS
Secrets of the I Ching, 1983
The Wishing Chair, 1985
In My Tribe, 1987
Blind Man's Zoo, 1989
Hope Chest: The Fredonia Recordings, 1982-1983,
   1990
Our Time in Eden, 1992
MTV Unplugged, 1994
Love Among the Ruins, 1997
Natalie Merchant solo
■ ALBUMS
Tigerlily, 1995
Ophelia, 1998

SEE ALSO: R.E.M.

John Tesh

BORN: Garden City, New York; July 9, 1952
FIRST ALBUM RELEASE: *Tour de France,* 1988
MUSICAL STYLES: New age, pop instrumental

John Tesh grew up in the musical family of John and Mildred Tesh and started playing piano and trumpet at age six. In junior and senior high school bands such as Daze of Night, he performed covers of progressive rock songs by Yes, Jethro Tull, Steppenwolf, and Emerson, Lake, and Palmer. After acceptance by the New York Symphonic Orchestra, he studied at the Juilliard School of Music. Tesh then went to North Carolina State University, where he double-majored in music and communication.

Tour de France. After graduation in 1975, Tesh worked as an investigative reporter in Durham, North Carolina, then as a news anchor for a New York City CBS television affiliate. A three-sport varsity athlete, Tesh was hired as a sports commentator by CBS in 1983 and covered the Tour de France bicycle race. He composed original music to accompany the televised race coverage, which resulted in a call-in campaign by viewers requesting copies of the score. After placing two advertisements in cycling magazines, he received five thousand orders within two weeks.

From 1986 to 1996, Tesh cohosted the syndicated television series *Entertainment Tonight* with Mary Hart and began his music career in earnest. In order to retain artistic control of his music, Tesh manufactured and distributed his Tour de France cassette from his home, selling over thirty thousand copies. After experiencing stage fright throughout 1986, Tesh underwent therapy, which left him able to perform more easily from 1987 onward.

After releasing the Grammy-winning *Tour de France* (1988) and *Garden City* (1989) albums on Private Music, Tesh founded GTS Records. Tesh then released several sports theme albums, notably *Ironman Triathlon* (1992) and *The Games* (1992), the latter a sound track of music used on the U.S. telecasts of the 1992 Summer Olympic Games in Barcelona, Spain. His 1983 music for the Pan-American Games won an Emmy Award, and Tesh earned two more Emmys in 1991 for the World Track and Field Championships. Subsequent million-sellers included *A Romantic Christmas* (1992) and *A Family Christmas* (1994). For his John Tesh Project, Tesh produced *Sax by the Fire* (1994), *Sax on the Beach* (1995), and *Discovery* (1996).

A Larger Audience. Tesh reached his widest audience with the 1995 *Live at Red Rocks* concert album, which quickly moved to number 1 on *Billboard*'s new age charts. The video of the event later aired on Public Broadcasting Service (PBS) stations. Independently produced by Tesh, the concert featured Olympic opening ceremony pageantry, gymnastic routines by former Olympic athletes, and performances by an eighty-piece orchestra. The PBS airings led to impressive financial support during pledge drives, earning more than one million dollars for the network, which forced Tesh to decide which of his two careers to pursue. In the same year, Tesh issued his first CD-ROM, *Backstage with John Tesh*, and appeared on a cable shopping network, where he sold nine thousand box sets in ninety minutes. He also appeared on the cover of *People* magazine and cohosted an infomercial.

In early 1996, after 2,800 shows with *Entertainment Tonight*, Tesh departed full-time television work, although later that year he provided sports commentary for NBC's coverage of the Summer Olympics. NBC also began using Tesh's music for its telecasts of professional basketball games. From June to October of 1996, the General Motors-sponsored Tesh Undiscovered America tour raised over $200,000 for the National Coalition for Music Education's campaign to fund school music programs and provide equipment, keyboards, and sheet music to elementary schools in selected cities. The tour opened with a free concert in Minneapolis to coincide with the Olympic torch relay on June 1. In March, 1997, Tesh produced a second PBS special, *John Tesh: The Avalon Concert*, filmed in Santa Catalina, California, which also yielded lucrative financial rewards for the network and Tesh. Tesh used the program to promote his music education support, dedicating the title song from his 1996 album, *Discovery*, as his anthem for music education in America.

While Tesh became categorized as a new age performer, some critics have deemed him an original synthesizer of jazz, rock, and classical music. Because of his mellow sound, his attention to his family, and his association with tabloid television, Tesh became the subject of widespread derision by detractors on the Internet, notably NATAS (the National AntiTesh Action Society), who picketed his Detroit concerts in June, 1997.

—*Wesley Britton*

SELECT DISCOGRAPHY
■ ALBUMS
Tour de France, 1988
Garden City, 1989
Monterey Nights, 1993
Winter Song, 1993
Sax by the Fire, 1994
Live at Red Rocks, 1995
Sax on the Beach, 1995
Discovery, 1996
Choirs of Christmas, 1996
Avalon, 1997
Sax All Night, 1997
Grand Passion, 1998

SEE ALSO: G, Kenny; Yanni.

Richard Thompson

BORN: London, England; April 3, 1949
FIRST ALBUM RELEASE: *Fairport Convention*, 1968 (with Fairport Convention)
FIRST SOLO ALBUM RELEASE: *Henry the Human Fly*, 1972
MUSICAL STYLES: Folk rock, rock and roll

Richard Thompson first recorded with the English folk-rock band Fairport Convention but eventually began a solo career that established him as one of rock music's most respected guitarists and songwriters. Although Thompson never had the commercial success that an artist of his stature deserved, he was able to carve out a meaningful recording career as both a solo performer and a guest artist on numerous other recordings.

The Beginnings. Richard Thompson was born in London and began playing an acoustic guitar when he was twelve years old. Before long, Thompson was playing an electric guitar in various bands with his school friends. He learned new guitar chords from his sister's boyfriends and his father. After leaving school in 1967, Thompson spent a short period of time as an apprentice to a stained-glass maker. Music was his first love, however, and when not practicing the guitar with friends, he was performing in local folk clubs. Thompson learned to perform the songs of Phil Ochs, Bob Dylan, Paul Butterfield, and Buddy Guy.

During 1967, Thompson joined Simon Nicol (guitar and vocals), Ashley Hutchings (bass), and Shaun Frater (drums) to form Fairport Convention. Frater was eventually replaced on drums by Martin Lamble, and vocalists Ian Matthews and Judy Dyble were invited to join the band. The group covered songs by Joni Mitchell and Bob Dylan while performing in London clubs. In 1968, Joe Boyd produced the group's first album, *Fairport Convention*, for Polydor Records. As lead guitarist, Thompson injected a brooding energy into his guitar solos. In addition to being a brilliant rock guitarist, he also ventured into folk styles with the same confident mastery. In the spring of 1968, vocalist Sandy Denny joined the band after Dyble decided to leave in order to join Giles, Giles, and Fripp. Denny was an incomparable singer and very knowledgeable about British folk music.

Early in 1969, Fairport Convention released its second album, *What We Did on Our Holidays*, which included some very strong original songs such as Denny's "Fotheringay" and Thompson's "Meet on the Ledge," "No Man's Land," and "Tale in a Hard Time." After the album's release, Matthews left the band in order to form Matthews Southern Comfort. With this album and its next one, *Unhalfbricking* (1969), Fairport Convention established themselves as the preeminent British folk rock band of the period. During their 1969 British tour, Lamble was killed in a traffic accident and was replaced by Dave Mattacks. Violin player Dave Swarbrick was also added to the band.

In 1969, the group released another fine album, *Liege and Lief*, which was more deeply rooted in the traditional folk vein. The group composed new arrangements for such traditional folk songs as "Matty Groves," "Tam Lin," and "The Deserter." Thompson wrote the moody "Farewell, Farewell" and cowrote "Crazy Man Michael" with Swarbrick. Thompson remained with Fairport Convention for only one more album. *Full House* was released in July, 1970, and contained three songs that Thompson cowrote with Swarbrick.

Time to Move On. Although Thompson's guitar prowess had reached prodigious heights during his tenure with Fairport Convention, it was his songwriting skill that had made the more remarkable progress. After leaving the group in January, 1971, Thompson worked on a couple of session projects. During one of the sessions, Sandy Denny

For the Record

Richard Thompson has been nicknamed the "Drizzle King" because he has used a wide variety of rain metaphors in more than two hundred of his songs.

introduced Thompson to Linda Peters, one of the backup singers, and the two became romantically involved. In 1972, Thompson began work on his first solo album, the eccentric *Henry the Human Fly* (1972). During that year, Peters and Thompson got married and also formed a musical partnership. Recording as Richard and Linda Thompson, they released six albums together. The duo's first album, *I Want to See the Bright Lights Tonight* (1974), included such somber songs as "Calvary Cross," "Withered and Died," and "End of the Rainbow." While Thompson wrote the songs for the duo, he shared lead vocals with his wife. Her mezzo-soprano voice added warmth to his often razor-edged lyrics. As with Fairport Convention, Thompson attempted to write material that mixed Celtic folk traditions with contemporary rock instrumentation. The duo's second album, *Hokey Pokey* (1974), had a somewhat lighter tone with such songs as "Smiffy's Glass Eye" and "Georgie's on a Spree."

During 1974, the couple converted to the Sufi Muslim faith. For the next few years, they went about establishing a Sufi community in rural England. After they recorded *Pour Down the Silver* in 1975, the Thompsons did not record again until 1978. While *First Light* (1978) and *Sunnyvista* (1979) contained some excellent songs, their sixth and final album together, *Shoot Out the Lights* (1982), was their boldest and most riveting recording. Their marriage was disintegrating around this time, and a good deal of anger and bitterness spilled over into the songs on the album.

Going Solo with Painful Baggage. After the 1982 divorce, Richard Thompson became a solo artist and released *Hand of Kindness* in 1983. A number of songs on the album dealt with failed relationships, including "Tear Stained Letter" and "A Poisoned Heart and a Twisted Memory." The album went to number 183 on the U.S. pop charts. In 1985, he married concert promoter Nancy Covey and released *Across a Crowded Room*, which also included some biting songs about troubled relationships such as "She Twists the Knife Again" and "When the Spell Is Broken." The album rose to number 102 on the U.S. pop charts.

Although almost universally praised by critics, Thompson's albums never sold well. In 1993, the box set *Watching the Dark: The History of Richard Thompson* was released. Highly respected by his peers, a tribute album *Beat the Retreat* was released in 1994. Among the artists who contributed cover versions of Thompson's songs were Bob Mould, Syd Straw, Graham Parker, R.E.M., Bonnie Raitt, David Byrne, and Los Lobos. For his 1996 double album *You? Me? Us?*, Thompson devoted one disc to acoustic ballads and the other disc to electric rock and roll. Famous for his crackling guitar solos and his poignant and sardonic songs, Thompson continued to brilliantly mix various musical traditions together to the amazement of the discriminating listener.

—Jeffry Jensen

SELECT DISCOGRAPHY
■ ALBUMS
Fairport Convention
Fairport Convention, 1968
What We Did on Our Holidays, 1969
Unhalfbricking, 1969
Liege and Lief, 1969
Full House, 1970
Richard and Linda Thompson
I Want to See the Bright Lights Tonight, 1974
Hokey Pokey, 1974
Pour Down the Silver, 1975
First Light, 1978
Sunnyvista, 1979
Shoot Out the Lights, 1982
Richard Thompson solo
Henry the Human Fly, 1972
Hand of Kindness, 1983
Across a Crowded Room, 1985
Daring Adventures, 1986
Amnesia, 1988

Rumor and Sigh, 1991
Watching the Dark: The History of Richard Thompson, 1993 (boxed set)
Mirror Blue, 1994
You? Me? Us? 1996

SEE ALSO: Byrds, The; Chieftains, the; Costello, Elvis; Jethro Tull; Los Lobos; Parker, Graham; Raitt, Bonnie; Reed, Lou; R.E.M.

George Thorogood and the Destroyers

ORIGINAL MEMBERS: George Thorogood (b. 1952), Ron Smith, Billy Blough, Jeff Simon
OTHER MEMBERS: Hank Carter, Steve Chrismar
FIRST ALBUM RELEASE: *George Thorogood and the Destroyers*, 1977
MUSICAL STYLES: Blues, rock and roll, rhythm and blues

The music of George Thorogood and the Destroyers has been called everything from ancestor worship to formulaic rehash. Fans live for their live shows—two hours of hard rocking, duck walking, boogie-down rock and roll. Their musical influences comprise a who's who of the blues: John Lee Hooker, Elmore James, Willie Dixon, Muddy Waters, and Howlin' Wolf. Thorogood once told an interviewer that he didn't really need to write any more songs, because "Chuck Berry already wrote them all."

The Beginnings. Not a lot is known about Thorogood's personal life, which is his preference. ("Write about someone who has really accomplished something," he has told interviewers.) He was born in Baton Rouge, Louisiana, but grew up in Wilmington, Delaware. He did not pick up a guitar until after high school, concentrating instead on sports and leisure activities. Thorogood first became interested in music and Chicago blues after seeing John Paul Hammond perform in 1970.

However, his first love was baseball. For a time, Thorogood played infield for a semi-professional baseball team, the Delaware Destroyers. According to an unconfirmed story, he formed a roots rock-and-roll band of the same name in order to raise money to buy uniforms for the team. The musical Destroyers comprised Thorogood on guitar and vocals, Ron Smith on guitar, bass player Billy Blough, and drummer Jeff Simon. They built a small but loyal local following, and soon Thorogood found himself spending more time with his guitar than with his baseball mitt. The band moved to Boston a few years later, where they augmented their own performances by playing backup for visiting blues artists.

Folk Meets Blues. In July, 1975, John Forward and his friends wandered into Joe's Place, a Cambridge blues club, in search of some old-fashioned rock and roll. None of them had ever heard of Thorogood and the Destroyers, but by the music coming from the building, they thought they might be in the right place. It turned out the club was nearly empty, yet Forward and his friends were treated to the best show they had ever seen. Forward was so impressed that he proclaimed himself "Fan Number One" and devoted the next two years to procuring the Destroyers a contract with Rounder Records. Forward described the experience in his note on the back of the debut album *George Thorogood and the Destroyers* (1977): "This group played as if they were in front of twelve thousand people instead of twelve and sounding like a whole band instead of the small combo they really are."

The album was a risk for all involved. Rounder was primarily a folk and bluegrass label, and the

For the Record

George Thorogood has taken his baseball very seriously. So seriously, in fact, that in some years Thorogood and the Destroyers would only tour during the baseball off-season. This kept them out of the lucrative summer circuit of outdoor venues and limited their exposure during the early part of their careers.

Destroyers were their first rock-and-roll act. Only two of the tracks were originals; the rest were heartfelt covers of songs by Thorogood's heroes: "Madison Blues" and "Can't Stop Lovin'" by Elmore James, John Lee Hooker's "One Bourbon, One Scotch, and One Beer," and "Kind Hearted Woman" from Robert Johnson.

Despite the concern, the first album received good reviews, and a second followed in 1978, *Move It On Over*. The title track, a cover of Hank Williams's classic, received heavy radio airplay. *Move It On Over* reached the Top 40 and became the Destroyers' first gold record. Thorogood also continued his tradition of cover songs, this time with "That Same Thing" from Willie Dixon and Chuck Berry's "It Wasn't Me." Following the success of the second album, MCA found an old demo that had been recorded and signed away by Thorogood in 1975. Capitalizing on the success of *Move It On Over*, MCA released the demo as *Better than the Rest*, against the wishes of the band.

The Big Time. Smith left the Destroyers in 1980 and was replaced by saxophonist Hank Carter. Thorogood took time off from music that season to play baseball but was back in time to open a few shows for the Rolling Stones during their 1981 U.S. tour. Playing stadiums was a new experience for the band, which until then had shunned large arenas for smaller clubs and had even played under false names to prevent overcrowding. Their own 1981 tour was called "50/50," because they visited fifty states in fifty days.

They moved to EMI in 1982 and released their breakthrough album, *Bad to the Bone*. The title song was featured in the 1983 film *Christine* and became the subject of the Destroyers' first music video. The video, which received heavy MTV airplay, featured Thorogood playing pool with the legendary Bo Diddley. The album went gold and spent nearly one full year on the charts.

In 1985, the Destroyers released *Maverick*, their best-selling album. *Maverick* featured the sardonic "I Drink Alone" and a cover of "Willie and the Hand Jive." The group also appeared at the Live Aid global relief concert playing backup for blues legends Albert Collins and Bo Diddley. A 1986 live album (*Live*) was followed by a string of studio albums, none of which repeated the success of *Maverick* or *Bad to the Bone*. The undaunted Destroyers continued to tour with a concert schedule that still left time for baseball.

Rock and Roll Never Forgets. Their 1997 album, *Rockin' My Life Away*, was their last for EMI, and they put their hearts into it. "It's gotten raunchier, tougher, tighter, meaner, and the songs have gotten funnier over the years," Thorogood told one interviewer. "Right now is vintage Destroyers." Any band that can put together an album of songs by John Hiatt, Frank Zappa, Merle Haggard, Slim Harpo, and Elmore James is clearly a force to be reckoned with. "I don't like commercial music and I don't like mainstream stuff," Thorogood continued. "We play rough. That's what we do."   —*P. S. Ramsey*

SELECT DISCOGRAPHY
■ ALBUMS
George Thorogood and the Destroyers, 1977
Move It On Over, 1978
More George Thorogood and the Destroyers, 1980
Bad to the Bone, 1982
Maverick, 1985
Live, 1986
Born to Be Bad, 1988
Boogie People, 1991
Haircut, 1993
Let's Work Together Live, 1995
Rockin' My Life Away, 1997

SEE ALSO: Berry, Chuck; Diddley, Bo; Dixon, Willie; Hooker, John Lee; Howlin' Wolf; Waters, Muddy.

Three Dog Night

ORIGINAL MEMBERS: Danny Hutton (b. 1942), Chuck Negron (b. 1942), Cory Wells (b. 1942), Mike Allsup (b. 1947), Jimmy Greenspoon (b. 1948), Joe Schermie, Floyd Sneed (b. 1943)
OTHER MEMBERS: Jay Gruska, Paul Kingery, Pat Bautz
FIRST ALBUM RELEASE: *Three Dog Night*, 1969
MUSICAL STYLES: Rock and roll, pop

From 1969 to 1974, Three Dog Night had eighteen Top-20 hits. Three Dog Night was one of the most popular bands in the United States during this time. By late 1975, the band had sold nearly fifty million records. The group wrote few songs themselves, preferring to showcase other songwriters.

Beginnings. Danny Hutton, born in Ireland and raised in the United States, had a minor hit in 1965 with "Roses and Rainbows," a song which he wrote and produced. Later that year, he became a producer for Metro-Goldwyn-Mayer (MGM). At MGM, he met Cory Wells, born in Buffalo, New York, who worked with the group the Enemies and later toured with Sonny and Cher. Hutton failed in his audition for the Monkees, and by 1968, Hutton and Wells decided to form Three Dog Night. Chuck Negron, a clear-voiced tenor, was added to the singing group along with instrumentalists Mike Allsup (guitar), Jim Greenspoon (keyboards), Joe Schermie (bass), and Floyd Sneed (drums). The group signed to Dunhill Records and had an immediate hit with "Try a Little Tenderness" in 1969, a reworking of the 1966 Otis Redding hit.

Hits. Other early hits included "Eli's Coming" in 1969, written by Laura Nyro; "Easy to Be Hard" in 1969, from the musical *Hair*; "One" also in 1969 and the group's first million seller, written by Harry Nilsson; and "Mama Told Me (Not to Come)," the ultimate party mood song, written by Randy Newman and recorded in 1970, which became the group's first U.S. number 1 hit. The band struck gold in 1971 with the hit single "Joy to the World," written by Hoyt Axton.

Some other hits of the early 1970's included "Liar" in 1971, written by Russ Ballard of Argent, a group organized by former Zombie member Rod Argent; "Just an Old Fashioned Love Song" in 1971 by Paul Williams; and "Never Been to Spain" in 1972 by Hoyt Axton. In 1972, the band recorded "Black and White," which had been written in 1954 by David Arkin (father of actor Alan Arkin) and Earl Robinson as a response to the U.S. Supreme Court decision banning segregation in U.S. public schools. Later hits included "Shambala" in 1973, "The Show Must Go On," by

Three Dog Night (Archive Photos/Frank Driggs Collection)

can Sportsman, as well as *Country Sportsman*, taped in New Zealand. Negron continued to perform with Wells and Jay Gruska as Three Dog Night.

Reunion. In 1981, the original group came together, and they discovered that their old sound and rhythm was still there. Unfortunately, the reunion did not last long. Negron did not stay with the group at that time due to personal problems and professional ambitions. Another attempt at a reunion with all three of the original members occurred in 1993. Once again, the reunion did not work, and Negron began a recording career as a solo artist, featuring Sneed and Greenspoon as instrumentalists.

In 1997, the Three Dog Night lineup consisted of Cory Wells and Danny Hutton (vocals), Jimmy Greenspoon (keyboards), Michael Allsup (guitar), Paul Kingery (bass), and Pat Bautz (drums). Three Dog Night fan clubs existed all over the world, and members ranged over all age groups. Three Dog Night also toured the United States regularly in the late 1990's.

Legacy. One of the most popular and influential bands of the 1970's, Three Dog Night provided an avenue for many upcoming songwriting artists, including Hoyt Axton, Laura Nyro, Elton

Leo Sayer, in 1974, and "Play Something Sweet," by Allen Toussaint, in 1974.

Three Dog Night consistently played to sold-out concert arenas, and acts such as Rod Stewart, Aerosmith, and Electric Light Orchestra served as their opening act. By 1975, the touring had taken its exhausting toll, and the members decided to leave the group and pursue their own interests.

Separation. Hutton went to Los Angeles, Central America, and England before returning to his hometown of Buncrana, Ireland. He formed a management and booking agency which managed such bands as Fear, the Go-Go's, and X. He also recorded two songs for motion-picture sound tracks, "Brand New Day" for 1985's *American Flyers* and "Wouldn't It Be Good" for 1986's *Pretty in Pink*.

Wells toured the United States with his family. An avid fisherman, in 1997 Wells worked as a field editor for *Outdoor Life* magazine, and he has appeared in segments of the television show *Ameri-*

For the Record

The odd name Three Dog Night was cause for much speculation in the band's early days; an aborigine term, "three dog night" is an expression for an extremely cold evening.

John, Paul Williams, and Randy Newman. Because of massive concert attendance, the band pioneered in the modern rock-tour concept of stadium-size shows. Three Dog Night also set the pattern for later groups that showcased multiple lead singers harmonizing.   —*Karan A. Berryman*

SELECT DISCOGRAPHY
■ ALBUMS
Three Dog Night, 1969
Suitable for Framing, 1969
Three Dog Night Captured Live at the Forum, 1969
It Ain't Easy, 1970
Harmony, 1971
Around the World with Three Dog Night, 1973
Joy to the World—Their Greatest Hits, 1974
    (compilation)
American Pastime, 1976
The Best of 3 Dog Night, 1982 (compilation)
Celebrate—The Three Dog Night Story, 1965-1975,
    1993 (compilation)

SEE ALSO: John, Elton; Newman, Randy.

Mel Tillis

BORN: Pahokee, Florida; August 8, 1932
FIRST ALBUM RELEASE: *Walk on By,* 1961
MUSICAL STYLES: Country

Lonnie Melvin Tillis was born in the small Florida town of Pahokee in 1932 in the midst of the Great Depression. His family was very poor, and Tillis's father, a baker by trade, frequently abused him and his three siblings. When he was three years old, Tillis was bitten by a mosquito and almost died from malaria. The illness left him with a stutter in his speech that made it difficult for him to say even the simplest words. His unstable and violent father eventually deserted the family and never returned. Tillis's speech impediment made life difficult for him, but a friendly teacher encouraged him to learn how to play the drums and the piano, the instrument for which he became most noted. He was also a star on his high-school football team even though he worked long hours picking strawberries to help his destitute mother.

In Nashville. Tillis began writing songs as a teenager and discovered that his stutter disappeared while he was singing. He entered the Air Force after high school and continued to write ballads. After leaving the Air Force, he went to Nashville to sell his music but experienced great difficulties. Music executives found his stutter distracting and told him there was no way he would ever become a country star. While waiting for a break, Tillis worked as a milkman and delivery truck driver. The legendary country singer Webb Pierce finally bought one of his songs because he liked the words and turned it into a hit called "I'm Tired." The success of this song enabled Tillis to get a job as a songwriter with the Cedarwood Publishing Company. A few years later he would buy the company.

Tillis recorded his first song in 1958 for Columbia Records. "The Violet and the Rose" made it to

Mel Tillis in 1977 (AP/Wide World Photos)

the Top 30 country list. He followed this success with performances of songs he had written, including the minor hits "Wine," "Who's Julia," and "These Lonely Hands of Mine." The songs he wrote and that were performed by other artists proved to be more successful, however, including Bobby Bare's great hit "Detroit City," and Kenny Rogers's best-selling "Ruby, Don't Take Your Love to Town."

Superstar. Tillis became one of the best-selling singers and writers in the history of country music. His primary success came between 1968 and 1978 when more than thirty of his songs became number 1 singles, including "The Arms of a Fool," "Commercial Affection," "Heaven Everyday," "In the Middle of the Night," and "Southern Rain." Tillis became a frequent guest on popular television shows such as *Hee Haw* and *The Glen Campbell Goodtime Hour*. In 1976 he was named Entertainer of the Year by the Country Music Association.

Following this success, Tillis tried to move into a style referred to as "country pop," a smoother, mellower sound that record producers hoped would appeal to a larger audience. Tillis's experiments in this direction included an album with Nancy Sinatra. He was very uneasy with this type of music, however, and quickly returned to the traditional country sound of his greatest hits. His road show, which included a seventeen-piece orchestra, became so popular he soon had little time to write songs anymore. He developed a successful

stage presence and became well known as a comedian along with being a great singer and songwriter. Tillis's autobiography, *Stutterin' Boy*, was published in 1985. He has been married twice and has four children. —*Leslie V. Tischauser*

SELECT DISCOGRAPHY
■ ALBUMS
Walk on By, 1961
The Violet and the Rose, 1962
Heart over Mind, 1970
After All This Time, 1983
The Best of Mel Tillis, 1985 (previously released material)
I Believe in You, 1985
Brand New Mister Me, 1988
American Originals, 1990
Greatest Hits, 1991 (previously released material)

SELECT AWARDS
Country Music Association Entertainer of the Year, 1976

SEE ALSO: Campbell, Glen; Clark, Roy; Rogers, Kenny.

TLC

ORIGINAL MEMBERS: T-Boz (b. Tionne Watkins, 1970), Chilli (b. Rozonda Thomas, 1971), Left Eye (b. Lisa Lopes, 1971)
FIRST ALBUM RELEASE: *Oooooooohhh . . . On the TLC Tip*, 1992
MUSICAL STYLES: Hip-hop, rap, soul

This Atlanta, Georgia-based hip-hop trio became pop stars with their first trip to the studio. Founded and managed by singer and producer Pebbles, TLC and their first album, *Oooooooohhh . . . On the TLC Tip* (1992), went triple platinum on the strength of three Top-10 hits: "Ain't 2 Proud 2 Beg" (number 6), "Baby-Baby-Baby" (number 2), and "What About Your Friends" (number 7). "Ain't 2 Proud 2 Beg" was notable for its extensive sampling, incorporating bits from James Brown's "Escape-ism," Kool and the Gang's "Jungle Boogie," Average White

For the Record

Mel Tillis is widely known for having a stutter, which he developed at the age of three. It made his life difficult as a youth, but he managed to overcome it when he sang: "I think the stutter made me work harder to become an entertainer. I would have done anything."
—*Mel Tillis*, quoted in Alanna Nash, *Talking with the Legends of Country Music*, 1988

Band's "School Boy Crush," Silver Convention's "Fly, Robin, Fly," and Bob James's "Take Me to the Mardi Gras." In 1993 they released "Get It Up" from the *Poetic Justice* sound track.

Top of the Charts. Their follow-up, *CrazySexyCool* (1994), hearkens back to Philly soul, minimizing TLC's early rap associations. With the help of Dallas Austin and Babyface in production, they created a mainstream sound which appealed across the pop spectrum. *CrazySexyCool* was even bigger than *Ooooooohhh . . . On the TLC Tip*, selling more than ten million copies and producing four Top-10 hits. Both "Creep" (1994) and "Waterfalls" (1995) hit the top of the pop charts, while "Red Light Special" (1995) reached number 2 and "Diggin' on You" peaked at number 5. All four singles also reached the U.K. Top 20. "Creep" samples Slick Rick's "Hey Young World."

Coming Apart. As they peaked, TLC began to disintegrate. Just before the release of *CrazySexyCool*, Lopes was arrested for burning down the house of erstwhile boyfriend Andre Rison of the Atlanta Falcons. She was eventually convicted, but in a defense in which her attorney highlighted her drinking problems, avoided prison with a five-year probated sentence. In 1995 the group filed for Chapter 11 bankruptcy. Ironically, TLC won Grammy Awards in 1995 for Best R&B Performance by a Duo or Group for "Creep" and Best R&B Album for *CrazySexyCool*. Financial conflicts with producer Dallas Austin delayed release of a third album. —*John Powell*

SELECT DISCOGRAPHY

■ ALBUMS
Ooooooohhh . . . On the TLC Tip, 1992
CrazySexyCool, 1994

TLC (Paul Natkin)

SELECT AWARDS
MTV Video Music Awards for Best Video of the Year, Best Group Video, Best R&B Video, and Viewer's Choice Video for "Waterfalls," 1995

For the Record

T-Boz, who battles sickle-cell anemia, is a spokeswoman for the national Sickle-Cell Association.

§

TLC's founder, Pebbles (Perri Alette McKissack) had four Top-20 hits between 1988 and 1991. "Girlfriend," "Mercedes Boy," and "Giving You the Benefit" also topped the rhythm-and-blues charts.

Grammy Awards for Best R&B Album for
CrazySexyCool and Best R&B Performance by
a Duo or Group with Vocal for "Creep," 1995

SEE ALSO: DJ Jazzy Jeff and the Fresh Prince; Salt-
n-Pepa.

Peter Tosh

(Winston Hubert McIntosh)

BORN: Westmoreland, Jamaica; October 9, 1944
DIED: St. Andrew, suburb of Kingston, Jamaica;
September 11, 1987
FIRST SINGLE RELEASE: "Simmer Down," 1964
(with the Wailers)
FIRST SOLO ALBUM RELEASE: Legalize It, 1976
MUSICAL STYLE: Reggae

Born Winston Hubert McIntosh, Peter Tosh,
along with Bob Marley and Bunny Wailer, was one
of the three original Wailers, the most influential
and controversial reggae group of the 1960's.
Tosh left the Wailers in 1974 to strike out on his
own after being relegated to backup singer for
Marley. He went on to record
eight solo albums before his
murder in 1987.

The Wailers. Peter Tosh and
Bob Marley met in Trenchtown,
Jamaica, at that time a chaotic
mixture of shacks and concrete
apartments poised on the edge
of the twentieth century. With
Neville "Bunny" Livingstone,
later Bunny Wailer, they formed
the reggae group the Wailers in
1963. During the years with the
Wailers, Tosh recorded some
solo singles, including "Selassie
Serenade" (1969) and "The Return of Al Capone" (1969), under the name of Peter Touch. In
the beginning, none of the
group ever heard their records
played on Jamaican radio. In
1973, the Wailers recorded two
albums, Catch a Fire and Burnin', and the group
finally caught the interest of the general public.

An extremely talented musician, Tosh was bitter and often hostile. Arrogant and inflexible,
both he and Marley rebelled against the system—
organized government, religion, business—and
promoted their Rastafarian belief system. When
Tosh wrote "Mark of the Beast" in 1972, it was in
response to a situation of police brutality against
him. Tosh considered "Mark of the Beast" a historical song in his life.

In 1973, Tosh drove his car off a bridge on the
Spanish Town Road, and his girlfriend died in the
accident. His rebellious and combative nature
intensified after this incident. Many people in the
reggae music community were suspicious of Mar-
lene Brown's role in the tragedy. Brown later became Tosh's common-law wife, and she provided
a support system for the rest of his life. Tosh left
the Wailers in 1974 because of the hectic touring
schedule and a clash with Chris Blackwell who,
although he was promoting the Wailers at that
time, would not produce a solo recording for Tosh.

Solo. When Tosh left the Wailers, he began
recording with his own label, Intel-Diplo H.I.M.,

Peter Tosh in 1979 (AP/Wide World Photos)

which proclaimed the Rastafarian faith that Tosh practiced and preached. Tosh recorded a series of uncompromising solo albums between 1974 and 1987. The albums, characterized by a sarcastic and caustic social commentary, featured innovative reggae arrangements in the style of Sly and Robbie, who combined reggae's African roots with a modern rhythm-and-blues pattern and attention to form.

His first solo album, *Legalize It* (1976), featured a title track that attacked the existing antimarijuana laws of the day. In 1977, Tosh recorded *Equal Rights*, which included a version of the Wailers' "Get Up, Stand Up." After the release of this album, Tosh and his Word, Sound, and Power band, which included Sly and Robbie, joined the Rolling Stones' world tour.

The turning point in Tosh's career occurred in 1978, when he performed at a peace concert in Kingston, Jamaica. All of Jamaica's top reggae groups had agreed to perform. During this concert, Tosh lectured the captive audience for more than forty-five minutes on the evils of oppression, neocolonialism, and the establishment. Jamaicans supported Tosh's views.

As a result of the Rolling Stones tour, Tosh signed with the Rolling Stones Records label. Following this changeover, *Bush Doctor* was recorded in 1978. Mick Jagger and Keith Richards were both featured on the album. In 1979, *Mystic Man* was recorded and released, and in 1981, *Wanted Dread and Alive* was released. In 1983, Tosh signed to the E.M.I. label and, with Chris Kinsey, produced *Mama Africa*, which featured soul singer Betty Wright. The album included the political commentary "Peace Treaty" as well as a reggae version of Chuck Berry's "Johnny B. Goode."

Tosh later recorded *Captured Live* in 1984 and *No Nuclear War* in 1987. Tosh wrote the song "No Nuclear War" in response to the situation between what he perceived as the superpowers of the world in 1987, the United States and the Soviet Union. His purpose in writing the song was to point out that no matter how "super" the powers might seem, a greater force existed in the universe that could ultimately destroy even the superpowers.

For the Record

Peter Tosh named his backup band Word, Sound, and Power to identify his Rastafarian beliefs and to bring his message of inspiration to the public.

Tosh's life and career ended abruptly in September, 1987, when he was gunned down in his home during a robbery.

Legacy. Peter Tosh was an extremely talented man, but often his personality obstructed his path to success. Tosh promoted the reggae style of music, and he was instrumental in the introduction of the reggae sound to the U.S. mainstream. Because of Tosh, the general public began to understand how reggae depended on emotion and spirit to keep the music alive.

By 1987, Tosh felt that the general public did not realize how dependent reggae music was on singers and musical instruments for the lyrics. When Tosh wrote a song, he felt that he had divine inspiration. He wrote and sang about his Rastafarian religion and his beliefs in his reggae songs. With Tosh, it became apparent that reggae music was not a reflection or derivation of American musical developments, but rather a distinctive Jamaican tradition that had survived for centuries. Throughout his short career, Tosh remained committed to his Rastafarian ideals and beliefs.

—*Karan A. Berryman*

SELECT DISCOGRAPHY
■ ALBUMS
Legalize It, 1976
Equal Rights, 1977
Bush Doctor, 1978
Mystic Man, 1979
Wanted Dread and Alive, 1981
Mama Africa, 1983
Captured Live, 1984
No Nuclear War, 1987
The Toughest, 1988 (compilation)

SEE ALSO: Cliff, Jimmy; Marley, Bob.

Toto

ORIGINAL MEMBERS: Bobby Kimball (b. Robert Toreaux, 1947), Steve Lukather (b. 1957), David Paich (b. 1954), Steve Porcaro (b. 1957), David Hungate, Jeff Porcaro (1954-1992)

OTHER MEMBERS: Dennis "Fergie" Frederikson (b. 1951), Mike Porcaro (b. 1955), others

FIRST ALBUM RELEASE: *Toto*, 1978

MUSICAL STYLE: Pop

One of the very few rock bands ever to be condemned for being too professional, these former studio musicians joined forces in the late 1970's to become one of the most successful rock bands of the 1980's. The early Top-10 hit "Hold the Line" presaged later success with "99," "Rosanna," "I Won't Hold You Back," and the number 1 hit "Africa." The continuing session work of the individual members added to the group's collective influence, which helped define the sound of popular radio in the 1980's.

A High School Rock-and-Roll Band. The years of session work by Toto's individual members preceding the formation of the band led many to believe that they were merely an assemblage of studio musicians of tremendous technical proficiency but without any creative identity. In fact, the group had been playing together for years. Keyboardist and principal songwriter David Paich remembered the group's beginnings in drummer Jeff Porcaro's garage: "We must have been about 15 years old then and we were mostly interested in bands from England, which was unusual for American teenagers. We . . . found that groups such as the Stones, Led Zeppelin, or Yes had more of an image. And, just to set the record straight again, we really started out as a high school rock-and-roll band. Later lots of people accused us of originally meeting up in some studio. That's rubbish."

It was no accident that the future band members had an early interest in music. Paich's father was Marty Paich, a noted Hollywood conductor and arranger for such performers as Mel Torme and Ray Charles, while Porcaro's father worked with Marty as a percussionist on Glen Campbell's television variety show in the late 1960's. He also ran a Los Angeles drum store and taught all of his children to read music. The fatherly effort paid off, because two more Porcaro brothers eventually became members of the band: Steve, on keyboards and vocals, and Mike, who replaced bassist David Hungate in 1982. Guitarist Steve "Luke" Lukather was another old friend of the Porcaros who once played in a band with his school friend Steve.

After high school the future bandmates honed their musical skills doing session work for established performers, eventually playing for Steely Dan, Hall and Oates, Joan Baez, Christopher Cross, Michael Jackson, and Olivia Newton-John. Paich established himself as a songwriter at the age of nineteen by writing "Houston" for his father's onetime boss, Glen Campbell. Paich, Hungate, and Jeff Porcaro eventually joined Boz Scaggs's band, playing on the five-million-selling *Silk Degrees* (1976) album. Paich also cowrote a number of songs for the album, including the hit song "Lowdown." With that success behind them and the added talents of vocalist Bobby Kimball, the musicians decided it was time to form their own band.

And Your Little Dog, Too! The group named themselves and their first album after Dorothy's dog in *The Wizard of Oz*. The decision evidently brought them luck, because they soon received a Grammy nomination for Best New Artist. By the beginning of 1979, their debut album was at number 9 in the charts, and their hit single "Hold the Line" had reached number 5. On their next album, *Hydra* (1979), the group fought against the perception that they were simply an all-star team of studio musicians by defining their musical roots. Of all of Toto's albums, this one may have the greatest musical depth, but as is often the case with an artist's sophomore effort, it failed to equal the commercial success of the debut album. *Hydra* nevertheless produced a Top-40 hit with the hauntingly enigmatic love song "99."

Toto's third album, 1981's *Turn Back*, failed to attract U.S. listeners; the strongest single on the disk, "Goodbye Eleanor," did not even appear on the charts. However, this was merely the trough before the tidal wave of their next album. The appropriately named *Toto IV* rose to number 4 in the charts during the summer of 1982, carried there by the infectious melody of the Grammy-winning hit "Rosanna." The song borrowed its name from that of Steve Porcaro's girlfriend, the gifted and stunningly beautiful actress Rosanna Arquette. "No, she was not the inspiration for 'Rosanna,'" Porcaro protested. "It was written by David . . . unless it was wishful thinking on his part."

The tremendous success of "Rosanna" was surpassed early in 1983, however, when the powerfully atmospheric "Africa" became a number 1 hit. The evocative lyrics and fluid melody contributed greatly to the song's effectiveness, but Jeff Porcaro's rhythm track was especially notable for its deftness and dexterity. *Toto IV* scored its third Top-10 single later in the year with "I Won't Hold You Back," but the album's highest achievement came at the Grammy Awards, where it won for Record of the Year and Album of the Year.

Filling the Void. The departure of lead singer Kimball the following year left a void that negatively affected the next few albums (the instrumental sound track to David Lynch's 1984 motion picture *Dune* being the major exception). Fergie Frederikson sang lead vocals on 1984's *Isolation*, but he was soon replaced by Joseph Williams, son of Boston Pops conductor and renowned film composer John Williams, who appeared on both *Fahrenheit* (1986) and *The Seventh One* (1988). Also lending their talents on *The Seventh One* were such noted musicians as Patti Austin, Tom Scott, and Linda Ronstadt. Yet another vocalist, Jean-Michel

For the Record

The inspiration for the Top-40 hit "99" came not from the Barbara Feldon character in the television series *Get Smart* but from the 1971 George Lucas film *THX-1138*, which depicts a future in which names have been replaced by numbers.

Byron, was brought in to record new versions of Toto's greatest hits on the album *Past to Present: 1977-1990* (1990).

Finally, guitarist Lukather stepped forward to assume lead vocal duties on Toto's next album, *Kingdom of Desire* (1992), which included every kind of music from conventional pop to the jazz-fusion instrumental "Jake to the Bone." Tragically, it was the last studio album to feature the talents of Jeff Porcaro, who passed away in the summer of 1992. Many rumors surrounded the sudden and untimely demise of Toto's gifted percussionist, but accidental exposure to a dangerous insecticide was the most likely cause of death.

Only one of the three albums released by Toto after Jeff Porcaro's death included any new material: 1995's *Tambu*, with Simon Phillips on drums. *Absolutely Live* captured some of Jeff Porcaro's last performances with the group on the *Kingdom of Desire* tour, while *Toto XX*, released in May of 1998, was a collection of rarities.　　—*Ed McKnight*

SELECT DISCOGRAPHY
■ ALBUMS
Toto, 1978
Hydra, 1979
Turn Back, 1981
Toto IV, 1982
Dune, 1984 (sound track)
Isolation, 1984
Fahrenheit, 1986
The Seventh One, 1988
Past to Present: 1977-1990, 1990 (previously released material)
Kingdom of Desire, 1992
Absolutely Live, 1993 (live)
Tambu, 1995
Toto XX: 1977-1997, 1998 (previously unreleased material)

SELECT AWARDS
Grammy Awards for Record of the Year for "Rosanna," Album of the Year for *Toto IV*, and Producer of the Year, all 1982

SEE ALSO: Hall and Oates; Jackson, Michael; Led Zeppelin; Newton-John, Olivia; Ronstadt, Linda; Scaggs, Boz; Steely Dan; Yes.

Traffic / Steve Winwood / Dave Mason

Traffic

ORIGINAL MEMBERS: Steve Winwood (b. 1948), Dave Mason (b. 1946), Jim Capaldi (b. 1944), Chris Wood (1944-1983)

OTHER MEMBERS: Rick Grech (1946-1990), Jim Gordon, Reebop Kwaku Baah (d. 1982), Roger Hawkins (b. 1945), David Hood (b. 1943)

FIRST ALBUM RELEASE: *Mr. Fantasy*, 1967

Steve Winwood

BORN: Birmingham, England; May 12, 1948

FIRST ALBUM RELEASE: *Steve Winwood*, 1977

Dave Mason

BORN: Worcester, England; May 10, 1946

FIRST ALBUM RELEASE: *Alone Together*, 1970

MUSICAL STYLES: Psychedelic rock, rock and roll, art rock, pop

Formed in 1967, Traffic was one of the premier progressive-rock bands of its era, combining superb musicianship, songwriting, and innovation. In its earliest incarnation, the band had hits penned by Steve Winwood and Dave Mason. Mason, more interested in pop music, left the band on several occasions before his final departure in 1971. From 1970, Traffic followed Winwood's lead into more experimental, jazz-oriented rock, which made them a staple on radio playlists throughout the 1970's. Winwood and Mason both went on to successful solo careers.

Phase One. All the members of Traffic were seasoned musicians from Birmingham, England-area bands when they united in 1967. Steve Winwood's remarkable rhythm-and-blues vocals, which led critics to compare him to Ray Charles, helped produce a series of Top-10 hits for the Spencer Davis Group between 1965 and 1967, including "Keep On Running," "Gimme Some Lovin'," and "I'm a Man." (At that time, Winwood was still a teenager.) Guitarist and vocalist Dave Mason, drummer Jim Capaldi, and saxophone player Chris Wood were already using vibraphones and flutes in their progressive band, Deep

Feeling, when they met Winwood in 1966. Still only eighteen and anxious to escape the commercial constraints that had come with early success, Winwood opted to join Mason, Capaldi, and Wood in a more artistically creative group.

In order to escape the influences of the club scene and professional producers, during 1967 Traffic retreated to an isolated cottage in rural Berkshire, England, to produce innovative rock records, fusing rythm and blues, rock, folk, and jazz. This collaboration led to three U.K. Top-10 singles before the end of the year: "Paper Sun" (number 5), "Hole in My Shoe" (number 2), and "Here We Go Round the Mulberry Bush" (number 8). Their early singles and first album, *Mr. Fantasy* (1967), featured a variety of unusual instruments, spoken word passages, and elements of the English music-hall tradition, much like the Beatles' *Sgt. Pepper's Lonely Hearts Club Band* (1967), which Traffic acknowledged as inspirational, though their earliest material had been written before that album's release.

Winwood and Mason, the band's two front men, proved how artistically different they were. Winwood, ever reticent on stage and uncomfortable with commercial success, pushed for greater collaboration and innovation. Mason, who had pleased Island Records executives by penning the commercially successful "Hole in My Shoe," proved that his image as a loner, earned by his erratic association with a number of mid-1960's bands, was well deserved. Mason left Traffic in December, 1967, but for the next four years remained a floating member of the band, sometimes contributing songs and occasionally playing

For the Record

Traffic's most successful single, "Hole in My Shoe," reached number 2 on the British charts in 1967. It also split the band, as Winwood, Capaldi, and Wood hated the Mason composition and refused to play it in concert.

live dates. In the United States Traffic was not discovered until 1968 and was usually thought of as a trio.

Traffic's self-titled second album in many ways best represents both the quality of the band's music and the chaotic nature of its development. *Traffic* made the *Billboard* charts in December, 1968, two months after Mason had left the group for a second time. Still, his "You Can All Join In," "Vagabond Virgin," and the often covered "Feelin' Alright" defined the group as much as Winwood and Capaldi's edgier and enigmatic "Pearly Queen" and "40,000 Headmen." By the time the combination live and studio album *Last Exit* reached the charts in May, 1969, it looked as if Traffic was finished. Winwood had joined former Cream members Eric Clapton and Ginger Baker to form Blind Faith, while Mason was touring with Delaney and Bonnie. Ironically, Winwood and Mason continued to see each other, because their respective groups were touring together.

Phase Two. Blind Faith lasted only long enough to tour the United States to sold-out audiences and to produce *Blind Faith*, which hit number 1 on the *Billboard* charts in August, 1969. After a brief stint with Ginger Baker's Air Force, in 1970 Winwood began work on a solo project, with former bandmates Capaldi and Wood sitting in on the sessions. This evolved into a Traffic reunion which yielded their best and most characteristic mature work.

John Barleycorn Must Die was their most successful album, climbing the charts in July of 1970 and peaking at number 5. Without Mason, there was little interest in producing hit singles, but the remarkable variety and quality of the music, from Winwood's New Orleans-style piano-driven "Glad" to the traditional folk title track to the rhythm-and-blues "Empty Pages," earned the band a large following on radio stations which were then emerging as the venue for serious rock music. *John Barleycorn Must Die* and follow-up *The Low Spark of High-Heeled Boys* (number 7, 1971) both became staples of progressive radio playlists. Decades later, the title track from the latter album would still define progressive music for many lis-

Steve Winwood (Ken Settle)

teners, a hauntingly simple Winwood piano and bass line evolving from the silence, gradually augmented by Wood's distant jazz saxophone, organ, and percussion, all gradually building to a vocal introduction by Winwood. At more than eleven minutes, "The Low Spark of High-Heeled Boys" allowed plenty of time for studio jamming by accomplished musicians, including bassist Rick Grech, previously of Blind Faith and Ginger Baker's Air Force, who had joined Traffic in 1970, and Ghanaian percussionist Reebop Kwaku Baah, who joined the following year.

While Winwood suffered through a bout of peritonitis, Capaldi recorded a solo album, *Oh! How We Danced* (1972), in Muscle Shoals, Alabama. This led to the addition of Muscle Shoals session players bassist David Hood and drummer Roger Hawkins to Traffic's successful *Shootout at the Fantasy Factory* (1973), which rose to number 6 on the *Billboard* charts. Though this lineup produced the live *Traffic on the Road* later that year (number 29), Hood and Hawkins then left the band. By the time Traffic produced its final studio album, *When the Eagle Flies* (number 9, 1974), the group had returned to something near its original composition, with Winwood, Capaldi, Wood, and bassist Rosco Gee.

Winwood and Mason Go Solo. Though Mason occasionally played with Traffic through 1971, he had effectively been pursuing a solo career since 1968. Preferring to work alone in songwriting, he ironically spent much of his career in performance collaborations, either on the road or in the studio. His various ventures saw him play with Delaney and Bonnie, Mama Cass Elliot, Derek and the Dominos, George Harrison, Graham Nash, and Stevie Wonder. His most successful solo album was *Alone Together* (1970), which peaked at number 22 and included the single "Only You Know and I Know" (number 42). Though his solo career has been solid rather than spectacular, "We Just Disagree" did reach number 12 on the *Billboard* singles chart in 1977. In 1994 he joined Fleetwood Mac for a brief stint.

Winwood, on the other hand, became more popular with time. Always shy and unobtrusive on stage, by the early 1980's he had become more accommodating to the press and to popular video formats. His *Steve Winwood* (1977) was a modest success, but *Arc of a Diver* (1980), which featured Winwood playing all instruments, went platinum, based in large part upon the strength of the Top-10 single "While You See a Chance" (number 7). The 1986 *Back in the High Life* (number 3) went triple platinum, and included three Top-20 hits. "Higher Love" became Winwood's first number 1 hit and earned Grammy Awards for Best Pop Vocal Performance and Record of the Year. *Roll with It* (1988), Winwood's first album for Virgin Records, went double platinum and reached the top of the album charts. In 1994, Winwood and Capaldi, the base of the classic Traffic band, reunited with Rosco Gee to produce the critically acclaimed *Far from Home* (number 33).

The Traffic Legacy. Unlike many progressive bands from the late 1960's and early 1970's, Traffic aged well. In part this was due to the presence of three talented songwriters in the band. Though Mason was at odds with Winwood, Capaldi, and Wood on the direction of the band, he nevertheless penned several of their biggest hits and helped them gain an audience from the beginning. The often covered "Feelin' Alright" (Joe Cocker did the most well-known version) would become a rock classic. Winwood and Capaldi, often with Wood, were a dynamic songwriting team, whose evocative and enigmatic lyrics, combined with creative fusions of rock, jazz, and rhythm-and-blues idioms, led to enduring songs such as "Heaven Is in Your Mind," "Dear Mr. Fantasy," "40,000 Headmen," and their trademark "Low Spark of High-Heeled Boys."

Traffic's music would remain fresh also because the music and production were part of an integrated process. Traffic was the first major band to retreat from the city during production, for the sake of artistic integrity. Because Winwood, Mason, Capaldi, and Wood were accomplished musicians on a variety of instruments who also played together as a band, they developed a style that could never be duplicated by studio musicians.

Chris Wood died in 1983. An underrated musician, Wood was not a flashy player, but his flute playing, in particular, worked beautifully to establish a song's appropriate mood. The flute lines on "40,000 Headmen" and the saxophone parts and overdubbed double-flute soloing in "Freedom Rider" (on *John Barleycorn Must Die*) typify his talents. Winwood once observed that he and Capaldi could "play and sing, but Chris [Wood] gave the band its character. . . . He was more responsible for the sound than anyone else." Despite Winwood's generous assessment, most critics agree that it was Winwood himself who was primarily responsible for the enduring success of Traffic. He was one of the great vocal stylists of the rock era who proved as adept at adjusting his classic rhythm-and-blues voice as the band was at fusing a wide variety of musical styles. —*John Powell*

SELECT AWARDS
Grammy Awards for Record of the Year and
Best Pop Vocal Performance, Male, for
"Higher Love," 1986 (Winwood)

SEE ALSO: Clapton, Eric; Cream; Fleetwood Mac.

Randy Travis

BORN: Marshville, North Carolina; May 4, 1959
FIRST SINGLE RELEASE: "She's My Woman," 1978
FIRST ALBUM RELEASE: *Randy Ray Live at the Nash-
ville Palace*, 1982
MUSICAL STYLE: Country

Randy Travis was born Randy Traywick, the son of
a horse trainer, and as a result, Randy developed
an early interest in riding and nurturing horses.
Because of his father's insistence, Travis learned
how to play a guitar and began performing publicly with his older brother Ricky when he was only
nine years old. As a child, his most memorable
Christmas present was a Gibson guitar he received

at the age of ten. With their father arranging the
bookings, Randy and Ricky were joined by brother
David, and they played at local clubs in a wide area
around their home in North Carolina.

Travis hated school but loved the wild life, and
he was frequently in trouble with the law for
varying offenses, including drunkenness, theft,
drug possession, speeding violations, and running away from home. Partway through ninth
grade, he quit school, worked on the family farm,
and did construction work. While on probation in
1977, Travis appeared under the name of Randy
Ray at a nightclub in Charlotte, North Carolina,
which was co-owned by Lib Hatcher. Impressed
with Travis's talent, Hatcher persuaded the judge
to release him into her custody, found him regular

Randy Travis (Paul Natkin)

work at her club, provided him a home with her and her husband, and financed his first recordings. The association with Travis soon led to Hatcher's divorce from her husband Frank. In 1981, Travis and Hatcher moved to Nashville, where she became manager of the Nashville Palace nightclub and hired Travis as the resident singer as well as a dishwasher and cook.

The New Crown Prince. In November of 1982, Travis recorded his first album, *Randy Ray Live at the Nashville Palace*, and with Hatcher's wise management, he began to establish himself in Nashville. His big break came in 1984 when he received a contract with Warner Bros. Records which led to the release of *Storms of Life* in 1986. The album reached gold status faster than any other debut release in the history of country music and spent more than 150 weeks on the charts, twelve of those as number 1. By the end of 1986, the album had reached the platinum level, a rarity for country music at that time, and Travis had his first number 1 country single, "On the Other Hand," which had been originally released a year earlier.

Fellow artists quickly recognized Travis's talents, and he received the award for New Male Vocalist of the Year from the Academy of Country Music (ACM) in 1985, and in 1986, the ACM named *Storms of Life* the Album of the Year, "On the Other Hand" the best Single of the Year, and Travis the Male Vocalist of the Year. Also in 1986, the Country Music Association (CMA) selected Travis for the Horizon Award. By early 1987, Travis had another huge album out, *Always and Forever*, which spent forty-three weeks at the number 1 position on country charts and was named Album of the Year for 1987 by the CMA. Four singles from the album, "Forever and Ever, Amen," "Too Gone Too Long," "I Won't Need You Anymore," and "I Told You So," became number 1 country hits, and Travis was named Male Vocalist of the Year by the CMA in 1988. With his baritone, down-home singing style, Travis dominated country music in the late 1980's and became known as "The New Crown Prince of Country Music."

The hits continued with his 1988 album *Old 8 x 10*, which won him a Grammy Award for Best Country Male Vocal Performance in 1988 and spawned two more number 1 hits, "Honky Tonk Moon" and "Deeper Than the Holler." With intensive touring, doing some 250 live shows year after year, as well as making numerous radio and television appearances, Travis maintained his status as "The New Crown Prince of Country Music."

After being involved in a serious car crash in 1989, Travis came back with two number 1 country hits, "Is It Still Over?" and "It's Just a Matter of Time," as well as two more albums, *An Old Time Christmas* (1989) and *No Holdin' Back* (1989). Travis's 1990 album, *Heroes & Friends*, included duets with George Jones, Tammy Wynette, B. B. King, and Roy Rogers.

Marriage and a Slower Pace. In late 1990, Travis began cutting back on his entertainment activities, giving up touring for several years because he tired of waking up in a different town each day. In 1991, he married his manager Lib Hatcher, and they established a home in Maui, Hawaii, as well as a large farm near Ashland City, Tennessee, and Travis began making selected television appearances. He appeared twice on *Matlock* with his friend Andy Griffith, and he also appeared on the television drama *Down Home*. In 1992, Travis had two number 1 country singles, "Better Class of Losers" and "If I Didn't Have You," and his album of *Greatest Hits, Volume 2* earned a gold record. In 1993, he completed his first one-hour television special, *Wind in the Wire*, which highlighted the music of the American West.

In the mid-1990's, Travis brought some of his childhood dreams to reality by appearing in some Western films, including a small part in *Young Guns* (1988) and more extensive parts in the 1994 hit film *Maverick* and 1995's *Frank & Jesse*. After fulfilling some of his acting desires, Travis had a new album on the country charts in May, 1994, titled *This Is Me*, which remained on the charts until early 1995, winning gold record status. Two number 1 singles from the album were "Before You Kill Us All" and "Whisper My Name," and in 1995, two of his 1992 albums, *Greatest Hits, Volume 1* and *Greatest Hits, Volume 2*, went platinum. With the release of *Full Circle* in 1996, Travis again had more country chart hits, including one he had written, "Future Mister Me." In 1998, Travis went on tour to publicize his new film, *Black Dog*, and his new album, *You and You Alone*, containing the country chart single "Out of My Bones."

—*Alvin K. Benson*

SELECT DISCOGRAPHY
■ ALBUMS
Storms of Life, 1986
Always and Forever, 1987
Old 8 x 10, 1988
Heroes & Friends, 1990
Greatest Hits, Volume 1, 1992 (compilation)
This Is Me, 1994
Full Circle, 1996

SELECT AWARDS
Academy of Country Music New Male Vocalist of the Year Award, 1985
Academy of Country Music Male Vocalist of the Year Award, 1986, 1987
Country Music Association Horizon Award, 1986
Country Music Association Male Vocalist of the Year Award, 1987, 1988
Grammy Award for Best Country Vocal Performance, Male, for *Always and Forever*, 1987
Grammy Award for Best Country Vocal Performance, Male, for *Old 8 x 10*, 1988

SEE ALSO: Frizzell, Lefty; Haggard, Merle; Jackson, Alan; Jones, George; Nelson, Willie; Tubb, Ernest; Wynette, Tammy.

Travis Tritt

BORN: Marietta, Georgia; February 9, 1963
FIRST ALBUM RELEASE: *Country Club*, 1990
MUSICAL STYLES: Country, country rock

In 1989, Travis Tritt's local band had been playing the American Legion and county fair circuit around his Marietta, Georgia, home for about four years, when the strong recommendation of an Atlanta, Georgia, promoter for Warner Bros. Records drew company executives to see and sign the young singer-songwriter.

Tritt Hits. Their investment paid dividends immediately, as Tritt's first single, "Country Club,"

made the country Top 10 in 1989 and would rank among the singer's top-selling songs. The resultant album *Country Club* followed in 1990. Its songs, such as "Put Some Drive in Your Country," earned the farmer's son a reputation as a country singer who paid musical homage to his southern boogie-band forebears, such as the Allman Brothers Band, the Marshall Tucker Band, Charlie Daniels, and Lynyrd Skynyrd.

Knowing a hot property when he saw one—Ken Kragen had guided the careers of Lionel Richie, Olivia Newton-John, the Smothers Brothers, and Kenny Rogers—Kragen agreed to manage Tritt. Soon the former air-conditioning installer Tritt was performing 280 concerts per year and appearing on national television with Kenny Rogers.

Tritt's Hits. His next three albums, *It's All About to Change* (1991), *t-r-o-u-b-l-e* (1992), and *Ten Feet Tall and Bulletproof* (1994), yielded trademark rowdy hits "Here's a Quarter (Call Someone Who Cares)," "The Whiskey Ain't Workin'," and "t-r-o-u-b-l-e." Tritt also revealed a tender side with heart-wrenching ballads such as "Anymore," "Can I Trust You with My Heart," and "Foolish Pride."

As owner of one of country music's most recognizable, if not particularly melodious, voices, Tritt has become one of the genre's most visible figures. He became the youngest member of the Grand Ole Opry in 1992 (the record did not last long; twenty-one-year-old Alison Krauss was inducted in 1993). Named *Billboard* magazine's Best New Male Country Artist in 1990, he boasts the Country Music Association's 1991 Horizon Award and a 1993 Grammy Award for his "The Whiskey Ain't Workin'" duet with Marty Stuart. That partnership led to several chart-topping hits, as well as the acclaimed "No Hats" tour in 1992.

From No Hats to Many Hats. Tritt grew to wear many hats: singer, songwriter, guitarist, producer, and even actor and author. Film and television beckoned when the country star landed a part in the 1993 made-for-television film *Rio Diablo*. That led to feature-film work in *The Cowboy Way* (1994) and *Sgt. Bilko* (1996) and a role in an episode of the Home Box Office (HBO) series *Tales from the Crypt*. He entertained his largest audience when he performed for a half billion people around the

For the Record

Since horseback riding and target shooting are two of Travis Tritt's favorite hobbies, his wife Lib bought Travis a colt from Roy Rogers that was sired by Trigger, Jr. She gave it to him as a Christmas gift.

world as part of the televised halftime entertainment at 1993's Super Bowl.

The *Rhythm, Country & Blues* compilation album, helmed by legendary producer Don Was, found Tritt dueting with Patti LaBelle on the distinctly uncountry "When Something Is Wrong with My Baby." He also hosted a gathering of the Eagles for the video "Take It Easy," Tritt's contribution to the tribute album *Common Thread: The Songs of the Eagles*. The singer released a 1992 holiday album titled *A Travis Tritt Christmas: Loving Time of the Year*. His autobiography, *Ten Feet Tall and Bulletproof*, was released in conjunction with the album of the same name in 1994.

During "Fan Fair '96" in Nashville (country music's annual meet-the-stars festival for its fans), Warner Bros. Records presented Tritt with a plaque commemorating his fourteen million album sales at the time. A self-described "ultimate control freak," the singer parted ways with longtime producer Gregg Brown in 1996 and took over as coproducer with Was for *The Restless Kind*. True to Kragen's description of Tritt as a walking encyclopedia of the history of country music, the album represented a step back to his youthful roots in the country styles of Porter Wagoner, Buck Owens, and George Jones. It was also a step forward to the adult concerns expressed in songs such as "The Restless Kind" and "Where Corn Don't Grow."

—*Tim Bradley*

SELECT DISCOGRAPHY
■ ALBUMS
Country Club, 1990
It's All About to Change, 1991
t-r-o-u-b-l-e, 1992

Ten Feet Tall and Bulletproof, 1994
The Restless Kind, 1996
No More Looking over My Shoulder, 1998

SELECT AWARDS
Billboard, named Best New Male Country Artist, 1990
Grand Ole Opry, became member 1991
Country Music Association Horizon Award, 1991
Grammy Award for Best Country Vocal Collaboration for "The Whiskey Ain't Workin'," 1992 (with Marty Stuart)
Country Music Association Vocal Event of the Year Award for "The Whiskey Ain't Workin'," 1992 (with Marty Stuart)

SEE ALSO: Allman Brothers Band, The; Daniels, Charlie; Jones, George; Lynyrd Skynyrd; Owens, Buck.

Ernest Tubb

BORN: Crisp, Texas; February 9, 1914
DIED: Nashville, Tennessee; September 6, 1984
FIRST SINGLE RELEASE: "The Passing of Jimmie Rodgers," 1936
MUSICAL STYLE: Country

Ernest Dale Tubb, always called simply E. T. by his friends, was born on February 9, 1914, on a cotton farm near Crisp, Texas, about forty miles south of Dallas. His father, Calvin, and mother, Sarah Ellen, had four other children. Ernest was the youngest. Sarah played the organ and encouraged him to listen to the recordings of Jimmie Rodgers, the most popular country singer of the 1920's. Ernest had limited schooling, less than four years all together, as was the case with many children of tenant farmers. The family always seemed to be moving, and when his mother and father divorced in 1926 Tubb went to work in the cotton fields.

Musical Beginnings. Tubb sang in the Baptist church and at country picnics, but he was almost twenty before he bought his first guitar. In 1933, during the worst days of the Great Depression, he won a construction job with the Works Progress Administration for one dollar per day. He spent almost all his first week's pay, $5.50, on a guitar he liked. He learned to play chords from a friend. In 1934 he married Lois Elaine Cook, from San Antonio, and their first child, Justin, was born one year later. He found his first radio job the same year, a fifteen-minute 5:30 A.M. twice weekly broadcast, and made his first record in 1936, with help from the widow of his idol, Jimmie Rodgers. Rodgers had died of tuberculosis in 1933 in San Antonio. Ernest looked up Mrs. Rodgers's name in a telephone book, called her, and asked for a picture of her husband. As it turned out she had heard Tubb sing on his early morning show, liked the way he sounded, and said she would help him get a record contract.

His first recording was made for RCA at the Texas Hotel in San Antonio. Mrs. Rodgers let Ernest use her husband's guitar to record four songs, including "The Passing of Jimmie Rodgers" and "The Last Thoughts of Jimmie Rodgers." RCA thought little of the songs, however, and the records did not sell well. Tubb moved to San Angelo, Texas, in 1937, where he got a job on a local radio station. He moved shortly after that to Fort Worth where he had another radio job sponsored by the makers of Gold Chain Flour. He was called the "Gold Chain Troubadour," eventually referring to himself as the "Texas Troubadour," a name that remained with him until the end of his career. In 1939 he had his tonsils removed, an operation that changed the quality of his voice and made it impossible for him to yodel like Jimmie Rodgers. Thus, he had to adopt a new style which was more raspy voiced and intense. He changed record companies, moving to Decca, and had his first session for that label in Houston on April 4, 1940.

Tubb recorded four songs in Houston, none of which became hits, but Dave Kapp, the head of the company's country-and-western division, was impressed with what he heard. Kapp encouraged Tubb to record more songs and in the fall of 1941 released the hit "I'm Walking the Floor over You." The record, which Tubb wrote in twenty minutes during a sleepless night in a Fort Worth hotel, sold more than three million copies, and it sold even more after Bing Crosby rerecorded it. This early success led to a brief film career. Tubb appeared in four Hollywood pictures by 1947: *Fighting Buckaroos* (1943) and *Ridin' West* (1944) with Charles Starrett, *Jamboree* (1944), and *Hollywood Barndance* (1947), his only starring role. More important, his success gave him an opportunity to appear at the Grand Ole Opry in 1942. He appeared as a regular on the Opry's radio program

Ernest Tubb (Archive Photos/Frank Driggs Collection)

almost every Saturday night from then until his retirement more than thirty years later.

Success and Influence. After 1945, Tubb became one of the greatest stars in the history of country-and-western music. He even managed to get Decca to use the term "country" rather than the standard term, "hillbilly," in promoting his kind of music. Tubb, in 1947, along with fellow country singer Red Foley, was responsible for making the first studio recording in Nashville. That same year he opened Ernest Tubb's Record Shop, just around the corner from the Ryman Auditorium, home of the Grand Ole Opry. Later that year he started a radio program called *The Midnight Jamboree.* Broadcast from his record store, it followed the three-hour Opry program each Saturday night and featured generally unknown musicians. Elvis Presley made an appearance on the show before he became famous.

Tubb headlined the first country music show ever to appear in New York's Carnegie Hall and in the late 1940's teamed with Red Foley for a series of recorded duets, including the number 1 hit from 1950, "Goodnight Irene." Tubb had written a song in 1938 after the sudden death of his second child, titled "Our Baby's Book," which became a major hit for him, as did "Waltz Across Texas." In 1949 he married Olene Adams of Old Hickory, Tennessee. His first marriage had ended in divorce a few years earlier. He had seven children, two from his first marriage and five with Olene.

Tubb returned to solo recordings in the 1950's

For the Record

Since Ernest Tubb frequently sang out of tune, missed chords and notes, and mispronounced words even in his own songs, musicians in Nashville used to explain his success in this manner: He was successful because of honky-tonk beer drinkers who liked to listen to him because they figured they could sing much better than he could, drunk or sober.

and maintained a long and difficult road schedule. He also hosted the *Grand Ole Opry* television show in the 1950's, which featured the most popular country stars. Heavy drinking and smoking began to take their toll, however, and he was diagnosed with emphysema in 1965. He did stop drinking and smoking after that, but his lungs were already very damaged. In the 1960's he teamed with Loretta Lynn for a series of five singles and three albums. The major hits for this duo included "Mr. and Mrs. Used-to-Be," "Our Hearts Are Holding Hands," and "Sweet Thang." Tubb continued to make solo records and had continuing success with songs such as "The Yellow Rose of Texas," "Two Rights Don't Make a Wrong," and "Another Story, Another Time, Another Place." Tubb's greatest hits always emphasized feelings of lost love, loneliness, and the importance of family and friends. As he liked to say, his performances were as humble, simple, and relaxed as his audience.

Dedication. Tubb had thousands of loyal fans and his concerts were almost always sold out. He was extremely devoted to his fans, usually playing more than three hundred shows per year at school gyms, small clubs, American Legion halls, and stadiums. His bus, called the Green Hornet, racked up more than two million miles from 1965 to 1969. By the 1970's, Tubb had to carry an oxygen bottle with him on his tours. He frequently would sing for thirty minutes, rush back to the oxygen tank on the bus, breathe for forty-five minutes, and then return to complete his concert.

Tubb's band was one of the first to use electric guitars, simply to increase the volume so the music could be heard in a dance hall. His voice had always been rough and undisciplined, and he sang very loudly, a style attributed to his early saloon-playing days where one had to shout out the lyrics just to be heard above the crowd noise. All the alcohol he drank and cigarettes he smoked made his voice rougher and more primitive sounding. He did not invent the honky-tonk style, but he was the singer who made it the dominant form of country music for much of the 1940's and 1950's.

Tubb made his last recording shortly before his death from emphysema in 1984. An album called

Legend and Legacy, it featured Tubb in duets with a host of his admirers, including Willie Nelson, Merle Haggard, Loretta Lynn, Johnny Cash, Hank Williams, Jr., and Waylon Jennings.

—*Leslie V. Tischauser*

SELECT DISCOGRAPHY
■ ALBUMS
Ernest Tubb: Retrospective, 1987
The Ernest Tubb Collection, 1990
Let's Say Goodbye Like We Said Hello, 1991
   (five-CD boxed set)
Walkin' the Floor over You, 1996 (eight-CD
   boxed set)

SELECT AWARDS
Country Music Hall of Fame, inducted 1965

SEE ALSO: Frizzell, Lefty; Lynn, Loretta; Nelson, Willie.

Tanya Tucker

BORN: Seminole, Texas; October 10, 1958
FIRST SINGLE RELEASE: "Delta Dawn," 1972
FIRST ALBUM RELEASE: *Delta Dawn,* 1972
MUSICAL STYLES: Country, country rock, pop

From the time that Tanya Tucker was a little girl, her parents encouraged her musical talents, and at the age of six, she was already singing some of Loretta Lynn's hits. Recognizing Tucker's potential to be a professional singer, her father, Beau, took her to numerous country music shows after the family moved to Arizona, and she got to meet several stars, including Mel Tillis and Ernest Tubb, and even sang with some of them. At age thirteen, Tucker had a small part in the 1972 film *Jeremiah Johnson.*

In 1970, the Tucker family moved to Las Vegas, Nevada, and Beau financed a demo tape for his daughter, which eventually caught the attention of music producer Billy Sherrill. Sherrill was impressed with what he heard and signed Tucker to a contract with Epic Records in Nashville. In March, 1972, Beau took Tanya to Nashville, where she taped her first song, "Delta Dawn," which

For the Record

In 1976, at the age of fifteen, Tanya Tucker received a Grammy Award nomination and was featured on the cover of *Rolling Stone* magazine with the prophetic headline, "Hi, I'm Tanya Tucker, I'm 15, You're Gonna Hear from Me."

quickly reached the Top 10 on the country charts. Her debut album, also titled *Delta Dawn,* became a country best-seller and yielded two other top hits, "Jamestown Ferry" and "Love's the Answer."

In 1973, Tucker released her first number 1 country hit, "What's Your Mama's Name," followed by three more number 1 songs, "Blood Red and Goin' Down," "Would You Lay with Me," and "The Man Who Turned My Mother On." At the age of sixteen, her album *Tanya Tucker* (1975) rose to number 10 on the country charts, and her 1975 hit, "Lizzie and the Rainman," became another number 1 single. In 1977, Tucker had the hit album *Ridin' Rainbows* and a Top-10 single, "It's Cowboy Lovin' Night."

A New Tucker Goes Wild. Sporting red tights and adding fuzz-tone guitars to her band in 1978, Tucker changed her singing style from conventional country to country rock and made *TNT* for Columbia Records. On November 1, 1978, she appeared at the Grand Ole Opry as the "new Tanya" and was heavily booed when singing some country favorites with a rock-and-roll sound. At the end of her performance, however, she received mostly cheers. Tucker's hit "Texas" was the best-selling single in 1979, and her album *Tear Me Apart* appeared on the country Top-50 charts from 1979 until early 1980, when Tucker returned to more traditional country music.

In the early 1980's, Tucker became almost as well known for her wild lifestyle as for her music, participating in almost nonstop partying and abusing alcohol and hard drugs. She had a romantic relationship with Glen Campbell, and they recorded a successful duet, "Dream Lover," in late

Tanya Tucker (Mark Tucker)

Tucker was nominated for the CMA Female Vocalist of the Year Award in 1989 and 1990, and she won the award in 1991 while she was in the hospital giving birth to her second child, Beau. In 1990, she had two number 1 singles, "My Arms Stay Open All Night" and "Walking Shoes," as well as two other best-sellers in "Don't Go Out" and "It Won't Be Me." *Tennessee Woman* was released in 1990, becoming certified platinum in 1995, and *Can't Run from Yourself* (1992) also reached the platinum level. A big number 1 country hit for Tucker in 1992 was "Two Sparrows in a Hurricane," which was written in tribute to her parents' fiftieth wedding anniversary, and it won her the Academy of Country Music Video of the Year Award in 1993. Tucker also had three other top hits in 1992, "What Do I Do with Me," "Some Kind of Trouble," and "If Your Heart Ain't Busy Tonight."

During the mid-1990's, billed as the "Black Velvet Lady," Tucker drew capacity crowds for her shows in arenas, civic centers, and fairs all over the United States, averaging about 250 appearances per year. Her 1993 works included the gold-selling album *Soon*, two top singles titled "It's Too Little Too Late" (a number 1 country hit) and "Tell Me About It" (a duet with Delbert McClinton), and an exercise video, *Tanya Tucker Country Workout*. The year 1994 brought three more top singles for Tucker, "We Don't Have to Do This," "Hangin' In," and "Somethin' Else," a duet with rock legend Little Richard that was deemed a standout by music critics.

Fire to Fire, released in 1995, exhibits Tucker's great versatility, ranging from country ballads to country rock. Hits from the album include "I Bet She Knows," "Come in out of the World," "Nobody Dies from a Broken Heart," "I'll Take the Memo-

1980. Tucker has said that their stormy relationship ended when Campbell knocked out Tucker's front teeth in a fight. (She also purportedly had flings with Merle Haggard, Andy Gibb, and television star Don Johnson.) Despite all her difficulties and a three-year hiatus from recording, Tucker managed to keep her career afloat, and in 1986, she had a *Billboard* Top-20 album, *Girls Like Me*, that spawned the number 1 country single "Just Another Love." In 1987, her single "I Won't Take Less than Your Love" was nominated for the Country Music Association (CMA) Vocal Event of the Year.

Back on Track. In 1988, Tucker found a new love in aspiring actor Ben Reed, and they had a daughter, Presley, in the next year. Tucker credited her approaching motherhood with her decision to enter the Betty Ford clinic to lose her cocaine and alcohol addiction, and 1988 brought two more Top-10 country singles, "If It Don't Come Easy" and "Strong Enough to Bend."

ries," and "The Love You Gave to Me." The hits kept coming for the energetic, hard working Tucker with *Complicated* (1997) and singles "Riding out the Heartache," "Hurts Like Love," "By the Way," and "Love Thing."

Variety and Service. Besides her musical career, Tucker has also appeared in a number of films, including *Amateur Night at the Dixie Bar and Grill* (1979) and *The Rebel* (1986), and she made a television appearance in *Shannon's Deal.* Tucker also runs her own designer denimwear company and sells her own salsa. In addition, Tucker finds time to raise funds for handicapped children and for research for multiple sclerosis, and she is actively involved in efforts dealing with environmental issues, which began in 1978 when she recorded "Save Me," dealing with saving seals on Canada's Magdalen Islands.   —*Alvin K. Benson*

SELECT DISCOGRAPHY
■ ALBUMS
What's Your Mama's Name, 1973
Would You Lay with Me, 1974
Ridin' Rainbows, 1977
Tear Me Apart, 1979
Girls Like Me, 1986
Strong Enough to Bend, 1988
Tennessee Woman, 1990
What Do I Do with Me, 1991
Can't Run from Yourself, 1992
Soon, 1993
Fire to Fire, 1995
Complicated, 1997

SELECT AWARDS
Academy of Country Music Most Promising Female Vocalist Award, 1972
Country Music Association Female Vocalist of the Year Award, 1991
Academy of Country Music Video of the Year Award for *Two Sparrows in a Hurricane,* 1993
Country Music Association Album of the Year Award for *Common Thread: The Songs of the Eagles,* 1994 (with others)

SEE ALSO: Campbell, Glen; Carpenter, Mary Chapin; Haggard, Merle; Little Richard; Mattea, Kathy; Nelson, Willie; Parton, Dolly.

Ike and Tina Turner / Tina Turner

Ike and Tina Turner

MEMBERS: Ike Turner (b. Izear Luster Turner, 1931); Tina Turner (b. Annie Mae Bullock, 1939)
FIRST ALBUM RELEASE: *The Soul of Ike and Tina Turner,* 1961

Tina Turner

BORN: Brownsville, Tennessee; November 26, 1939
FIRST ALBUM RELEASE: *Acid Queen,* 1975
MUSICAL STYLES: Rhythm and blues, pop, rock and roll

Ike and Tina Turner stunned the music world in the late 1960's with a combination of soul and sensuality. Amid American racial turmoil and social unrest, the Ike and Tina Turner Revue would help unify soul with rock music. The duo officially disbanded in 1976 after a much-publicized divorce. Tina remained active in record production and concert tours, while Ike's career faded into obscurity.

The Kings of Rhythm. Izear "Ike" Luster Turner, Jr., was born November 5, 1931, in Clarkesdale, Mississippi. Ike worked as a disc jockey and formed his first band, the Kings of Rhythm, while in high school. The Kings of Rhythm teamed with singer-saxophonist Jackie Brenston at Sam Phillips's Sun Studio in Memphis, Tennessee, on March 5, 1951, to record "Rocket 88." Although neither Ike nor the Kings of Rhythm would receive any credit for the recording, "Rocket 88" is often cited as the first rock-and-roll recording. Aside from his studio work, Ike was successful as a talent scout and producer for the Modern Records label.

In 1956, Ike met Annie Mae Bullock while performing in a nightclub in St. Louis, Missouri. Bullock, an amateur gospel singer, was able to convince Ike to let her sing with his group and soon became a regular member. He changed her name to Tina, and they recorded their first single, "A Fool in Love," in 1960. An instant hit, "A Fool in Love" was followed by "It's Gonna Work Out Fine" and "Idolize You" in 1961. They became the Ike and Tina Turner Revue and were married in 1962.

The Ike and Tina Turner Revue. From the onset, it was obvious that Tina was a sensational asset. She evoked a synthesis of strength and sensuality on the stage, her shapely legs as much a topic of conversation as her raw vocals. The Ike and Tina Turner Revue included three "Ikettes," who provided background vocals, and nine musicians. There were a few setbacks, such as the critically disappointing American release of "River Deep, Mountain High." Overall, however, the Ike and Tina Turner Revue was a success, leading to their opening for the 1969 Rolling Stones tour. Early 1970's hits included "Come Together," "I Want to Take You Higher," an energetic version of Creedence Clearwater Revival's "Proud Mary," and "Nutbush City Limits," which reached number 4 on England's pop charts in 1973 and thrust Tina into the spotlight. Tireless energy, powerful vocals, and raw sexuality became her trademarks. Ike and Tina Turner recorded more than thirty albums before their separation in 1976. According to Tina's 1986 autobiography *I, Tina*, Ike's constant physical and emotional abuse, infidelity, and addiction to cocaine and alcohol ultimately led to their divorce. After the separation, Ike became involved in studio management, while Tina continued to pursue a successful solo performing career.

Tina's Solo Career. Tina's first solo success came in 1975 with her portrayal of the Acid Queen in the film adaptation of the Who's rock opera *Tommy*. Critics hailed the raw energy and passion of her performance. After several unsuccessful albums for United Artists in the late 1970's, Tina's future looked dismal. Her manager, Roger Davies, staged a phenomenal career comeback.

The rejuvenation of Tina's career began in 1981 when she opened several shows for both the Rolling Stone's tour in the United States and Rod Stewart's world tour. In 1983, she was approached by members of the British group Heaven 17 to revive the Temptation's "Ball of Confusion" for an album with the British Electric Foundation (BEF)

project. The BEF album, *Music of Quality and Distinction Volume 1*, was a critical success in Britain. Impressed with Tina's recent success, Capitol Records offered her a recording contract. The result was one of 1984's most critically and financially successful albums, *Private Dancer*, which sold more than twelve million copies worldwide and remained on the Hot 100 charts for over two years. The first single release, a remake of Al Green's 1971 single "Let's Stay Together," reached the Top 20 in the United States early in 1984. The next single, "What's Love Got to Do with It," became one of the year's biggest hits, staying number 1 for three weeks. In addition, the singles "Private Dancer" and "Better Be Good to Me" reached the

Tina Turner (Ken Settle)

Top-10 charts. In 1984, Tina also participated in the recording of the benefit single, "We Are the World."

In 1985, Tina landed a prominent acting role in George Miller's futuristic film, *Mad Max: Beyond Thunderdome*. "We Don't Need Another Hero" and "One of the Living" were two successful single releases from the motion picture's sound track. Tina also teamed up with the Rolling Stones' Mick Jagger in 1985 to perform for the U.S. Live Aid concert. She recorded the rock duet "It's Only Love" with Bryan Adams in 1986, which climbed to number 15 on the U.S. charts.

In 1986, Tina released her second solo album, *Break Every Rule*, which was certified platinum. *Break Every Rule* included her next number 1 hit, "Typical Male," as well as "What You See Is What You Get." The album initiated a successful world tour and broke box-office records in thirteen countries. A concert tour recording, *Tina Live in Europe*, was released in 1988.

The 1989 platinum album *Foreign Affair* rose to number 1 on the British charts and to a respectable number 31 in the United States. Including hits such as "The Best" and "Steamy Windows," the album launched a 121-day world tour. By the tour's end in 1990, Tina had performed in front of more than three million fans. *Simply the Best*, a greatest hits collection, was released in 1991. It contained three new cuts, including Tina and Rod Stewart performing a remake of the Marvin Gaye-Tammi Terrell hit "It Takes Two." *Simply the Best* rose to number 1 on the British charts.

The 1993 Touchstone Pictures motion picture *What's Love Got to Do with It* was based on Tina's best-selling autobiography *I, Tina*. Although she did not act in the movie, Tina was a consultant, contributing new numbers for the sound track. The sound track single "I Don't Wanna Fight," cowritten by Steve DuBerry and Lulu, once again placed Tina on the Top-10 charts.

Wildest Dreams was released in 1996 and ultimately launched a worldwide tour. The album featured duets with Sting and actor Antonio Banderas, and includes the hits "Whatever You Want," "Missing You," and Sheryl Crow's "All Kinds of People." *Wildest Dreams* also includes the title track

---

For the Record

According to her autobiography, *I, Tina*, Tina Turner was offered the starring role in the film *The Color Purple* by director Stephen Spielberg. Tina declined, stating, "I've *lived* that story."

---

of *Goldeneye*, a James Bond motion picture released the previous year.

Ike Turner. In the 1970's, Ike attempted to create a solo career, unsuccessfully releasing a couple of albums from his own studio, Bolic. The studio was destroyed by fire in 1982. After a series of arrests, Ike was convicted in 1988 to a four-year prison term for drug abuse. In this same year he began writing his autobiography, *My Confessions*. He was released from prison after serving eighteen months and kept a low public profile. As of 1998, *My Confessions* had yet to be published.

—*Brent Register*

SELECT DISCOGRAPHY
Ike and Tina Turner
■ SINGLES
"A Fool in Love," 1960
"It's Gonna Work Out Fine," 1961
"River Deep, Mountain High," 1966
"Proud Mary," 1971
"Nutbush City Limits," 1973
■ ALBUMS
The Soul of Ike and Tina Turner, 1961
Dynamite, 1963
Live! Ike and Tina Turner Show, 1965
Live at Carnegie Hall/What You Hear Is What You Get, 1971
Ike Turner solo
■ ALBUMS
Blues Roots, 1972
I'm Tore Up, 1978
Tina Turner solo
■ SINGLES
"Acid Queen," 1975 (from *Tommy* sound track)
"Let's Stay Together," 1983

"What's Love Got to Do with It," 1984
"We Don't Need Another Hero
    (Thunderdome)," 1985 (from *Mad Max:
    Beyond Thunderdome* sound track)
"I Don't Wanna Fight," 1993
"Goldeneye," 1995 (from *Goldeneye* sound
    track)

■ ALBUMS

Acid Queen, 1975
Private Dancer, 1984
Break Every Rule, 1986
Tina Live in Europe, 1988
Foreign Affair, 1989
Simply the Best, 1991
Tina: The Collected Recordings—Sixties to Nineties,
    1994 (three-CD anthology)
Wildest Dreams, 1996

SELECT AWARDS:

Grammy Award for Best R&B Vocal Perfor-
    mance by a Duo or Group for "Proud Mary,"
    1971 (Ike and Tina Turner)
Grammy Awards for Record of the Year for
    "What's Love Got to Do with It" (Tina
    Turner with Terry Britten) for Best Pop Vo-
    cal Performance, Female, for "What's Love
    Got to Do with It" (Tina Turner), and for
    Best Rock Vocal Performance, Female, for
    "Better Be Good to Me" (Tina Turner), all
    1984
Grammy Award for Best Rock Vocal Perfor-
    mance, Female, for "One of the Living,"
    1985 (Tina Turner)
American Music Award for Favorite Female Art-
    ist, Pop/Rock, 1986 (Tina Turner)
Grammy Award for Best Rock Vocal Perfor-
    mance, Female, for "Back Where You
    Started," 1986 (Tina Turner)
Grammy Award for Best Rock Vocal Perfor-
    mance, Female, for *Tina Live in Europe*, 1988
    (Tina Turner)
Rock and Roll Hall of Fame, inducted 1991 (Ike
    and Tina Turner)

SEE ALSO: Creedence Clearwater Revival; Crow,
Sheryl; Green, Al; Rolling Stones, The; Stewart,
Rod; Sting; Who, The.

The Turtles

ORIGINAL MEMBERS: Howard Kaylan (b. Howard
    Kaplan, 1945), Mark Volman (b. 1944), Al
    Nichol (b. 1946), Chuck Portz (b. 1945), Don-
    ald Ray Murray (b. 1945)
OTHER MEMBERS: Jim Tucker (b. 1946), John Bar-
    bata, Chip Douglas, Jim Pons (b. 1943), John
    Seiter
FIRST ALBUM RELEASE: *It Ain't Me Babe*, 1965
MUSICAL STYLES: Pop, rock and roll, folk

In the early 1960's, Los Angeles's Westchester
High School students Howard Kaylan, Chuck
Portz, and Al Nichol formed the Nightriders and
started playing local school shows. Adding drummer Don Murray and saxophonist Mark Volman,
within two years the newly christened Crossfires
had earned a Southern California following and
released several undistinguished singles. By 1965
they had become the house band at a club owned
by disc jockey Rebel Foster. Disheartened by their
lack of progress, they thought about disbanding.
As a result, Foster invited record distributors Ted
Feigan and Lee Laseff to hear the group. The two
liked what they heard and signed the Crossfires as
the first act on their new White Whale label, with
the stipulation that they change their name. Thus
the Turtles were born.

Change in Sound. Because White Whale was
looking for a folk-rock group, they steered the
Turtles away from their surf sound, choosing Bob
Dylan's "It Ain't Me Babe" (1965) as the group's
first release. Within a few weeks it broke the Top
10. The next four releases were relatively sophisticated pop singles, distinguished by the strong
vocals of band leaders Kaylan and Volman, but
none went higher than number 20 on the pop
charts. Just as they were again about to quit, they
released "Happy Together," which spent three
weeks on top of the charts in the spring of 1967.
"Happy Together" reinvigorated the Turtles, who
had three other hits in 1967: "She'd Rather Be
with Me" (number 3), "You Know What I Mean"
(number 12), and "She's My Girl" (number 14).
Their *The Turtles! Golden Hits* peaked at number 7
on the album chart and was certified gold.

Despite good sales, the Turtles had never been very cohesive as a group. Kaylan and Volman were ambitious for more than commercial success, which led to frequent personnel changes. Only Kaylan, Volman, and lead guitarist Al Nichol were with the band throughout their career.

Their creative instincts led to an unusual 1968 album, *The Turtles Present the Battle of the Bands*. Each of the eleven songs on the album was meant to sound as if it had been sung by a different group, and the sleeve showed the Turtles dressed as eleven different groups. Though it produced two Top-10 hits ("Elenore," 1968; "You Showed Me," 1969), *The Turtles Present the Battle of the Bands* did not capture the public's imagination, going only as high as number 128 on the charts. Their next effort, *Turtle Soup* (1969), was produced by the Kinks' Ray Davies but did not fare much better (number 117).

The End of the Turtles. The Turtles finally disbanded in 1970 and were promptly taken to court by White Whale records. In order to avoid further complications, Kaylan and Volman took the aliases the Phlorescent Leech (Flo) and Eddie when they joined Frank Zappa's band. They left Zappa in 1972 with bassist Jim Pons and drummer Aynsley Dunbar to form the group Phlorescent Leech and Eddie, later Flo and Eddie. Their albums and shows, featuring both regular songs and lampoons of rock pretensions, became cult hits, though they were never popular with the general public. Their work was nevertheless in character with the history of Kaylan and Volman. As Volman once said, "We've never catered to the industry we were trying to succeed in." Flo and Eddie's smoothly blending voices allowed them to do backup singing for other artists; they sang, for example, on Bruce Springsteen's "Hungry Heart," his first Top-10 single.

Since 1976, Kaylan and Volman have produced several albums, contributed dialogue to an X-rated animated film, written columns for music magazines, hosted radio and television programs, and provided background vocals for numerous recording artists, including T. Rex, Stephen Stills, John Lennon and Yoko Ono, David Cassidy, Alice Cooper, Blondie, Sammy Hagar, Roger McGuinn, and Bruce Springsteen. In the 1980's they produced children's records for the popular *Strawberry Shortcake* and *Care Bears* sound tracks. Occasionally, during the mid-1980's and into the 1990's, Kaylan and Volman revived the Turtles name to participate in oldies tours with other 1960's acts.

—John Powell

SELECT DISCOGRAPHY
the Turtles
■ SINGLES
"It Ain't Me Babe," 1965
"Happy Together," 1967
"She'd Rather Be with Me," 1967
"Elenore," 1968
"You Showed Me," 1969
■ ALBUMS
It Ain't Me Babe, 1965
You Baby, 1966
Happy Together, 1967
The Turtles! Golden Hits, 1967 (compilation)
The Turtles Present the Battle of the Bands, 1968
Turtle Soup, 1969
Happy Together Again, 1975
Out of Control, 1981 (material recorded in the early 1960's as the Crossfires)
The Best of the Turtles, 1987 (compilation)
Captured Live, 1992
Flo and Eddie
■ ALBUMS
Phlorescent Leech and Eddie, 1972
Flo and Eddie, 1973

For the Record

After a group called the Crossfires signed a record contract with White Whale, they were asked to find a new name. Strongly influenced by British groups, they considered calling themselves Six Pence until Rebel Foster, a Los Angeles disc jockey at whose club they had been playing, suggested the Tyrtles. The band accepted the name but not the artificial spelling.

Illegal, Immoral, and Fattening, 1975
Rock Steady with Flo and Eddie, 1982

SEE ALSO: Zappa, Frank / The Mothers of Invention.

Shania Twain

BORN: Windsor, Ontario, Canada; August 28, 1965
FIRST ALBUM RELEASE: *Shania Twain,* 1993
MUSICAL STYLES: Country, country rock, pop

One of the biggest-selling female artists of the early 1990's, Canadian singer-songwriter Shania Twain gained international attention through a combination of slickly produced records combining country, rock, and pop styles and a sexy, video-driven image. Twain's success underscored the country music industry's tendency in the 1990's to feature younger artists, uptempo songs, and a highly produced pop style rather than a more traditional country sound.

Hard Times. Twain, born Eileen Edwards, was raised in the northern Canadian town of Timmins, Ontario. Her parents divorced when she was two; her mother later married Jerry Twain, an Ojibwa Indian. The Twains loved country-and-western music, and little Eileen harmonized along with country songs on the radio when she was still a toddler. The Twains encouraged their daughter to sing, eventually pushing her to perform in public. Twain recalls being awakened in the early morning and taken out to sing in local bars when she was eight years old (as a minor, she could not appear until after 1:00 A.M., when the bars had stopped serving alcohol). In her teens, Twain continued to perform with country and rock bands.

When Twain was twenty-one, her mother and stepfather were both killed in an automobile accident. Left to support three of her four brothers and sisters, Twain found a job performing at an Ontario resort, singing everything from country-and-western songs to pop standards and Broadway show tunes. Twain's friend Mary Bailey, who had had a brief career as a Nashville-based country singer, became Twain's manager and called upon her remaining Nashville connections to bring representatives from a record company to hear Twain sing. Twain was offered a recording contract, and when her younger brothers were old enough to live on their own, she headed for Nashville.

Twain had by this time changed her first name to Shania, an Ojibwa word meaning "on my way." However, her 1993 self-titled debut album of standard country and western tunes was not a success. Although Twain had written songs for the album, the producers rejected her original material, and only the single "God Ain't Gonna Getcha for That" was cowritten by "Eileen" Twain.

Cinderella Story. Twain's otherwise lackluster debut caught the attention of British fans, among them Robert John "Mutt" Lange, a successful producer of rock acts such as AC/DC, Bryan Adams, and Def Leppard. Lange tried to contact Twain after seeing one of her videos; however, Twain had never heard of the Grammy-winning producer. Initially Twain and her management company thought he was simply a fan; accordingly, Twain sent him an autographed photo.

Twain and Lange eventually spoke and developed a friendship over the telephone. Lange encouraged Twain's songwriting efforts, and the pair began writing songs together over the telephone. They finally met in 1993 at Nashville's annual Fan Fair and were married six months later.

Lange produced and cowrote the songs on Twain's second album. He also partially financed what was rumored to be the most expensive country album ever made. Released in 1995, *The Woman in Me* showcased Twain's original material. Her lyrics were often quirky and humorous and seldom lamented the lost loves and broken hearts that frequently typify country music. With the songs on *The Woman in Me* and its accompanying music videos, Twain began promoting herself as a playfully flirtatious woman with a spunky, independent attitude.

The Woman in Me quickly became one of the fastest-selling records by any female artist in popular music, eventually selling over ten million copies (only Whitney Houston, Alanis Morissette, and

Shania Twain at the 1996 Country Music Awards (Reuters/Lee Celano/Archive Photos)

have enough original songs for a complete show, critics speculated that Twain's voice was too weak to carry her through a live performance. Twain countered that she had been singing before live audiences since she was a child but wanted her first tour to set her apart from spectacular shows by more established artists such as Wynonna Judd and Reba McEntire.

Twain worked hard to promote her album through other avenues. She made frequent personal appearances, sang on national television programs, and gave radio interviews. Thousands of potential record buyers flocked to her appearances at fan appreciation days in shopping malls, where she cheerfully posed for pictures and signed autographs for hours at a time.

Twain was subjected to personal censure because of her claim to Ojibwa heritage. Twain had been adopted as a child by her Ojibwa stepfather and was therefore considered one of the Ojibwa tribe. Twain identified herself as half Ojibwa, and her image was somewhat tarnished when her hometown newspaper published an article revealing that her ethnic heritage was actually Irish-Canadian.

While *The Woman in Me* remained a fixture on the *Billboard* charts, Twain's oft-repeated stories of growing up in poverty were also called into question. Twain spoke of her family having nothing to eat but potatoes or bread and milk for days at a time and of hiding her hunger from schoolteachers for fear that she and her siblings would be placed in foster care. Critics questioned and even mocked her sometimes melodramatic tales of her hardscrabble northern Canadian childhood.

Rock This Country! In 1997, Twain released a third album, *Come On Over*. The new album and its accompanying videos built on the sexy, independent, and fun-loving image Twain had created with *The Woman in Me*. Twain and her husband wrote all of the sixteen songs on *Come on Over*, which offered a few standard country ballads among several danceable songs featuring colloquial lyrics ("My pantyline shows/ got a run in my hose") that were touted as a Twain trademark. Her declarations of feminine independence were frequently punctuated with her speaking voice as she

Carole King had sold as many records) and remaining on the *Billboard* album charts well into 1998.

Criticism and Controversy. Twain's phenomenal success with *The Woman in Me* was attributed to her husband's production and to her own penchant for wearing skintight pants, as much as to her abilities as a singer or songwriter. Twain was also criticized because she did not tour to promote the album. She had sold enough records to headline a tour, but while she said that she did not

For the Record

The original title of Shania Twain's hit song "Gets Me Every Time" (from *Come On Over*) was "Gol' Darn Gone and Done It." Twain changed it so disc jockeys would not have to struggle with a tongue-twisting title when the song was released as a single.

either recited lyrics or inserted vocal hiccups and supposed exhoratations to her studio musicians. As Twain explained, "What a lot of people would clean up on records are the things that I like to keep in . . . It just makes it more fun."

Twain's phenomenal success with *The Woman in Me* indicated that her potential audience extended far beyond country music fans. *Come On Over* was released to both country and pop markets, with an early single release ("You're Still the One") successfully crossing over to pop radio. Between her second and third albums, Twain fired long-time friend and manager Bailey and hired Bruce Springsteen's manager, Jon Landau, charting her course for success on a grander scale. In 1997, Twain assembled a backup band and began rehearsing for a planned 1998 world tour.

—*Maureen J. Puffer-Rothenberg*

SELECT DICOGRAPHY
■ ALBUMS
Shania Twain, 1993
The Woman in Me, 1995
Come On Over, 1997

SELECT AWARDS
Academy of Country Music Album of the Year for *The Woman in Me*, 1995 (with Robert "Mutt" Lange)
Academy of Country Music Top New Female Vocalist, 1995
Grammy Award for Best Country Album for *The Woman in Me*, 1995

SEE ALSO: McEntire, Reba; Rimes, LeAnn; Tucker, Tanya.

Conway Twitty

BORN: Friars Point, Mississippi; September 1, 1933
DIED: Springfield, Missouri; June 5, 1993
FIRST ALBUM RELEASE: *Conway Twitty Sings*, 1959
MUSICAL STYLES: Country, pop, rockabilly

During Conway Twitty's forty-year musical career, he earned more number 1 records than any other artist in the history of popular music. Twitty's voice and music knew no boundaries, crossing over from pop into country, with influences ranging from rockabilly and gospel to Dixieland and blues. Twitty had a song somewhere on a chart for five consecutive decades, including fifty-five number 1 songs. He is the only singer in history, including Elvis Presley and the Beatles, to have more than fifty number 1 hits. "It's Only Make Believe," "Hello Darlin'," "You've Never Been This Far Before," and "Linda on My Mind" are among the Twitty songs that have become country standards.

The Beginnings. Twitty, born Harold Lloyd Jenkins, grew up in Friars Point, Mississippi, where his father was a riverboat pilot. His father taught him guitar chords at the age of four, but he was equally influenced by the gospel music he heard on Sundays from a nearby black church. At the age of ten, he moved with his family to Helena, Arkansas, and formed his first band, the Phillips County Ramblers, which led to his own radio show two years later. He sang the music of Eddy Arnold, Roy Acuff, and Bill Monroe over the airways of KFFA-radio, first with the Ramblers and then with the Arkansas Cotton Choppers. Despite this early success, Jenkins was determined to become a preacher because he wanted to help young people. He began working at youth revivals in Arkansas and Alabama, where he later moved.

After graduating from high school and moving to Chicago, he was recruited by the Philadelphia Phillies baseball team but then was drafted by the Army and sent to Japan. Two years later, he returned to Memphis, and his life was forever changed when he turned on the radio and heard Elvis Presley's "That's Alright."

Jenkins began writing rockabilly songs and took them to Sun Records, home of Presley, Carl

Perkins, and Jerry Lee Lewis. He wrote "Rockhouse" for Roy Orbison and recorded several songs for Sun's owner, Sam Phillips, but they were never released. When he was given a deal with Mercury Records, he decided that if he wanted to be a rock star, he should sound like a rock star, so he changed his name to Conway Twitty, borrowing the names of two local towns: Conway, Arkansas, and Twitty, Texas. Twitty's first single, the rockabilly-pop song "I Need Your Lovin'," was released in 1957, but it only reached number 93 on the charts. He lost his deal with Mercury after several other singles failed to capture attention.

Success Begins. Twitty found success in 1958, when he wrote and sang "It's Only Make Believe," which sold eight million copies and earned the number 1 spot in twenty-two countries. Previous Twitty songs were very similar to those of Presley,

but in this song he unveiled a deep, throaty growl that became his lifelong trademark. The smash hit made Twitty a teen sensation and secured him spots on television's *American Bandstand* and tours with Fabian and Frankie Avalon. He even starred in a few Hollywood films, while enjoying several more hits, including "Danny Boy" in 1959 and "Lonely Blue Boy" in 1960. However, Twitty's songs soon stopped climbing the charts, reaching only the bottom half of the Top 40. Twitty asked MGM to allow him to record several country songs, but the label refused.

Move to Country. In 1965, Twitty crossed over into the country realm during a concert in New Jersey. He stopped singing mid-song, walked off the stage, laid his guitar down, and never played rock and roll again. He moved to Oklahoma City and began his search for a record company that would take him seriously. He soon met with Owen Bradley, who had produced such legends as Patsy Cline and Loretta Lynn. Bradley agreed to work with Twitty after songwriter Harlan Howard played Twitty's tape for Bradley without telling him whose it was.

Twitty spent the next few years touring constantly to promote his songs, though he did not find the success he had enjoyed in the rock world. All that changed with "The Image of Me," which became a Top-5 country song in 1967. He had several more hits and then released "Hello Darlin'" in 1970, capturing the number 1 spot on the country charts for one month.

Conway Twitty (Archive Photos)

For the Record

"I never make a change either in my career or personal life without giving it a lot of thought. I believe in change. It's the only thing I know of that's constant. When things stop changing, they die. . . . "I'm an artist who's always tried to change before the changes come. It keeps me fresh, too, as an artist, when I don't sing the same old thing all the time." —*Conway Twitty*

Bradley then teamed Twitty with Loretta Lynn to create a duo whose success has not been repeated. Their first duet, "After the Fire Is Gone," reached country music's number 1 position in 1971 and won a Grammy Award. That was followed by the number 1 country songs "Lead Me On" and "Louisiana Woman, Mississippi Man," "Feelins'," and four Country Music Association Awards for Vocal Duo of the Year. While their solo careers remained a priority, the two toured and sang together for more than a decade.

By the mid-1970's, Twitty had twenty-three consecutive number 1 country songs and a reputation for impressive record production and solid songwriting. Not only did he become known as the best friend a song ever had, but he emerged as one of the few romantic singers who truly understood women. In fact, his 1973 song "You've Never Been This Far Before" created controversy from critics who thought the song was too racy for the wholesome country music audience. However, women loved it.

In 1979, Twitty took another career risk by leaving Bradley to produce his own music and create a more contemporary country sound. Again, that risk paid off and his string of number 1 country hits continued. By 1981, he had nearly forty number 1 songs and four years later, he scored his fiftieth. Unlike many singers' voices, Twitty's voice improved with age, boasting a maturity and low blues range that was unparalleled. His unforgettable voice often overshadowed his impressive songwriting ability. Many never realized that he wrote "Hello Darlin'," "Linda on My Mind," and other hits. Twitty carried a portable tape recorder on the road so he could write songs whenever he had free time.

Twitty continued to reach the top of the charts through the 1980's and into the 1990's. "I Couldn't See You Leavin'" made the Top 10 in 1991, nearly thirty-five years after his first number 1 single. He turned pop songs such as "The Rose" and "Slow Hand" into bona fide country hits by adding his distinctive touch. In 1993, Twitty recorded one of his most memorable performances when he sang "Rainy Night in Georgia" with Sam Moore. Tragically, that turned out to be his last recording, because one month later, on June 4, 1993, Twitty was returning from Branson, Missouri, to his home in Nashville when he became ill on his bus. He suffered an abdominal aortic aneurysm and died in a Springfield, Missouri, hospital the next day at the age of fifty-nine.

—*Beverly Keel*

SELECT DISCOGRAPHY
■ ALBUMS
Conway Twitty Sings, 1959
Greatest Hits, 1960 (compilation)
Hello Darlin', 1970
We Only Make Believe, 1971 (with Loretta Lynn)
Southern Comfort, 1982
House on Old Lonesome Road, 1989
The Best of Conway Twitty Volume I: The Rockin' Years, 1991 (compilation)
The Conway Twitty Collection, 1994 (compilation)

SELECT AWARDS
Grammy Award for Best Country Vocal Performance by a Group for "After the Fire Is Gone," 1971 (with Loretta Lynn)
Country Music Association Vocal Duo of the Year Award, 1972, 1973, 1974, 1975 (with Loretta Lynn)

SEE ALSO: Lynn, Loretta; Orbison, Roy; Presley, Elvis.

2 Live Crew

ORIGINAL MEMBERS: Luke Skyywalker (b. Luther Campbell, 1960), Fresh Kid Ice (Christopher Wong-won), Brother Marquis (Mark Ross), Mr. Mixx (David Hobbs)
OTHER MEMBERS: Verb (Larry Dobson), Dolomite (Rudy Ray Moore)
FIRST ALBUM RELEASE: *The 2 Live Crew Is What We Are*, 1986
MUSICAL STYLE: Rap

Inspired by the off-color party records of Richard Pryor and Redd Foxx, Luther Campbell helped launch the bass-heavy Miami, Florida, sound with his 1984 single, "Throw the D." One year later he

For the Record

Luther Campbell, 2 Live Crew's founder, had to change the name of his record company from Skyywalker Records to Luke Records after *Star Wars* film creator George Lucas filed a lawsuit.

formed his own label, Skyywalker Records (later changed to Luke Records), and the band 2 Live Crew. Both their debut *The 2 Live Crew Is What We Are* and follow-up *Move Somethin'* (1987) featured explicit sexual raps that gained an underground following, but neither was a commercial success.

Obscenity. Their quintessential third album, *As Nasty as They Wanna Be* (1989), defined the career of 2 Live Crew. It contained more than seven dozen references to oral sex alone. Their first hit single, "Me So Horny" (number 26), earned both widespread airplay and the wrath of Jack Thompson, an evangelical Christian attorney who took 2 Live Crew to court on obscenity charges. In 1990 the group was arrested for performing material from the album. Campbell did not help his cause by claiming on network television in 1992 that he had had oral sex on stage with female fans in Japan.

For four years, Campbell and 2 Live Crew were in and out of the courts on a series of charges and countercharges over obscene lyrics and the right to parody. When a Florida federal court declared *As Nasty as They Wanna Be* obscene, the group was publicly defended by performers as diverse as Bruce Springsteen, Mötley Crüe, and Sinéad O'Connor. Ultimately, the group was acquitted of obscenity charges filed after they performed the album's songs in a Florida nightclub, and an appeals court overturned the obscenity ruling on the album.

Popularity. The group's popularity was directly linked to the novelty of their lewdness. The "clean" version of *As Nasty as They Wanna Be* sold only one-eighth as many albums as the original. *Banned in the U.S.A.* (1990), based upon Bruce Springsteen's *Born in the U.S.A.*, and *Sports Weekend (As Nasty as They Wanna Be Part II)* (1991) both went gold, but 2 Live Crew's market was increasingly being taken by more explicit and more creative rappers such as Shabba Ranks and the Mad Cobra.

Meanwhile, Campbell's label, Luke Records, had great success with a new Houston, Texas, rhythm-and-blues vocal group, H-Town, whose *Fever for Da Flavor* (1993) reached number 16 on the pop charts, largely on the strength of the hit single "Knockin' da Boots" (number 3). By 1994, with Ross and Hobbs having left the group and Larry Dobson joining on vocals, Campbell proclaimed the New 2 Live Crew, which produced *Back at Your Ass for the Nine-4*, which briefly landed in the rhythm-and-blues Top 10. In 1995 Campbell filed for bankruptcy over 1.6 million dollars in back royalties owed to rapper M.C. Shy D.

—*John Powell*

SELECT DISCOGRAPHY
2 Live Crew
■ ALBUMS
The 2 Live Crew Is What We Are, 1986
Move Somethin', 1987
As Nasty as They Wanna Be, 1989
As Clean as They Wanna Be, 1989
Banned in the U.S.A., 1990 (as Luke Featuring the 2 Live Crew)
Sports Weekend (As Nasty as They Wanna Be Part II), 1991
2 Live Crew's Greatest Hits, 1992 (compilation)
Back at Your Ass for the Nine-4, 1994
2 Live Bass, 1994
Original 2 Live Crew, 1995
Goes to the Movies: Decade of Hits, 1997 (compilation)
The Real One, 1998
Luke Skyywalker solo
■ ALBUMS
In the Nude, 1993
Freak for Life 6996, 1994

U

U2

MEMBERS: Paul "Bono" Hewson (b. 1960), Dave "the Edge" Evans (b. 1961), Larry Mullen, Jr. (b. 1961), Adam Clayton (b. 1960)

FIRST ALBUM RELEASE: *Boy*, 1980

MUSICAL STYLES: Rock and roll, alternative

U2 rose from their roots as a punk-influenced, alternative rock band to become one of the most popular musical groups of the 1980's and 1990's, selling millions of albums and drawing thousands of fans to sold-out concerts on their worldwide tours.

Dublin. The four members of U2 hailed from Dublin, Ireland, a city that is not generally considered an important center for rock music. Heavily influenced by punk bands such as the Sex Pistols and art rockers such as David Bowie, the four teenage schoolmates started their own band in 1976. Dave Evans, who was nicknamed "the Edge," played guitar, Larry Mullen played drums, Adam Clayton played bass guitar, and Paul Hewson, who was known as "Bono," sang. First called Feedback and then the Hype, the band took the name U2 in 1977. Their early performances included covers of Rolling Stones and Beach Boys songs. The band spent the next two years working clubs, writing original songs, and releasing singles such as "Out of Control," which met with success in Ireland but was ignored elsewhere. Most observers agreed that the band members needed to work on their musicianship but also noted that the enthusiasm and energy that U2 exhibited during live performances showed promise.

After an impressive 1980 concert, Island Records offered the band a recording contract, and U2 recorded their first album, *Boy* (1980). Although clearly influenced by punk, the album featured the Edge's unusual guitar playing, which relied on subtlety and careful sound effects instead of the slashing roar that marked many punk efforts of the time. The album only reached number 94 on the *Billboard* pop charts, but it caught the attention of music critics who were intrigued by the album's texture. Paul McGuinness, the band's manager, knew that the band's success depended on a positive reception in the United States, so U2 began their first U.S. tour shortly after *Boy*'s U.S. release.

U2 recorded material for the second album during the summer of 1981. Released in late fall, *October* did not contain any hit singles, and the album stalled at number 104 on the pop charts. However, it received significant airplay on college radio stations. It also revealed U2's willingness to examine spiritual issues usually ignored in rock music. The single "Gloria," which contained a brief but brilliant repeated guitar riff, had lyrics that expressed religious devotion, most unusual for a pop song. U2 was also becoming a band capable of expressing anger, as shown in the song "I Threw a Brick Through a Window," and ecstasy, as revealed in "Rejoice."

Breakthrough. The band's weak album sales spelled trouble, and U2 worked hard to make their third album a powerful musical and lyrical statement that would nonetheless be commercially viable. Well over a year passed while their fans awaited new material. They were not disappointed when *War* was released in March, 1983. The track "Sunday, Bloody Sunday" was an angry indictment of Ireland's tragic history and, by extension, a condemnation of all violence. However, the album did not fare well initially. The music television station MTV played the video for the track "New Year's Day," but the single did not break into the Top 40. The band toured the United States in order to bolster sales, with Bono whipping the crowds when he ran about the concert halls waving a white flag. During this tour, the band filmed a concert performance at Red Rocks in Denver, Colorado, which was later released as the video *Under a Blood Red Sky* (1983). An EP with the same title contained live performances from Red Rocks and a European venue. Although the recording and performance were uneven, the EP reached number 28 on the U.S. charts.

The strength of the material on *War* and the high quality of the supporting concert tour made the album a best-seller. It would remain on the album charts for over three years. In March, 1984, *Rolling Stone* magazine declared that U2 was the 1983 Band of the Year. The band negotiated a new contract with Island Records that ensured that the four members would have artistic control over their material and rights to their music. U2 had retained their artistic integrity while achieving their dream of popular success.

The next album, *The Unforgettable Fire* (1984), marked a change in the band's direction that received a negative response from many critics. The title came from a museum exhibit of drawings by survivors of the atomic bomb blasts that had destroyed the Japanese cities of Hiroshima and Nagasaki during World War II. Intentionally seeking to create a sound far different from that on earlier albums, U2 called upon the eclectic musician Brian Eno to produce the new material. Eno was well known for his work with tape loops and other experimental techniques. Eno gave the new songs, which were recorded in a castle outside Dublin, an ethereal, almost atmospheric feeling. Unfortunately, many of the songs lacked the focus and dynamism of the band's previous work. The single "Pride (In the Name of Love)," an ode to civil rights leader Martin Luther King, Jr., again evidenced the band's commitment to spiritual needs in a chaotic world; it also provided the band with a minor hit in the United States.

The tepid critical response to *The Unforgettable*

For the Record

Bono took his name from a Dublin hearing aid store called Bonovox. He did not realize that the term was Latin for "good voice."

Fire did not weaken the band's popularity, which continued to grow throughout the world. In 1985, *Rolling Stone* again sang U2's praises, calling them the "Band of the Eighties." This enthusiasm for a group that had never reached number 1 on the record charts stemmed from the positive response to U2's belief that rock music still had the power to change people's lives for the better, a value system that many fans and record company executives had abandoned during the 1970's and 1980's.

The Joshua Tree. U2 continued to perform in 1985, touring extensively and appearing at the Live Aid concert. The only 1985 release was the EP *Wide Awake in America*, which appropriately contained live performances, including an outstanding version of "Bad," which received some radio airplay. In 1986, the group began recording material for the next album but had to stop work because of a commitment to perform in Amnesty International's Conspiracy of Hope tour. After the tour, U2 returned to the studio, working with Eno and completing the new album, *The Joshua Tree*, in early 1987. Hoping to generate excitement around the impending release of the new material, Island Records banned radio stations from playing any promotional copies before the official release date in March.

The album exceeded everyone's expectations and provided U2 with the best-selling hits that they had not produced in the past. The collaboration with Eno, which had resulted in the mixed performance on *The Unforgettable Fire*, now proved to be inspired. The songs revealed a group with diverse interests and capabilities. "Where the Streets Have No Name" featured a synthesizer and guitar opening that harkened back to the ethereal tone that had pervaded the previous studio album. Bono's vocals on "I Still Haven't Found What I'm Looking For" had a gospel tinge. The Edge opened "Bullet the Blue Sky" with a heavily distorted guitar sound but added delicate slide guitar riffs to "Running to Stand Still." The album was an artistic triumph, and the American public responded enthusiastically. Within four weeks of its release, *The Joshua Tree* reached number 1 on the record charts. The single "With or Without

You" reached number 1 in May, 1987. The second single from the album, "I Still Haven't Found What I'm Looking For," reached the top spot later that year.

Backlash. The success of *The Joshua Tree* made U2 the most prominent band in rock music. Their concerts, now often performed in huge stadiums, sold out all over the world, and their videos went into heavy rotation on MTV. However, the band members did not rest on their laurels. During their U.S. tour, they explored various aspects of American music, which they incorporated into their work. Bono performed "I Still Haven't Found What I'm Looking For" with accompaniment from a Harlem gospel choir. The Memphis Horns, who had performed on many great rhythm-and-blues hits, provided the brass section on "Angel of Harlem." The band also recorded with blues great B. B. King and the legendary Bob Dylan. The new songs appeared on the 1988 double album *Rattle and Hum*, which also included live performances from their concerts.

Like its predecessor, the new album shot to the top of the chart, reaching number 1 only two weeks after its release. The single "Desire" eventually reached the number 3 spot. The success of the album heightened anticipation regarding the feature-length film made during U2's most recent tour, set to premiere in November, 1988. Also entitled *Rattle and Hum*, the film included both black and white and color concert footage, as well as clips of the band discussing their music. Fans flocked to the theaters to see U2, and the film did well on its opening weekend.

However, there were signs that the critics and the public had wearied of the U2 phenomenon.

U2's the Edge and Bono (Paul Natkin)

The album received mixed reviews, and many critics found the film either boring or even offensive, arguing that U2 had become pretentious in their attempts to exploit American music. The public's interest in the movie tapered off in a few weeks, indicating that only the band's dedicated fans had paid to see it. U2 was experiencing a critical and popular backlash to their success. The release of so much material in less than two years, the constant video rotation on MTV, and the film had saturated the market. The band's commitment to a large number of charities such as Amnesty International now seemed to reflect a "cause of the moment" attitude. U2 stood in danger of becoming a parody of themselves.

In response to the growing negative response to their image, U2 retreated from the public eye, waiting nearly three years to release *Achtung Baby* (1991), an album recorded in part in a former Nazi ballroom in Berlin, Germany. The band had intentionally set out to write music that departed from the texture of *The Joshua Tree*, and the new album featured shorter songs with lyrics that examined personal relationships instead of major social issues. Rather than engage in a massive promotional effort, U2 remained quiet prior to the album's release. This low-key approach had no impact on the album's sales, and it debuted at number 1 on the *Billboard* charts.

However, the supporting concert tour was anything but low key. The 1992 Zoo TV concert tour featured an elaborate stage presentation, including giant video screens and props. It was one of the most successful rock tours of the year, filling stadiums throughout the world and confirming U2's status as one of the most popular bands in rock history. In 1993, Island Records signed a new contract with the group that guaranteed a reported $170 million for their next six albums, placing U2 among the world's wealthiest entertainers and making the band one of the leading business concerns in Ireland.

Pop. The group's next release, *Zooropa* (1993), took many fans and critics by surprise. Committed to keeping their sound fresh, U2 again experimented with different genres, this time examining electronic programming and industrial rock.

One track, "Daddy's Gonna Pay for Your Crashed Car," made use of sampling, a studio technique that evidenced the band's desire to remain in step with new trends; however, the song sounded out of place on an album by a band that usually relied on the Edge's guitar to drive the music. Many critics praised the album, but the final result was uneven, and *Zooropa* did not yield any hit singles.

Fans were even more surprised with *Pop* (1997), which again reflected the band's interest in technology. The release of the album was accompanied by a promotional blitz, including a prime-time special on the ABC television network. However, this effort held little attraction for fans, and the special was one of the lowest rated programs in the network's history. Although it opened at number 1, the album quickly slipped off the record charts. Some reviews lauded *Pop* for its inventiveness, but others declared that commercialism, not art, was now determining the nature of U2's output. Some critics argued that U2 had abandoned their high principles and commitment to "rock that matters" for gaudy and meaningless spectacle. They argued that wealth and fame had made it impossible for the band to relate to their fans.

The divided critical response and the ambivalent fan reaction to *Pop* indicated that U2 had reached another important crossroads in their career. While remaining one of the leading bands in the music industry, still drawing thousands of fans to their concerts and selling hundreds of thousands of albums, U2 risked losing their position as a symbol of integrity and optimism in an industry that focused on profit and fame. In the past, U2 had always rebounded from crises, releasing *War* when their viability as a rock act was in doubt, using the *The Unforgettable Fire* as a learning experience to craft the magnificent *The Joshua Tree*, and prudently leaving the U.S. market during the late 1980's in order to avoid fan burnout. U2 was never a band to ignore, and the weakness of *Pop* did not necessarily spell a decline in their importance or impact.

However, U2's past successes had been based in large measure upon their ability to connect emotionally with fans, to express feelings of hurt and rage in an uplifting spiritual context without seeming preachy or maudlin. If critics were right in their charge that U2 had succumbed to commercial impulses, it seemed unlikely that the band would be able to motivate fans to the levels of excitement and loyalty generated during the 1980's. —*Thomas Clarkin*

SELECT DISCOGRAPHY
■ ALBUMS
Boy, 1980
October, 1981
War, 1983
Under a Blood Red Sky, 1983 (EP)
The Unforgettable Fire, 1984
Wide Awake in America, 1985 (EP)
The Joshua Tree, 1987
Rattle and Hum, 1988
Achtung Baby, 1991
Zooropa, 1993
Pop, 1997
Best of 1980-1990, 1998

SELECT AWARDS
Grammy Awards for Album of the Year for *The Joshua Tree* (with Daniel Lanois and Brian Eno) and for Best Rock Performance by a Duo or Group with Vocal for *The Joshua Tree*, 1987
Grammy Awards for Best Performance Music Video for "Where the Streets Have No Name" (with others) and for Best Rock Performance by a Duo or Group with Vocal for "Desire," 1988
Grammy Award for Best Rock Performance by a Duo or Group with Vocal for *Achtung Baby*, 1992
Grammy Award for Best Alternative Music Album for *Zooropa*, 1993
Grammy Award for Best Music Video, Long Form, for *Zoo TV—Live from Sydney*, 1994

SEE ALSO: Bowie, David; Eno, Brian; Sex Pistols, The.

V

Ritchie Valens

BORN: Pacoima, California; May 13, 1941
DIED: Near Mason City, Iowa; February 3, 1959
FIRST ALBUM RELEASE: *Ritchie Valens*, 1959
MUSICAL STYLES: Rock and roll, Mexican folk, pop, rhythm and blues

Ritchie Valens was born Richard Stephen Valenzuela in Pacoima, California, in Los Angeles's San Fernando Valley. Today at Pacoima Junior High School, an 8-foot by 15-foot mural portrait honors the first Chicano rock star. During the brief seventeen years of his life, Valens witnessed the birth of rock and roll and helped guide its direction. On February 3, 1959, Valens's life was tragically cut short when he died in a plane crash along with rock legends Buddy Holly and the Big Bopper (J. P. Richardson), of "Chantilly Lace" fame. Valens had been touring the country with several other rock stars the day he boarded the small plane chartered by Buddy Holly and bound for Fargo, North Dakota. According to Valens's manager and record producer, Bob Keene, Valens and Holly's guitarist Tommy Allsup flipped a coin to decide who would ride in the plane. The plane crashed shortly after takeoff in Mason City, Iowa, killing all aboard on a cold and snowy evening that people in the music industry called "the day the music died."

Succeeding Against the Odds. As a child, Valens played on a homemade toy guitar and later on a secondhand guitar with only two strings. In junior high school, he made his own electric guitar in woodshop and helped to form a neighborhood band called the Silhouettes. Playing at dances at San Fernando's American Legion Hall, Ritchie soon became the Silhouettes's main attraction with his Little Richard covers. In 1958, Ritchie came to the attention of Bob Keene, who owned a small Hollywood record label called Del-Fi. Keene recalled a popular, friendly, bull-like kid with a flattop haircut who sang in a pure, high tenor and played guitar excellently. Keene helped Valens transform many of his musical ideas into complete songs and hired experienced musicians to play with him in the studio. Next, Keene shortened Ritchie's last name either to sound more catchy or to conceal his ethnicity, as was common practice in the 1950's.

"Come On, Let's Go" (1958) was Ritchie Valens's first single, which reached number 42 on the charts and earned him a gold record. "Come On, Let's Go" is an upbeat guitar rock song that was backed on the B side by the excellent "Framed," a pop-blues tune originally written by Jerry Leiber and Mike Stoller for the Coasters. Valens struck double-gold with his next record, the two-sided hit single "Donna," (1959) which reached number 2 on the charts, backed by "La Bamba" which reached number 22. The slow tempo of "Donna," sung in an expressive high voice, is a classic 1950's teenage lament composed after Valens was rejected by the parents of his girlfriend, Donna Ludwig, for being of Mexican descent. Interestingly, Bob Keene initially thought "La Bamba" was a throwaway B side.

Keene soon had Valens touring the country with major rock stars such as Bo Diddley and Eddie Cochran and arranged a television appearance on *American Bandstand*. Valens also sang "Ooh My Head" in the 1959 rock film *Go Johnny Go*, starring teen idol Jimmy Clanton and famed disc jockey and rock promoter Alan Freed. "Ooh My Head" is a near copy of Little Richard's "Ooh! My Soul" that was covered by Led Zeppelin in 1975 on their epic *Physical Graffiti* album under the title "Boogie with Stu."

All five songs mentioned above are on Valens's first album, *Ritchie Valens*, released after his death, in 1959. This album also includes excellent covers of the rock classics "We Belong Together" and "Boney Maronie." To have so many excellent songs on the same album was unusual at a time when most rock albums contained only one or two high-quality songs and considerable "filler" material. A third single from the album, "That's My Little Susie"/"In a Turkish Town," reached number 55 on the charts. Like "Donna," "In a Turkish Town" displays Valens's sentimental love for slow, sad songs, a style that also surfaced on three songs from his second album, *Ritchie* (1963), such as "Stay Beside Me." In addition to a couple of good rock tunes, such as "Hurry Up," there are two very good instrumental blues tunes on this album that were pressed into a single record and mysteriously released under the name Arvee Allens.

In 1985, Rhino Records released the definitive *History of Ritchie Valens* boxed set, which includes the two albums mentioned above in addition to

Ritchie Valens (AP/Wide World Photos)

Ritchie Valens in Concert at Pacoima Junior High (1960). This third album contains the live concert on side 1 and studio recordings on side 2 that Bob Keene described as "fragments of ideas not yet polished or completed." While the concert recordings are of poor sound quality, they capture fresh and spontaneous versions of Valens's hit songs as well as the excited screams of his hometown teenage fans.

What Ritchie Valens accomplished before his untimely death is extraordinary considering the times and the extremely slim chances that a poor Chicano teenager would become a rock star. Who could have predicted, for example, that a rock-and-roll version of a Mexican folk song, sung in Spanish, would become an enduring rock-and-roll classic? In addition to Valens's bad luck (which led to his untimely death), he was blessed with good luck, much talent, and a dedicated manager.

The "La Bamba" Sound. In the 1989 book *The Heart of Rock and Soul: The 1001 Greatest Singles Ever Made*, noted rock critic Dave Marsh listed "La Bamba" among the top 100 greatest rock singles. He also ranked "Donna" at number 121 and "Come On, Let's Go" among the top 500 greatest singles. In the book *The Sound of the City* (1970, rev. 1983), considered one of the best histories of rock and roll, author Charlie Gillett noted that "La Bamba" was an important song that pushed rock-and-roll music forward by introducing a new sound—a distinctive rhythm and repeating three-chord sequence—that became the basis for many hits to follow. The most obvious examples include "Twist and Shout" by the Isley Brothers in 1962 (popularized by the Beatles), "Hang on Sloopy" by the McCoys in 1965, and "Good Lovin'" by the Young Rascals in 1966. The "La Bamba" chord changes were slowed slightly and altered to serve as the basis for the Kingsmen's 1963 classic "Louie Louie" and were slowed down considerably for "You've Lost That Lovin' Feelin'" by the Righteous Brothers in 1964.

Ritchie Valens, the Motion Picture. In 1987, Valens was immortalized on the big screen in Columbia Pictures' biographical film *La Bamba*. This surprise hit was created by Chicano director

Luis Valdez, who also wrote the screenplay. Valens's music was faithfully re-created by the rock band Los Lobos at the insistence of Valdez and Valens's family. Both the film sound track and the "La Bamba" single reached number 1 on the charts. The film falsely portrays Valens as coming from a migrant farmworker background, having a mystic meeting with a curandero (Mexican healer) in Tijuana, and engaging in an exaggerated sibling rivalry with his older brother. However, Beverly Mendheim, author of the 1987 biography *Ritchie Valens: The First Latino Rocker*, viewed these fabrications as the director's successful attempt to create a Hollywood legend. The picture was beautifully filmed and well acted, and Valdez skillfully captured the Chicano culture in family scenes that secretly included Valens's real mother and family members. Even Los Lobos made a cameo appearance as a Mexican string band in a Tijuana nightclub. Finally, even though actor Lou Diamond Phillips was too trim and boyish-looking to play the heavyset and mature-looking Valens, the film proves true to the spirit, memory, and legacy of Ritchie Valens.   —*Kurt C. Organista*

SELECT DISCOGRAPHY
■ SINGLES
"Come On, Let's Go," 1958
"Donna"/"La Bamba," 1958
■ ALBUMS
Ritchie Valens, 1959
Ritchie Valens in Concert at Pacoima Junior High, 1960
Ritchie, 1963
The History of Ritchie Valens, 1985 (compilation)

SEE ALSO: Holly, Buddy / The Crickets; Los Lobos.

Luther Vandross

BORN: New York, New York; April 20, 1951
FIRST ALBUM RELEASE: *Never Too Much*, 1981
MUSICAL STYLES: Pop, soul, rhythm and blues

Luther Vandross began his professional singing career in the 1970's as a backup vocalist and arranger for some of the biggest names in show business and went on to become one of the most successful solo artists of the 1980's. His string of platinum pop and rhythm-and-blues (R&B) albums placed him among the elite of the music industry of the 1980's.

The Beginnings. Luther Vandross became interested in pop and soul music while growing up in the Alfred E. Smith Housing Project in lower Manhattan. His father and mother, both musically gifted, encouraged him to cultivate his musical talent. His genius was evident at such an early age that Vandross took piano lessons when he was only three years old. His sister, who sang in a vocal group known as the Crests during the 1950's, is also credited with influencing his early interest in music.

While attending William Howard Taft High School in the Bronx, Vandross formed a group with friends Carlos Alomar and Robin Clark. He went on to attend college at Western Michigan University in the late 1960's but dropped out of school after only two semesters in order to pursue his dream of a career in music. He had already written several original songs and was extremely confident that his musical talent would provide adequate employment while he waited for his big break.

His first big break came in 1974 when his old friend Alomar invited Vandross and Robin Clark to watch David Bowie record the *Young Americans* album. Bowie was so impressed with Vandross that he allowed the young composer to work all of the vocal arrangements for the album already in progress. Bowie also introduced Vandross to Bette Midler, who was also very struck with his talents. Vandross was invited by Midler to join her on tour and sing backup vocals, an offer Vandross gladly accepted. During the 1970's, he tried to form, and also join, several groups, including Luther, Bionic Boogie, and Change. The group Luther made two albums for Catillion Records that produced hit singles but were not very successful albums. Luther was eventually dropped by Catillion Records, which forced Vandross to continue working as a backup singer.

In the late 1970's, Vandross worked with several popular disco groups, including Chic. During

For the Record

Although he has never had difficulty maintaining success as a music star, Vandross has always had difficulty maintaining his weight. He claims to have lost more than 120 pounds on nine different occasions while on various diets.

Luther Vandross in 1984 (Paul Natkin)

those years, besides session and concert performances with big-name talent, Vandross made a name as a songwriter and a commercial jingle writer and singer. His distinctive voice was heard promoting many corporate television and radio sponsors. Products and services such as AT&T, Burger King, Kentucky Fried Chicken, and the U.S. Army were promoted using his creative talents.

Recording Classics. In 1980, Columbia Records gave Vandross his first solo recording contract when he signed with its subsidiary, Epic Records. Vandross wrote and arranged nearly all of the material for his first album, *Never Too Much* (1981), which became a huge commercial success for the label and was eventually certified platinum. The title song became a number 1 hit on the rhythm-and-blues charts. As a popular new artist with a large following, Vandross performed as an opening act for Frankie Beverly and Maze, often drawing more ticket sales than the headline act. The huge success of his debut album encouraged even more artists to consider Vandross when looking for someone to collaborate with on new projects. He worked with Aretha Franklin on *Jump to It* (1982), which would prove to be her most successful album since the mid-1970's. He also worked with Dionne Warwick and soul superstar Teddy Pendergrass. His 1982 album, *Forever, for Always, for Love,* was a hit on both rhythm-and-blues and pop charts. During 1982, Vandross had four singles on *Billboard* soul charts, including "Bad Boy/Having a Party." He followed this up in 1983 with three more hit singles.

Vandross always played to racially mixed crowds, but, prior to the mid-1980's, he had limited success breaking onto the pop charts. His recording popularity continued to increase with his next platinum album, *Busy Body,* released in 1983. In 1985 Vandross released *The Night I Fell in Love* and three hit singles, including "Till My Baby Comes Home," which reached number 29 on the pop charts.

In 1986, Vandross's platinum album *Give Me the Reason* rose to number 1 on the *Billboard* soul chart and into the Top 20 on the pop charts. In 1987, with several singles on the soul charts, Vandross served with Dionne Warwick as cohost of the First Annual Soul Train Music Awards in Hollywood, California. He was recognized not only as host but also as recipient of the Album of the Year Award for a male performer. Utilizing his stardom as a means of making a political statement, he cancelled two sellout concerts that year in Arizona in protest of the state government's refusal to recognize Martin Luther King Day. In 1988, his fifth straight platinum-selling album, *Any Love*, was released. He was recognized that year by the American Music Awards as the Favorite Male Soul/R&B Vocalist.

It was not until 1989, however, when Epic Records released *The Best of Luther Vandross, the Best of Love*, a greatest-hits album containing the song "Here and Now," that Vandross finally achieved his first Top-10 pop hit. That breakthrough album led the way for Vandross's 1991 album, *Power of Love*, featuring the hit singles "Power of Love/Love Power" and "Don't Want to Be a Fool." His fifty-five-date U.S. tour of the same year, which included four sellouts at Madison Square Garden, was one of the most successful by any artist in the 1990's. He received 1991 Grammy Awards for Best R&B Song and Best R&B Vocal Performance, Male, for *Power of Love*.

Vandross's commercial success continued well into the 1990's, beginning with the release of *Never Let It Go* in 1993, which added to his ever-growing list of platinum albums. *Songs* (1994), *Greatest Hits: 1981-1995* (1995), and *One Night with You: The Best of Love Volume 2* (1997), were also well received by his fans and continued his string of successful releases.   —*Donald C. Simmons, Jr.*

SELECT DISCOGRAPHY
■ ALBUMS
Never Too Much, 1981
Forever, for Always, for Love, 1982
The Night I Fell in Love, 1985
The Best of Luther Vandross, the Best of Love, 1989 (previously released material)
One Night with You: The Best of Love Volume 2, 1997 (previously released material)

SELECT AWARDS
Grammy Award for Best R&B Vocal Performance, Male, for "Here and Now," 1990
Grammy Awards for Best R&B Song for "Power of Love/Love Power" (with Marcus Miller and Teddy Vann) and for Best R&B Vocal Performance, Male, for *Power of Love*, 1991
Grammy Award for Best Male R&B Vocal Performance for "Your Secret Love," 1996
Image Award for Outstanding Male Artist, 1994

SEE ALSO: Bowie, David; Chic; Midler, Bette; Pendergrass, Teddy.

Vangelis
(Evangelos Odyssey Papathanassiou)
BORN: Valos, Greece; March 29, 1943
FIRST ALBUM RELEASE: *The Dragon*, 1971
MUSICAL STYLES: New age, pop

Because of his desire to keep his personal life private, his reluctance to grant interviews, and his policy to rarely give live performances, limited information is available about Greek composer Vangelis. It is known that the composer and keyboardist started playing the piano at age four and gave his first public performance of original compositions at the age of six. As a teen, he formed his first Greek band, the Forming, followed by the progressive rock band Aphrodite's Child with singer Demis Roussos and drummer Lucas Sideras.

Recording. Moving to Paris, the group issued the single "Rain and Tears," followed by three albums, *End of the World* (1968), *It's Five O'Clock* (1969), and the controversial *666* (1972), the last issued two years after the group's breakup. Primarily a keyboardist, Vangelis also became proficient on percussion, flutes, vibraphone, and tubular bells.

After the band's breakup, Vangelis began a career of composing primarily instrumental music that became widely used in film and television sound tracks, including his 1975 *Heaven and Hell*, which yielded the theme for astronomer Carl Sagan's *Cosmos* series for the American Public Broadcasting System. Scores written specifically for the screen included *Crime and Passion* (1976), *Missing* (1982), *Blade Runner* (1982), *The Bounty* (1984), *Francesco* (1989), and *Bitter Moon* (1994).

Chariots of Fire. While most of Vangelis's scores did not attain popularity in their own right, major mainstream success came with his 1981 main theme for Hugh Hudson's film *Chariots of Fire*, which won an Academy Award for Original Score and became the theme for the Olympic Games in Sarajevo, Yugoslavia, in 1984. In 1982, the album went platinum, staying at number 1 on the charts for eighteen weeks.

Vangelis's greatest success came with the score of *1492: Conquest of Paradise* (1992). In the United States, the score was nominated for a Golden Globe Award. Three years later in 1995, German boxer Henry Maske used the "Conquest of Paradise" passage as his personal theme on television, which resulted in a renewed interest in the score in Europe; the music broke sales records in Germany, Austria, Portugal, England, Spain, Switzerland, France, the Netherlands, Canada, Korea, Hungary, Argentina, and Belgium.

The president of East/West, Vanglis's record label, immediately sponsored a campaign of tie-in videos and advertising which resulted in both the sound track and the "Conquest of Paradise" single reaching number 1 in Germany. In February of 1995, the label honored Vangelis for his international sales of *1492*, which surpassed two million copies.

Throughout his career, Vangelis's income was supported not only by commissioned studio work, but also by passages from his classically oriented album pieces not intended for informal performances. These also became well-known commercial backgrounds and television themes. In the United States, Gallo wine commercials used "Hymn" from the album *Opera Sauvage* (1987). Vangelis's *China* (1979) yielded "Chung Kuo" for Ford Motors commercials in the early 1980's, and "The Little Feet" from the same album was used to promote Chanel perfume. Vangelis also wrote the theme for the British series *Great River Journeys*, and for oceanographer Jacques Cousteau, Vangelis composed the music for "We Cannot Permit," a documentary about the destruction of the sea.

Other Projects. Vangelis composed one ballet, *Elektra* (1983), and the opera *M D E de Euripide* (1992), which featured his frequently used singer and friend, Greek actress Irene Papas. Vangelis also experimented with synthesizer rock-flavored music on four albums with former Yes singer Jon Anderson, including *The Best of Jon and Vangelis* (1984).

It has been claimed Vangelis was once married to Vana Veroutis, a Greek vocalist who performed on *Heaven and Hell*. He lived with photographer Veronique Skawinska, who designed his album artwork during the late 1970's and early 1980's. With brother Nico, a music producer, Vangelis worked on an album by the Italian band Chrisma, recorded in Vangelis's Nemo studio in London. Later, he built a studio in Paris, the Epsilon Laboratory, with the roof and walls made of glass. An in-depth interview with Vangelis, filmed in 1992 by French television station France 2, was subsequently broadcast throughout Europe.

—*Wesley Britton*

For the Record

When Vangelis was nominated for the Best Original Score Academy Award for his work on *Chariots of Fire* in 1982, he did not believe that he had a chance of winning. Not only did he not bother attending the awards ceremony, but he did not even watch the ceremonies on television. The moment his award was announced, friends called to congratulate him, only to find he was in bed asleep.

SELECT DISCOGRAPHY
■ ALBUMS
Direct, 1988
The City, 1990
Voices, 1995
Oceanic, 1996

SELECT AWARDS
Academy Award for Original Score for *Chariots of Fire*, from *Chariots of Fire*, 1981

SEE ALSO: Yanni; Yes.

Van Halen

ORIGINAL MEMBERS: Michael Anthony (b. 1955),
David Lee Roth (b. 1955), Alex Van Halen
(b. 1953), Eddie Van Halen (b. 1955)
OTHER MEMBERS: Sammy Hagar (b. 1947), Gary
Cherone (b. 1961)
FIRST ALBUM RELEASE: *Van Halen*, 1978
MUSICAL STYLES: Pop, rock and roll

A generation of fans grew up with Van Halen.
Teenagers who listened to self-taught guitar hero
Eddie Van Halen and original front man David
Lee Roth were listening to Sammy Hagar's Van
Halen as adults. These fans' teenage children
then heard Gary Cherone's voice leading the
group. Through all their personnel changes, the
power trio of Eddie, brother Alex on drums, and
Michael Anthony on bass, has survived more than
two decades and recorded twelve albums that have
sold more than seventy million copies.

The Beginnings. Born in the Netherlands,
Alex and Eddie Van Halen took classical music
lessons throughout most of their childhood.
When the boys were in their early teens, the Van
Halens moved to Pasadena, California, where
their musician father supported his family by playing at weddings. Once in the United States, Alex
and Eddie discovered rock and roll, effectively
ending their father's classical ambitions for them.
Originally, Eddie played drums and Alex played
guitar, but by the time they reached high school,
they had traded instruments.

Roth came from a wealthy California family
and had his first stage experience with a band
called Redball Jet. He met and ultimately joined
with Alex and Eddie in a band called Mammoth.
Soon after, bassist Anthony left Snake to complete
the foursome. As the shows grew more professional, they learned there was another band already performing under the name Mammoth and
renamed themselves Van Halen after fifty percent
of their membership.

No overnight success, Van Halen played hundreds of bars and small clubs throughout Southern California, developing a small but intense
local following. Their intensity and Eddie's guitar
technique earned notice from Los Angeles disc
jockey Rodney "The Killer B" Bingenheimer, who
helped arrange dates and brought them to the
attention of record company executives. In 1977,
Gene Simmons of Kiss saw the band at the Star-
wood club and agreed to finance a demo. On the
strength of that demo and Simmons's recommendation, Warner Bros. signed Van Halen.

The Roth Era. Van Halen's 1978 self-titled debut album was well received by both fans and
critics eager for something other than disco. The
first single was a cover of the Kinks classic "You
Really Got Me," with front man Roth's trademark
over-the-top panting, yelps, and groaning delivery
and Eddie's rapid-fire riffs and groundbreaking
technique, which stunned guitar aficionados. Two
more singles followed; "Jamie's Crying" and "Run-
nin' with the Devil." *Van Halen* made the charts
worldwide, was certified gold in a matter of weeks,
and went platinum five months later. *Van Halen II*
followed in 1979 and contained their first Top-20
single, "Dance the Night Away."

Neither *Women and Children First* (1980), nor
Fair Warning (1981) spawned a hit single, though
the former did reach number 6 on the album
charts. Nevertheless, Van Halen reached head-
liner status, based on strong album sales, Eddie's
guitar playing, and Roth's larger-than-life onstage
antics. It was not until 1982 and *Diver Down* that
Van Halen reached the singles charts again. This
time, it was with another cover, Roy Orbison's
"Oh, Pretty Woman."

The album *1984* propelled Van Halen into the
video age and into superstardom. The first single,
"Jump," was significant for many reasons. It was
Van Halen's first number 1 single, their first video,
and most important, it featured Eddie, not on
guitar, but on synthesizer. Though the move was
well received by most fans and critics, an outraged
few likened it to the day Bob Dylan picked up an
electric guitar. More hit singles followed; "I'll
Wait," "Panama," and "Hot for Teacher," which
was supported by a clever video which inter-
spersed a teenage version of the band with their
grown-up counterparts wearing pink suits and
dancing like the Four Tops.

Despite the success of *1984*, a schism was devel-

Van Halen in 1986: Michael Anthony, Sammy Hagar, Eddie Van Halen, Alex Van Halen (Paul Natkin)

oping between "Diamond Dave" and the rest of the band. He stepped away to record a cover-laden solo extended-play single, 1985's *Crazy from the Heat*, featuring "California Girls" and "Just a Gigolo/I Ain't Got Nobody," both of which received extensive MTV airplay. At first, the extended-play single was just a side project, a claim Roth backed up by pointing out the lack of guitars (he said he did not want it to be mistaken for a Van Halen project). Anthony and the Van Halen brothers countered by stating that they wanted a lead singer who was dedicated to the band. When Roth's solo activities delayed the follow-up to *1984*, he was fired from Van Halen.

The Hagar Era. Arena-rock veteran Sammy Hagar took over as lead singer in 1985, giving rise to tongue-in-cheek rumors that the band would be renamed "Van Hagar." The choice of Hagar, a former front man for Montrose and a solo artist in his own right, surprised many and even angered a few. The success of the new lineup proved to be an even greater surprise. Their first album, *5150*, was released in 1986 and was named for the California police code for an escaped mental patient (it was also the name of Eddie's new home studio). The album reached number 1 and spawned several hit singles: "Why Can't This Be Love," "Dreams," and "Love Walks In."

OU812 (1988) reached number 1 on the *Billboard* charts within a week of its release. This second outing by the new lineup was well received by fans and critics, and Hagar began to sound comfortable with the band. Singles included "When It's Love" and "Finish What You Started." That summer, Van Halen headlined the "Monsters of Rock" tour with Dokken, Scorpion, and Metallica.

The third album with Hagar, 1991's *For Unlawful Carnal Knowledge*, also reached number 1 and featured "Right Now," a hit on both radio and MTV. Where the songwriting was less than stellar, the music more than made up for it with a return to straightforward rock and roll. A double album, *Van Halen Live: Right Here, Right Now*, followed in 1993.

Balance, in 1995, proved to be the breaking point for the second incarnation of Van Halen. Though it debuted at number 1, *Balance* did not sit well with the critics, who accused the band of becoming formulaic. Eddie had finished a well-publicized substance abuse rehabilitation, while Hagar continued the unending rock-and-roll party lifestyle that was growing less compatible with the rest of the band and their new manager. Stories varied: the rest of the band claimed Hagar left to resume his solo career, but Hagar maintained that he was pushed to quit (his first solo release following the breakup was called "Little White Lie").

Gary Cherone Makes Three. In 1997 Van Halen was again in need of a lead vocalist. In a bizarre twist, Roth reunited with the band for two songs on *Best of Van Halen, Vol. I* in 1996, and there were published reports that he was back in the band. Unfortunately for the faithful, the reunion was short-lived, ending on live television during the MTV Video Music Awards ceremony. After contractual negotiations, Gary Cherone became Van Halen's third lead singer. If the transition from Roth to Hagar was rocky, the Hagar to Cherone transition was even more so. Cherone, known mainly as half of the duo Extreme, had two pop hits in the early 1990's, "Hole Hearted" and "More than Words," that had teenage girls swooning and hard-rock fans rolling their eyes.

The first album from the third incarnation, *Van Halen III* (1998), debuted to lukewarm reviews, selling 100,000 fewer copies than *Balance* in its first week. In addition to Cherone's debut, *Van Halen III* was notable because Eddie performed the role of lead vocalist on the final track, "How Many Say I."

—*P. S. Ramsey*

SELECT DISCOGRAPHY
■ ALBUMS
Van Halen, 1978
Van Halen II, 1979
Women and Children First, 1980
Diver Down, 1982
1984, 1984
5150, 1986
OU812, 1988
For Unlawful Carnal Knowledge, 1991
Van Halen Live: Right Here, Right Now, 1993
Balance, 1995
Best of Van Halen, Vol. I, 1996
Van Halen III, 1998

SELECT AWARDS
Guitar Player, Eddie Van Halen named Best Rock Guitarist, 1979
Grammy Award for Best Hard Rock Performance with Vocal for *For Unlawful Carnal Knowledge*, 1991

SEE ALSO: Kinks, The; Kiss; Metallica.

For the Record

Van Halen might have featured Eddie on drums and Alex on guitar. When the boys' discovery of rock and roll effectively ended their interest in classical music, their parents compromised by letting Alex take flamenco guitar lessons. Not wanting to be left out, Eddie bought a drum kit with money from his paper route. However, every time his younger brother went out to deliver papers, Alex commandeered the drum set. Eventually Eddie relented and picked up the guitar.

Stevie Ray Vaughan

BORN: Dallas, Texas; October 3, 1954
DIED: East Troy, near Milwaukee, Wisconsin; August 27, 1990
FIRST ALBUM RELEASE: *Texas Flood*, 1983
MUSICAL STYLES: Texas blues, blues rock

Born to a musical family, Stevie Ray Vaughan grew up imitating his brother Jimmie (three years older than Stevie), another fine blues guitarist. Their father primarily supported Jimmie in his music, buying him instruments and records, a situation that drove Stevie to excel on his own.

The Vaughans and the Blues. The boys immersed themselves in the blues and copied songs and guitar parts from the latest singles. Stevie's prowess led to rivalry, but the brothers' tastes were similar. They disregarded the racial boundaries of the day by adopting the expressive style of the old acoustic-guitar tradition of Leadbelly and Blind Lemon Jefferson. However, they followed T-Bone Walker and Chuck Berry to the electric guitar.

Stevie was especially impressed with Lonnie Mack's hit singles of the mid-1960's, "Wham" and his version of Chuck Berry's "Memphis." Both were instrumentals in the blues tradition that displayed Mack's impressive double picking. "Wham" was a twelve-bar blues (the traditional blues form), but "Memphis" showed that the blues form could be expanded and the blues feeling kept intact. Mack recorded vocals, but the guitar stayed in front. Even more important, Mack's style was an early blues fusion: The newer blues styles accommodated fast playing and other technical displays over rock rhythms. The Vaughans became important contributors to the blues style. Though their devotion to the blues kept them in the background while British rock was at its peak, their blues-rock promised eventual fame and fortune. Jimmie Vaughan was a founder of the Fabulous Thunderbirds in 1974; they had a hit record with "Tuff Enuff" in 1986.

Career. Vaughan remained in Texas throughout his youth, working his way through several Dallas bands in which he pursued the Texas style and gained local fame. Like Jimi Hendrix,

Vaughan played a Fender Stratocaster guitar through Marshall amplifiers. Vaughan used a flat pick and relatively heavy strings on his Stratocaster, which was customized with jumbo frets for enhanced tone and sustain. The guitar's "heavy action" demanded a strong technique, but it enabled Stevie to play the clean phrases that became his trademark.

Vaughan formed several groups in Dallas while still in high school, and he played occasionally with his brother. Then Jimmie moved to Austin, the state capital and home of a thriving music scene. The lure of the limelight, adoring women, and unlimited substance abuse brought Stevie to Austin soon afterward, in 1972. Playing in groups that featured his guitar, he got up the courage to begin singing. Vaughan's guitar technique steadily improved, and as his groups had steadily fewer members he was able to fill out the sound by playing harmonies on guitar. The group Triple Threat became Double Trouble after the female singer left in the late 1970's. It was with Double Trouble that Vaughan finally achieved wide acclaim. Double Trouble began as a three-piece group with Chris Layton on drums and Jackie Newhouse on bass, but Tommy Shannon replaced Newhouse in 1981. Vaughan toured the Southwest often in the 1970's. With Double Trouble he eventually toured across the nation and finally played in Europe. In 1979 Vaughan married

---

For the Record

"He affected the way blues will be played and heard forever. . . . I've said that playing the blues is like having to be black twice. Stevie missed on both counts, but I never noticed." —*B. B. King*

§

"I didn't get to see or hear Stevie play near enough, but every time I did I got chills. . . . He seemed to be an open channel and music just flowed through him." —*Eric Clapton*

Lenora Baily in Austin (they were divorced in 1988).

In 1982 Vaughan and Double Trouble took the Montreux (Switzerland) Jazz Festival by storm, and David Bowie hired Vaughan to play on his *Let's Dance* album. Having just met legendary talent scout John Hammond, who promised a recording contract on Epic, Stevie declined Bowie's offer to tour worldwide in order to record Double Trouble's debut album, *Texas Flood*, released in 1983. Double Trouble released an album a year from 1983 to 1986. Keyboard player Reese Wynans joined the band in 1985. Late in 1986, Vaughan entered a treatment program and managed to beat his problems with drug and alcohol dependency. The group's, and Vaughan's, reputation steadily grew.

Vaughan's last concert was at Alpine Valley, a ski resort just south of Milwaukee that served as a summer concert venue. Eric Clapton organized the event for the last weekend in August, 1990, which was to stage outdoor performances in an amphitheater before thirty thousand fans. Several groups performed, including Jimmie Vaughan's band. Double Trouble performed the final night, on August 26, and stole the show. The evening ended in a blues jam with the entire cast (including such musicians as Clapton, Buddy Guy, and Robert Cray) and concluded with "Sweet Home, Chicago." Afterwards, the artists flew back to Chicago by helicopter. There was dense fog that night. Vaughan's helicopter got lost en route and hit a hill in East Troy, killing him, the crew, and several musicians in Clapton's band. Stevie Ray Vaughan was dead at the age of thirty-five.

Style. Though Stevie recorded and collaborated with many other performers, his masterworks came out with Double Trouble. A posthu-

Stevie Ray Vaughan (Paul Natkin)

mous sampler compact disc entitled *Greatest Hits* is representative. All its songs are worthy of note, and some contained historical precedents. "Texas Flood," the title track from his first album and his smash hit at Montreux, won Vaughan his first Grammy Award. It is a slow twelve-bar blues with triple subdivisions of the beat. The guitar plays a verse before the vocal entrance. Then as Vaughan sings, his guitar fills the ends of each phrase while Shannon on bass and Layton on drums walk along behind. The solo riffs cascade into vibrant phrases full of intense vibrato and soulful pitch-bending.

"The House Is Rockin'" is fast-paced, old-fashioned country rock with a honky-tonk piano tinkling in the background. To keep time, Shannon walks the bass on every eighth note. After the piano solo, Vaughan delivers a guitar lead full of double and triple stops.

"Pride and Joy" begins with a fragment from Robert Johnson's delta blues song "Hellhound on My Trail" but settles into a medium-tempo shuffle with the trio. Vaughan not only doubles the walking bass line with Shannon but also strums the chords on the upbeat to form a busy backup. On top of this, he fills in short riffs whenever he takes a breath in the vocal. "Little Wing," a Hendrix tune, won Vaughan another Grammy, this time for Best Rock Instrumental. It is a slow, hypnotic rock ballad. Vaughan's brilliant guitar tone sings on its own, and with it he explores such effects as suddenly changing dynamics, harmonics, octaves on the blues scale brushed with his thumb, cascading leads, and long trills. On "Couldn't Stand the Weather" Jimmie plays rhythm guitar and doubles the bass pattern. The song's chord voicings (its 7#9 chords) are a tribute to Hendrix.

Like rock's Jimi Hendrix or jazz's Charlie Parker (who also died at thirty-five), Stevie Ray Vaughan established a unique sound and technique. He imposed major technical innovations on the blues and left a legacy in his recordings that will forever be viewed as a turning point of Texas blues guitar. Vaughan has attracted a host of authors whose efforts will facilitate further study into his life and works. Admirers have transcribed his solos, first in guitar magazines, then in books from publisher Hal Leonard. Two detailed biographies appeared in 1993: Joe Nick Patoski and Bill Crawford's *Stevie Ray Vaughan: Caught in the Crossfire* and Keri Leigh's *Stevie Ray: Soul to Soul*. Each contains an index and a long list of articles, recordings, and videos. —*Richard Pinnell*

SELECT DISCOGRAPHY
■ ALBUMS
Texas Flood, 1983
Couldn't Stand the Weather, 1984
Soul to Soul, 1985
Live Alive, 1986
In Step, 1989
Family Style, 1990 (with Jimmie Vaughan)
The Sky Is Crying, 1991
In the Beginning, 1992

SELECT AWARDS
Grammy Award for Best Traditional Blues Recording for *Blues Explosion*, 1984 (with others)
W. C. Handy Blues Foundation Entertainer of the Year Award, 1985

Grammy Award for Best Contemporary Blues Recording for *In Step*, 1989
Grammy Awards for Best Rock Instrumental Performance for "D/FW" and Best Contemporary Blues Recording for *Family Style*, 1990 (both with Jimmie Vaughan)
Grammy Award for Best Rock Instrumental Performance for "Little Wing," 1992
Grammy Award for Best Contemporary Blues Album for *The Sky Is Crying*, 1992

SEE ALSO: Clapton, Eric; Cray, Robert; Hendrix, Jimi; Johnson, Robert; King, B. B.

Suzanne Vega

BORN: Santa Monica, California; July 11, 1959
FIRST ALBUM RELEASE: *Suzanne Vega*, 1985
MUSICAL STYLES: Alternative, folk, pop rock

One of the most respected and brilliant songwriters of her generation, Suzanne Vega has progressed in a short amount of time from a folk musician singing in coffeehouses to an artist few musicians can equal. Her influence has extended to such musicians as Edie Brickell, Michelle Shocked, Tracy Chapman, and Shawn Colvin, and she is credited with paving the way for the next generation of female artists. A careful lyricist, Vega is more interested in the quality of her music than in having a catchy, radio-ready single, and it is this self-piloted determinism that has established Vega as a true artist in a field populated by people simply hoping for the next hit record.

Early Influences. Vega's parents divorced shortly around her first birthday. Her mother would remarry in 1960 and the family would move to New York City, living in Hispanic neighborhoods. Vega learned to speak Spanish as well as English and flourished in a home environment that was a haven to artistic creativity. She began picking out guitar chords at age eleven and by age twelve was writing songs. She wrote down her thoughts in journals, discovering a natural ability to rhyme, and her stepfather advised her not to write with cliches but to be as honest as she could.

Vega had many influences early in her life. She sought inspiration from the great folk musicians of her day, including Joan Baez, Laura Nyro, and Woody Guthrie. Like many other musicians, she was also inspired by Bob Dylan, but her other major influence was Buddhism, which she credits as both being influential in her songwriting and enabling her to see her potential. In 1979 she began performing in Greenwich Village nightclubs including Gerde's Folk City, the club where Dylan made his professional debut. That same year, Vega attended a concert by veteran rock artist Lou Reed, whose style shocked her into realizing that she could write songs about her experiences and the people she saw around her. She also learned from Reed that music does not always have to make sense or tell a complete story.

First Recordings. Vega graduated in 1982 from Barnard College with a degree in English and continued her nighttime performing schedule in Greenwich Village, gaining the notice of critics. She was immediately compared to Joan Baez and other female folksingers, but she was also recognized as someone with a unique musical style, sound, and subject matter. She soon made her first album for A&M Records, *Suzanne Vega* (1985), which gained immediate attention. Critics hailed Vega as the clearest and freshest voice on the music scene in years. More than 750,000 copies were sold worldwide and *Rolling Stone* listed *Suzanne Vega* as one of the one hundred best albums of the 1980's. Despite all of this, Vega spent much of 1985 and 1986 in a state of writer's block, surprised by the sudden success she had achieved.

Luka. In 1987 things improved. Her writer's block lifted, Vega resumed writing and released *Solitude Standing*. Even though many of the songs on the album were written years earlier, they showed a consistent strength in her writing and proved that the fans and critics were not wrong. The album is best known, however, for one single it contained: "Luka," a song about child abuse. To everyone's surprise, "Luka" became a hit single around the world, receiving Grammy Award nominations for Record and Song of the Year and garnishing Vega with praise from children's advocates everywhere.

Vega's goal with "Luka" was not to create a song of self-pity but to write a song about a child who faces his sad situation with dignity. The situation in the song is never resolved, with the ambiguity causing the listener to consider all the possible outcomes that might occur. "The audience in the song is the neighbor," Vega said. "So it was kind of like writing a play. First of all, how do you introduce the character? You do that by saying, 'My name is Luka. I live on the second floor.' And then you get the audience involved, saying, 'I live upstairs from you. So you've seen me before.' You're incriminating . . . and you're involving the audience in it and that was what I wanted to do." "Luka" would become Vega's biggest hit.

New Styles and Directions. Vega has described her writing style as an association of random words and phrases, finding inspiration in children's nursery rhymes, street games, scientific and medical textbooks, and her own personal experiences and dreams. These sources are prominent in the 1990 release *Days of Open Hand*, an album that stretched Vega into new directions musically and stylistically. A mixture of folk and experimental melodies, the album was themed by songs of fortune-telling and dream imagery, with Vega utilizing exotic instruments such as the dumbek, tiple, and bouzouki to create the atmosphere she wanted.

For the Record

Suzanne Vega once worked with Pat DiNizio of the Smithereens at a typesetting sales and service company. "I was a receptionist/office administrator," Vega said, "and his job was to answer the phones in the morning. Sometimes people would call complaining . . . [because] he sounded like he didn't care about their problems with the equipment." Vega eventually had to fire him, but she later sang backup vocals on the Smithereens' *Especially for You* album.

With the 1992 release of *99.9F°*, produced by Mitchell Froom, Vega again entered new musical territory. While retaining some folk elements in songs such as "Bad Wisdom" and "Blood Sings," many of the songs combined Vega's sharp lyrics with an industrial sound that makes the album come alive. Some of the dance rhythms were inspired by the *Tom's Album* release the previous year, a collection of remakes of the "Tom's Diner" track from *Solitude Standing*. *99.9F°* has been compared to the Beatles' *Sgt. Pepper's Lonely Hearts Club Band* as being "a slice of perfection."

Vega and Froom married in March of 1995, and in 1996 she released *Nine Objects of Desire*, an album that added bossa nova rhythms and jazz themes to Vega's trademark style. Vega has described the album as being about seductions, and it is both more casual and intimate, reflecting Vega's marriage and the birth of her daughter, Ruby.

Vega has contributed to many projects over the years, including tribute albums of music originally recorded by the Grateful Dead, Leonard Cohen, and, in 1997, Laura Nyro. Nyro was one of her primary influences. Vega sang "Buy and Sell" and contributed a poem she wrote for Nyro in 1971 to the liner notes. In 1997 Vega also participated in the highly publicized Lilith Fair tour created by fellow musician Sarah McLachlan.

As one critic has written, Vega's songs are "cooly observed moments of deep emotion." Vega has continued to chart her own path regardless of whether she loses some of her audience or ever has another radio single. Vega shares a close kinship with musicians such as Tom Waits and Elvis Costello in the way she continually evolves her musical style, and she constantly pushes ahead while other musicians are just starting to catch up to her. —*Kelly Rothenberg*

SELECT DISCOGRAPHY
■ ALBUMS
Suzanne Vega, 1985
Solitude Standing, 1987
Days of Open Hand, 1990
99.9F°, 1992
Nine Objects of Desire, 1996

SEE ALSO: Baez, Joan; Chapman, Tracy; Costello, Elvis; Dylan, Bob; Jones, Rickie Lee; McLachlan, Sarah; Reed, Lou; Waits, Tom.

Velvet Underground

ORIGINAL MEMBERS: John Cale (b. 1942), Sterling Morrison (1942-1995), Lou Reed (b. 1942), Maureen "Moe" Tucker (b. 1945)
OTHER MEMBERS: Nico (born Christa Päffgen, 1938-1988), Doug Yule, others
FIRST ALBUM RELEASE: *The Velvet Underground and Nico*, 1967
MUSICAL STYLES: Rock and roll

Taking their name from a trashy pulp novel, the Velvet Underground formed in New York City in 1966. Despite the help of pop artist Andy Warhol, who produced the group's first album, the Velvet Underground failed to achieve commercial success and were relatively short lived. While the group's flame burned briefly, it also burned extremely brightly. Few groups can claim to be as historically important as the Velvet Underground, who were a primary influence on David Bowie, the Sex Pistols, R.E.M., the Violent Femmes, and virtually every other punk rock or alternative musician who has picked up an instrument since the late 1960's. Their importance stems from the extraordinary fusion of Lou Reed's poetic vision of despair and decay in urban America, John Cale's unflinchingly experimental approach to music, and the inventive support lent by Sterling Morrison and Maureen Tucker. The group provided an important musical expression of the dark side of New York and other large cities during the 1960's. Their songs explored difficult themes and provided a striking contrast to the generally positive tone of counterculture bands coming out of the West Coast during that time.

The Band Before Andy Warhol. The band formed around the talents of Cale and Reed. Reed studied creative writing at Syracuse University, while Cale, a classically trained violist and composer, was studying at the nearby Eastman School of Music. Cale provided a viola line for one of

Reed's songs, and the two began collaborating more frequently. In time, Morrison, another student at Syracuse University, joined the group. After the band had already been through several names, drummer Angus MacLise suggested that they name themselves the Velvet Underground. Soon after, he quit the group at a time when they were beginning to get paid for appearances at happenings in New York City because he opposed making money with their music. MacLise was replaced by Tucker, a childhood friend of Morrison.

Finally settling into a lineup made up of Reed (guitar and lead vocals), Cale (viola, bass, and piano), Morrison (guitar, organ, and bass), and Tucker (drums), the band began working more extensively in New York City at clubs catering to the avant-garde. Cale, who had worked previously with avant-garde composer La Mont Young, brought a profound experimental energy to the band that meshed extremely well with Reed's grounding in rhythm and blues. This fusion of experimentation and tradition earned the band a small but fanatically devoted following.

The Velvet Underground and Nico. On hearing the band, pop artist Andy Warhol agreed to promote them. Warhol had a brilliance for generating publicity and a wonderfully sly take on fame. One of his passions was promoting total unknowns. Toward this end, Warhol convinced the band to accept model and Warhol "superstar," Nico, as a singer. Nico's statuesque beauty, indifferent intonation, husky voice, and marginal grasp of English pronunciation combined to make her an unlikely vocalist. For many fans, however, Nico's work with the group resulted in some of their most outstanding songs. They began playing at Warhol's events, including the infamous Exploding Plastic Inevitable Media Show (1966).

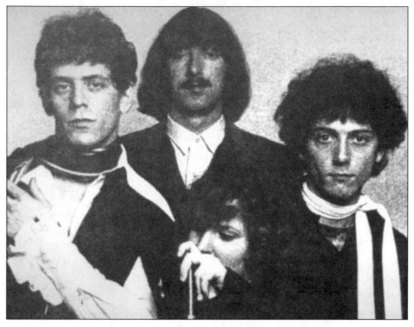

The Velvet Underground: Lou Reed, Sterling Morrison, Maureen Tucker, Doug Yule (Michael Shulman/Archive Photos)

The band's first album, *The Velvet Underground and Nico*, was recorded during the spring of 1966. The recording was rejected by several companies before landing with MGM/Verve Records. The album contained several controversial elements. The cover, designed by Warhol, featured a banana-shaped screen print that could be peeled off the sleeve. The band's frenetic instrumental postlude to "European Son" gave listeners a dose of atonal, screeching music that exuded a pure energy never heard before in popular music. Moreover, several songs dealt with delicate issues: "Venus in Furs" dealt with sadomasochism, and the title of the album's most powerful track, "Heroin," spoke for itself. Once released, the album climbed to only number 171 on the charts, was banned in New York City, and prompted a copyright suit initiated by an actor whose picture from a Warhol film appeared on the back cover without the actor's permission.

Critics spewed vitriol at the album, and radio executives steered almost entirely away from the band. Now considered a landmark album, *The Velvet Underground and Nico* constitutes one of the outstanding achievements in innovative rock and

For the Record

The song "Sister Ray" from the album *White Light/White Heat* was recorded on a single take and seems to have been loosely planned only minutes before the tape began rolling. The band was running out of studio time for their second album, but they only had five songs, barely enough for one side of an album. For "Sister Ray," they agreed to turn up their amplifiers all the way and just play around a loose framework. The result was much more interesting than the inauspicious circumstances would suggest. Lou Reed called the enterprise a homage to superb free jazz saxophonist Ornette Coleman.

roll. Tucker and Morrison were very credible and imaginative musicians, and every track benefited from their presence. Nico, who sang on only selected tracks, provided a singular contribution. Her slightly askew rendering of "I'll Be Your Mirror" revealed her at her best. Reed's lead guitar and imaginative songwriting were riveting. The song "I'll Be Your Mirror" best revealed Reed's asymmetrical and bleak lyric vision: "When you think the night has seen your mind/ Then you know you're twisted and unkind/ Let me stand to show that you are blind/ Please put down your hands/ 'Cause I see you." The song's vague poetry, simple and direct melody, and quiet, folklike guitar work hinted at the direction of Reed's eventual solo career. His somewhat traditional "There She Goes" demonstrated that his grounding in rock and roll was thorough and persuasive. Cale's experimentation shined brightest on "European Son" and in patches of improvisation on "Heroin." His reeling viola line on "The Black Angel's Death Song" hinted at his roots in the folk music of the British Isles.

Departures. Nico's unpredictable work habits prompted her exclusion from the band for their second album, *White Light/White Heat* (1968). She went on to an interesting solo career until her untimely death in 1988. With Nico's dismissal, Warhol lost interest in the band and played no further role. *White Light/White Heat* contained only six tracks, all of which offered a relentless intensity. Cale's experimental sensibility was especially in evidence in "Sister Ray," a seventeenminute song that was almost entirely improvised. The manic album topped out on the charts at number 199. Cale and Reed had been experiencing increasing dissatisfaction with each other. After the release of the album, their clash of styles led to Cale's removal from the band and the introduction of a more traditional bassist named Doug Yule.

With Cale's unhappy departure, the band changed direction. Their next two albums, *The Velvet Underground* (1969) and *Loaded* (1970), featured a much less aggressive musical style and little atonal experimentation. However, the same despairing lyricism from the earlier efforts remained. After reshaping the band around his vision, Reed quit even before the release of *Loaded*. With the departure of Reed, the band was essentially finished, although Yule recorded one more album under the Velvet Underground name. The album was so poor that it is almost never included on Velvet Underground discographies.

Legacy. During the 1970's, continued interest in the Velvet Underground prompted the release of two live recordings made during the 1960's while Cale and Reed were still in the band. The band released another album of previously unreleased material, *VU*, in 1985. This album became their most commercially successful release, hitting number 87 on the charts. This unlikely success fifteen years after the group effectively disbanded demonstrates how the Velvet Underground's stature has risen over the years. In 1993, a live recording was released that was made when the band reformed briefly with their original lineup and played several European shows. This reunion thrilled a new generation of fans with their frenzied and despairing music. In 1995, the band's five studio-recorded albums were released in a box of compact discs titled *Peel Slowly and See*. The death of Morrison in 1995 made future projects for the band unlikely as he was the only member to figure into every performance and recording since the band's inception. —*Michael Lee*

SELECT DISCOGRAPHY
■ ALBUMS
The Velvet Underground and Nico, 1967
White Light/White Heat, 1968
The Velvet Underground, 1969
Loaded, 1970
Live at Max's Kansas City, 1972
1969—Velvet Underground Live with Lou Reed, 1974
VU, 1985
Live MCMXCIII, 1993

SELECT AWARDS
Rock and Roll Hall of Fame, inducted 1996

SEE ALSO: Bowie, David; Reed, Lou; Sex Pistols, The; Violent Femmes, The; X.

The Ventures

ORIGINAL MEMBERS: Bob Bogle (b. 1937), Nokie Edwards (b. 1939), Don Wilson (b. 1937), Howie Johnson (d. 1988)
OTHER MEMBERS: Gerry McGee, Mel Taylor (1933-1996)
FIRST ALBUM RELEASE: *Walk, Don't Run*, 1960
MUSICAL STYLES: Rock and roll, pop

The best-selling instrumental group in rock-and-roll history, the Ventures helped standardize the four-piece format of the guitar band: lead guitar, rhythm guitar, bass, and drums. Their distinctive sound and deft interplay of guitars placed the group at the head of a burgeoning instrumental-rock movement in the early 1960's. After a string of groundbreaking hits, the group relied more on its marketing talents than musical vision to promote itself, but its lasting influence can be heard in the work of three decades of guitar bands ranging from the Beatles to the B-52's.

Classic Period. The Ventures were formed in Seattle, Washington, in 1959. The initial lineup consisted of cofounders Bob Bogle and Don Wilson on lead and rhythm guitars, respectively, Nokie Edwards on bass, and Howie Johnson on drums. Originally named the Versatones, the group issued its first single, the instrumental "Cookies and Coke," on its own Blue Horizon label after being turned down by Seattle's Dolton Records. To celebrate this joint financial undertaking, the group rechristened itself the Ventures. The single received little airplay until Bogle and Wilson convinced a Seattle disc jockey to use it as a lead-in to news breaks. After hearing the song on the radio, Dolton president Bob Reisdorff changed his mind and signed the group to his label. Their first single for Dolton was "Walk, Don't Run," a hard-driving rendition of the Jazzy Johnny Smith classic. The song soon became an international hit, peaking at number 2 on the *Billboard* singles chart in August, 1960. Sales of their premiere album, *Walk, Don't Run* (1960), were also strong, establishing the Ventures in a relatively new format.

The success of follow-up singles "Perfidia" (number 15) and "Ram-Bunk-Shush" (number 29), both included on the hit album *The Ventures* (1961), set the group apart from the one-hit bands common to the instrumental genre. Even without Top-40 singles, albums such as *Another Smash!!!* (1961) and *The Colorful Ventures* (1961) managed to sell a respectable ten thousand copies each. The latter album, a collection of songs with colors in the title (such as "Yellow Bird" and "White Sands") perhaps qualifies as one of the first rock-and-roll concept albums. The group was also quick to exploit the latest musical and social fads with releases such as *Twist with the Ventures* (1962), *Surfing* (1963), and *The Ventures in Space* (1964). By their ninth album, *The Ventures Play Telstar, the Lonely Bull* (1963), the group had largely abandoned singles to focus on the album market; a compilation of covers of other instrumental bands' hit singles, *The Ventures Play Telstar, the Lonely Bull* was both a bravura performance and an admission that the group's moment had passed. Their last groundbreaking release was the instructional *Play Guitar with the Ventures* (1965), a three-album set (plus one bass book) which included slow- and regular-speed versions of their songs and a booklet with chord diagrams, making it one of the first instructional records.

By 1964 the Ventures' four-piece format had become typical of the rock guitar band. The group's crisp, riff-laden sound had a direct influence on Beatles hits such as "I Feel Fine" and "Day Tripper" and the complex interplay of twin guitars provided a model for the Rolling Stones' Keith Richards and Brian Jones. While the Ventures briefly recaptured their former glory with the single "Walk, Don't Run '64" (number 8), a surf-guitar remake of their first and biggest hit, the instrumental era was coming to a close. The group itself was in a period of transition: Drummer Mel Taylor had replaced Howie Johnson, who was injured in an auto accident, and Edwards traded instruments with Bogle to become lead guitarist. Edwards's twangy blend of blues and country licks temporarily revived the group with searing guitar work on covers such as "The House of the Rising Sun" and Ventures-penned originals such as "Bird Rockers," both included on *Knock Me Out!* (1965). Yet Edwards's guitar work soon came to dominate the band, turning the other Ventures into a back-up band. Moreover, the group increasingly relied upon keyboards, horns, and a variety of stringed instruments to augment their sound—abandoning their original theory that less is more. As the 1960's continued, the group released albums with Dolton's parent company Liberty Records and tried to maintain its relevance with a string of ill-conceived albums such as *Super Psychedelics* (1967) and *Underground Fire* (1968).

Discovering Japan. While the Ventures were languishing domestically, they were more popular than ever in Asia. The group had first toured Japan in 1962 as a backup band for singer Bobby

Vee. However, by 1965 "Venturemania" rivaled "Beatlemania" in the island nation. The album *Live in Japan '77* captures the energy of the period and showcases the group's technical expertise. While instrumental music transcended the language barrier, the group also won favor with the Japanese for its emphasis on teamwork rather than individuality. No doubt the song arrangements, bare melodies with simple embellishment, also conformed to a musical tradition defined by the koto (a Japanese zither) and samisen (a Japanese instrument resembling a banjo). In 1972 the Ventures became the first foreign inductees in the Music Conservatory of Japan and by the 1990's had sold fifty million records in that nation alone. The group would remain a primary influence on Japanese rock and roll, and they have spawned a score of popular imitation bands such as the Osaka Ventures.

Hawaii Five-O and After. In 1968 Nokie Edwards left the band to pursue a solo career and to dabble in horsebreeding; he was replaced by Gerry McGee, a session musician who had recorded with Barbra Streisand and Elvis Presley. Ironically, the newcomer McGee played lead on the group's most well-known single, "Hawaii Five-O." The theme song for the television program reached number 4 on the *Billboard* singles chart in September, 1969, but did little to revive interest in the group, which had been buried by a twenty-eight-piece orchestra, complete with kettle drums. The group reached its creative nadir in the early 1970's when it recorded an album of television themes for United Artists, then released *New Testament* (1971), touted as the album on which "the Ventures sing!" After being dropped by United Artists, the Ventures established their own Tri-Dex label, but even with the return of Edwards in 1972, their recordings remained an uninspiring mix of easy listening and country-and-western covers. While the group would remain popular in Japan and Europe, interest in the United States only revived periodically: Bogle, Wilson, Taylor, and McGee recorded "Surfin' and Spyin'," written by Go-Go Charlotte Caffey in 1981, and the classic lineup's "Surf Rider" was included in the influential sound track of the 1994 film *Pulp Fiction*.

—*Luke A. Powers*

For the Record

The Ventures were the first group in rock-and-roll history to have a Top-10 hit with a remake of one of its own previous Top-10 hits: "Walk, Don't Run '64" (number 8) was a rerecording of the group's 1960 hit walk, Don't Run" (number 2).

SELECT DISCOGRAPHY
■ SINGLES
"Walk, Don't Run," 1960
"Perfidia," 1960
"Walk, Don't Run '64," 1964
"Hawaii Five-O," 1969
■ ALBUMS
Walk, Don't Run, 1960
The Ventures, 1961
Another Smash!!! 1961
The Colorful Ventures, 1961
The Ventures Play Telstar, the Lonely Bull, 1963
Surfing, 1963
Walk, Don't Run, Volume 2, 1964
The Ventures in Space, 1964
Play Guitar with the Ventures, Volumes 1-3, 1965
Knock Me Out! 1965
Super Psychedelics, 1967
Underground Fire, 1968
Hawaii Five-O, 1969
New Testament, 1971
Live in Japan '77, 1977

SEE ALSO: B-52's, The; Beatles, The; Eddy, Duane; Go-Go's, The.

The Village People

ORIGINAL MEMBERS: Victor Willis, Felipe Rose (b. 1954), Alex Briley (b. 1951), David Hodo (b. 1947), Glenn Hughes (b. 1950)
OTHER MEMBERS: Ray Simpson (b. 1952), Miles Jay, Randy Jones
FIRST ALBUM RELEASE: *Village People*, 1977
MUSICAL STYLES: Disco, pop

The Village People were never really a band in the traditional sense. There were no early days of artistic struggle, no desperate long climb to the top, and none of its members ever even tuned an instrument. The Village People were a concoction created by disco producer Jacques Morali. All of the group members were cast, much the way actors are cast for a film or play. Regardless, the Village People made a huge mark on the world of popular music, selling more than twenty-eight million albums at the height of their popularity.

A Producer's Work. The 1970's saw the advent of disco, which gave rise to the notion of producer as artist. Traditionally, in pop music, a band would bring in a producer to shape their albums and to help orchestrate arrangements during recording. However, with disco, the producer often wrote the songs, brought in vocalists and musicians for hire, and essentially was the driving force behind the release. The idea was not completely new; in the 1960's, Phil Spector, known for his wall-of-sound productions, brought in outside artists, such as Tina Turner, to perform on his own productions. In 1970's disco, this was standard procedure. Jacques Morali was one such producer cum artist.

In 1976, Morali moved from his native France to New York. His first hit was performed under the name the Ritchie Family, which was never an actual group. Their biggest song was a disco version of "Brazil" by Arriba Rosa. It earned him respect and some serious record label interest, but he needed an actual full-time group for any sort of true visibility and a record deal.

Morali first spotted Felipe Rose at a Greenwich Village, New York, gay bar called the Anvil. What set Rose apart was his outfit—full Native American garb complete with headdress and bells on his feet. Inspired by this, and a couple of other men dressed as a cowboy and a construction worker, Morali made a decision to come up with a group of macho stereotypes. This group would be the Village People.

Macho Men. For lead vocals, Morali brought in Broadway actor Victor Willis. Willis had previously starred in Broadway's *The Wiz* and became the Village People's first police officer character. Alex Briley, who assumed the role of soldier, provided backup vocals on the tracks. Morali immediately started work on two songs for his envisioned disco group, "Fire Island" and "San Francisco," which became their first hit single. The songs were designed for gay audiences. Greenwich Village itself had a large gay population, which is why the group was named the Village People. Their 1977 album, *Village People*, sold more than 200,000 copies. Mor-

The Village People (Archive Photos)

ali's next step was to find a permanent, complete lineup.

Auditions. Glenn Hughes, a toll-collector at Brooklyn's Battery Tunnel, went to the Village People audition on a dare and was chosen four hours later, becoming the group's biker character. David Hodo, who became the group's construction worker character, was an unemployed Off-Broadway performer. Randy Jones picked up the role of cowboy, while Felipe Rose, Morali's inspiration, completed the lineup with his American Indian role.

Life in Casablanca. Now a solid troupe of entertainers, the Village People's second album was released in 1978. *Macho Man* was a huge success at discos nationwide, staying on the pop charts for sixty-nine weeks. Several huge hits followed, including the international phenomenon "Y.M.C.A." Cowritten by Morali, Victor Willis, and Henri Belolo (one of Morali's frequent collaborators and the executive producer of the Village People), it went to number 2 on the charts.

In 1978 came a tremendous amount of activity for the Village People and Morali. He continued to produce works for the Ritchie Family and a male disco singer, Patrick Juvet. The Village People, meanwhile, had their hits. "In the Navy" reached number 3 in the United States and number 2 in the United Kingdom. Their record sales rose to the eighteen million mark.

Casablanca Records, the Village People's label, was a leading disco label in the 1970's. Home of such acts as Donna Summer and P-Funk, it lost steam early in the 1980's, when disco had passed its peak. Perhaps hoping to avoid an inevitable downfall and profit from the Village People while they were still big sellers, Morali sold his rights to the group to Bill Aucoin, manager of another high-profile group, Kiss. The Village People released another album, *Go West* (1979), and then a live album, *Live and Sleazy*.

In 1979, not long before the opening of their semiautobiographical film, *Can't Stop the Music*, starring the Village People as themselves, Bruce Jenner, and Steve Guttenberg, lead vocalist Willis left the band, hoping to begin a solo career. Ray Simpson, the brother of singer Valerie Simpson, took Willis's place. Simpson had previously sung backup on the Village People's recordings, and he made a smooth transition to main member.

After the Music. The film was a box office failure, released just as disco was falling out of favor. Rather than disband, the Village People shifted gears and discarded their disco sound and image. With 1980's *Renaissance* album, the Village People became "new romantics" along the lines of Duran Duran and Adam and the Ants. They now sported robotic makeup, flashy haircuts, and neon neckties. The album went gold in spite of this change in direction, but on 1982's *In the Street*, the Village People returned to their former macho-man images.

The single "Sex over the Phone" (1985) proved a minor hit for the band, and in 1989, disco became popular again in the southern United States. The group resumed touring, performing a seventy-five-city world tour in 1991. On Novem-ber 15, 1991, Morali died in his native France of complications from acquired immunodeficiency syndrome (AIDS).

By the 1990's, several members of the Village People had been replaced. Jones, the cowboy, was replaced by Jeff Olson, a former singer for the band Step Child. Hughes, the biker, retired from the group in 1997, with Eric Anzalone filling his shoes and leather chaps. Still touring into the late 1990's, the Village People would be one of disco's most endearing and enduring acts. A group which was created as a front for a disco producer managed to become a successful, independent musical entity.

—*Lawrence Ferber*

SELECT DISCOGRAPHY
■ ALBUMS
Village People, 1977
Macho Man, 1978
Cruisin', 1978
Go West, 1979
Live and Sleazy, 1979
Renaissance, 1980
In the Street, 1982
Greatest Hits, 1988 (compilation)

SEE ALSO: Duran Duran; KC and the Sunshine Band.

For the Record

Victor Willis, the Village People's lead vocalist until 1980, was married to *The Cosby Show*'s Phylicia Rashad. In fact, Jacques Morali produced her 1978 album, *Josephine Superstar*, on which the Village People sang backup vocals. She was known as Phylicia Allen at the time. Her marriage to Willis lasted from 1978 to 1980, during which time she opened for the Village People's shows.

The Violent Femmes

ORIGINAL MEMBERS: Gordon Gano (b. 1963), Brian Ritchie (b. 1960), Victor DeLorenzo (b. 1954)
OTHER MEMBERS: Guy Hoffman (b. 1954)
FIRST ALBUM RELEASE: *Violent Femmes*, 1983
MUSICAL STYLE: Alternative

The Violent Femmes was founded by bassist Brian Ritchie in Milwaukee, Wisconsin, in 1981. Much of the band's identity comes from the uniquely nasal voice of vocalist, guitarist, and songwriter Gordon Gano. Gano's songs cover a range of musical genres, from folk and bluegrass to reggae and gospel. The subject matter is equally diverse, ranging from ballads about psychotic behavior such as "Country Death Song" to exposés of society's failures in "America Is." Primarily an acoustic band, the Violent Femmes occasionally have brought in outside musicians to play specific instrumental parts to accent their jazzlike improvisational style. Influences include avant-garde composer Pierre Henry, experimental jazz composer and bandleader Sun Ra, and the Velvet Underground.

The First Decade. Gano, Ritchie, and drummer Victor DeLorenzo had been together as the Violent Femmes for less than one year when, in 1981, Pretenders guitarist James Honeyman-Scott heard them playing and asked them to open for a Pretenders concert. The Violent Femmes attracted more attention after *The New York Times* published a positive review of their 1982 performance as the opening act for Richard Hell at the Bottom Line in New York City. The band signed with Slash Records and, in 1983, released their self-titled debut album. *Violent Femmes* was a raw acoustic album filled with songs that humorously yet fearlessly explored themes of adolescent angst and sexuality. With anthems to teenage frustration such as "Add It Up," "Blister in the Sun," and "Kiss Off," the album quickly became an early alternative classic and eventually achieved impressive sales.

The follow-up album, 1985's *Hallowed Ground*, was somewhat less quirky than the debut, as the band moved toward a more traditional folk style. Lyrically, the album perplexed some of the Violent Femmes' fans, as Gano began introducing

For the Record

The Violent Femmes were the first alternative band to play Carnegie Hall in New York City. Their 1986 performance was apparently a little more than the Carnegie Hall staff was prepared to handle. Scores of fans rushed the stage, and the ushers were powerless to stop them. The band had to stop the show and clear the stage themselves.

Christian themes that harkened back to his strict Baptist upbringing. Songs such as "It's Gonna Rain," a lighthearted retelling of the story of Noah's Ark, were mixed in with darker songs about murder and suicide. The album also introduced the Horns of Dilemma, an ever-changing collection of backup musicians who played instruments ranging from traditional woodwinds and strings to toy pianos and combs with wax paper. The Violent Femmes' third album, *The Blind Leading the Naked*, was released in 1986 and continued the band's move toward a more mainstream sound while Gano toned down the Christian content of his lyrics. The songs themselves were stylistically more diverse than those on the previous albums, and the Horns of Dilemma became a major feature of the band's sound. Among the songs was a cover of T. Rex's "Children of the Revolution."

After a three-year lull during which band members worked on side projects, the Violent Femmes fulfilled their obligation to Slash Records with the release of *3* (1989), which marked an uninspired return to a simpler acoustic sound, and *Debacle: The First Decade* (1991), a compilation of songs culled from their first four albums. *Why Do Birds Sing?*, released on Reprise Records in 1991, continued where *3* had left off but stood as a more successful return to the three-piece acoustic style. The album included a cover version of Culture Club's hit song "Do You Really Want to Hurt Me?"

Rebirth. Shortly after the Violent Femmes released the compilation album *Add It Up (1981-1993)* on Warner Bros. Records in 1993, long-time drummer DeLorenzo quit the band to pursue a solo career. He was replaced by former BoDeans and Oil Tasters drummer Guy Hoffman. The following year, the new version of the Violent Femmes recorded *New Times* (1994) and released the album on Elektra Records. The album signaled the beginning of a new era for the band. Unlike Slash Records, which, according to Gano, kept pushing the band to "sound like R.E.M.," Elektra Records seemed to accept the Violent Femmes for who they were and gave them more creative control over their recordings. The result was an eclectic album produced by Gano and Ritchie that gained inspiration from such diverse musical styles as rock and roll, avant-garde jazz improvisation, and polka music.

In 1997, the Violent Femmes rerecorded "Blister in the Sun" from their debut album for the film *Grosse Point Blank* and its sound-track album on London Records. Because the original master recordings of the song had been lost after Castle Recording Studios in Wisconsin shut down and threw the tapes out, the song was rerecorded rather than simply remixed. The band and its anthem "Blister in the Sun" continued to rate highly among American youth. In an interview with the *Los Angeles Times*, Gano noted, "As I get older, the people listening to my music keep getting younger."   —*Donna Addkison Simmons*

SELECT DISCOGRAPHY
■ ALBUMS
Violent Femmes, 1983
Hallowed Ground, 1984
3, 1988
Why Do Birds Sing? 1991
Add It Up: 1981-1993, 1993
New Times, 1994

SEE ALSO: Velvet Underground, The.

Tom Waits

BORN: Pomona, California; December 7, 1949
FIRST ALBUM RELEASE: *Closing Time*, 1973
MUSICAL STYLES: Alternative, blues, folk, jazz, rhythm and blues, rock and roll

Born in the back of a taxi cab on the anniversary of the bombing of Pearl Harbor, Tom Waits holds the musical distinction of being enormously popular and respected while never having had a hit song on the radio. One of the most creative and talented songwriters in music, Waits's style puts him in a category that sets him apart from nearly all other musicians.

The Skid-Row Singer. Thomas Alan Waits was born December 7, 1949, in Pomona, California. At a young age Waits was already fascinated with music, teaching himself to play piano at a friend's house and recording lyrics he thought of in the middle of the night. Waits also taught himself to play a Gibson guitar and paid careful attention to the music he was listening to at the time—Cole Porter, Bing Crosby, and especially Bob Dylan, the wordsmith of his generation. Waits was also influenced by jazz greats Charlie Parker and Miles Davis, but would later be most inspired by Beat generation author Jack Kerouac.

In the early 1970's, Waits worked a variety of odd jobs, including one that would inspire a song on his second album: pizza maker at Napoleone's Pizza House in San Diego. He began recording the conversations he heard onto paper and discovered the music hiding within the stories by arranging them into songs. While playing at the Troubadour night club in Los Angeles, he was discovered by Herb Cohen, who was managing Frank Zappa's band the Mothers of Invention. Cohen offered Waits a recording contract.

Closing Time debuted in 1973 to critical acclaim but was most notable for the track "Ol' 55," later covered by fellow Elektra Entertainment/Asylum Records group the Eagles. A low-key combination of folk and blues, *Closing Time* introduced the persona with which Waits would be identified: a beatnik balladeer with a penchant for the down-and-out. His next album, *The Heart of Saturday Night* (1974), featured a tighter collection of songs and Waits as a performer more confident in his abilities. His singing and musical style on these first two albums resembled those of Randy Newman, but this would change by his next album.

Nighthawks at the Diner, Waits's first live album, appeared in 1975. A commercial and critical failure at the time of its release, the album captures Waits in his element at the point in his career where he had perfected his raconteur persona. Waits's natural penchant for storytelling and drawing the audience into his stories of frustrated love and sadness are nowhere better captured than here. It is on this album that Waits's signature "vocal sound" first appears, a rough, gravelly sound reminiscent of Louis Armstrong.

"Bad Liver and a Broken Heart." Waits began touring again in 1976 and found it harder and harder to write. Facing hostile audiences and ill treatment by fellow musicians, Waits fled to Europe. He performed in Amsterdam, Holland, and Copenhagen, Denmark, before going to London, England, where he spent two weeks writing songs. The results culminated in the brilliant 1976 recording *Small Change*. None of Waits's previous albums more eloquently captured the atmosphere Waits was painting with his music. The album reflected his experiences of the previous year in loungy sentiments, with the saving grace being the wonderfully evocative lyrics and Waits's own voice, gravelly from cigarettes, booze, and perhaps his own crafted persona. Recorded in five days, the album featured such songs as "Step Right Up" and "Bad Liver and a Broken Heart," Waits's response to people who thought he was a drunk simply because he sang about drunks.

His popularity and fame beginning to rise,

Waits released *Foreign Affairs* in 1977. Also recorded in five days with no overdubs, the album featured the instrumental "Cinny's Waltz" and a guest vocal by Bette Midler on "I Never Talk to Strangers." Even though Waits's sound was more polished on this album, he continued experimenting. *Blue Valentine* (1978) began incorporating rhythm and blues, though he continued to write about society's outcasts. *Blue Valentine* is perhaps most famous for having a photograph of Waits's then-girlfriend Rickie Lee Jones on the back cover. It also continued Waits's tradition of recording albums in less than a week, causing critics to respond that his albums sounded rushed.

Heartattack and Vine (1980) was the last album Waits recorded for Elektra Entertainment. By 1983 Waits had signed with Island Records and was producing his own music. During this period Waits began scoring motion pictures and met Kathleen Brennan, who was a script editor for Twentieth Century-Fox, while working on the film *One from the Heart* (1983). They subsequently married.

Reinvention. *Swordfishtrombones*, released in 1983, again radically redefined Waits's musical style much in the same way *Small Change* had seven years earlier. The album was a mixture of heavy rhythms, experimental noises, and a larger, full sound. Despite the at-times unconventional sounds and noises on the album, Waits held the songs together with his powerful lyrical ability and vocal style. In 1985 *Rain Dogs* was released, which featured Rolling Stones' guitarist Keith Richards on the song "Big Black Mariah" and also included the track "Downtown

Train," later a hit for Rod Stewart. With the 1987 release of *Frank's Wild Years* (taken from a song on *Swordfishtrombones* and based on a play written by his wife), Waits completed his initial trilogy of albums based on "found sound." His 1992 release *Bone Machine* received a Grammy Award for Best Alternative Album.

During this time Waits started accepting small acting roles in motion pictures. He played a drunken vagabond named Rudy, who was the quintessential Waits character, opposite Jack

Tom Waits (Archive Photos/Sandra Johnson)

Nicholson and Meryl Streep in the film *Ironweed* (1987) and continued to work on film scores, recording *Night on Earth* in 1992. Waits also collaborated with theater composer Robert Wilson on what came to be called "art musicals": *The Black Rider* (1993), which included a collaboration with writer William S. Burroughs, and *Alice* (1995), which was based on author Lewis Carroll and the rumors concerning his relationships with young girls. Both pieces premiered at the Thalia Theater in Hamburg, Germany. —*Kelly Rothenberg*

SELECT DISCOGRAPHY
■ ALBUMS
Closing Time, 1973
The Heart of Saturday Night, 1974
Nighthawks at the Diner, 1975
Small Change, 1976
Foreign Affairs, 1977
Blue Valentine, 1978
Heartattack and Vine, 1980
One from the Heart, 1982 (motion picture sound track)
Swordfishtrombones, 1983
Rain Dogs, 1985
Frank's Wild Years, 1987
Big Time, 1988
Night on Earth, 1992 (motion picture sound track)
Bone Machine, 1992
The Black Rider, 1993

SELECT AWARDS
Grammy Award for Best Alternative Album for *Bone Machine*, 1992

SEE ALSO: Dylan, Bob; Jones, Rickie Lee; Midler, Bette; Newman, Randy; Vega, Suzanne; Zappa, Frank / The Mothers of Invention.

Jerry Jeff Walker

BORN: Oneonta, New York; March 16, 1942
FIRST ALBUM RELEASE: *Circus Maximus*, 1967 (with Circus Maximus)
FIRST SOLO ALBUM RELEASE: *Mr. Bojangles*, 1968
MUSICAL STYLES: Folk, country, country rock

Jerry Jeff Walker helped create the progressive country sound in the early 1970's, a musical movement that included artists such as Willie Nelson and Kris Kristofferson.

Early Years. Given the name Ronald Clyde Crosby at birth, Walker came from a musical family. His grandparents performed in a square-dance band, and his mother and sister sang in a vocal group similar to the Andrews Sisters. Walker was inspired by the music of country pioneer Jimmie Rodgers and folk singer Woody Guthrie. After receiving his first guitar, a gift from his grandmother, at age thirteen, he played in several high school bands until he turned sixteen, when he dropped out of high school to travel around the United States. He earned money by "passing the hat" around to the customers after performing in bars.

Walker returned home to New York to complete his high school degree, which he earned in 1959. The following year, he left New York again to perform on the road, adopting the stage name Jerry Ferris before settling on Jerry Jeff Walker in 1966. Walker formed a band called Circus Maximus, which received a recording contract from Vanguard Records in 1967. The band settled in New York City and established a regional following for its "psychedelic folk-rock" but never earned a national reputation. The group disbanded in 1968.

Walker's first real success in the music industry came about as a result of his arrest for public intoxication in New Orleans in 1965. While in jail, he met a street dancer called "Bojangles." The encounter inspired him to write the song "Mr. Bojangles." In 1968, he performed the song live at a New York radio station with his friend Dave Bromberg. The disc jockey recorded the performance and played it regularly. Walker soon recorded a studio version of the song that did not sell well, but the Nitty Gritty Dirt Band's 1970 cover was a hit. Several performers, including Sammy Davis, Jr., later released versions of the song, which provided Walker with royalty income.

Walker released his first solo album, *Mr. Bojangles* (1968), and two other solo albums on the Atlantic Records label, but his career remained at

Jerry Jeff Walker in 1980 (Paul Natkin)

a standstill until he moved to Austin, Texas, in 1971. Distant from the demands of record company executives in New York, Los Angeles, and Nashville, the musical scene in Austin was relaxed, freewheeling, and experimental. Walker found the Austin environment congenial, and he played a leading role in the development of a new style of music, later called progressive country, that blended elements of country, folk, and rock music. In 1972, he recorded several tracks on a portable tape recorder with some friends. The resulting album, released in 1972 under the title *Jerry Jeff Walker*, captured the laid-back atmosphere of the Austin sound. The single "L.A. Freeway" became a minor hit.

¡Viva Terlingua! Walker established himself as one of the leaders of the progressive country movement in 1973 with the release of the live album *¡Viva Terlingua!* The album was recorded in a tiny bar in Luckenbach, a small town in the Texas Hill Country. Walker's announcement of a live concert costing only one dollar per person brought almost nine hundred people to the bar, including future Texas governor Ann Richards. The crowd grew so large that people hung from the rafters and stood outside the bar's windows to hear the music.

Far from marring the album, the crowd noise contributed to the loose, partying atmosphere that marked the progressive country attitude. Backed by a group of freelance Austin musicians billed as the Lost Gonzo Band, Walker sang in a rough voice that wandered out of tune. Two songs from the album became Texas anthems. Ray Wylie Hubbard's rowdy "Up Against the Wall Redneck Mother" inspired honky-tonk audiences to sing along. Gary P. Nunn's "London Homesick Blues," which sang the praises of Texas, became the theme song of the television program *Austin City Limits*.

The live album, which became Walker's best-selling record, entered the pop charts and made Walker a regional hero. Constant touring with the Lost Gonzo Band brought in substantial sums of money, allowing Walker to travel by private plane. However, Walker abused drugs and alcohol to such a degree that it damaged his reputation. While this casual attitude toward performing reflected yet another facet of the Austin music scene, fans grew weary of arriving at concerts only to discover that Walker was in no condition to play live. On a few occasions, angry fans beat him. Although he continued to release albums, including four with the Lost Gonzo Band before they went their separate ways in 1977, Walker saw his career faltering.

His difficulties were not merely the result of his substance abuse. During the late 1970's and early 1980's, Austin became an increasingly cosmopoli-

For the Record

The title of the album *¡Viva Terlingua!* was taken from a bumper sticker celebrating the annual chili cookoff held in Terlingua, Texas, that was slapped on the wall of the bar in Luckenbach.

tan city, and the small-town atmosphere that launched the progressive country movement faded as the city grew and its population became more urban in its outlook. In addition, Walker was frustrated with large record companies, which he believed were more interested in turning a profit than in producing quality music. He switched to Elektra Entertainment in 1978, and returned to MCA Records in 1981, recording his last album with that company in 1982.

Walker continued to tour, but he did not record again for another four years. In 1986, he and his wife Susan formed their own record label, Tried and True Music. In addition to starting his own company, Walker abandoned the wild life, taking up jogging, golf, and health food. The Walkers had two children, and Walker found family life and parenthood satisfying. He recorded most of his 1986 album, *Gypsy Songman*, in the family home. Fans discovered the impact of Walker's lifestyle change in 1989, when they gathered in Gruene, Texas, for the recording of another live album. Audience members were asked to remain seated, sing along only if invited, and abstain from alcohol for the first half of the concert. Walker included several romantic ballads in the show, an indication of the importance of his wife Susan in his life.

During the 1990's, Walker remained a popular performer, playing at one of President Bill Clinton's inaugural balls and touring in Europe and the Caribbean. His fan club claimed over forty thousand members known as the Tried and True Warriors. He was also a prolific recording artist, releasing his twenty-eighth album, *Cowboy Boots and Bathin' Suits*, in 1998. His continued success

was the result of his adherence to the singer-songwriter tradition and his willingness to depart from the recurring fads that typify the country music industry.   —*Thomas Clarkin*

SELECT DISCOGRAPHY
■ ALBUMS
Circus Maximus, 1967 (with Circus Maximau)
Mr. Bojangles, 1968
Jerry Jeff Walker, 1972
¡Viva Terlingua! 1973
Contrary to Ordinary, 1978
Cowjazz, 1982
Gypsy Songman, 1986
Live at Gruene Hall, 1989
Great Gonzos, 1991 (previously released material)
Hill Country Rain, 1992
¡Viva Luckenbach! 1993
Cowboy Boots and Bathin' Suits, 1998

SEE ALSO: Guthrie, Woody; Kristofferson, Kris; Nelson, Willie.

The Wallflowers

ORIGINAL MEMBERS: Jakob Dylan (b. 1969), Tobi Miller, Rami Jaffee (b. 1969), Barrie Maguire, Peter Yanowitz
OTHER MEMBERS: Michael Ward (b. 1967), Greg Richling (b. 1970), Matt Chamberlain, Mario Calire (b. 1974)
FIRST ALBUM RELEASE: *The Wallflowers*, 1992
MUSICAL STYLES: Rock, pop, alternative

Fronted by singer-songwriter and guitarist Jakob Dylan, son of the legendary Bob Dylan, the Wallflowers were part of a wave of roots-oriented rock bands that emerged in the late 1990's. The group scored a big success with their sophomore effort, *Bringing Down the Horse*, which spawned several hit singles and won two Grammy Awards.

The Beginnings. The youngest of five children raised by Bob Dylan and his wife, Sara Lowndes, Jakob Dylan grew up in California and was eight years old when his parents divorced. After high school graduation, he headed east to attend the Parsons School of Design in New York. While there, he played guitar in various bands. In 1989, after moving back to California, Dylan started a band, with guitarist Tobi Miller, called the Wallflowers. The duo added drummer Peter Yanowitz, keyboardist Rami Jaffee, and bassist Barrie Maguire to the lineup and began to play the Los Angeles club circuit.

They found a second home in an unlikely spot, the Kibitz Room at Canter's Deli, a famous L.A. spot, regularly appearing at the Tuesday-night jam sessions there. At this point in his fledgling career, Dylan was reluctant for the audience to discover his famous heritage; one of his bandmates, the story goes, did not even learn the identity of Dylan's famous father until nearly two months after joining the group.

A Shaky Debut. The Wallflowers signed a contract with Virgin Records, and in August, 1992, they released a self-titled debut album, which featured the single "Ashes to Ashes" (the song was an original tune, not a cover of the David Bowie song of the same name.) Although the release garnered generally good reviews, the album sold only forty thousand copies.

The band decided to leave Virgin a few months later, when the executives who had signed them left the label. This was followed by a period of growing pains common to young bands. Drummer Yanowitz moved on to play with Natalie Merchant, and other personnel changes followed. Core members Dylan and Jaffee began to search for a new label and to recruit new bandmates—lead guitarist Michael Ward, a founding member of the L.A. band School of Fish, and bassist Greg Richling, a high school friend of Dylan. Drum-

mer Matt Chamberlain, who had briefly played with Pearl Jam, later joined the group. Despite these major lineup changes, the members agreed to keep their original name.

Their Big Break. The revamped Wallflowers, using Dylan's songwriting, began playing gigs around Los Angeles and marketing a demo of a song called "6th Avenue Heartache." They were signed by Interscope Records and headed into the studio. This time, they had T-Bone Burnett, a longtime friend of the Dylan family, as producer,

The Wallflowers: Michael Ward, Mario Calire, Greg Richling, Jakob Dylan, Rami Jaffe (Reuters/Stringer/Archive Photos)

along with a slew of guest musicians, including Adam Duritz of Counting Crows, Mike Campbell of the Heartbreakers, Gary Louris of the Jayhawks, Michael Penn, and Sam Phillips. Also contributing was veteran musician Leo LeBlanc, who died shortly after the recording was finished; the album is dedicated to him.

Released in 1996, *Bringing Down the Horse* produced three hit singles, "6th Avenue Heartache," "One Headlight," and "The Difference," and went on to sell more than three million copies. The group won two Grammy Awards, for Best Rock Song and Best Rock Performance, for "One Headlight." After the album was recorded, drummer Chamberlain left the band and was replaced by Mario Calire.

Newfound Success. The band spent much of 1996 and 1997 on the road, capitalizing on the album's success. They also began to enjoy the trappings of their newfound celebrity. They taped an episode of *MTV Unplugged* and welcomed guest stars such as Carly Simon, Levon Helm, and Bruce Springsteen to their live shows.

In 1998, the band recorded a cover of David Bowie's "Heroes" for the sound track to the movie *Godzilla.*　　　　　*—Robert DiGiacomo*

SELECT DISCOGRAPHY
■ ALBUMS
The Wallflowers, 1992
Bringing Down the Horse, 1996

For the Record

Jakob Dylan usually declines to discuss his famous father publicly. "I've chosen not to," he has said. "I'm never running away from anything. I always found it to be a distraction—the questions of what he was like as a parent. That's asking what the parent is like, not what the child is like. They should ask him. I find myself crossing the lines if I choose to talk about it. It could be disrespectful."

SELECT AWARDS
Grammy Awards for Best Rock Song and Best Rock Performance by a Duo or Group with Vocal for "One Headlight," 1998

SEE ALSO: Dylan, Bob.

War

ORIGINAL MEMBERS: Harold Brown (b. 1946), Papa Dee Allen (b. Thomas Sylvester Allen, 1931-1988), B. B. Dickerson (b. 1949), Leroy "Lonnie" Jordan (b. 1948), Charles Miller (1939-1980), Eric Burdon (b. 1941), Lee Oskar (b. 1948), Howard Scott (b. 1946)
OTHER MEMBERS: Peter Rosen, Alice Tweed Smith, Luther Rabb, Pat Rizzo, Ronnie Hammon, Ricky Green, Tetsuya "Tex" Nakamura, Rae Valentine (b. Harold Rae Brown, Jr.), Sal Rodriguez, Charles Green
FIRST ALBUM RELEASE: *Eric Burdon Declares "War,"* 1970
MUSICAL STYLES: Funk, jazz

A unique combination of funk, jazz and Latin strains—and the help of an Animal—made War one of the hottest funk bands of the 1970's. War began as a high school band in California in 1962. By 1965, cofounders Harold Brown and Howard Scott had teamed with Lonnie Jordan, B. B. Dickerson, and Charles Miller to form the Creators, who played West Coast nightclubs and opened for acts such as Ike and Tina Turner. When Scott was drafted and Dickerson moved to Hawaii, the band expanded its horn section, added percussionist Papa Dee Allen (who had worked with Dizzy Gillespie), and continued to work under the name Nightshift.

War Forms. Around 1969, producer Jerry Goldstein invited Eric Burdon, former lead singer of the Animals and a bona fide star, to hear the band. He liked what he heard, and after some initial sessions, he and friend Lee Oskar, a gifted Danish harmonica player, joined Nightshift to form War. (Scott and Dickerson had also returned.) Their first album, *Eric Burdon Declares*

For the Record

When producer Jerry Goldstein introduced Eric Burdon to War, they were backing Los Angeles Rams hall-of-famer Deacon Jones in his ill-fated attempt to establish a singing career.

"War," (1970), went to number 18. "Spill the Wine" (number 3, 1970) was a Top-10 hit. With a hugely successful European tour in the fall of 1970, War seemed poised to become one of the dominant pop bands of the 1970's. With the sudden death of Jimi Hendrix in September, 1970, however, Burdon abruptly left the band, and they finished the tour on their own.

Overnight, War lost the dynamic lead singer who had seemed to be the key to their success. Forced to rely upon the innovative musical style which had initially attracted Burdon's attention, they nevertheless proved adept at creating a musical experience that did not require a dominant vocal lead. In part this was a result of the group's stability, for they kept the entire band intact from the time Burdon left until the departure of Dickerson in 1979.

Between 1972 and 1977, they produced seven Top-20 albums, all of which went gold or platinum. Their big breakthrough came in 1972 when *The World Is a Ghetto* went to number 1 for two weeks and spawned hit singles "The World Is a Ghetto" (number 7) and "The Cisco Kid" (number 2). Over the next four years, they had four more Top-10 hits: "The Gypsy Man" (number 8, 1973), "Why Can't We Be Friends?"(number 6, 1975), "Low Rider" (number 7, 1975), and "Summer" (number 7, 1976). Their last significant single was "Galaxy," which went to number 39 in 1977.

Rise and Fall. With commercial success came the inevitable flood of special projects, including work on the sound track for the film *The River Niger* (1978). Their only album for Blue Note records, *Platinum Jazz* (number 23, 1977), was a compilation of three tracks from *The River Niger* and other previously released or recorded cuts. Having lost their audience to disco in the late 1970's and having been disrupted by numerous personnel changes after 1979, War was unable to regain their mass appeal and eventually split with producer Goldstein in the mid-1980's. They nevertheless continued to tour.

By the late 1980's, War's reputation was being enhanced by the frequent sampling of their tunes by a variety of rappers. This led to the album *Rap Declares War* (1992), featuring a bevy of hip-hop stars. After adding several musicians, including Harold Brown's son, Rae Valentine, and reuniting with Goldstein, War returned to the recording studio in 1994 with *Peace Sign*, featuring harmonicist Lee Oskar and singer José Feliciano.

—John Powell

SELECT DISCOGRAPHY
■ ALBUMS
The Black-Man's Burdon, 1970
War, 1971
Deliver the Word, 1973
War Live! 1974
Why Can't We Be Friends, 1975
War's Greatest Hits, 1976 (compilation)
Love Is All Around, 1976 (session music recorded with Eric Burdon in 1969)
Galaxy, 1977
The Music Band, 1979
Outlaw, 1982
Peace Sign, 1994
War Anthology 1970-1994, 1994 (compilation)

SEE ALSO: Animals, The / Eric Burdon.

Dionne Warwick

BORN: East Orange, New Jersey; December 12, 1940

FIRST SINGLE RELEASE: "Don't Make Me Over," 1962

MUSICAL STYLES: Pop, jazz, gospel, rhythm and blues

A Grammy Award-winning singer with a distinctive, captivating voice, Marie Dionne Warwick was

Dionne Warwick (Archive Photos)

born the eldest of three children to Marcel and Lee Warwick. She was raised in a pious Methodist home located in a racially integrated community in Orange, New Jersey. Warwick's parents were associated with the music business. Her mother served as business manager for the Drinkard Singers, a popular gospel group which consisted of family members and relatives. Her father worked for Chess Records as a gospel music promotion director. Since Warwick's parents recognized her musical talent early, they arranged for her to take vocal training during most of her youth.

Gospel Influence. When Warwick was growing up, she was always surrounded by gospel music, which influenced her musical development. She was only six when she joined the New Hope Baptist Church choir in Newark, New Jersey, where her parents were members. Later, during her teenage years, she occasionally served as a pianist, an organist, and a substitute vocalist with the Drinkard Singers. Professionally the group toured

for several years and gained recognition as one of the most successful gospel groups in the United States, becoming the first of its type to record for RCA Victor and the first to perform at the Newport Jazz Festival. In 1954, Warwick, Dee Dee (her sister), and Cissy Houston (her cousin and later mother of Whitney Houston) started their own group, the Gospelaires. Since Warwick was the only one in the group who could read music, she became the leader. The trio performed together for seven years, mostly as backup singers.

Aspiring to become a music teacher, Warwick, in 1959, enrolled in the Hartt College of Music at the University of Hartford on a four-year scholarship. Meanwhile, she kept singing with the group during her spare time, especially during the summers. The Gospelaires performed as backup singers for several groups, which included the Drifters and Sam "The Man" Taylor at the Apollo Theatre in Harlem, New York, as well as at several other black theaters and recording studios.

Achieved Recognition. In 1960 Warwick attracted the attention of Burt Bacharach, a composer-arranger, during a recording session, while he was conducting the Drifters along with the Gospelaires as backup singers. They were doing a rendition of Bacharach's "Mexican Divorce." Warwick's voice and persona made an impression on Bacharach; he started a partnership with Warwick and Hal David, his lyricist. (Because of some business disagreements, the trio later split up in 1972. In 1986 Bacharach and Warwick reconciled, since Warwick was among the few who could sing some of Bacharach's unusual compositions to his satisfaction.) In 1962 the trio entered into an agreement with Scepter Records and recorded "Don't Make Me Over," which made the Top 40 on the pop charts. The trio continued to be successful, recording about thirty other hits. In 1963 Warwick decided to terminate her studies at Hartt School and concentrate on her career. Warwick, with the influence of Paul Cantor, her manager, and Bacharach, embarked on a series of successful concert tours. Her first major tour was in France, where she was tremendously well received. She spent most of 1963 there. While in Paris, she became known as "Paris's Black Pearl."

Transitional Period. The mid-1970's marked a transitional period for Warwick. In 1972 she terminated her relationship with Bacharach and David when she learned of the Bacharach-David breakup from a newspaper article. Deeply hurt and disappointed, she began legal procedures which involved a suit for breach of contract. There were also changes in her personal life. In 1975 she divorced Bill Elliot, a drummer-actor and father of their two sons, whom she had married in 1967. Subsequently, in 1977 Warwick learned of the unexpected death of her father, followed by the stroke of her mother the next day. From a professional viewpoint, Warwick was not having as many hits as she had anticipated. Formerly, during the course of a year, she would have two or three hits. Between 1972 and 1979, she had only three hits, which included "Then Came You" (number 1, 1974) and "I'll Never Love This Way Again" (number 5, 1979).

Warwick also showed concern for political and social issues. She sang, along with forty-four other performers known as USA for Africa, "We Are the World" (1985), a song which was recorded for the purpose of raising funds for hunger relief in Africa. Moreover, Warwick, along with Elton John, Gladys Knight, and Stevie Wonder, recorded "That's What Friends Are For" (1985), written by Burt Bacharach and his wife, Carole Bayer Sager. The proceeds, which netted in excess of 1.5 million dollars, were given to the American Foundation for Acquired Immunodeficiency Syndrome (AIDS) Research (AMFAR). Two years later, she organized several concerts with friends to further support AIDS research; she also started the Warwick Foundation to provide additional support.

Dionne Warwick, who has shared her distinctive talent unwaveringly and altruistically, is truly a remarkable woman. Her musical talent has earned her international acclaim.

—*Nila M. Bowden*

SELECT DISCOGRAPHY

■ SINGLES
"Walk on By," 1964
"Message to Michael," 1966
"Alfie," 1967
"I Say a Little Prayer," 1967
"(Theme from) *Valley of the Dolls*," 1968
"Do You Know the Way to San Jose," 1968
"Promises, Promises," 1968
"I'll Never Fall in Love Again," 1970
"Then Came You," 1974 (with the Spinners)
"I'll Never Love This Way Again," 1979
"That's What Friends Are For," 1985 (with Elton John, Gladys Knight, and Stevie Wonder)

■ ALBUMS
The Windows of the World, 1967
Dionne in the Valley of the Dolls, 1968
Dionne Warwick's Golden Hits Part I, 1968
Dionne Warwick's Golden Hits Volume 2, 1970
The Dionne Warwick Story, 1971
Then Came You, 1975
Dionne, 1979
Hot! Live and Otherwise, 1981
How Many Times Can We Say Goodbye, 1983
Friends, 1985
Reservations for Two, 1987
Dionne Warwick Sings Cole Porter, 1990

SELECT AWARDS
Grammy Award for Best Contemporary Pop Vocal Performance, Female, for "Do You Know the Way to San Jose," 1968
Grammy Award for Best Contemporary Vocal Performance, Female, for "I'll Never Fall in Love Again," 1970
Grammy Awards for Best Pop Vocal Performance, Female, for "I'll Never Love This Way

For the Record

Dionne Warwick's albums sold five million copies, and her singles sold more than six million copies six years after she signed with Scepter Records in 1962. "Valley of the Dolls," a single, and three of the albums became gold records.

§

In 1968 Warwick set an attendance record by attracting an audience of nineteen thousand at the Newport Jazz Festival.

Again" and Best R&B Vocal Performance, Female, for "Deja Vu, 1979
Hollywood Walk of Fame, star awarded 1985
Grammy Award for Best Pop Performance by a Duo or Group with Vocal for "That's What Friends Are For," 1986 (with Elton John, Gladys Knight, and Stevie Wonder)
National Association for the Advancement of Colored People (NAACP) Key of Life Award, 1990

SEE ALSO: Drifters, The; Houston, Whitney; John, Elton; Knight, Gladys, and the Pips; Wonder, Stevie.

Muddy Waters

(McKinley Morganfield)

BORN: Rolling Fork, Mississippi; April 4, 1915
DIED: Chicago, Illinois; April 30, 1983
FIRST SINGLE RELEASE: "Rollin' Stone," 1950
MUSICAL STYLE: Blues

Born McKinley Morganfield on a Mississippi cotton plantation, Muddy Waters became the most influential blues guitarist and songwriter in post-World War II Chicago by adding electric guitar to creative ensembles he organized in Chicago's South Side clubs. He began his career in 1930 as a country-blues singer with an acoustic guitar, and he became considered a seminal figure in the creation of the urban rhythm-and-blues (or Chicago blues) style linking traditional blues to the new urban blues genre.

Early Life. Waters, who was raised by his grandmother after his mother died when he was three, learned to sing in the Mississippi cotton fields and the Baptist church. The African call-and-response forms, field hollers (improvised work songs of African Americans), and work songs characteristic of the blues influenced much of his music. He could play harmonica by age eight and acoustic guitar by age thirteen. Known as Muddy as a boy for playing on a muddy river bank, he was recorded by folklorists John and Alan Lomax for the Library of Congress Archives of American Folksong in 1942, long before he became popular. These were Waters's first recordings and document his roots as a Mississippi Delta blues man.

Chicago. His performing career began at house parties and fish fries with a Clarksville, Mississippi, band, while working on a farm for fifty cents per day. Influenced by Delta blues masters Robert Johnson, Willie Brown, and Son House on the slide guitar, Waters discovered his professional ambition playing on Clarksville street corners. He moved to Chicago's South Side ghetto in 1943. Living with relatives and working in a paper factory, he played Saturday night house parties and quickly moved to local clubs and lounges patronized by Deep South audiences lonesome for their Delta homes. In order to make his music heard in the noisy and sometimes violent clubs, Waters switched to an electric guitar in 1943 and added harmonica, drums, and piano to his group, which defined the new blues sound.

His importance in transforming Mississippi Delta folk blues into Chicago's electrified city blues cannot be overlooked. His broad sound, robust rhythm, and steely electric guitar virtuosity expanded with an ensemble including Little Walter, who first played an amplified harmonica, and blues greats such as Big Walter Horton, James Cotton, Jimmy Rodgers, A. C. Reed, and Willie Dixon. From 1947 to 1952 Waters played Chicago clubs and made records, at the urging of his sideman Dixon, for Chess Records in Chicago,

For the Record

After Muddy Waters performed at the annual White House staff picnic in 1978, President Jimmy Carter said of him, "Muddy Waters is one of the great performers of all time. He's won more awards than I could name. His music is well known around the world, comes from a good part of the country, and represents accurately the background and history of the American people."

changing the old-time rural blues style with a melodic pattern matching the rhythm. Dixon also wrote some of his best songs for Waters, especially "The Seventh Son," "Hoochie Coochie Man," and "I Just Want to Make Love to You." Together they wrote "Whole Lotta Love."

As black radio stations played these hit records, his fame spread to other cities. With Junior Wells on the harmonica and Otis Spann on the piano, the group prospered in 1953, when Waters took the band to Nashville and St. Louis for the first time. His sidemen over the years comprise a who's who of the blues. Waters did not have an agent until 1954, when he began developing black audiences while on tours in the South, sometimes with Betty Carter or Sarah Vaughan, as well as one-night performances in small clubs and dance halls. Although his career was well established, like most blues men, he earned few record royalties and performed continually to make a home in Chicago for his wife Geneva and their children.

Muddy Waters (Michael Ochs Archive)

The Blues. As segregation subsided in the 1950's, black or "race" records were played on some white radio stations, and for a time Muddy Waters became a crossover rhythm-and-blues star, but his raw and muscular style used a slow beat too heavy for rock-and-roll dancing, thus denying it mainstream popularity. He toured England in 1958 but found Elvis Presley and Jerry Lee Lewis were more popular with young British audiences who considered Waters's sound too loud. However, his records aroused interest in some British clubs that specialized in rhythm and blues, and his influence was significant on the Beatles, the Rolling Stones, Led Zeppelin, and Eric Clapton, well before rock musicians in the United States discovered the rich Chicago blues sound cultivated by

Record Row studios, distributors, and night clubs on South Michigan Avenue.

In 1960 Waters played the Newport Jazz Festival to great acclaim, and Chess Records released *Muddy Waters at Newport* later that year, attracting new white, middle-class jazz and folk audiences. In 1962 Waters made a second tour of England and received a much warmer reception than the first time. When Mick Jagger named his Rolling Stones group after Waters's 1950 hit song "Rollin' Stone" and recorded his song "Just Make Love to Me," Waters's fame spread to young American audiences.

Live. The blues revival was in full swing in 1962, when Bob Messinger scheduled Waters at a Boston jazz club, his first club date in the Northeast. He was an immediate hit with young audiences who discovered the blues from rhythm-and-blues and folk records. Messinger became Waters's manager, opening college and folk coffeehouses to his band and others from Chicago. After the

Newport Folk Festival, Waters played both the Apollo Theatre in Harlem, New York, and college campuses.

White blues artists such as Mike Bloomfield and Jeff Beck imitated Muddy Waters with a thunderous beat and volume unlike his own. The advent of soul music in the 1970's cost Waters much of his black audience, but he remained popular with whites, especially when he performed with guitarist Buddy Guy and Junior Wells on harmonica. However, black audiences preferred soul to the blues, which were considered low class or old-fashioned. Although popular, Waters never achieved the commercial success many of his imitators earned, sometimes by covering his own songs.

On stage, Muddy Waters was sober, well dressed, and eloquent, despite his lack of formal education. He was a compelling physical performer singing about joy, suffering, love, and work with a rocking backbeat and down-home intensity. His album *They Call Me Muddy Waters* won a Grammy Award (the first of six) for Best Ethnic or Traditional Recording in 1971, and his career enjoyed a resurgence with his productive collaboration with producer-guitarist Johnny Winter in the mid-1970's. Muddy Waters made international tours throughout the 1970's and early 1980's, recapturing his place as the dominant force in modern blues. Winter produced four of his albums for Blue Sky records, and three of them, *Hard Again* (1977), *I'm Ready* (1978), and *Muddy "Mississippi" Waters Live* (1979), won Grammy Awards and revived his career. Only after his death from heart disease was he recognized as the patriarch of the Chicago blues and a major influence on modern American music. Musicians from Chuck Berry to Bob Dylan, Jimi Hendrix, and Mick Jagger paid respect to Muddy Waters's legacy as a guitarist, songwriter, singer, stage performer, and recording artist.   —*Peter C. Holloran*

SELECT DISCOGRAPHY
■ ALBUMS
Electric Mud, 1968
The London Muddy Waters Sessions, 1972
Hard Again, 1977
I'm Ready, 1978
King Bee, 1981

SELECT AWARDS
Grammy Award for Best Ethnic or Traditional Recording for *They Call Me Muddy Waters*, 1971
Grammy Award for Best Ethnic or Traditional Recording for *The London Muddy Waters Sessions*, 1972
Grammy Award for Best Ethnic or Traditional Recording for *The Muddy Waters Woodstock Album*, 1975
Grammy Award for Best Ethnic or Traditional Recording for *Hard Again*, 1977
Grammy Award for Best Ethnic or Traditional Recording for *I'm Ready*, 1978
Grammy Award for Best Ethnic or Traditional Recording for *Muddy "Mississippi" Waters Live*, 1979
Rock and Roll Hall of Fame, inducted 1987
Grammy Award for Lifetime Achievement, 1992

SEE ALSO: Berry, Chuck; Clapton, Eric; Dixon, Willie; Dylan, Bob; Guy, Buddy; Hendrix, Jimi; Howlin' Wolf; Rolling Stones, The.

Doc Watson

BORN: Stoney Fork Township, North Carolina; March 2, 1923
FIRST ALBUM RELEASE: *Doc Watson and His Family*, 1963
MUSICAL STYLES: Folk, country

Arthel "Doc" Watson is one of the United States' renowned and influential folk and country guitar players. Watson was born in Stoney Fork Township near what is now Deep Gap, North Carolina. His father, General Dixon Watson, was a laborer and farmer who played banjo and sang, and his mother, Annie Watson, instilled in Arthel a love for church hymns at an early age. While music was an important part of the Watson family's life, it is unlikely that Arthel Watson would have become a professional musician had he not gone blind as a baby as a result of an eye infection.

Playing Music. Watson was given his first instrument, a harmonica, when he was five years old. At age eleven, he started playing the banjo. As a teenager, Watson attended the North Carolina School for the Blind in Raleigh, North Carolina, where a friend taught him several guitar chords. After his father heard Watson playing on a borrowed guitar, he went off to town, promising to buy his son a guitar if Watson could learn a song before his father returned. Watson figured out the chords for "When Roses Bloom in Dixieland," and the next week Watson was given his first guitar. Later, he earned enough money cutting wood to buy a guitar from Sears, and soon he was playing along with his older brother, Linny.

When Watson was nineteen, he appeared for the first time on a local radio show. The announcer felt that his name, Arthel, was too dull, so he asked the audience for suggestions. Someone shouted out, "Call him Doc," and the nickname stayed with him.

When he was twenty-three, Watson married Rosa Lee Carlton, a fifteen-year-old third cousin. Carlton's father, Gaither Carlton, was a well-known fiddle player. The Watsons had two children, Eddy Merle, who was named after the famous guitar player Merle Travis, and Nancy Ellen.

Professional Career. It was not until Watson was thirty that he began to make a living playing music. In 1953, Watson met up with Jack Williams and started playing electric guitar with Williams's western-swing and rockabilly dance band. Since the band did not have a fiddle player, Watson developed an ability to pick out the melody lines of dance tunes on the guitar, thereby developing his trademark flat-picking style. Although he earned his living playing electric guitar, Watson continued to play traditional acoustic music with a number of local musicians.

In the late 1950's and early 1960's, many Americans grew interested in traditional rural music during what was known as the folk revival. In 1960, Ralph Rinzler and Eugene Earle went south to record the music of Tom Ashley, a well-known musician who lived near the Watson family. Rinzler and Earle were amazed at Watson's guitar playing and introduced him and his unique flatpicking style to the emerging folk music audience. In 1961, Watson began to tour the coffeehouse circuit in the Northeast. After Watson's appearances at the 1963 Newport Folk Festival and at New York City's Town Hall in 1964, he became one of the United States' most famous traditional southern musicians.

Family Ties. In 1964, upon returning from a tour, Watson was surprised to find that his son, Merle, had taken up the guitar and seemed to play almost effortlessly. Soon, Doc and Merle Watson began touring and recording together. Doc was

Doc Watson (Ken Settle)

the front man, talking with the audience and singing, while Merle remained quiet, distinguishing himself with his exceptional guitar-picking skills. Although folk and traditional country music lost popularity in the 1970's, the Watsons continued to play together. Doc and Merle Watson recorded twenty albums and won four Grammy Awards, including one in 1973 for *Then and Now* and another in 1974 for *Two Days in November*.

On October 23, 1985, tragedy hit the Watson family when Merle was killed when his tractor flipped over on a steep hill near his home. Several years later, area musicians approached Doc with the idea of creating a benefit concert in Merle's memory. The first Merle Watson Memorial Festival took place in 1988, and the gathering, now known as "MerleFest," would bring together more than one hundred artists and draw crowds of more than forty thousand.

Legacy. Doc Watson's guitar playing has influenced virtually every country and folk musician since the 1960's, and his extraordinary ability to overcome the adversity of childhood blindness is a lesson to all. A legend, Watson would continue to entertain audiences with lightning-fast flat-picking and the delicate melodies of old-time ballads, gospel songs, and traditional, acoustic country music. *—Daniel Rothenberg*

SELECT DISCOGRAPHY
■ ALBUMS
Doc Watson, 1964
Doc Watson & Son, 1965
The Elementary Doc Watson, 1972
Then and Now, 1973
Two Days in November, 1974 (with Merle Watson)
Live and Pickin', 1979
Riding the Midnight Train, 1986
On Praying Ground, 1990
Elementary Doctor Watson/Then & Now, 1997 (compilation)

SELECT AWARDS
Grammy Award for Best Ethnic or Traditional Recording for *Then and Now*, 1973
Grammy Award for Best Ethnic or Traditional Recording for *Two Days in November*, 1974 (with Merle Watson)
Grammy Award for Best Traditional Folk Recording for *Riding the Midnight Train*, 1986
Grammy Award for Best Traditional Folk Recording for *On Praying Ground*, 1990

Weather Report

ORIGINAL MEMBERS: Joe Zawinul (b. 1932), Wayne Shorter (b. 1933), Miroslav Vitous (b. 1947), Alphonse Mouzon (b. 1948), Airto Moreira (b. 1941)
OTHER MEMBERS: Jaco Pastorius (1951-1987), Alphonso Johnson (b. 1951), Peter Erskine (b. 1954), Omar Hakim (b. 1959), others
FIRST ALBUM RELEASE: *Weather Report*, 1971
MUSICAL STYLES: Jazz rock, jazz fusion, funk

Saxophonist Wayne Shorter and keyboardist Joe Zawinul united to create Weather Report in 1971. Both had played in the experimental jazz-rock group led by Miles Davis in the late 1960's. Besides their innovative talents on their instruments, each was an accomplished composer who had contributed original compositions to the Davis group. It could be argued that Weather Report was an outgrowth of the Miles Davis group because Zawinul was a chief arranger for the classic 1969 Davis albums *In a Silent Way* and *Bitches Brew*. Both were pioneering ventures in the jazz-rock idiom. The collaboration between Zawinul and Shorter resulted in a successful blend of amplified rock and synthesized sounds with modal jazz. The partnership resulted in sixteen albums by Weather Report and numerous live concerts over a fifteen-year period, 1971-1986.

Zawinul and Shorter. Although a considerable number of personnel came and went over the years, the duo of Zawinul and Shorter remained a constant. Their association had begun long before the formation of Weather Report and lasted until the breakup. Zawinul moved to the United States from his native Vienna, Austria, in 1959. After brief stints with Maynard Ferguson, Slide Hampton, and Dinah Washington, he achieved prominence and recognition through his work with the Cannonball Adderley Quintet from 1961

Weather Report (Archive Photos)

to 1970. One of the band's signature pieces was Zawinul's "Mercy, Mercy, Mercy," which won a Grammy Award for Best Instrumental Performance in 1967. While with Adderley, Zawinul developed as a soul-jazz and blues performer, incorporating the sounds of the Fender Rhodes electric piano. After leaving the Adderley Quintet, Zawinul recorded with Miles Davis and then launched Weather Report. One of Zawinul's lasting contributions to the success of Weather Report was his composition "Birdland," recorded in 1977 on the *Heavy Weather* album. The vocal group Manhattan Transfer later recorded a version of the piece with lyrics. The appealing repeating riffs and uplifting melody of "Birdland" have made it a perennial favorite with jazz bands, marching bands, jazz choirs, and listeners.

After graduating from New York University in 1956 with a bachelor of music education degree, Wayne Shorter played briefly with pianist Horace Silver before he was drafted into the Army. Upon his discharge, Shorter joined Maynard Ferguson's band and met Joe Zawinul for the first time in 1958. Next he became a member of Art Blakey's Jazz Messengers from 1959 to 1963, eventually becoming the group's music director. After much coaxing and prodding from Miles Davis, Shorter finally joined the Davis band in 1964 and stayed until 1970. During this period Shorter composed many jazz standards such as "Nefertiti," "Footprints," and a piece that seemed descriptive of Davis—"Prince of Darkness."

Instrumental Textures. The original group's instrumentation was standard—piano, bass, drum set, and saxophone (soprano and tenor), but it also included a percussionist. The first of these was Airto Moreira, who performed on a variety of exotic instruments such as Moroccan clay drums and Israeli jar drum. The group's formative period lasted from 1971 to 1973, culmi-

For the Record

It is believed that Joe Zawinul named the group Weather Report because he described its music as "changing from day to day like the weather."

nating with the successful *Sweetnighter* album (1973). On this recording, Zawinul's influence on the group's direction increased, and there was less free improvisation and more emphasis on arranged structure. Short phrases were continually repeated and accompanied by a funk-style rhythm section. This approach was an effective attempt to increase record sales. The combination of rock rhythms, emphasis on collective improvisation, and the use of electric bass and synthesizers resulted in an exciting new style of music, a "fusion" of jazz and rock elements. This formula also made their next album, the sometimes danceable, sometimes ethereal *Mysterious Traveller* (1974), popular and artistically successful.

Fusion represented the blending of two musical styles, jazz and rock, into a new creation. Weather Report was successful in capturing—and helping define—the essence of fusion music in a number of ways. They incorporated electronically amplified and modified instrument sounds. They were among the first jazz-derived groups to use synthesizers in recording and live performances. Weather Report also augmented the ensemble with Latin-influenced percussion, utilized both pronounced rock rhythms and swing jazz elements, and employed sophisticated studio recording techniques.

Almost exclusively an instrumental group, Weather Report created new and unusual textures through modifying traditional jazz instrumentation. Zawinul orchestrated musical colors by employing an arsenal of keyboards, which grew as technological improvements made new sounds available. On the first Weather Report album, he played acoustic piano and Fender Rhodes electric piano. Subsequently he added an ARP 2600 synthesizer, a second ARP 2600, an Oberheim polyphonic synthesizer, a Prophet 5, and more. (The ARP 2600 was among the first generation of portable synthesizers, and it could play only two notes at a time; the Oberheim could play four, with richer orchestral textures; the Prophet 5 and later devices dramatically increased the range of sounds and could store programmed sounds and recall them at the touch of a button.) Zawinul proved to be a master at creating unique musical timbres by combining the various keyboards into layered sounds. Also, he would sometimes play a bass line on synthesizer, freeing the bassist to play as a soloist.

Shorter's husky, uniquely personal tone on saxophone was easily recognizable within the ensemble. Rather than playing extended, improvised solos with accompanied rhythm section, Shorter contributed in a more supportive manner as an ensemble improviser, sometimes carrying the melody and other times playing single-note punctuations or fragmented lines. Shorter frequently played the soprano saxophone rather that the more common alto or tenor, adding another distinctive aspect to his playing with Weather Report. Bassist Miroslav Vitous (and others later) refrained from the "walking" bass lines (outlining the chord changes) that are typical of a jazz rhythm section. Instead, the bass was a melodic instrument, engaging in musical conversations with other group members, creating moods and sound textures through both plucked and bowed strings. The possibilities and infinite number of tone colors on the drum set and auxiliary percussion were endless. The percussionists contributed to the collective improvisation of the ensemble rather than assuming the traditional role of "timekeeper."

Jaco. Following the release of the first album, *Weather Report*, the band underwent personnel changes with each succeeding album (particularly percussionists). After *Sweetnighter* Alphonso Johnson replaced Vitous on bass and remained with the group until an extraordinarily talented twenty-five-year-old bass virtuoso named Jaco Pastorius joined. Pastorius first appeared on the 1976 album *Black Market* and performed on the next five recordings. The group had already begun to shift direction toward a funk-oriented style. The threads of collective improvisation were still there, but now most compositions were based on repetitious motifs and selected themes or patterns that served as the basis for a rock-funk oriented sound. Shorter's and Zawinul's roots were solidly in jazz. Pastorius had experience in both jazz and rock. Together, this trio altered the destiny of Weather Report and of fusion music in general. By the release of *Heavy Weather* in 1977 Pastorius was a full-fledged member of the group, as a player, composer, and coproducer (with Zawinul). *Heavy Weather* was the group's best-selling album and garnered for them their first gold record. Pastorius rapidly became a jazz superstar who was idolized by bassists everywhere. Students of the electric bass practiced "Jaco licks" in the hope of emulating the man who was setting a new standard for bass performance. Within the framework of the group, Pastorius continued the established roles of the bass player: playing chord changes in time, utilizing selective improvisation while interacting with others, and playing repetitive funk patterns. In addition, Pastorius contributed as a composer and excelled as a soloist. His creative use of a fretless bass, combined with a dazzling technique and warm, singing tone, transformed the sound of Weather Report. He also produced electronically altered tones with phase shifting and tape loops. The group was more popular than ever. Pastorius eventually left the band in 1982 to form his own group, Word of Mouth. Only five years later Pastorius's personal problems—his abuse of drugs and alcohol and bouts of manic depression—led to his death at the age of thirty-six. He was killed in the summer of 1987 after a fight in a bar.

The follow-up to *Heavy Weather* was *Mr. Gone*, and it introduced new drummer Peter Erskine. Erskine possessed such facility and power on the drum set that he replaced both a drummer and a percussionist, making Weather Report a four-piece group. A few years later, Erskine left the group shortly after Pastorius, between the *Night Passage* and *Procession* albums.

Breakup. It would be easy to assume that the departures of Jaco and Erskine would have trig-

gered a musical collapse or at least created morale problems within Weather Report. Actually, their replacements—Victor Bailey, bass, Omar Hakim, drums, and Jose Rossy, percussion—provided a needed stimulus to the group. Zawinul increasingly desired to emphasize Third World rhythms and textures. The new personnel were in agreement with Zawinul's intentions. Shorter, however, had lost most of his artistic influence on the group's direction and sensed that the end was near. In 1985 he took a leave of absence. He returned to perform on a final album, *This Is This* (1985), although in a minimal role. Zawinul toured in 1986 with his new group, Weather Update (and later with the Zawinul Syndicate). Shorter, still committed to fusion music that incorporated traditional jazz elements, recorded with his own groups. The collaboration of two giants of jazz was over, resulting in the demise of a truly trailblazing musical ensemble.

Weather Report and many of its individual members consistently won various jazz polls (such as *Down Beat* magazine's). The group was tremendously influential throughout the 1970's. The terms "fusion" and "jazz fusion" became widely applied; among the other best-known pioneers of the fusion movement were guitarist John McLaughlin's Mahavishnu Orchestra and keyboardists Herbie Hancock and Chick Corea. Like any genre, fusion has produced some first-rate music and much that is of lesser quality. By the 1980's much watered-down jazz and fusion music was being recorded in artists' attempts to reach a wider audience. The derogatory pun "fuzak" was coined to refer to this lightweight genre. Moreover, the entire "new age" genre of the 1980's and 1990's owes a large debt to the early fusion bands, particularly Weather Report. —*Douglas D. Skinner*

SELECT DISCOGRAPHY
■ ALBUMS
Weather Report, 1971
Live in Tokyo, 1972 (Japanese release)
Sweetnighter, 1973
Mysterious Traveller, 1974
Tale Spinnin', 1975
Black Market, 1976

Heavy Weather, 1977
Mr. Gone, 1978
8:30, 1979
Night Passage, 1980
Record, 1982
Procession, 1983
Sportin' Life, 1985
This Is This, 1985

SEE ALSO: Adderley, Julian "Cannonball"; Davis, Miles; Hancock, Herbie; McLaughlin, John; Manhattan Transfer.

Kitty Wells
(Muriel Deason)

BORN: Nashville, Tennessee; August 30, 1919
FIRST SINGLE RELEASE: "Death at the Bar"/"Gathering Flowers for the Master's Bouquet," 1949
MUSICAL STYLE: Country

A 1952 recording by Kitty Wells called "It Wasn't God Who Made Honky-Tonk Angels" changed country music forever, set a pattern for women performers, and started this shy mother and housewife on the way to a long-term career which earned her the unofficial title of "Queen of Country Music."

The Beginnings. Kitty Wells was born Muriel Deason in Nashville, Tennessee. Her stage name came from the title of a Carter Family song. Growing up in a musical family, Wells sang old sentimental and gospel songs. With her cousin, she began to sing on a local Nashville radio station in 1936. She lived in the hometown of the Grand Ole Opry, which, beginning in 1925, featured a variety of rural musicians and singers. As a radio show with a powerful signal and with a policy of letting people from downtown Nashville attend its broadcasts, the Opry was a mecca for all those who had ambitions to make music a profession. Wells attended the show and began to hone her basic rhythm-guitar playing and her clear, piercing soprano.

In 1935, Wells met a neighbor, Johnnie Wright, also a musician and singer who had moved to Nashville from the nearby rural community of Mt.

Juliet. Born in 1914, Wright picked up the same old-time folk and country music as Wells. Wells and Wright fell in love and were married in 1937. Wright soon met the Anglin brothers, Van, Jim, and Jack, who performed on the same radio station as Wells and her cousin. Jim Anglin became a prolific songwriter and wrote many songs for the band that Wright and Jack Anglin formed around 1939. By the early 1940's, they became known as Johnny and Jack and the Tennessee Mountain Boys and formed the nucleus of the band which accompanied Wells when she became a soloist. Struggling to establish themselves on radio throughout the Southeast, the band featured Wells on harmony or singing old-time or religious songs. These would always remain central to the music of both Wells and Wright.

Kitty Wells (Archive Photos)

Wells tried to divide her time between motherhood and performing with her husband. She did record solo with RCA Victor starting in 1949, without much success. In 1952, she signed a contract with Decca, where she did her most famous recordings. It was in the same year that Wells recorded her signature song, "It Wasn't God Who Made Honky-Tonk Angels." After the song became a number 1 hit, the first number 1 country record for a woman, Wells was regarded as an equal with Johnny and Jack on their road show. Over the next decade, she became recognized as the first genuine female country singer.

Context of the Times. The post-World War II era witnessed great social upheaval. Men had seen war and death; women had gone to work in defense plants. Families were broken; farms and rural life were abandoned as the move to towns and cities accelerated. Divorce rates soared. There was the baby boom and the birth of television. As the nuclear family became status quo over the old extended rural family structure, isolation and alienation from roots were common. In terms of country music, the older songs of innocent romance and sentiments of home, family, and religion seemed to many to be outdated. In their places were new songs about marital difficulties, divorce, and adultery. These dominant themes emerged in the new honky-tonk style. This louder and harsher sound, with wailing steel guitars, heavy bass, and later, piano and drums, came to epitomize modern country music. The honky-tonk, or barroom, was the perfect setting for cheating and infidelity.

Stardom. In this context, Wells became the spokesperson for women besieged by the changes in working-class life. Fronting the Johnnie and Jack band with backup of steel guitar, fiddle, acoustic rhythm guitar, and upright bass, she began to sing of the hard-edged realities facing women in a changed world. Older folk and country songs did sometimes address issues of broken love and the problems of marriage, but the modern songs dealt more exclusively with these themes. While there had been women singers in family bands or as novelty acts, Wells represented a full-fledged star whose crystalline tones and

For the Record

Kitty Wells's "It Wasn't God Who Made Honky-Tonk Angels" was written as an "answer song" to "The Wild Side of Life," a number 1 hit for country singer Hank Thompson in 1952. The lyrics of "The Wild Side of Life" blamed immoral women for leading married men astray and suggested that they were put on earth solely to seduce good men. Songwriter Jay Miller (a male) responded by writing "It Wasn't God Who Made Honky-Tonk Angels." The title says it all: Honky-tonk angels are not born bad but turn that way after being mistreated by men. A defiant song from a woman's perspective, it was a new theme in country music.

clearly articulated words stood out distinctly from the backup band. Her words and sentiments came across with a searing intensity. Unlike later singers such as Loretta Lynn and Dolly Parton, Wells did not write songs, but her husband was a master at selecting songs for her, mostly from male songwriters who became adept at writing compelling songs from a female perspective.

From 1952 through the 1960's, Wells dominated the country field as a female singer. Although acting and dressing in a conservative manner, seeming demure in gingham dresses, Wells sang of heartbreak, unrequited love, and broken marriages. She did sing positive songs celebrating marriage and true love as well, songs that reflected her own life. The titles of some of her hit songs evoke the themes she favored: "Paying for That Back Street Affair," "Cheatin's a Sin," "Release Me," "Makin' Believe," "Whose Shoulder Will You Cry On," "Lonely Side of Town," "Searching for Someone Like You," "The Other Cheek," and "Heartbreak U.S.A."

Wells also recorded a number of duets with male singers that recall an old tradition of the dialogue song, in which opposing or similar viewpoints can be articulated by two characters in one piece. Songs which convey broken relationships included "One by One" (a number 1 hit), "I'm a Stranger in My Home," "I Can't Tell My Heart That," and "Broken Marriage Vows." Positive songs about enduring love and marriage include: "You and Me," "As Long as I Live," "Oh, So Many Years," "No One But You," and the older song "Have I Told You Lately That I Love You." Like many country songs, they are really minidramas set in realistic situations that reflect social conditions.

Style. For the most part, Wells remained consistent in her style. On stage she has sung with a controlled yet deeply emotional voice which can soar and hold notes for intensifying effects. She strums an acoustic guitar and barely moves while she sings, a traditional Appalachian style of performing. In songs chastising men for their ways, she is able to combine a vocal sweetness with an edge. Hers is a voice that often cuts to the emotional core—both on record and in live performances. While the musicians who accompany her remain in the background, so the words are easily heard, the use of bluesy solo breaks by the steel guitar contributes to the intensity and emotional impact of the songs of lost love that are her specialty.

Legacy. In the 1950's and early 1960's, only singer Jean Shepard rivaled Wells as a singer of songs depicting false dreams and promises. Together they sang of vexed marriage and single women who endure a double standard by which men could—or imagined they could—be free to cheat and lie to their women. The postwar period witnessed the rise within country music of assertive female voices that responded to this sort of dilemma. As Wells and Shepard succeeded, others began to voice in song the same problems.

After Jack Anglin's death in 1963, Wells and Wright remodeled their show to feature Wells. The durability of her career (she continued to tour through the 1990's) is itself a tribute to the enduring relevance of the themes of her songs. Her music and career became models and inspiration for the careers of women such as Loretta Lynn, Patsy Cline, Dolly Parton, and Reba McEntire. Wells set the standard for women to sing realistically about their lives and the complexities of living in a world vastly changed during their generation. —*Frederick E. Danker*

SELECT DISCOGRAPHY
■ ALBUMS
Country Hit Parade, 1956
Winner of Your Heart, 1957
Dust on the Bible, 1959
Seasons of My Heart, 1960
Heartbreak U.S.A., 1961
Lonely Street, 1965
Country Music Hall of Fame Series, 1991
   (compilation)

SELECT AWARDS
Country Music Hall of Fame, inducted 1976
Academy of Country Music Pioneer Award, 1985
Grammy Award for Lifetime Achievement, 1991

SEE ALSO: Cline, Patsy; Lynn, Loretta; McEntire, Reba; Parton, Dolly; Wynette, Tammy.

Barry White

BORN: Galveston, Texas; September 12, 1944
FIRST ALBUM RELEASE: *I've Got So Much to Give*, 1973
MUSICAL STYLES: Rhythm and blues, soul

An unlikely sex symbol, the portly Barry White excited audiences in the 1970's with his passionate, gravelly voiced declarations of love. White, who learned the music business by guiding the careers of others while working in the artists and repertoire department of a record company, was also the creative force behind the Love Unlimited Orchestra, a forty-piece instrumental ensemble that accompanied him on his 1970's disco hits and recorded some hits of its own. White continued to score new hits in the 1990's, following a career lull in the previous decade.

The Beginnings. White started singing in a church in Galveston, Texas, when he was eight, later becoming the organist and part-time director of the choir. His family later moved to Los Angeles, where he joined the Upfronts, a rhythm-

and-blues band, as a singer-pianist when he was sixteen. In 1966, he joined Mustang Records in the artists and repertoire department. His most notable discovery was Love Unlimited, a female vocal trio consisting of Diana Taylor and the sisters Linda and Glodean James, White's future wife. White produced the trio's gold single "Walking in the Rain with the One I Love" (number 14, pop; number 6, rhythm and blues) in 1972 for Uni Records.

A Golden Recording Debut. White was an immediate success upon his signing with Twentieth Century Fox Records in 1973. His first three singles were major hits: "I'm Gonna Love You Just a Little More Baby" (number 3, pop; number 1, rhythm and blues), "Never, Never Gonna Give Ya

Barry White (Ken Settle)

Up," (number 7, pop; number 2, rhythm and blues), and "I've Got So Much to Give," (number 32, pop; number 5, rhythm and blues). His Love Unlimited Orchestra also scored its first hit that year with the instrumental "Love's Theme," (number 1, pop; number 10, rhythm and blues).

Despite his reputation for lush orchestrations, White says his production credo has been "simplicity." "Even though I use violins and French horns, basses, guitars, keyboards, and drums," White told *The Boston Globe*, "I think you can sit down and listen to Barry White's arrangements and hear the distinction of everybody. Because no two instruments speak at the same time. Everybody takes their time."

The Hits Keep Coming. The gold hits continued through the mid-1970's, among them, Love Unlimited Orchestra's "Rhapsody in White" and White's "Can't Get Enough of Your Love, Babe," "You're the First, the Last, My Everything," and "Just Another Way to Say I Love You." He compiled his first greatest-hits collection in 1975 and continued to chart new material. In 1977, his album *Barry White Sings for Someone You Love*, featuring the single "It's Ecstasy When You Lay Down Next to Me," went platinum. Other hits of the late 1970's included "Playing Your Game, Baby," and "Your Sweetness Is My Weakness."

1980's Fadeout. For most of the 1980's, White's career slowed considerably as disco faded in popularity. By the end of the decade, he began to make a comeback. His 1987 release, *The Right Night and Barry White*, yielded the rhythm-and-blues hits "Sho' You Right" and "For Your Love (I'll Do Most Anything)." An auspicious begin-

For the Record

"My life has truly been rewarding," Barry White told *The Boston Globe*. "I'm not a zillionaire. I don't own jets and things, but as a human being, I've had a beautiful life, man. Even when it was hard, it ended up nice and smooth, believe me."

ning to 1989, White joined a long list of guest stars, including Al B. Sure!, James Ingram, and El De-Barge on Quincy Jones's *Back on the Block* album; their song, "The Secret Garden (Sweet Seduction Suite)," topped the rhythm-and-blues charts and went to number 31 on the pop charts.

1990's Comeback. His 1994 release, *The Icon Is Back*, lived up to its billing: The album sold nearly two million copies and produced the hit singles "Practice What You Preach" (number 18, pop; number 1, rhythm and blues) and the title track (number 20, pop; number 1, rhythm and blues).

—*Robert DiGiacomo*

SELECT DISCOGRAPHY
■ ALBUMS
Stone Gon', 1973
Can't Get Enough, 1974
Barry White's Greatest Hits, 1975 (compilation)
Let the Music Play, 1976
Barry White Sings for Someone You Love, 1977
I Love to Sing the Songs I Sing, 1979
Barry White's Greatest Hits, Vol. 2, 1980
    (compilation)
Sheet Music, 1980
Barry and Glodean, 1981 (with Glodean White)
Dedicated, 1983
The Right Night and Barry White, 1987
The Man Is Back! 1989
Put Me in Your Mix, 1991
Just for You, 1992
All-Time Greatest Hits, 1994 (compilation)

SEE ALSO: Ingram, James.

The Who / Pete Townshend

The Who

ORIGINAL MEMBERS: Pete (Peter Dennis Bland-ford) Townshend (b. 1945), Roger Daltrey (b. 1944), John Entwistle (b. 1944), Keith John Moon (1947-1978)
OTHER MEMBERS: Kenney Jones (b. 1948), John "Rabbit" Bundrick
FIRST ALBUM RELEASE: *The Who Sings My Genera-tion*, 1965

Pete Townshend

BORN: London, England; May 19, 1945
FIRST ALBUM RELEASE: *Who Came First*, 1971
MUSICAL STYLE: Rock and roll

One of the most influential rock bands in the history of popular music, the Who and its main songwriter and resident philosopher Pete Town-shend became a force on the music scene begin-ning in the 1960's. The Who are known for their generation-defining lyrics, their use of synthesiz-ers, their pioneering musical formats, including the rock opera, their use of power chords, their outrageous, set-destroying stage antics, and their extremely loud concerts. The lyrics to their early hit single "My Generation," written by Town-shend, became an anthem for the 1960's genera-tion: "People try to put us d-down/ Just because we get around/ Things they do look awful c-cold/ Hope I die before I get old." This rebellious re-frain shouted out open defiance and rejection of those who did not share the music or the moment.

The Early Years. Townshend, Roger Daltrey, and John Entwistle grew up together in a working-class London neighborhood. Playing together as the Detours, they teamed up with drummer Keith Moon in 1963. The band began calling itself the Who the following year. Their first manager, Pete Meaden, packaged the group to capitalize on the "mod" fashion scene popular in the mid-1960's in Great Britain, renaming them the High Numbers. After releasing a forgettable single, the band re-placed Meaden with new managers, Kit Lambert and Chris Stamp, changing their name back to the Who and refining their look and act. Early on, Townshend and Moon acquired reputations for their wild stage presence, which sometimes in-cluded set demolition. Lambert and Stamp sug-gested that the group incorporate their antics into their act. Thus was born the band's distinctive finale of drum-set trashing and guitar bashing.

The band recorded "I Can't Explain" in 1965 (with backup guitar work by Jimmy Page, later of Led Zeppelin). The single was ignored until the band appeared on the popular British TV show *Ready, Steady, Go.* Something about their distinc-tive style registered with the audience. Entwistle

The Who c. 1967: Keith Moon, Pete Townshend, John Entwistle, Roger Daltrey (MCA)

performed stiffly, as was his manner, Daltrey strutted across camera range while belting out the vocals, Moon pushed over his drum kit, and Townshend smashed his guitar to pieces. Soon after, the single reached number 8 on the British charts, and the band had defined itself and its sound. This recording was followed by "Anyway, Anyhow, Anywhere" and "My Generation."

Landmarks. After the release of their second album, *Happy Jack*, in 1966, the Who went after the American audience. Although their earlier hits had flopped in the United States, their flamboyant stage presence quickly won them a following among American teens. The pivotal event in the Who's career was their performance of a blister-

ing rendition of "My Generation" at the 1967 Monterey International Pop Festival in San Francisco's Golden Gate Park before twenty thousand fans. Monterey, one of the first mass rock festivals, served to launch the "British invasion" of America as well as the Who's international success. Their newfound popularity was followed by the release of the concept album *The Who Sell Out*, which featured trendy pop art and songs inspired by popular-culture advertisements and fads. This album also contained a miniopera conceived by Townshend and a Top-10 hit, "I Can See for Miles." The follow-up release, *Magic Bus* (1968), contained mostly a compilation of past hits and B-sides.

For the Record

The Who's reputation for wild stage antics began early in the band's career. Townshend, after finishing a particularly rough set in the Railway Tavern early in 1964, poked his guitar through the low pub ceiling and smashed it to bits in frustration. The audience loved it. Later, their new managers, Kit Lambert and Chris Stamp, young filmmakers with a flair for theatrics, urged the band to incorporate the bashing into the final piece of their act, where it soon became one of the most well-known and imitated signature gestures in rock and roll.

Following years of experimentation with new rock genres and longer musical forms, Townshend began to devote much of his creative energies to the production of rock's first full-length opera, Tommy, released as an album in 1969. Pretension and obscure spiritual message notwithstanding, this quirky ninety-minute story of a blind, deaf, and mute pinball wizard turned visionary became an immediate hit. The Who performed the piece occasionally over the years, and Ken Russell directed a controversial feature film version of it in 1975, with Roger Daltrey in the title role, Hollywood actress Ann Margaret as Tommy's mother, and rhythm-and-blues icon Tina Turner as the Acid Queen. In 1969, right after the release of Tommy, the Who made an appearance at the now-historic Woodstock concert. In one of the festival's most dramatic sets, a bare-chested Daltrey delivered his vocals in an exotic fringed costume. The stage presence of the lead singer and the rest of the band ignited the crowd. This single performance did more than anything else to define the Who's place within the countercultural music scene of that era.

Townshend continued to experiment with interesting arrangements, introducing synthesizers into his next composition, the 1971 Who's Next.

This recording produced several hits that would later become staples of classic rock: "Baba O'Riley," "Bargain," and "Won't Get Fooled Again." Townshend's next attempt at writing a rock opera, Quadrophenia (1973), was less well received than Tommy and uninteresting musically or as a stage production. Its less-than-successful release also coincided with the eruption of long-simmering tensions among the band members.

The Who in Crisis. Although the band still enjoyed tremendous popularity throughout the 1970's, it was clearly considered to be in rock's older generation. The world of pop music had recently been riveted by the advent of punk, whose anarchic lyrics and antiestablishment attitude far surpassed the Who's onstage pranks. Groups such as the Sex Pistols replaced the Who and the Rolling Stones as rock's "bad boys." Townshend and Daltrey, whose personal rivalries exploded into public feuding, each flirted with solo projects, and Moon pursued a reckless lifestyle, flagrantly abusing alcohol and drugs. Despite the turmoil, however, the band's Who Are You, recorded in 1978, quickly went double platinum in sales, and its title single reached number 14 on the charts. Only one month after the album's release, Moon was found dead in London from an overdose of medication he had been taking to curb his alcoholism. Having long enjoyed a well-deserved reputation as "the madman of rock and roll," Moon's wild onstage persona was often overshadowed by his offstage excesses. He had experimented with every type of mind-altering substance available to him (at one time suffering temporary paralysis after ingesting an elephant tranquilizer), and his long-standing addictions had begun to affect his performance in the years before his death. Although the band hired Kenney Jones as their drummer just a few months after Moon's death and continued to perform together for another three years, they never recovered from the loss. Their projects during this period included a documentary about the band, The Kids Are Alright, and a soundtrack version of Quadrophenia. The Who, with Jones and another new member on keyboards, John "Rabbit" Bundrick, began a tour in 1979 when another tragedy befell them.

On December 3, 1979, eleven fans were crushed to death at a Who concert at Cincinnati's Riverfront Coliseum. The accident occurred as the result of the then-widespread industry practice of general-admission ("festival") seating, when the crowd rushed to the front of the arena as soon as the gates opened. This tragic incident was devastating to the band (they were not told about the deaths until after the show). Although they continued to perform together for a few years after, their unity was clearly damaged. Entwistle developed an interest in heavy metal; Daltrey, who began feuding with Jones, got into movie acting; and Townshend entered a period of personal instability. The composer, who also fancied himself a rock philosopher, continued to make ambiguous pronouncements on both the importance and the triviality of his music. By the early 1980's, his substance abuse had burgeoned out of control, and he was seen falling asleep onstage at a concert in 1981. For at least one year before, Townshend had been regularly abusing alcohol, cocaine, and freebase cocaine mixed with heroin. After a near-fatal overdose in 1982, he underwent a lengthy acupuncture treatment and reportedly overcame his addiction.

The Who in the 1980's and 1990's. The Who officially disbanded in 1982, but, like other bands of this period, they came together sporadically to perform. The band first reassembled for the Live Aid concert in 1985 and again in 1989 for a very successful silver anniversary tour that included concert renditions of *Tommy*, with young Simon Phillips replacing Jones on drums. Townshend, to cope with his damaged hearing, had to perform much of the tour from behind a special plastic buffer to filter out stage noise. A memorable appearance in 1994 saw the three surviving original members reunited for two concerts at Carnegie Hall in New York in honor of lead singer Daltrey's fiftieth birthday. Distributed internationally on cable television, the concert featured a sixty-five-piece orchestra and guest cameos by other rock icons.

Townshend, in particular, made it a point to separate himself from the group. Always given to cryptic philosophical musings about the Who's music and the general state of rock and roll, he wrote in the liner notes to the 1994 retrospective album *The Who: Thirty Years of Maximum R&B* that he "didn't like the Who much." He has worked as an editor, published a collection of short stories, and done some solo recording, most notably *Empty Glass* (1980), which sold a half million copies and included the Top-10 song "Let My Love Open the Door." Despite pursuing separate musical interests as well as other endeavors farther afield artistically, Townshend, Daltrey, Entwistle, and the late Moon will always be connected in the public memory for the music, the lyrics, the performance art, and the good times they created together as one of the best rock-and-roll bands in history.

—*Janice Monti-Belkaoui*

SELECT DISCOGRAPHY
■ ALBUMS
The Who Sings My Generation, 1965
Happy Jack, 1966
Magic Bus, 1968
Tommy, 1969
Who's Next, 1971
Quadrophenia, 1973
Who Are You, 1978
The Kids Are Alright, 1979
Who's Last, 1984
The Who: Thirty Years of Maximum R&B, 1994

SELECT AWARDS
Rock and Roll Hall of Fame, inducted 1990
Tony Award for Best Score, Musical, for *The Who's Tommy*, 1993 (Pete Townshend)

SEE ALSO: John, Elton; Led Zeppelin; Rolling Stones, The; Sex Pistols, The; Turner, Ike and Tina / Tina Turner.

Hank Williams

BORN: Mt. Olive, Alabama; September 17, 1923
DIED: Oak Hill, West Virginia; January 1, 1953
FIRST SINGLE RELEASE: "Move It on Over," 1947
MUSICAL STYLES: Blues, country, rock and roll, rockabilly

Hank Williams was country music's first superstar and legend. He also won great acclaim in the pop-music world. Songs written by him, such as "Cold, Cold Heart," "Hey, Good Lookin'," and "Your Cheatin' Heart," are classics of American music history. Williams is known for his simple, beautiful melodies, straightforward lyrics, and thick Alabama twang. Many of his hits became hits for other performers as well. Williams has been called the most influential country-and-western singer and songwriter, and he helped spread the popularity of country music across the United States.

His story is legendary—rags-to-riches, a stormy relationship with his mother, an unhappy marriage, alcoholism and drugs, a tragic ending, and a larger-than-life popularity after his death. The secret of his success, he once said, was his sincerity. Williams threw himself completely into his music.

The Beginnings. Hiram Williams (his real name) was born on September 17, 1923, in Mt. Olive, Alabama, to a poor family. Williams was always scarecrow-thin and suffered from chronic back problems caused by spina bifida. School bored him, but music did not. Williams taught himself to play the guitar at age eight. The church music his strong-willed mother played influenced him. It was from this music that he gained a sense that life is foreordained. Another major influence on his development was a black street singer named Rufus "Tee-Tot" Payne, who taught him guitar chord progressions and blues rudiments. Williams credited Payne with giving him all the music training he ever had. Payne is the source of the noticeable blues thread that runs through Williams's music. In fact, Williams described his vocal style as "moanin' the blues." When asked what kind of music he played, he called his music folk music. Other musical influences include gospel hymns and performers Ernest Tubb and Roy Acuff. His melodies were simple and sincere, like the hymns and folk songs he learned as a child.

Williams won an amateur contest in Montgomery, Alabama, for his own composition, "WPA Blues." (The title refers to a Depression-era government agency called the Work Projects Administration, or WPA.) This was probably his first original song, which he modeled on an old Riley Puckett song. In 1937 Williams formed his own band, the Drifting Cowboys, which played in Alabama honky-tonks. In 1942, during World War II, he tried to enlist in the Army but was rejected because of his back problems. He worked on and off at the shipyards in Mobile, Alabama.

Williams had his first success as a songwriter in 1943 when he sold the tune "I Am Praying for the Day Peace Will Come" to singer-songwriter Pee Wee King. By the early 1940's Williams was a successful regional performer, but he had a reputation for drinking and being unreliable. In 1943 steel guitarist Don Helms joined Williams and his Drifting Cowboys band. Helms is credited with providing Williams' trademark sound—high-pitched chords.

Williams's big break came when he moved to Nashville in 1946 and became associated with Fred Rose, Nashville's most successful songwriter, record producer, and publisher (Acuff-Rose Pub-

Hank Williams (Freddie Patterson Collection/ Archive Photos)

lications). Under Rose's guidance, Williams got a contract with MGM Records. In 1947 he had his first hit ("Move It on Over") and his first *Billboard* chart entry. This Williams song influenced the writers of Bill Haley's early rock-and-roll hit, "(We're Gonna) Rock Around the Clock" (1955). Rose (whom he called "Pappy") often helped Williams shape his songs and gave him career advice. For example, it was Rose who helped Williams land a job on the *Louisiana Hayride*, a program on a 50,000-watt radio station (KWKH) in Shreveport. The program helped Williams promote his music to a wider audience.

Rose and Williams worked well together. Rose's genius lay in his songwriting and editing and in his sure sense of the market. He helped Williams craft his songs so that they would attract pop music fans and musicians. Pop singer Tony Bennett, for example, had a number 1 hit with "Cold, Cold Heart." Jo Stafford had a number 1 hit with "Jambalaya" and big hit in a duet with Frankie Lane, "Hey, Good Lookin'."

The song that brought Williams to the Grand Ole Opry in 1949 and propelled him to superstardom was "Lovesick Blues," which, ironically, was not one he wrote. It was a show tune recorded in the 1920's by yodeler Emmett Miller and sung since by vaudeville and country performers. Williams added his touch, including the yodels. The song stayed at number 1 for sixteen weeks and ignited his career. Because of the song and his love affair with blues music, he was often called "that Lovesick Blues boy." On June 11, 1949, Williams made his debut on the Grand Ole Opry stage. The audience loved his performance so much that he did six encores.

The Opry appearances and backing helped Williams launch his career. His records consistently hit the charts. Eleven of his songs reached the number 1 spot on the country charts. When he performed, he wore western clothes with handpainted ties and hand-tooled boots. Of all the songs he wrote, Williams often said that "I'm So Lonesome I Could Cry" (1949) was his personal favorite. Using the name "Luke the Drifter," Williams recorded "Men with Broken Hearts" (1951), "Ramblin' Man" (1951), and other recitations

For the Record

In only four years Hank Williams had eleven records reach number 1, another sixteen become Top-5 singles, and nine other releases make the Top 10. At one time he had five of the top twelve pop songs.

that were little homilies, usually with a strong moral undertone, narrated to a musical accompaniment. He recorded these under a different name so as not to upset the jukebox operators who primarily serviced bars. His jukebox and radio audiences wanted toe-tapping music.

Williams life was coming apart by mid-1952. Plagued by worsening back pain, he became ever more dependent on drugs and alcohol. He was fired from the Grand Ole Opry in 1952 for failing to show up for scheduled shows and sometimes being too drunk to perform. That year he briefly returned to the *Louisiana Hayride*, divorced his first wife, and remarried. Williams was happiest when he was performing or fishing with a cane pole on Kentucky Lake.

Death. On New Year's Day, 1953, Williams died of a heart attack at age twenty-nine in the back seat of a Cadillac on the way to a show in Canton, Ohio. Drug and alcohol abuse apparently hastened his death. At the time he died, Williams ironically had a hit record on the charts called "I'll Never Get out of This World Alive." His memorial service at the Municipal Auditorium in Montgomery, Alabama, drew twenty thousand mourners. Williams is buried at Oakwood Cemetery Annex in Montgomery. Three of his songs reached the top of the charts in the year following his death— "Your Cheatin' Heart," "Kaw-Liga," and "Take These Chains from My Heart." In 1961 Williams was one of the first to be elected to the Country Music Hall of Fame.

Williams' son, Hank, Jr., has become a successful country star in his own right. In 1989 Hank Williams, Jr., used electronics to record a duet and produce a video featuring him singing with his father. Both recording and video won awards, including a Grammy Award for Best Country Vocal Collaboration and the Country Music Association's Vocal Event of the Year and Music Video of the Year Awards.

Legacy. Hank Williams recorded 129 songs that have been bought and heard by millions of fans. Many of his songs have become standards of the country music repertoire. Amazingly, his stardom lasted less than four years (from 1949 to 1953). The man behind the legend was a triple threat—a great songwriter, singer, and performer—who put sincerity and authenticity into his songs. Whether he was entertaining audiences over the radio or in person, Williams performed with passion and a go-for-broke intensity. Some music-industry polls have voted him the most popular country-and-western singer of all time. Other country musicians have written songs in his honor, including "I Don't Think Hank Done It This Way" by Waylon Jennings. Many country musicians have stated that Williams strongly influenced their music. Country musicians most influenced by Williams include Ferlin Husky, George Jones, Faron Young, and Ray Price.   —*Fred Buchstein*

SELECT DISCOGRAPHY
■ SINGLES
"Lovesick Blues," 1949
"Long Gone Lonesome Blues," 1950
"Why Don't You Love Me," 1950
"Moanin' the Blues," 1950
"Cold, Cold Heart," 1951
"Hey, Good Lookin'," 1951
"Jambalaya (on the Bayou)," 1952
"I'll Never Get out of This World Alive," 1952
"Your Cheatin' Heart," 1953
"Kaw-Liga," 1953
"Take These Chains from My Heart," 1953
■ ALBUMS
Forty Greatest Hits, 1978
The Original Singles Collection . . . Plus, 1992
    (3-CD compilation)

SELECT AWARDS
Country Music Hall of Fame, inducted 1961
Academy of Country Music Pioneer Award, 1973
National Academy of Recording Arts and Sciences Lifetime Achievement Award, 1982
Rock and Roll Hall of Fame, inducted 1987

SEE ALSO: Bennett, Tony; Jones, George; Tubb, Ernest; Williams, Hank, Jr.

Hank Williams, Jr.

BORN: Shreveport, Louisiana; May 26, 1949
FIRST SINGLE RELEASE: "Long Gone Lonesome Blues," 1964
MUSICAL STYLES: Country rock, country

Groomed from the age of three to fill the immeasurable musical void left by the tragic and premature death of his father, Hank Williams, Hank Williams, Jr. (born Randall Hank Williams), eventually emerged as an outstanding composer, performer, and entertainer in his own right. Even with the advantage of the Williams name, however, his journey to stardom was difficult and painful and led to at least one suicide attempt. His lofty position in the country music hierarchy is a tribute to both his substantial talent and his perseverance.

The Beginnings. A product of the tempestuous marriage of Hank and Audrey Williams, Hank Williams, Jr. (also known by his nickname of Bocephus), was to have no memory of his often absent father. The death of Hank Williams on January 1, 1953, the result of an alcohol- and drug-induced heart attack, left the rearing of the little boy to his mother, the unrelenting and determined Audrey Williams. Audrey had two all-consuming goals: to preserve the memory, and hence record sales, of her husband, and to create a musical career for her son. She made sure her son learned to play the guitar while he was still in grade school, being taught by Audrey's many musician friends who often visited the Williams's home. A stage act was developed which featured Williams wearing miniature versions of the performing costumes his father had worn. His mother also insisted that her son sing nothing but his father's songs, performed in a manner as close as possible to the old recordings. The idea, apparently, was to make fans feel that in watching Hank Williams, Jr., they were actually observing the reincarnation of Hank Williams, Sr.

At the age of eight, Williams made his professional debut on a stage in Swainsboro, Georgia, and earned a warm reception. Three years later he made his first appearance at the legendary Grand Ole Opry, singing his father's classic hit "Lovesick Blues." By the time he turned fourteen, young Hank had signed a recording contract, headlined national tours, and appeared on *The Ed Sullivan Show.*

Battling the Demons. In 1964, Williams scored the sound track for the film biography of this father, titled *Your Cheatin' Heart.* At the strong urging of his mother, he also named his backing band the Cheatin' Hearts, thus cementing his career and reputation even more closely with that of his father's. Even though his career was flourishing, Williams's private life was becoming progressively more miserable. Although he loved his father's music, he desperately wanted to perform and record some of his own songs or at least perform the classics in his own style. As long as the younger Williams was a minor, however, the obstinate Audrey demanded her son's performances sound like her deceased husband's recordings.

Hank also had difficulty in maintaining healthy relationships with women. He did try marriage twice as a young man, but by the age of twenty-five, he had been divorced twice. Williams also developed an ongoing problem with alcohol, primarily whiskey and beer, perhaps in a subconscious attempt to carry the emulation of his father even further.

On August 8, 1975, while hiking on Ajax Mountain in Montana, he took a wrong step on the snow-covered slope and fell five hundred feet. The horrifying plummet ended only when the singer's head collided with a group of boulders. When his hiking companion finally reached him, Williams appeared dead. Every single bone in his face was broken, one of his eyes was detached, and part of his brain lay exposed as a result of a massive skull fracture. For two weeks he lay near death, and his survival was far from certain. Almost miraculously, he avoided a usually fatal brain infection, but there had occurred some slight brain damage, and his entire face needed to be rebuilt through reconstructive surgery. His recovery would be both frustrating and painfully slow.

Recording Classics. Shortly before the accident, Williams had finally broken completely with his mother and had left the ultra-conservative Nashville environment. He had also recorded a country rock album titled *Hank Williams, Jr, and Friends* (1976), which featured Charlie Daniels and members of the Allman Brothers Band. During his long recovery, Williams was thrilled to see the album's success. By 1978, his comeback was in full swing with the release of the hit single "I Fought the Law" and two gold albums. The next year he wrote a best-selling autobiography, *Living Proof,* which later became a made-for-television film. During this time, he continued his musical evolution by identifying himself with the "outlaw" movement led by Willie Nelson and Waylon Jennings, with the latter producing Williams's hit album *The New South* (1977).

Although he only rarely made the pop charts, Hank compiled a long string of country hits from the late 1970's through the 1980's. Some of his largest selling records were "Family Tradition," "All My Rowdy Friends (Have Settled Down)," "Ain't Misbehavin'," and "Young Country." One of his best received and most interesting singles was "There's a Tear in My Beer," which produced a video, via modern technology, featuring both Williams and his father together. The American Broadcasting Company evidently believed that

For the Record

In the late 1960's, Hank Williams, Jr., recorded a series of albums under the pseudonym Luke the Drifter, Jr. (His father had used the name Luke the Drifter on occasion.) These albums consisted of emotional recitations, not totally dissimilar from later rap music.

Williams's fans were also football fans and hired him to write and perform a new theme song for Monday Night Football, a move which guaranteed widespread national attention. Despite his huge commercial success, Williams received little to no formal recognition from the music industry until the mid-1980's. The reasons for the shunning were widely believed to be the Williams family's reputation for substance abuse and Williams's avowed disgust for the musical constraints imposed by the stodgy Nashville music scene.

Legacy. From the time of his first public appearance while still a child, Hank Williams, Jr., was the living embodiment of a musical legacy. While he certainly enjoyed the benefits of the Williams name, he was also faced with the tremendous burden of living up to that name. Another of his problems was the perceived need to pay homage to his father and to his father's beloved music while simultaneously trying to carve a niche for himself. In this task, he was very successful, as the younger Williams helped to create the music genre known as country rock. While Williams recognized from the start that he could never be a clone of his father (a realization accepted only later and begrudgingly by his mother, record company, and many fans), he has excelled at being Hank Williams, Jr., as witnessed by the release of over sixty albums and millions of record sales.

—*Thomas W. Buchanan*

SELECT DISCOGRAPHY

■ ALBUMS

Songs My Father Left Me, 1969
Family Tradition, 1979
The Pressure Is On, 1981
Hank Williams Jr.'s Greatest Hits, 1982 (compilation)
Born to Boogie, 1987
Out of Left Field, 1993

SELECT AWARDS

Country Music Association Music Video of the Year Award for "All My Rowdy Friends (Have Settled Down)," 1985
Country Music Association Music Video of the Year for "My Name Is Bocephus" and Entertainer of the Year Awards, 1987
Country Music Association Album of the Year for *Born to Boogie* and Entertainer of the Year Awards, 1988
Grammy Award for Best Country Vocal Collaboration for "There's a Tear in My Beer," 1989 (with Hank Williams, Sr.)
Country Music Association Vocal Event of the Year and Music Video of the Year Awards for "There's a Tear in My Beer," 1989 (with Hank Williams, Sr.)

SEE ALSO: Cash, Johnny; Jennings, Waylon; Nelson, Willie; Williams, Hank.

Vanessa Williams

BORN: Bronx, New York; March 18, 1963
FIRST ALBUM RELEASE: *The Right Stuff,* 1988
MUSICAL STYLES: Pop, rhythm and blues

Vanessa Williams and her younger brother Christopher grew up in suburban Milwood, New York, about twenty miles north of New York City. They were the only African American family in their middle-class neighborhood, and Vanessa was the first black student to go through the local public school system. Her home environment was ideal for a future pop singer, since both of her parents were elementary school music teachers who had a particular fondness for musical theater.

Intensive Training. They supported their daughter's interest in music and the arts, seeing to it that she had years of training in music (including French horn, piano, and mellophone) and six years in the study of dance. As a teenager, she toured parts of the United States and Caracas, Venezuela, and Nassau, Bahamas, with the Horace Greeley High School orchestra. In addition to playing musical instruments and dancing, Williams had developed the ability to sing and act. She was interested in a career on Broadway, and she majored in musical theater at Syracuse University.

Sudden Fame. Williams was also very beautiful. With startling green eyes and a svelte figure, she was able to help pay for her education by

Vanessa Williams (Paul Natkin)

modeling and working as a professional makeup artist. Almost as a fluke, she agreed to compete in a beauty contest, the Miss Greater Syracuse Pageant, when plans to appear in a stage production misfired. Williams won this contest and entered the next level, the Miss New York pageant. She won this one as well, defeating twenty-one competitors.

The next level of competition was the famous Miss America Pageant in Atlantic City, New Jersey. With her eye on the generous scholarship money (as much as three thousand dollars even for semifinalists at that time), as well as valuable publicity, Williams agreed to enter.

Although it had been over twenty years since the civil rights struggles and desegregation of the 1960's, cultural patterns changed more slowly. In 1970, Cheryl Browne had become the first African American to compete in the pageant, and in 1983, some new records were set, including the entry of four black contestants in the Miss America Pageant. Williams won the talent and swimsuit components of the competition. Although many of the contestants had entered many beauty contests and had trained for years to prepare for this moment (just as Williams had trained for a career in musical theater), she had only entered four pageants and won three of them.

When Williams won the 1983 contest, appearing before a television audience of about seventy-five million people, she realized that the nation's eyes were upon her, especially because she was making history. Because she had become the first African American to win the Miss America crown, there was a great deal of political symbolism involved, and she was under pressure from many directions.

Fall from Grace. As many celebrities have found, fame and privacy tend to exclude each other. Someone found nude photos of Williams from her days as a part-time model, and they were published in *Penthouse* magazine. In the midst of international publicity, her crown was taken away, making her the first Miss America to be dethroned, and her future seemed less than promising. However, Williams refused to be defeated. She hired Ramon Hervey, a Los Angeles publicist, as a manager. After moving to Los Angeles and marrying Hervey in January, 1987, she attempted to find work as an actress, but found acceptance difficult at that time.

Comeback. A return to singing, however, became very successful. Her debut album, *The Right Stuff* (1988), earned a gold record and won three Grammy Award nominations. The title track was

For the Record

The song "Happiness" from Vanessa Williams's album *Next* was written when a songwriter asked her how she felt about her life.

a hit single, soon followed by three more hit singles: "He's Got the Look," "Dreamin'," and "Darling I." Her second album, *The Comfort Zone*, which was released in 1991, included the single "Save the Best for Last," which sold more than one million copies and topped the pop, adult contemporary, and rhythm-and-blues charts for weeks. *The Comfort Zone*, which went double platinum, also included four other hit singles.

Since her childhood, Williams had dreamed of starring in musicals on Broadway. She realized this goal in 1994, when she starred in John Kander, Fred Ebb, and Terrence McNally's *Kiss of the Spider Woman*. To prepare for the rigors of the stage, she worked out with a trainer and performed in the show eight times per week for nine months. After her Broadway experience, she was ready to give Hollywood, which had rejected her earlier attempts, another try. She agressively pursued the leading role in the 1996 film *Eraser* and eventually starred in the film with Arnold Schwarzenegger.

Williams's rhythm-and-blues album *Next*, which was critically acclaimed, was released in 1997. Her performance of the song "Colors of the Wind" at the end of the 1995 animated film *Pocahontas* also generated a hit single. Along with her careers in music, film, television, and theater, Williams took care of her daughters Melanie and Jillian and her son Devin, often bringing them to work with her when schedules permitted. Two more of her films, *Hoodlum* and *Soul Food*, were released in 1997. In 1998, Williams returned to the New York stage in a revival of the musical *St. Louis Woman*, in which she played the character of Della Green. She also released the film *Dance with Me* that year.

Musical Style. Williams's vocal style reflects her diverse musical interests and years of study. She has sung many styles, including show tunes, swing, dance, soft rock, and others. Her strong voice and clear pronounciation reflect her theatrical background, but her delicate inflections and carefully controlled bends in pitch are reminiscent of blues and gospel singers. On her albums and on the screen, she has proven repeatedly that she is not just a beautiful woman, but a true artist.

—*Alice Myers*

SELECT DISCOGRAPHY
■ ALBUMS
The Right Stuff, 1988
The Comfort Zone, 1991
The Sweetest Days, 1994
Star Bright, 1996
Next, 1997

SEE ALSO: McKnight, Brian.

Bob Wills and His Texas Playboys

BORN: near Kosse, Texas; March 6, 1905
DIED: Fort Worth, Texas; May 13, 1975
ORIGINAL MEMBERS: Bob Wills, Herman Arnspiger, Jesse Ashlock, Tommy Duncan (1911-1967), William "Smokey" Dacus, Art Haines, Clifton "Sleepy" Johnson (d. 1976), Son Lansford, Leon McAuliffe (1917-1988), Zeb McNally, Al Stricklin (d. 1986), Johnnie Lee Wills (1912-1984), Everett Stover (members of the first "classic" 1936 band)
FIRST SINGLE RELEASE: "Right or Wrong"/"Steel Guitar Rag," 1936 (first release of the 1936 band)
MUSICAL STYLES: Western swing, country

Bob Wills almost singlehandedly invented the genre of music now known as western swing, that blend of 1930's big-band jazz, blues, Texas cowboy songs, rowdy Panhandle country ballads, popular ballroom dance rhythms, and old-time string-band fiddle tunes. Though the era of the big swing bands died after World War II, Bob Wills and His Texas Playboys continued to work in the decades that followed until 1973, just before his death. He has influenced country stars from Merle Haggard to John Denver to Charlie Daniels, and he won an international following.

Early Years. Born James Robert Wills in East Texas, "Jim Bob" was the first of nine children of poor farmers. Both his father and mother's families, however, had local reputations as excellent fiddlers. Fiddle tunes were popular all over the American South, being brought over by Anglo-

Celtic immigrants ever since the early days of colonization. The music was carried by settlers during the great westward expansions in the late nineteenth century. As this music went west—or deeper into the southern mountains—it became more Americanized, with Irish jigs, English reels, and Scottish airs becoming everyday American folk songs or fiddle tunes for dances. Rural social life centered around the local barn or school-house dance, and the Wills family supplemented their tight income by playing for these occasions. Bob played fiddle for his first dance at the age of ten when his father failed to arrive.

Another influence on Wills's musical development was African American song and culture. By picking cotton in the fields and playing with his neighborhood friends (who were all African Americans), Wills naturally acquired, at an early age, many black musical idioms, such as ragtime jazz, Delta blues, and black spirituals and work songs. As Wills grew older he also acquired a taste for recorded jazz, Tin Pan Alley pop tunes, and blues artists such as Bessie Smith. "She was the greatest thing I ever heard," he once told his biographer. In fact, it was his attempt to make his slurred fiddle imitate the blues that gave his music its special quality.

Doughboys, Playboys, and Radio Days. After briefly forming a duet with guitarist Herman Arnspiger in 1929, Wills formed a radio band sponsored by the Light Crust Flour company in 1931. The Light Crust Doughboys, as they called themselves, played all kinds of music, from current pop standards to waltzes to novelty songs. Often for their personal appearances they wore quasi-military uniforms similar to that of the U.S. doughboys (infantrymen) of World War I. After continued drinking caused Wills to get fired, he formed his own band, the Texas Playboys, in late 1933.

From 1934 to 1942, Wills had one of the most popular U.S. dance bands—first in the Southwest, then nationally. The addition of a young steel–guitar player in 1935, Leon McAuliffe, enhanced the depth of the band tremendously as well as kept the band current with the latest trends in musical instrumentation. Other improvements included adding drums, a horn section of trumpet and saxophone, and additional fiddles and strings. By the late 1930's Bob Wills was out-selling many established artists such as Louis Armstrong, Lawrence Welk, and Gene Autry.

Doorway to Success. It was around this time that Wills composed the tune that would later become his trademark, "San Antonio Rose." This one song alone propelled the Texas Playboys into international prominence. Three million copies were sold in 1940, and other artists, such as Bing Crosby, also achieved great success with it. As Wills's biographer Charles Townsend has said, "Without ['San Antonio Rose'] . . . probably Wills and western swing would have gone into oblivion." Their popularity increased, however, with film offers coming frequently and talented musi-

Bob Wills (Archive Photos/Frank Driggs Collection)

cians begging to join the band. Part of this popularity was likely due to the ability of the Texas Playboys to perform in any style, from big band to Dixieland, as well as from Wills's own personal charisma.

World War II broke up the tight Wills band in the 1930's. Personal problems (including six marriages and bouts of alcoholism) also took their toll on Wills. In 1964 he suffered a heart attack, and a number of strokes followed. In 1973, Wills was directing his band for the last time from a wheelchair for a two-day recording session. After the first day he suffered another stroke and went into a coma. He died fifteen months later, never having regained consciousness.

The Legacy of Western Swing. There is little doubt that the swinging jazz style of country music of Bob Wills heavily influenced both rock and roll and modern country music. In 1970, Merle Haggard's album, *Tribute to the Best Damn Fiddle Player in the World* introduced western swing to a new generation of post-World War II fans. In 1994, the revival band Asleep at the Wheel did the same for the 1990's generation with their *Tribute to the Music of Bob Wills and the The Texas Playboys* (1994). This album featured almost every big name in country music, young or old (including Chet Atkins, Garth Brooks, Lyle Lovett, Willie Nelson, Dolly Parton, and George Strait, among others), together with surviving Playboy stars such as Johnny Gimble and Eldon Shamblin. This album won two Grammy Awards and no doubt helped increase the popularity of country line dancing. Today, western swing is an internationally recognized musical style, and Bob Wills is commonly accepted as an American cultural icon.   —*James Stanlaw*

SELECT DISCOGRAPHY
■ ALBUMS
The Best of Bob Wills, 1973 (1965-1968 material)
Bob Wills: Columbia Historic Edition, 1982 (1930's and 1940's material)
The Tiffany Transcriptions Vol 1-9, 1982-1990 (9 CDs of 1946-1947 material)
Fiddle, 1987 (1935-1942 material)
Bob Wills, Anthology 1935-1973, 1991
The Essential Bob Wills, 1935-1947, 1992

For the Record

"In putting the swing back into country music, Bob not only energized the form itself, but opened the door to exploration of other possibilities as well, through the mutant rockabilly to the core of what became rock and roll."   —*John McEuen*
§
"Rock and roll? Why man, that's the same kind of music we've been playing since 1928!"   —*Bob Wills*, c. 1958

Bob Wills: Country Music Hall of Fame Series, 1992 (1955-1967 material)
The Longhorn Recordings, 1993 (1960's material)
Bob Wills, Encore, 1994 (1960-1973 material)
Classic Western Swing, 1994
For the Last Time, 1994 (1973 material)

SELECT AWARDS
Country Music Hall of Fame, inducted 1968
Rock and Roll Hall of Fame, inducted 1999

SEE ALSO: Daniels, Charlie; Denver, John; Haggard, Merle; Haley, Bill; Jennings, Waylon; Nelson, Willie; Strait, George.

Jackie Wilson

BORN: Detroit, Michigan; June 9, 1934
DIED: Mount Holly, New Jersey; January 21, 1984
FIRST SINGLE RELEASE: "Reet Petite (The Finest Girl You Ever Want to Meet)," 1957
MUSICAL STYLES: Rhythm and blues, pop, light classical

As a vocal stylist and showman-entertainer, Jackie Wilson was without peer. James Brown could match Wilson's showmanship, but few could match his ability to couple vocal virtuosity with sheer dynamic electricity and theatrically. Ironically, Wilson's athleticism and showmanship on stage probably contributed to his untimely death.

At the height of his career, he was considered one of pop music's most spectacularly gifted artists.

Early Life. Wilson was reared in a tough part of Detroit, where he first earned attention for his skills as a boxer. Although he had some real success in the ring, at one point capturing a title in the prestigious Golden Gloves amateur championship, he quit boxing at the behest of his mother, who disapproved of the sport. He subsequently focused his energies on the pursuit of an entertainment career. As a child, he had sung gospel music in Detroit churches and had acquired a local reputation as a gifted vocalist. In 1951, he was discovered by Johnny Otis after participating in a talent show. As a teenager, he sang at nightclubs in the Detroit area and became a member of the Thrillers, a predecessor group of the Royals. Although he made some minor recordings at this stage of his career, his first significant single would not be made until 1957.

His stature as a nationally recognized entertainment personality began to rise in 1953, after he auditioned for Billy Ward to replace Clyde McPhatter as lead singer of the Dominoes. At that point, his career began in earnest. Ward was a stern taskmaster who demanded perfection from his vocalists. Under his tutelage, Wilson's raw talent blossomed into a dynamite package of musicianship and showmanship. After a few years, however, Wilson parted ways with the strict discipline of Ward and the management of the Dominoes.

Solo Career. Wilson began a solo career in 1957 from his home base in Detroit. Al Green, an entrepreneur who had an interest in the Flame Show Bar, became his manager. Green, who also managed nationally prominent artists Johnny Ray and La Vern Baker, died shortly after taking over as Wilson's manager. Following Green's death, his assistant Nat Tarnapol became Wilson's manager. Berry Gordy, Jr., had worked for Green and served as house pianist for the Flame Show Bar. During his spare time, he wrote a string of hit singles for Wilson. Gordy, like Wilson, was rooted in gospel, and the vivid imagery and emotional vitality of gospel were fused into Gordy's secular compositions. He teamed with Tyran Carlo (later known as Roquel "Billy" Davis) to write the music and

lyrics to Wilson's first significant recording, "Reet Petite (The Finest Girl You Ever Want to Meet)." Released on September 8, 1957, on the Brunswick label, the record initially failed to attract much attention in the United States and was unlisted on the rhythm-and-blues charts; however, it reached number 6 on the British pop charts.

In 1958, Wilson had a significant U.S. hit with Gordy and Carlo's "Lonely Teardrops." Thereafter, Gordy devoted his attention to developing Motown Records. Although Gordy and Wilson were close friends and collaborators, Wilson never signed a contract for Motown. This proved unfortunate for Wilson, because Motown had a superior stable of composer-arrangers and studio musicians on its staff. Brunswick Records, for which Wilson recorded, seemed to lack the creativity and imagination to support Wilson's talent.

Although Wilson's recordings failed to capture the expressive emotionalism and vitality of his live performances, his showmanship catapulted him to a place of preeminence among popular entertainment artists. The public loved him, as evidenced by the sold-out houses where he performed. He lived up to his nickname "Mr. Excitement" at virtually every performance.

Onstage, Wilson, wearing skin-tight mohair or silk suits, would strut and dance with his coat slung over his shoulder, then suddenly spin and jump from one level of the stage to another, landing in a perfect split. His athleticism often stirred female fans into a frenzy, and many fans who saw Wilson perform have remarked that his energy and dramatic flair remain etched in their memories. He also impressed his fellow entertainer, and he has been cited as an important influence on the stage shows of Elvis Presley, among others.

Wilson's star continued to rise, and on December 25, 1958, he appeared in Alan Freed's "Christmas Rock and Roll Spectacular" at Loew's State Theater in Manhattan along with Chuck Berry and others. He also performed with Irving Field's "Biggest Show of Stars," which featured Frankie Avalon, Paul Anka, the Crescendos, Jimmy Reed, and Sam Cooke. His career was almost derailed in 1961 when a female fan shot and seriously wounded him at a New York hotel, but he recovered and returned to performing. On January 21, 1962, he made a coveted appearance on the prestigious Ed Sullivan Show, the showcase for artists who had arrived at the zenith their careers.

In 1963, Wilson released "Baby Workout," which reached number 5 on the pop charts, but his career then stalled. He collaborated with producer Carl Davis for a 1966 comeback that included the number 11 pop hit "Whispers" and the number 6 pop hit "(Your Love Keeps Lifting Me) Higher and Higher," which would also provide a 1977 hit for Rita Coolidge. His subsequent recordings met with indifferent receptions, however, and by the mid-1970's he had become a fixture on the nostalgia circuit.

In September, 1975, at the Latin Casino in Cherry Hill, New Jersey, he suffered a near-fatal onstage heart attack while performing in a Dick Clark revue. On falling, he struck his head and suffered brain damage. He remained hospitalized in a comatose condition until his death on January 21, 1984. —*Warren C. Swindell*

SELECT DISCOGRAPHY
■ SINGLES
"Reet Petite," 1957
"To Be Loved," 1958
"Lonely Teardrops," 1958
"Night/Doggin' Around," 1960
"Baby Workout," 1963
"(Your Love Keeps Lifting Me) Higher and Higher," 1966
■ ALBUMS
Mr. Excitement, 1992 (previously released material)

SELECT AWARDS
Rock and Roll Hall of Fame, inducted 1987

SEE ALSO: Brown, James; Cooke, Sam; Drifters, The.

The Winans

ORIGINAL MEMBERS: Carvin Winans (b. 1958), Marvin Winans (b. 1958), Michael Winans (b. 1959), Ronald Winans (b. 1955)

OTHER MEMBERS: Benjamin "BeBe" Winans (b. 1962), Priscilla "CeCe" Winans (b. c. 1964), Daniel Winans, Debbie Winans (b. c. 1972), Angie Winans, Vickie Winans
FIRST ALBUM RELEASE: *Introducing the Winans*, 1981
MUSICAL STYLES: Gospel, rhythm and blues

In the field of Christian music, where family groups are common, no family was more consistently impressive in the 1980's and 1990's than the Winans. From the traditional gospel sounds of the early Winans to the contemporary rhythm-and-blues gospel of BeBe and CeCeWinans, the ten children of David and Dolores Winans (known as Mom and Pop), in various combinations, were regulars on the gospel and contemporary Christian charts. BeBe and CeCe Winans became crossover stars in the early 1990's, logging two number 1 rhythm-and-blues hits.

Gospel Roots. David and Dolores Winans met in the early 1950's while singing in the Lemon Gospel Chorus. David's own group, the Nobelaires, were a traditional gospel quartet in the tradition of the Dixie Hummingbirds and the Soul Stirrers, of which Sam Cooke was a part. The young couple were poor, and each had to work two or three jobs in order to raise their family in the Parkside projects on the west side of Detroit, Michigan. As a Pentecostal minister, David Winans made sure there was plenty of gospel singing and music around his home. The children were not allowed to attend films or theater or listen to secular music.

The four oldest brothers, Ronald, Carvin, Marvin, and Michael, briefly formed a group as adolescents but stopped singing as an act of rebellion. While their parents were on vacation in 1973, however, Ronald encouraged Michael, BeBe, and CeCe to perform in a high school talent show, where they thrilled their first secular audience. In 1975 the four brothers regrouped as the Winans and began performing in the Detroit area. They were soon offered a recording contract. Legendary producer Quincy Jones began working with them in 1984, and that year they released *Tomorrow and More* (1984), which earned the first of four consecutive Grammy Awards, for Best Soul Gospel Performance.

Many Styles. Though the Winans began singing the traditional quartet music of their father, they evolved in the late 1980's toward rhythm and blues and incorporated elements of hip-hop into their performances. Collaborations with Michael McDonald ("Love Has No Color"), Anita Baker ("Ain't No Need to Worry), Stevie Wonder, Kenny G, and Ricky Skaggs gave them a sizable secular presence, while at the same time eroded some of their more conservative support. Their 1990 album, *Return*, featured the production work of "new jack swing" master Teddy Riley, then at the peak of his influence.

As the Winans became more involved in church-related activities in the 1990's, their younger siblings were emerging as professional musicians. Vickie and Daniel went solo, while the youngest, Debbie and Angie (sometimes billed as the Sisters), formed a partnership. The most successful Winans, however, would prove to be BeBe and CeCe, who together earned seven Grammy awards, seven Dove awards, five Stellar awards, and three National Association for the Advancement of Colored People (NAACP) Image awards. In addition to their superstar status in the contemporary Christian music scene, they earned six rhythm-and-blues Top-10 hits, with two going to number 1 ("Addictive Love" and "I'll Take You There"). Their 1991 platinum *Different Lifestyles* album was the first to head both the gospel and rhythm-and-blues charts.

All in the Family. In 1992, Winans parents and all ten children toured together for the first time on the "Winans' One Family World Tour." As on their recordings, each group or artist performed

Angie and Debbie Winans in 1997 (AP/Wide World Photos)

their own material, though they also worked in various combinations and occasionally as an entire family. In 1995 BeBe and CeCe separated to work on solo projects but planned to eventually return as a duo.   —*John Powell*

SELECT DISCOGRAPHY
The Winans
■ ALBUMS
Long Time Comin', 1983
Tomorrow and More, 1984
Let My People Go, 1986
Decisions, 1987
Live at Carnegie Hall, 1988

For the Record

BeBe Winans's self-titled solo debut features duets with sister Debbie, backing vocals by Luther Vandross, and guitar work by Eric Clapton.

Return, 1990
All Out, 1993
Mom and Pop Winans
■ ALBUMS
Mom and Pop Winans, 1989
Angie and Debbie Winans
■ ALBUMS
Angie & Debbie, 1993
BeBe Winans
■ ALBUMS
BeBe Winans, 1997
BeBe and CeCe Winans
■ ALBUMS
Lord Lift Us Up, 1984
BeBe & CeCe Winans, 1987
Heaven, 1988
Different Lifestyles, 1991
First Christmas, 1993
Relationships, 1994
Greatest Hits, 1996 (compilation)
CeCe Winans
■ ALBUMS
Alone in His Presence, 1995
Everlasting Love, 1998
Daniel Winans
■ ALBUMS
And the Second Half, 1987
Brotherly Love, 1988
Not in My House, 1994
Vickie Winans
■ ALBUMS
Live in Detroit, 1997

SELECT AWARDS
The Winans
Grammy Award for Best Soul Gospel Performance by a Duo or Group for *Tomorrow*, 1985

Grammy Award for Best Soul Gospel Performance by a Duo or Group, Choir or Chorus, for *Let My People Go*, 1986
Grammy Award for Best Soul Gospel Performance by a Duo, Group, Choir, or Chorus for "Ain't No Need to Worry," 1987 (with Anita Baker)
Grammy Award for Best Gospel Performance by a Duo or Group, Choir or Chorus, for *The Winans Live at Carnegie Hall*, 1988
BeBe and CeCe Winans
Grammy Award for Best Contemporary Soul Gospel Album for *Different Lifestyles*, 1991
Dove Award for Contemporary Gospel Recorded Song of the Year for "Up Where We Belong," 1997
BeBe Winans
Grammy Award for Best Soul Gospel Performance, Male, for "Abundant Life," 1988
Grammy Award for Best Gospel Vocal Performance, Male, for "Meantime," 1989
CeCe Winans
Grammy Award for Best Soul Gospel Performance, Female, for "For Always," 1987
Grammy Award for Best Gospel Performance, Female, for "Don't Cry," 1989
Dove Awards for Female Vocalist of the Year and Traditional Gospel Recorded Song of the Year for "Great Is His Faithfulness," 1995
Grammy Award for Best Contemporary Soul Gospel Album for *Alone in His Presence*, 1995

SEE ALSO: Cooke, Sam; Patti, Sandi.

Bobby Womack

BORN: Cleveland, Ohio; March 4, 1944
FIRST SINGLE RELEASE: "Looking for a Love," 1962 (with the Valentinos)
MUSICAL STYLES: Rhythm and blues, rock and roll, soul, jazz

Bobby Womack, a dynamic individual who exerted a lasting influence on black music in the 1960's, 1970's, 1980's, and 1990's, did not receive recognition until late in his career. A writer and singer, Womack listened to and performed gospel music when he was young, and he used this early influence to launch and establish his career.

Beginnings. Womack's father, Friendly Womack, Sr., a steelworker in Cleveland, Ohio, organized his sons Cecil, Curtis, Friendly, Jr., Harris, and Bobby into the Womack Brothers Gospel Quartet. In 1960, due largely to the influence of Sam Cooke, who was moving from gospel to a more secular musical style, the group renamed themselves the Valentinos. The mixing of gospel music of their youth with the soul music of Cooke developed the Valentinos' style into one of shouting lead vocals mixed with blues and gospel harmonies, predating late 1960's soul music. Under Cooke's Sar label and with his financial backing, the Valentinos recorded Bobby's two compositions, "Looking for a Love" in 1962 (later a J. Geils Band hit) and "It's All over Now" (later a Rolling Stones hit) in 1964.

In 1964, after Cooke's violent shooting death, Bobby decided to branch out and become a solo performer. During this time, he also incurred great disapproval in the music community by marrying Cooke's widow. For the next several years, Womack wrote songs and provided backup material for, among others, Wilson Pickett ("People Make the World" and "I'm a Midnight Mover"). Womack had a minor hit with "Fly Me to the Moon" (1967). He worked with Janis Joplin and later with Sly and the Family Stone on the album *There's a Riot Goin' On* (1971). Womack's guitar can be heard on the Aretha Franklin hit "Lady Soul" and on Wilson Pickett's "Funky Broadway." Another rhythm-and-blues single of Womack's that became a hit during the 1970's was "Check It Out" (1975).

Influence. Womack, one of the most renowned guitarists in the history of rhythm and blues, collaborated with some of the greatest musicians of the 1960's, 1970's, 1980's, and 1990's. Wilson Pickett, Ray Charles, Aretha Franklin, Jimi Hendrix, Janis Joplin, Patti LaBelle, Joe Tex, jazzman Gabor Szabo, and the Rolling Stones have used his music or been influenced by his style and incorporated it into their own performances and recordings.

In the early years, on a soul package tour in 1962, Womack and Hendrix became friends.

Womack's guitar style influenced Hendrix's later use of the wa-wa effects pedal. In turn, Womack would use that feature in 1971 on Sly Stone's album *There's a Riot Goin' On* and on the single "Family Affair."

Womack was one of the first black artists to make an impact on the British rock scene, as evidenced by the Rolling Stones hit "It's All over Now." The influence was lasting, as Womack was invited to record with the Stones in 1986 on *Dirty Work*. He also produced a solo album for Ron Wood.

Comeback. In 1976, Womack had a dispute with United Artists over the title of his collection of country songs. As a result, he moved to Arista. Due largely to personal difficulties, his work with this company was less than spectacular. Known throughout the industry as a wild soul man, Womack partied often with several music industry giants.

In 1980, Womack once again emerged as a presence in the music industry, performing as the vocalist on the Crusaders' "Inherit the Wind." In 1981, his album *The Poet* returned him to the forefront of the music industry. Soon after its release, *The Poet* rose to the Top 10 on *Billboard*'s soul charts. *The Poet* unfashionably highlighted soul roots in the age of disco. Since the album was such a big rhythm-and-blues hit, it prompted Womack to record *The Poet II* in 1984, an equally successful production. *The Poet II* sold especially well in Europe and became his first platinum recording.

For the Record

Bobby Womack's father, Friendly Womack, Sr., had told his son specifically not to play his guitar. Consequently, right-handed Bobby learned to play the guitar with his left hand while on the lookout for his father. One day his father caught him playing with the guitar. His father told him that he would not be in trouble if young Bobby could actually play the instrument. Bobby amazed his father with his ability to play the guitar in several different styles.

In 1985, Womack moved to MCA. Following this move, *So Many Rivers*, *Womagic*, and *The Last Soul Man*, which featured a guest appearance by Sly Stone, appeared in quick succession. The *Dirty Work* album with the Rolling Stones in 1986 served to reestablish Womack as a dynamic and lasting performer, one who would remain consistently productive over the years.

In 1992, Womack organized two tribute concerts in Redondo Beach, California, for Temptation Eddie Kendricks, who died from lung cancer. The concerts, which raised twenty-five thousand dollars for Kendrick's survivors, featured such performers as Chaka Khan and Bill Withers.

In 1997, he produced his thirty-third album, *Resurrection*, which included special performances by Keith Richards, Ron Wood, and Charlie Watts of the Rolling Stones, Stevie Wonder, Michael Compton of Journey, Brian May of Queen, Gerald Albright, and rapper May May Ali, boxer Muhammad Ali's daughter. Even with all these stellar performers on the album, Womack remained the star.

With a career spanning three decades, Womack represents the ultimate performer. He has provided a body of work that ranks among the best in modern pop and rock music. As a songwriter, singer, and guitarist, his influence will be felt for many years to come. Womack has assumed the role of the guardian of the soul tradition that stresses passionate singing and well-written songs.

—*Karan A. Berryman*

SELECT DISCOGRAPHY

■ ALBUMS

Communication, 1971
Understanding , 1972
BW Goes C&W, 1976
The Poet, 1981
The Poet II, 1984
Womagic, 1986
The Last Soul Man, 1987
Save the Children, 1989 (with the Womack Brothers)
Lookin' for a Love: Best of Bobby Womack, 1994 (compilation)
I Feel a Groove Comin' On, 1995
The Soul of Bobby Womack: Stop on By, 1996

SEE ALSO: Cooke, Sam; Pickett, Wilson; Rolling Stones, The.

Stevie Wonder

BORN: Saginaw, Michigan; May 13, 1950
FIRST ALBUM RELEASE: *Tribute to Uncle Ray*, 1962
MUSICAL STYLES: Rhythm and blues, soul

A career as long as Stevie Wonder's is an anomaly in U.S. popular music. For the maker of that career to have staved off the self-destructive excesses of musical stardom may be rarer still. Stevie Wonder has been one of the finest keyboard players in popular music and arguably one of its most accomplished musicians on nearly every score. Exploring virtually every form of popular music, he has defied the most determined efforts to categorize his style or to imitate his sound. A paragon of philanthropy and a champion of human rights, the black elder statesman of music has erased the boundaries between black and white music.

The Beginnings. Given the stage name Little Stevie Wonder by Berry Gordy, Jr., of Motown Records in 1961, he was born Steveland Judkins but called himself Steveland Morris. From age five, when his mother moved him and his five brothers and sisters to Detroit, Michigan, Wonder showed an amazing aptitude for music. He sang in the Whitestone Baptist Church choir and learned piano by the time he was seven, composed his first song at age eight, and was an accomplished drummer and harmonica player before the age of nine. An avid fan of rhythm and blues as well as gospel, he listened to Sam Cooke and especially to Ray Charles, with whom he felt a close kinship, as both were African American, blind, and prodigies.

Wonder might have become just one of many talented but unheralded ghetto children, had he not been living in Detroit while musical entrepreneur Berry Gordy was building the Motown empire. By chance, Ronnie White of the Miracles heard him playing harmonica for White's children in 1961 and took him to Gordy who, stunned by Wonder's supple, gymnastic voice and his virtuoso playing, signed him at age ten to his subsidiary label, Tamla. In 1962, Wonder recorded his first single, "I Call It Pretty Music (but the Old People Call It the Blues)." In the same year he released two albums, *Tribute to Uncle Ray* and *The Jazz Soul of Little Stevie*, the former capitalizing on the comparison to Ray Charles and the latter showing off his instrumental prowess. In August of 1963, his fourth single, the rousing "Fingertips, Part 2," recorded in Chicago at the Regal Theater, sold more than one million copies and became the first live recording to go to number 1 on the *Billboard* charts. With the success of his third album, *Little Stevie Wonder, the 12 Year Old Genius Recorded Live* (1963), Wonder became the first musician to have the number 1 single on the pop charts, the top rhythm-and-blues single, and the best-selling rhythm-and-blues album all at the same time. Few child acts had fledged so quickly.

Stevie Wonder in 1995 (AP/Wide World Photos)

Foreseeing the "British invasion" months ahead of its arrival, Gordy sent Wonder and other Motown acts to Great Britain in 1963 to head off the most dangerous threat to the company's future. In December, Wonder appeared on the popular televison shows *Ready, Steady, Go* and *Thank Your Lucky Stars*. (He would return in 1965 for an hour-long special, *The Sound of Tamla Motown* and again in 1966 for a concert tour.) These promotions paid dividends for years to come as Wonder's records often climbed higher in Great Britain than in the United States. Back home, he was in the first wave of another preemptive strike, debuting on *The Ed Sullivan Show*, the popular television variety show, just one week before the Beatles made their historic appearance on February 9, 1964.

Growing Up. Searching for their musical signatures, Motown and Stevie Wonder had been growing up together in the early 1960's. In 1964 Wonder took a brief hiatus while his voice changed and dropped the "Little" from his name (it took years for fans to follow suit). Motown's voice had also changed by 1964 as its trademark sound emerged. Although Wonder tried to conform to the company ethic, Gordy wisely allowed him the freedom to depart from the Motown formula when it suited him. His singing retained a uniquely ecstatic quality, exemplified in the exuberant and breathlessly spontaneous "I Was Made to Love Her" (1967). Yet, to demonstrate how difficult it was to confine Wonder's musical interests or to fathom Motown's marketing strategy, he had a hit covering the Tony Bennett standard "For Once in My Life" at the high-water mark of a musical and social revolution in 1968. Shortly thereafter he issued a touching but tame instrumental version of "Alfie," oddly attributed to Eivets Rednow, his name spelled backward.

Motown's clever promotion and Wonder's own boundless talent ignited a skyrocketing career. Beginning with "Uptight (Everything's Alright)," in June of 1966, Wonder's songs stormed the Top 40 almost without interruption into the mid-1970's, a chain of successes rivaling both the Beatles and Elvis Presley at the summits of their popularity. Even his B-sides became hits when "My Cherie Amour" peaked at number 4 in 1969.

The 1970's. Wonder's first feverish decade in show business closed in August 1970, with a number 3 single, "Signed, Sealed, Delivered, I'm Yours," from the album of the same name. Significantly, it was the first that he entirely self-produced, and he played most of the instruments and sang all the vocal tracks.

In May, 1971, Wonder, just married and twenty-one, was steering a new course. Like Marvin Gaye, he had been granted tacit privileges denied other Motown performers; still, he chafed to have his autonomy made legally binding. Moreover, having attained his majority, he was due his share of the thirty million dollars his music had earned. Perturbed that his allocation came to only one million dollars, he determined to seize control of his business affairs and guarantee his musical independence. Motown went to great pains to keep Wonder in its fold and offered him his own production company (Taurus Productions), his own publishing rights (Black Bull Publishing Company), and his artistic freedom. Now completely at liberty to choose his own material, Wonder thereafter recorded few numbers not entirely from his own pen and pocketed his well-earned reward. Fittingly, just weeks before cementing his new deal he released an especially persuasive rendition of the Beatles' "We Can Work It Out." Validating his business and musical astuteness, in early 1972, *Music of My Mind*, his first album independent of Motown resources, charged up the charts to number 3.

At the behest of Gordy, Wonder early in his career had bowed to a demeaning scheme to pander to white teenage audiences by accepting cameo roles in two uninspiring films of the era, *Bikini Beach* and *Muscle Beach Party* (both 1964). As a grown man, he was proud of his racial heritage and attracted a large following among white listeners without resorting to obsequious marketing contrivances. His exposure to this audience broadened enormously when he toured with the Rolling Stones in 1972 and then performed with John and Yoko Lennon. In November, the notable *Talking Book* album arrived in record stores and his new fans helped take it to number 3 in sales. In 1973 Wonder, who had not had a number 1 single in ten years, scored two from *Talking Book*, "Superstition" and "You Are the Sunshine of My Life."

Tragedy and Comeback. At the top of his game, however, he was nearly killed when his car collided with a log truck near Winston-Salem, North Carolina, on August 6, 1973. During his convalescence, which included four days in a coma, his hit album *Innervisions* advanced to number 4. Fortunately, it was not his swan song, for Wonder struggled from his bed in late September to sing with Elton John at the Boston Garden and then fulfilled a concert date at the Midem festival in France in January, 1974.

Restored to health, Wonder went from triumph to triumph through the remainder of the decade. In September, 1974, his new album, *Fulfillingness' First Finale*, was the best-selling album in the United States. Not only had his musicianship reached its zenith, so also had his business acumen; once again renegotiating his contract, he shrewdly extracted thirteen million dollars from Motown in 1976, the highest salary paid any musician to that time. Another great album quickly resulted. *Songs in the Key of Life* (1976) stayed atop the charts for three and a half months, and generated two number 1 singles ("I Wish" and "Sir Duke," a tribute to Duke Ellington).

Later Career. In the late 1970's Wonder spent two years laboring over a film score called *Stevie Wonder's Journey Through the Secret Life of Plants*, which failed to provoke much excitement, unlike

For the Record

Although most references to Stevie Wonder state that he was born blind, he was not. Born with normal vision, he was administered too much oxygen in an incubator and thus rendered sightless. Ironically, in 1973, after his near-fatal automobile accident, he suffered severe head injuries that deprived him of another of his senses, that of smell.

the less cerebral and brisk-selling *Hotter Than July* in 1980. Busy with benefit concerts, charity work, and humanitarian enterprises, he produced only five albums of original material and one compilation album between 1984 and 1996. Much of this esoteric and experimental music won critical praise but no longer caused the stir of his earlier work. Although they sold respectably (*Conversation Peace* from 1995 was certified gold), these albums were probably more talked about than listened to. However, his older albums would remain profitable and their example would long be revered. Rapper Coolio's use of Wonder's "Pastime Paradise" from *Songs in the Key of Life* as the basis of his own Grammy Award-winning hit "Gangsta's Paradise" (1995) is a case in point.

Recording Classics. Stevie Wonder's first hit, "Fingertips, Part 2," best exhibited the raw rhythmic drive that his music shared more with Memphis funk and soul than with Motown pop and soul. As a live recording it also captured the excitement and perilousness of improvised music making. Wonder's bravura harmonica solo modulated so far afield harmonically that a member of his band could not follow the eleven-year old and can be heard calling out, "What key? What key?" This single was his best selling until "I Just Called to Say I Love You," composed for the film *Woman in Red* (1984), which was number 1 on both sides of the Atlantic Ocean and one of the ten best-selling singles in the history of British popular music.

Noteworthy for its orchestral use of synthesizers, the hit album *Innervisions* was a convincing demonstration that the prodigy had matured into a genius. Among the four hit singles it launched, "Living for the City" summarized in eight mind-searing minutes the cruel indignities of ghetto existence and stands comparison with Marvin Gaye's *What's Going On* as the most significant musical example of social criticism in the 1970's.

Legacy. In a profession of self-important and self-indulgent poseurs, Stevie Wonder was self-deprecating and selflessly authentic. Hosting television's *Saturday Night Live* in May, 1983, he spoofed himself as a blind tennis player barraged by a hail of unseen tennis balls. His social conscience was evident as early as 1966, when he recorded Bob Dylan's "Blowin' in the Wind." In 1980 he dedicated *Hotter Than July* to Martin Luther King, Jr., and was at the forefront of the movement to have King's birthday declared a national holiday, which occurred in 1986. With Paul McCartney, he recorded "Ebony and Ivory" in 1982 as an appeal for racial harmony, and in 1985 he gave over his acceptance speech at the Academy Awards to a plea for the release of political leader Nelson Mandela from a South African prison.

Few entertainers have been as generous with their time and talent. His benefit performances have been numerous, including concerts for Ruben "Hurricane" Carter, the family of David Ruffin, Mary Wells, and for many other non-celebrities. In 1982 he performed at the "Peace Sunday: We Have a Dream" rally to voice his concern over the dangers of the nuclear arms race. To support famine relief in Africa he was integral to the all-star recording of "We Are the World" in 1985. An early spokesman for acquired immunodeficiency syndrome (AIDS) awareness, he and others recorded "That's What Friends Are For" in 1986 to further AIDS research. Along with supporting the Audubon Society, antidrug groups, and Recording Artists Against Drunk Driving (RAADD), he has underwritten organizations promoting the interests of the handicapped. In 1976, he financed the Stevie Wonder Home for Blind and Retarded Children and later endowed the Stevie Wonder Vision Awards for the integration of handicapped people into the workplace. In music and in all else, vision is Stevie Wonder's truest legacy.   —*David Allen Duncan*

SELECT DISCOGRAPHY

■ SINGLES

"Fingertips, Part 2," 1963
"Uptight (Everything's Alright)," 1966
"I Was Made to Love Her," 1967
"For Once in My Life," 1968
"My Cherie Amour," 1969
"Signed, Sealed, Delivered, I'm Yours," 1970
"Superstition," 1972
"You Are the Sunshine of My Life," 1973
"You Haven't Done Nothin," 1974
"Boogie On Reggae Woman," 1974
"Sir Duke," 1977
"Master Blaster (Jammin')," 1980
"Ebony and Ivory," 1982 (with Paul McCartney)
"I Just Called to Say I Love You," 1984
"Part-Time Lover," 1985
"That's What Friends Are For," 1985 (with Dionne Warwick, Elton John, and Gladys Knight)

■ ALBUMS

Tribute to Uncle Ray, 1962
The Jazz Soul of Little Stevie, 1962
Little Stevie Wonder, the 12 Year Old Genius Recorded Live, 1963
Up-Tight, Everything's Alright, 1966
I Was Made to Love Her, 1967
For Once in My Life, 1968
My Cherie Amour, 1969
Signed, Sealed and Delivered, 1970
Music of My Mind, 1972
Talking Book, 1972
Innervisions, 1973
Fulfillingness' First Finale, 1974
Songs in the Key of Life, 1976
Hotter than July, 1980
Stevie Wonder's Original Musiquarium I, 1982
In Square Circle, 1985
Characters, 1987
Conversation Peace, 1995
Song Review: A Greatest Hits Collection, 1996 (compilation)

SELECT AWARDS

Grammy Awards for Album of the Year for *Innervisions*; for Best Vocal Performance, Male, for "You Are the Sunshine of My Life"; for Best R&B Song and Best R&B Vocal Performance, Male, for "Superstition," all 1973
American Music Award for Favorite Male Artist, Soul/R&B, 1974
Grammy Awards for Album of the Year and Best Pop Vocal Performance, Male, for *Fulfillingness' First Finale*; for Best R&B Vocal Performance, Male, for "Boogie On Reggae Woman"; for Best R&B Song for "Living for the City," all 1974
Grammy Awards for Album of the Year and Best Pop Vocal Performance, Male, for *Songs in the Key of Life*; for Best R&B Vocal Performance, Male, for "I Wish"; for Producer of the Year, all 1976
Nashville Songwriters Hall of Fame, inducted 1983
Academy Award for Best Song for "I Just Called to Say I Love You," from *The Woman in Red*, 1984
Grammy Award for Best R&B Vocal Performance, Male, for *In Square Circle*, 1985
Grammy Award for Best Pop Performance by a Duo or Group with Vocal for "That's What Friends Are For," 1986 (with Elton John, Gladys Knight, and Dionne Warwick)
Rock and Roll Hall of Fame, inducted 1989
Nelson Mandela Courage Award, 1991
National Academy of Songwriters Lifetime Achievement Award, 1992
Grammy Awards for Best Male R&B Vocal Performance and Best R&B Song for "For Your Love," 1995

SEE ALSO: Charles, Ray; Cooke, Sam; Gaye, Marvin.

Tammy Wynette

(Virginia Wynette Pugh)

BORN: near Tupelo, Mississippi; May 5, 1942
DIED: Nashville, Tennessee; April 6, 1998

FIRST SINGLE RELEASE: "Apartment #9," 1966
MUSICAL STYLE: Country

Born Virginia Wynette Pugh, country music star Tammy Wynette experienced a life which contributed both to her ability to connect with fans and to her ability to express the feelings so evident in her music. As a child, Wynette helped pick her grandparents' cotton in the Mississippi bottomlands. She was the mother of two by the time she was twenty, and in 1965, when she was pregnant with her third child, she divorced her husband Euple Byrd and moved from Mississippi to Birmingham, Alabama. In Birmingham, Wynette lived with her three children in a government housing project. Having graduated from beauticians' training school in Tupelo, Mississippi, Wynette supported her children by working as a beautician.

By the time she died in 1998, Wynette had been married five times; however, her marriage to George Richey in 1978 lasted until her death. She was beaten and abducted in 1978, was treated for drug addiction in 1986, filed for bankruptcy in 1988, had a smash dance hit with a British rock group in 1992, and received an apology from the First Lady-to be of the United States, Hillary Clinton, in 1992. Wynette's life definitely provided material for country songs.

Substance and Style. Wynette's life experiences made it possible for her to sing about modern male-female relationships. However, unlike female country stars who had come before her, Wynette did not take the viewpoint of the passive victim. She, rather, took the viewpoint of an active participant in the relationship. Her songs about romantic relationships revealed as wide a range of feelings and experiences as any male country singer had. She produced music of the same emotional type made popular by Kitty Wells. However, while Wynette kept the emotional center to her music, she changed the delivery from Wells's high-pitched, ragged, nasal voice to the breath control and wide dynamic range that Patsy Cline had made popular a decade before Wynette began recording. Wynette's producer Billy Sherrill worked with her to combine her emotional content with her controlled voice to produce the same sort of polished glamour that Cline had produced.

The Beginnings. Wynette began her singing career in 1965 when she appeared regularly on an early morning television program in Birmingham. In 1966 she moved to Nashville, Tennessee, where she auditioned for Billy Sherrill of Epic Records. That year Epic released Wynette's first single, "Apartment #9," which was written by Johnny Paycheck. In 1967 Wynette recorded a duet with David Houston, "Your Good Girl's Gonna Go Bad," which became her first Top-10 hit. That year she also recorded "I Don't Wanna

Tammy Wynette in 1977 (Frank Edwards/Fotos International/Archive Photos)

Play House," which became her first number 1 hit and the first recording for which she won a Grammy Award. In 1968 Wynette had three number 1 hits on the *Billboard* charts, "Stand by Your Man," "Take Me to Your World," and "D-I-V-O-R-C-E." These three songs, all about women whose lives are falling apart, have been seen as most representative of Wynette's work, but "Stand by Your Man" has been regarded as her signature tune. In 1968, 1969, and 1970 Wynette was named the Country Music Association's Female Vocalist of the Year. Wynettte's music was showcased on the sound track of the film *Five Easy Pieces* (1970).

From 1970 to 1975 Wynette recorded a series of duets with her third husband, George Jones. (She had married her second husband, Don Chapel, in 1967 and divorced him in 1968, then married Jones in 1969.) These included such songs as 1973's "We're Gonna Hold On" and 1974's "(We're Not) the Jet Set." She and Jones divorced in 1975, but they did record together until 1980. In 1976 two of the Wynette and Jones duets, "Golden Ring" and "Near You" became number 1 hits. In 1994 Wynette and Jones reunited professionally to rerecord "Golden Ring" for Jones's *Unplugged* album.

Later Work. While Wynette is best-known for her songs of deep emotional despair, she was also involved in many types of musical and entertainment projects. In 1979 she published her autobiography, *Stand by Your Man*, which was later made into a successful television film. In 1992 she cre-

ated an international sensation when she joined British rock group the KLF to record "Justified and Ancient," which hit number 1 in eighteen countries. Also in 1992, Wynette received homage from other country musicians in the television special *The Women of Country*.

Wynette recorded with a host of other entertainers. *Higher Ground* (1987) included many performers such as Vince Gill and Ricky Shelton, who were then young in their careers. In 1989 she recorded a duet, "While the Feeling's Good," with Wayne Newton, and she and Randy Travis recorded "We're Strangers Again" in 1991. In 1993 she recorded, with Loretta Lynn and Dolly Parton, *Honky Tonk Angels* which included the single release (with Wynette as lead singer) "Silver Threads and Golden Needles," which premiered to a standing ovation at the 1993 Country Music Association Awards. Wynette was a special guest for Sting's Rainforest Foundation Benefit in 1994, and her 1994 album *Without Walls* teamed her with such diverse performers as Sting, Wynonna Judd, and Elton John.

Wynette's works were often rerecorded by other performers. In 1991, Highway 101 released its version of Wynette's 1973 number 1 hit "'Til I Get It Right." Lyle Lovett recorded "Stand by Your Man" in 1989.

Wynette and Politics. In 1992, presidential candidate Bill Clinton, having been accused of having an extramarital affair with Arkansas television personality Gennifer Flowers, appeared on the news program *60 Minutes* with his wife Hillary, in an effort to save his candidacy. Hillary, trying to show that she really cared about her husband, made a comment stating she was not like Tammy Wynette, passively standing by her man. Subsequently, Wynette, having taken offense at Hillary's remarks, sent a note to her, pointing out that while she might not have had the formal education which Clinton had, she was still an intelligent woman. Clinton responded to Wynette's note with an apology.

Legacy. Prior to Wynette's appearance on the country music scene, most female country singers sang about emotional despair in the high-pitched style made famous by Kitty Wells. Wynette

For the Record

Speaking of her 1994 album *Without Walls*, on which such diverse stars as Elton John, Smokey Robinson, Lyle Lovett, Sting, Wynonna Judd, and Joe Diffie appeared, Wynette said, "They're all excellent singers. This is such an exciting project for me. Good Lord, I never dreamed that something like this would ever happen in my life."

changed that; she kept the emotional subject matter, but she adopted the smooth, controlled style and big voice closely associated with Patsy Cline. Wynette became known as "the First Lady of Country Music" because she was the first female country artist to sell one million copies of an album. From the 1960's through the 1980's, she had thirty-nine Top-10 hits. By the time of her death in 1998 she had sold more than thirty million albums.

Funeral. After Wynette died in her sleep in April, 1998, fifteen hundred people attended her funeral in Nashville. Randy Travis, Wynonna Judd, Dolly Parton, and the Oak Ridge Boys performed, and Lorrie Morgan sang "Stand by Your Man."   —*Annita Marie Ward*

SELECT DISCOGRAPHY
■ SINGLES
"D-I-V-O-R-C-E," 1968
"Stand by Your Man," 1968
"Golden Ring," 1976 (with George Jones)
"Sometimes When We Touch," 1985 (with Mark Gray)
■ ALBUMS
Tears of Fire: The 25th Anniversary Collection, 1992 (boxed set, compilation)
Honky Tonk Angels, 1993 (with Dolly Parton and Loretta Lynn)
Without Walls, 1994

SELECT AWARDS
Grammy Award for Best Country & Western Solo Vocal Performance, Female, for "I Don't Wanna Play House," 1967
Country Music Association Female Vocalist of the Year, 1968, 1969, 1970
Grammy Award for Best Country Vocal Performance, Female, for "Stand by Your Man," 1969

SEE ALSO: Cline, Patsy; Jones, George; Lynn, Loretta; Parton, Dolly; Wells, Kitty.

X

ORIGINAL MEMBERS: John Doe (b. John N. Duchac, 1954); Billy Zoom (b. Tyson Kindell, 1947); Exene Cervenka (b. Christine Cervenkova, 1956); D. J. Bonebrake (b. Don J. Bonebrake, 1955)
OTHER MEMBERS: Dave Alvin (b. 1955), Tony Gilkyson (b. 1952)
FIRST ALBUM RELEASE: *Los Angeles*, 1980
MUSICAL STYLES: Punk rock; rock and roll

The fortuitous meeting of future spouses Exene Cervenka and John Doe in a Venice, California, poetry class in 1977 spawned the West Coast chapter of a rugged new kind of music called punk rock. With the Germs, the Minutemen, Fear, the Circle Jerks, Bad Religion, Social Distortion, and Black Flag, the elemental music of their band X was a bracing assault on the polished performers of the day who dared call themselves rock musicians. Though most fans and players of the 1990's postpunk/alternative/grunge movements might not realize it, there is a direct line from their music back to X.

Los Angeles. The members of X distinguished themselves from their counterparts on the scene by actually being able to play their instruments and write affecting songs. Guitarist Billy Zoom, famous for his Cheshire-cat grin and perfect yellow pompadour, was the virtuoso veteran of many rockabilly bands, including the Alligators and Gene Vincent's group. Drummer D. J. Bonebrake lived up to his name with a pounding, aggressive style. With its vivid imagery, unconventional song forms, and off-center harmonies, X's music was an original amalgam of the sentiments of the American roots music of the Weavers and Johnny Cash and the delivery of rock and roll gone berserk. Their songs captured the ethos of working-class Los Angeles and what it was like scraping by on the bottom in a town ruled by money and glamour.

The group began playing at Hollywood's landmark punk club the Masque and soon developed a local following. In 1979, erstwhile Doors keyboardist Ray Manzarek saw them at Los Angeles's fabled Whisky a Go-Go club and offered to become their producer. The result was the album *Los Angeles*, released in 1980 on Slash Records (one of only two label choices for punk bands in Los Angeles at the time). Selling more than sixty thousand copies, a stunning debut for a small label and an unknown band, the record was anchored by such signature songs as "Johny Hit and Run Pauline" and "Sex and Dying in High Society."

X Takes Off. The even more brilliant follow-up, 1981's *Wild Gift*, again with Manzarek at the controls, sold equally well and gave the world "We're Desperate," "Adult Books," and "Back 2 the Base," while 1982's *Under the Big Black Sun* included "The Hungry Wolf" and "Riding with Mary." Both albums made many "best of the year" lists, and X became local stars and critical darlings. The group was also featured in two concert films, *Urgh! A Musical War* (1981) and Penelope Spheeris's benchmark punk documentary *The Decline of Western Civilization* (1981). The *Los Angeles Times* proclaimed X one of the city's most important bands, and, in the mid-1990's, the influential California music paper *BAM* called the first album the second-best album ever to come out of California, second only to the Beach Boys' *Pet Sounds*.

X played in front of large, enthusiastic crowds on tour dates around the United States and, in

For the Record

"I wish we were simple enough people to be able to write something like Hank Williams. We know too much for our own good."
—*John Doe*

1981, signed with Elektra Records, which released their next three albums. Despite their critical accolades, historical significance, and cult following, the West Coast's "great punk hope" never received significant airplay (they arrived just after "underground" radio had died and was replaced by the much more restrictive "album-oriented rock" formats) or great material rewards. They took one cynical stab at commercial radio success with a cover of the fraternity-rock anthem *Wild Thing* in 1984.

Personnel Changes. Fans could tell the end was near by the sound of 1985's *Ain't Love Grand* album, the final recording by X's original lineup. Manzarek's replacement as producer, Michael Wagener, gave the record the very slick sheen that X had earlier rebelled against. The band was finally getting some airplay with its single "Burning House of Love," but it did not sound much different from the Journeys or Def Leppards of the day. Billy Zoom left the group, led his own band for a while, did a short stint in the Blasters, and supervised the release of some of his pre-X recordings. By 1988, he had quit performing and opened an amplifier customizing and repair shop in Orange County, California, where some of his customers were the very bands he had inspired.

He was replaced by Blasters guitarist Dave Alvin, who, with Doe and Cervenka, had been members of a side project, the acoustic country-rock band the Knitters. In early 1986, X became a quintet with the addition of guitarist Tony Gilkyson, formerly of Lone Justice, and recorded *See How We Are* (1987), whose title track was as powerful and insightful as anything X had ever recorded. Alvin soon left the band, leaving the remaining members to record a double performance album *Live at the Whisky a Go-Go on the Fabulous Sunset Strip* (1988). Gilkyson departed shortly thereafter to work with writer Michael Blake (*Dances with Wolves*) on a spoken-word album and to work on his own country-flavored music.

Hiatus. The pride of the Los Angeles punk scene had lost its direction. Band members pursued individual projects that soon took more of their time and inspiration than X; the band subsequently announced a hiatus. Exene went back to her natal surname Cervenkova, issued several spoken-word recordings (including a recitation of the *Unabomber Manifesto* to music and sound), divorced Doe, opened a store in Los Angeles called You've Got Bad Taste, and, with D. J. Bonebrake and bassist Matt Freeman (on loan from retropunk band Rancid), formed a new punk-influenced trio called Auntie Christ. The group originally contained L7's Donita Sparks on lead guitar, but her L7 duties prevented her from staying, so Cervenkova began learning rock guitar. John Doe continued his burgeoning movie career (doing both acting and music for films) and recorded with his band the John Doe Thing. He also

X: Billy Zoom, D. J. Bonebrake, Exene Cervenka, John Doe (Elektra/Ken Marcus)

worked on music projects with Beck sidemen Smokey Hormel and Joey Waronker, and Foo Fighter Dave Grohl.

X Exits. In 1993, X reunited and, on another new label, released *Hey Zeus!*, followed two years later by the acoustic *Unclogged*. The albums were praised by critics but went virtually unnoticed by the public. In mid-1996, after nineteen years, X decided to break up for good.

October, 1997, saw the release of *Beyond and Back: The X Anthology*, a forty-six-song collection spanning X's entire career. It leaned heavily on the early years, with demos, rarities, alternate takes, and live performances as well as comprehensive liner notes and recollections from Cervenkova and Doe. The original lineup of the band reunited momentarily in early 1998 to promote the anthology.　　　　　*—Tim Bradley*

SELECT DISCOGRAPHY
■ SINGLES
"Wild Thing," 1984
■ ALBUMS
Los Angeles, 1980
Wild Gift, 1981
Under the Big Black Sun, 1982
More Fun in the New World, 1983
Ain't Love Grand, 1985
See How We Are, 1987
Live at the Whisky a Go-Go on the Fabulous Sunset Strip, 1988
Hey Zeus! 1993
Unclogged, 1995
Beyond and Back: The X Anthology, 1997

SEE ALSO: Black Flag / Henry Rollins; Clash, The; Doors, The; Foo Fighters, The.

XTC

ORIGINAL MEMBERS: Andy Partridge (b. 1953), Colin Moulding (b. 1955), Terry Chambers (b. 1955)
OTHER MEMBERS: Barry Andrews (b. 1956), Dave Gregory (b. 1951)
FIRST ALBUM RELEASE: *White Music*, 1978
MUSICAL STYLE: Alternative, rock and roll, pop

Exploding onto the British music scene at the height of the punk era, XTC forged a new direction with its infusion of humor, charm, and intelligence into the audacious and vigorous punk rock aesthetic. Even at the outset, the social relevance of their music was made all the more compelling by the band's sophisticated combination of intricate melodies, quirky harmonic twists, and well-wrought lyrics. As a result, XTC became one of the most influential and imitated rock bands of their era.

The Early Days. In 1975, vocalist, guitarist, and songwriter Andy Partridge, bassist-songwriter Colin Moulding, and drummer Terry Chambers formed the band Helium Kidz in their hometown of Swindon, in north Wiltshire, England—an industrial town about seventy miles west of London. With the addition of keyboardist Barry Andrews in 1977, the foursome became XTC, releasing its first two albums (*White Music* and *Go 2*) with Virgin Records the following year. In 1979, Andrews left the band and was replaced by guitarist Dave Gregory, another Wiltshire native. Later that year, the new group released the album *Drums and Wires* (which included their first hit single, "Making Plans for Nigel"), followed by *Black Sea* in 1980.

The End of the Tours. Following the release of the more accessible album *English Settlement* in 1982 and after five years of grueling tours, Partridge suffered a severe attack of stage fright in the middle of the band's 1982 tour, which was subsequently cancelled. Partridge has claimed that his condition was the result of an increasing awareness that the impact of XTC's music was most effective in the more intimate club settings and less suitable for large crowds; others have speculated that Partridge suffers from an innate fear of success. The situation was serious enough that Chambers left the group, which became strictly a studio band from that point onward. Rather than find a permanent replacement for Chambers, however, the group decided to enlist a different drummer for each of their subsequent projects.

The following releases, *Mummer* (1983) and the more hard-edged *The Big Express* (1984), included some attractive tunes but were rather un-

For the Record

XTC's hit single "Dear God" was not included on the original U.S. release of *Skylarking*, ostensibly for fear that the contentious subject matter would not be appreciated by American audiences. However, after the unexpected and overwhelming success of the song (which appeared on the B side of the single release of "Grass"), "Dear God" was included on subsequent issues of the album, replacing the innocuous "Mermaid Smiled."

even. During this period, Gregory made the transition from guitarist to keyboardist in an effort to provide balance and add variety to the group's sound. A contentious but fruitful collaboration between the band members and producer Todd Rundgren resulted in *Skylarking* (1986), XTC's first major release in the United States and arguably their strongest album. The hit single from this album, "Dear God," is essentially a diatribe against organized religion, culminating in a pounding climax that gets to the core of Partridge's own philosophy on the subject: "I won't believe in heaven and hell/ No saints, no sinners, no devil as well/ No pearly gates, no thorny crown/ You're always letting us humans down." These controversial lyrics created some commotion in the United States but actually fueled XTC's rise in popularity.

It would be three years before the band followed up on the success of *Skylarking*. Both *Oranges and Lemons* (1989) and *Nonsuch* (1992) continued the group's penchant for clever lyrics and sharp social commentary, but the popular success of these albums was somewhat diminished by the public perception of overt intellectualism. Nonetheless, the albums yielded such hits as "The Mayor of Simpleton" and "The Ballad of Peter Pumpkinhead," the latter of which is a political statement raising the issue of ethics and integrity of governmental and spiritual leaders. The pro-

tagonist is ultimately brought down by his detractors, chillingly described just before the final chorus: "Peter Pumpkinhead was too good/ Had him nailed to a chunk of wood/ He died grinning on live TV/ Hanging there he looked a lot like you/ and an awful lot like me."

Other Projects and Hiatus. Besides their work as XTC, Partridge, Moulding, and Gregory formed an alter-ego band by the name of Dukes of Stratosphear in 1985, adopting playfully absurd pseudonyms for themselves as well. This project allowed them the freedom to explore their interest in 1960's psychedelic pop music (especially the Beatles), a significant inspiration for XTC's work that is particularly evident on the *Skylarking* album.

Following the release of *Nonsuch*, the group became entangled in contract renegotiations with Virgin Records and Geffen Records, resulting in the band's refusal to release any more albums. In 1996, after a four-year hiatus, the record labels finally relented, releasing XTC from its contractual obligations in return for two compilation albums: Virgin released the two-compact-disc chronicle *Fossil Fuel* (1997) in the United Kingdom, while Geffen released the more superficial single-disc *Upsy Daisy Assortment* (1997) in the United States.

—*Joseph Klein*

SELECT DISCOGRAPHY
■ ALBUMS
White Music, 1978
Go 2, 1978
Drums and Wires, 1979
Black Sea, 1980
English Settlement, 1982
Waxworks: Some Singles 1977-1982, 1982
Mummer, 1983
The Big Express, 1984
The Compact XTC: The Singles 1978-1985, 1985
Skylarking, 1986
Psonic Psunspot, 1987 (as Dukes of Stratosphear)
Oranges and Lemons, 1989
Rag and Bone Buffet: Rare Cuts and Leftovers, 1990
Nonsuch, 1992
Fossil Fuel: The XTC Singles 1977-1992, 1997
Upsy Daisy Assortment: The Sweetest Hits, 1997

SEE ALSO: Beatles; Rundgren, Todd.

Yanni

(Yanni Hrisomallis)

BORN: Kalamata, Greece; November 14, 1954
FIRST ALBUM RELEASE: *Keys to Imagination*, 1986
MUSICAL STYLE: Contemporary instrumental

Yanni's musical career is the result of a firm family foundation based on love and his conviction that music is the ultimate language of communication. Believing that a child must begin molding his talents at the "right moment" in life, Sotiris and Felitsa Hrisomallis bought a piano for their-six-year old son, Yanni. Although Yanni does not read or write music, he has established himself as an innovative composer and uses music as a way of sending a message of love, unity, acceptance, and tolerance.

Early Years. Yanni spent his childhood in his homeland of Greece. However, his parents sold their home and rented a small apartment so they could afford to give their son the opportunity to be educated in the United States. In 1972, Yanni registered at the University of Minnesota where he received his undergraduate degree in psychology. He graduated in 1976 and became the keyboardist for Chameleon, a rock band in Minneapolis, Minnesota.

Yanni's creativity flourished. It was further enhanced when he was introduced to synthesizers in his early twenties and became enamored with the enormous amount of sound synthesizers could generate. In his live performances he and his keyboard player Ming Freeman use thirty-five to forty synthesizers. The first thing Yanni does after purchasing a synthesizer is erase the factory presets. He then begins "sculpting" his own sounds. As a youth, Yanni developed self-taught hieroglyphics that he used to help him compose music. Despite this personal musical map and his ability to hear all the parts of a composition in his head, it is necessary for him to communicate the music to other musicians through an orchestrator. He believes that musicians should not be reading music while they are playing and tells them, "you have to make the music yours and then use it to express yourself."

Major Influences. As a composer, Yanni's most important attachment is to classical music. As a young boy in Greece, he enjoyed music written by composers such as Ludwig van Beethoven, Frédéric-François Chopin, and Wolfgang Amadeus Mozart. Other musical influences are Eastern music and progressive rock. His nonmusical inspiration includes powerfully creative people such as Socrates, Leonardo da Vinci, and Albert Einstein.

Yanni's love of music and his unwavering optimism about life is evident in all of his compositions. He prefers the term "instrumental music" rather than "New Age" in describing his music and believes that instrumental music transcends the inhibitions and limitations of lyrics and allows the listener to personalize the powerful emotional messages conveyed by the music. His album *Reflections of Passion* (1990) reached platinum status and stayed at the top of *Billboard*'s adult alternative chart for a record-breaking forty-seven weeks. Yanni composed the Grammy Award-nominated *Dare to Dream* (1992) to urge people to use their imagination and inherent power to dream. Both he and fellow artist and friend John Tesh have used their imaginative talents to become increasingly popular instrumental musicians by playing digital synthesizers and pianos along with symphony orchestras.

Successful Meshing of Sounds. After working ten years as a solo artist with a small, five-piece rock band, Yanni decided to hand-pick musicians and form his own orchestra. After two years of planning, Yanni's dream of performing live at the two-thousand-year-old Herod Atticus Theater in Athens, Greece, came true on September 25, 1993. His band, along with the Royal Philharmonic Concert Orchestra from London, England, conducted by Shardad Rohani, gave a spectacular performance to a sold-out audience. Yanni described the occasion as "a once in a lifetime experience and a very emotional event." The resulting album, *Live at the Acropolis* (1994), sold over seven million copies worldwide and reached platinum status in thirty-one countries. The video of the event was the third-largest-selling music video of all time.

In 1997, Yanni released *Tribute*, the live recording of his performances at the Taj Mahal in India and the Forbidden City in Beijing, China. He was the first Western artist permitted to stage a major concert at either landmark. To assist Yanni with concert preparations in India, the government of Uttar Pradesh and the Indian military constructed a temporary road and bridges that transformed the flood plains around the Taj Mahal into a concert site for the sold-out shows. While serving as a gesture of respect to two historical sites, *Tribute* marked the first compositions by Yanni since 1994. The nine new songs, including his first lyric song, "Love Is All," were performed by Yanni and his forty-five-piece symphony orchestra, who played modern, classical, and ancient instruments.

—*Elizabeth B. Graham*

SELECT DISCOGRAPHY
■ ALBUMS
Keys to Imagination, 1986
Out of Silence, 1987
Chameleon Days, 1988
Niki Nana, 1989
Reflections of Passion, 1990 (previously released material)
In Celebration of Life, 1991 (previously released material)

For the Record

At age 14, Yanni broke the national free-style swimming record as a member of the Greek National Swimming Team.

Dare to Dream, 1992
In My Time, 1993
Live at the Acropolis, 1994 (live)
Devotion: Best of Yanni, 1997 (previously released material)
Tribute, 1997 (live)

SEE ALSO: Tesh, John.

The Yardbirds

ORIGINAL MEMBERS: Keith Relf (1943-1976), Chris Dreja (b. 1945), Jim McCarty (b. 1943), Paul Samwell-Smith (b. 1943), Anthony "Top" Topham (b. 1947)
OTHER MEMBERS: Eric Clapton (b. 1945), Jeff Beck (b. 1944), Jimmy Page (b. 1944)
FIRST ALBUM RELEASE: *Five Live Yardbirds*, 1964
MUSICAL STYLES: Rhythm and blues, rock and roll, psychedelic rock, jazz fusion, pop

Best known for their covers of rhythm-and-blues classics and improvisational guitar solos, the Yardbirds launched the careers of three of Britain's greatest rock guitarists: Eric Clapton, Jeff Beck, and Jimmy Page.

The Beginnings. London in 1963 was on the verge of a cultural explosion in art, fashion, and music. The city's art colleges were natural gathering places for the growing ranks of blues aficionados, disaffected young men who sought to play like their American heroes, Howling Wolf, Bo Diddley, and Robert Johnson. They traded records and taught each other guitar chords, feeding off one another's energy.

In this atmosphere, the original members of the Metropolis Blues Quartet met. Keith Relf (harmonica) would become vocalist for the quartet. Chris Dreja's rhythm guitar filled out the sound generated by bassist Paul Samwell-Smith. Gifted drummer Jim McCarty completed the lineup. Soon, the Quartet hired Anthony "Top" Topham as lead guitarist, necessitating a name change. The fivesome took saxophonist Charlie "Bird" Parker's nickname, and the Yardbirds were born.

As the band played small clubs in London,

building a following, it became apparent they could rise to national prominence. When the Rolling Stones moved onto the national scene, the position of house band at Giorgio Gomelsky's Crawdaddy Club fell vacant. Gomelsky sought out new talent, showcasing them and acting as an informal manager. When he offered this opportunity to the Yardbirds, he was careful not to repeat his previous mistakes. The Rolling Stones never signed a management contract with him, so when they became famous, they left him for corporate management. Realizing the Yardbirds' potential, Gomelsky signed them immediately. He felt they had the musical ability to improvise that had eluded the Rolling Stones.

Guitar Heroes. Anticipating success, the Yardbirds made a hard decision to fire Topham. Relf's art schoolmate, Eric Clapton, had come to see the Yardbirds on occasion, approaching Relf about Topham's shortcomings. When Clapton suggested himself as a replacement, the band jumped at his offer. During these formative days for the second lineup, the band felt a fresh infusion of blues enthusiasm. Clapton shone as guitarist, bending notes, frequently shredding strings. The speed with which he played earned him a new nickname, "Slowhand," which persisted throughout Clapton's career.

The Yardbirds' next step was to make a recording. Their first album, *Five Live Yardbirds* (1964), brought them a larger audience but did not capture the excitement of the band on stage. A tour backing American bluesman Sonny Boy Williamson resulted in another album, *Sonny Boy Williamson and the Yardbirds* (1965). Williamson openly derided these white Englishmen, who were thrilled to play with one of their idols (Clapton, ever more focused on the blues, sometimes reviled them himself).

In swinging London, the focal point of popular culture, the music business was fueled by the release of singles. Thus the Yardbirds developed a more commercial sound. Their 1964 single, "A Certain Girl"/"I Wish You Would," had not fared well. It evidenced the growing rift in the band: Clapton wanted the Yardbirds to remain true to their rhythm-and-blues roots, while Samwell-

Smith was moving them toward pop. Just as their first successful single was released ("For Your Love," 1965), Clapton left the Yardbirds. Seeking to replace him, the group first approached Jimmy Page. Known as the best session guitarist in London, he had played on records for bands such as the Who and the Kinks, and was a producer for Mickie Most's Immediate Records. Making a comfortable living, Page was not interested in joining the struggling band at that time.

New Guitarist. London was home to another rising guitar hero, Jeff Beck, who had played lead guitar with the Tridents. Page nominated him to replace Clapton. Beck's tenure with the Yardbirds ushered in their most commercially successful period. "Heart Full of Soul" (1965), "Over Under Sideways Down," "Shapes of Things," "Train Kept a-Rollin'," and "Happenings Ten Years Time Ago" (all 1966), were singles which peaked high on the charts.

The Yardbirds had done package tours in Great Britain, but opportunities soon came to play Europe and the United States. Early in 1965, eager to break into the U.S. market, the Yardbirds arrived, only to find they had no work permits. Returning in August, 1965, with proper paperwork in hand, they played their first official U.S. dates. Simon Napier-Bell had begun managing the band, putting more pressure on them to work nonstop, touring, recording, and doing photo sessions and interviews.

In 1966, Samwell-Smith left the band to become a full-time producer. The Yardbirds turned once more to Jimmy Page, who was by then disillusioned with life as a session musician. He joined, taking over duties as bassist. Soon, Dreja switched to bass, and both Beck and Page played lead guitar, weaving their sounds. The Yardbirds became famous for the dual guitar, but only three songs were recorded featuring the pair.

Film director Michelangelo Antonioni, entranced by London's burgeoning art and music scene, wanted to make a film featuring the Who. Because the Who would have nothing to do with the film, Antonioni substituted the Yardbirds. Their four-minute segment in *Blowup* (1966) showed them imitating the Who's trademark of

The Yardbirds c. 1965: Jeff Beck, Jim McCarty, Chris Dreja, Paul Samwell-Smith, Keith Relf (Archive Photos/John Platt Collection)

destroying their equipment. By the time the film premiered, Beck had left the band. During a U.S. tour, he did not show up for a concert. Page played the show solo, and the fans did not seem to mind Beck's absence. When Beck returned, the Yardbirds said they no longer needed his services.

Transitions. By 1967, the Yardbirds were running out of enthusiasm. Arguments were more frequent, and alcohol and drug use were more prevalent. Napier-Bell had given management of the band to associate Peter Grant, warning that he would need to fire the "troublemaker" Page. Having known Page since 1962, Grant was surprised to hear that the introverted Page was causing problems. Grant was even more surprised when he found the reason: for two tours and for the film, band members had each made only 112 pounds (the equivalent of 330 U.S. dollars at the time). A good business manager, Grant did not

fire Page, but guided the Yardbirds through their last year together.

The End. In July, 1968, the Yardbirds played their final date at Luton Technical College. Backstage, Page asked Relf and McCarty to give him rights to the name Yardbirds, as they indicated they were leaving the band. A string of commitments in Scandinavia would fall to Page alone to honor. Relf and McCarty would go on to play folk music, calling themselves Renaissance. Clapton had moved on to a solo career, periodically joining bands such as Cream and Blind Faith. Beck formed the Jeff Beck Band (which included Rod Stewart and Ron Wood), continuing later as a solo artist. The most unexpected transition would be accomplished by Page, who assembled a band to play Scandinavia as the New Yardbirds; following that tour, they changed their name to Led Zeppelin. With Grant as their manager, they changed the way rock groups did business, generating profits on a scale never before seen in rock.

In 1976, Relf died in an accident, electrocuted by a set of headphones. When the Marquee Club hosted its twenty-fifth anniversary celebration in 1983, Samwell-Smith, Dreja, and McCarty reformed the Yardbirds for the night. Good feelings carried over, and McCarty, Dreja, and Samwell-Smith formed Box of Frogs with guitarist John Fidler. Their subsequent recordings displayed an eclectic style well received by old and new fans alike. —*Cynthia R. Kasee*

SELECT DISCOGRAPHY
■ SINGLES
"For Your Love," 1965
"Heart Full of Soul," 1965
"Shapes of Things," 1966
"Over Under Sideways Down," 1966
■ ALBUMS
Five Live Yardbirds, 1964
Roger the Engineer, 1966
Little Games, 1968
Live Yardbirds, 1971

SELECT AWARDS
Rock and Roll Hall of Fame, inducted 1992

SEE ALSO: Clapton, Eric; Cream; Led Zeppelin.

Trisha Yearwood

BORN: Monticello, Georgia; September 19, 1964
FIRST ALBUM RELEASE: *Trisha Yearwood*, 1991
MUSICAL STYLES: Country, country rock

Trisha Yearwood was the first female country artist to attain platinum status or better on her first four albums. In the first six years of her career, she sold ten million records and had eight number 1 singles.

When she signed with MCA Records in 1991, the company made a financial and marketing commitment to ensure that she became one of the top country female recording artists. She lived up to MCA's confidence by capturing the Academy of Country Music and the American Music Awards new artist awards, and in 1997 was crowned Country Music Association's Female Vocalist of the Year.

Musical Beginnings. Trisha was born Patricia Lynn Yearwood on September 19, 1964, in Monticello, Georgia, a small town sixty miles southeast of Atlanta. She grew up on a farm with her sister, Beth, her banker father, Jack, and her school-teacher mother, Gwen. Her parents were always very involved in their daughter's career, running her fan club, which was based in her hometown. From an early age, Trisha was an Elvis Presley fan. Her other early musical influences were her parents' record collection of country artists, southern rock she heard on area radio stations (particularly singers such as Linda Ronstadt), and the choral groups in which she participated during her high school years at Piedmont Academy. Yearwood's first two years of college were spent in the northern Georgia mountains at Young Harris, a small Methodist junior college. There she had roles in a few musicals and was a member of the traveling chorus. To further her education, she chose Belmont College (now University), a small Baptist college located at the end of Music Row in Nashville. During her Belmont years, she married fellow student Chris Latham; worked as an intern, then as receptionist, at MTM Records; began singing demos for songwriters and doing background vocals for artists; and earned her music business degree.

One of the budding recording artists who furthered Yearwood's career was Garth Fundis, who helped her put together a showcase performance which resulted in a contract offer from MCA. Fundis became her record producer. Another Garth was also very instrumental in her early career: Garth Brooks. In 1989, Yearwood recorded a duet with an unknown named Garth Brooks. (Yearwood and Brooks had met while both were doing demos and background vocals in Nashville.) The experience was so successful that Brooks promised he would help Yearwood if he ever became successful. By 1991, Brooks had been signed by Capitol Records, had already produced four or five number 1 hits on the country chart, and was the world's hottest country act. He called to invite Yearwood to open his shows on his next tour, which gave this new artist incredible exposure. The tour was extremely successful for both singers.

Platinum Career. Yearwood's recording career was launched in 1991 with the album *Trisha Yearwood*, which became a certified double-platinum album. The blockbuster hit from the album was her debut single, "She's in Love with the Boy." It shot up the charts and spent two weeks at number 1. Four chart hits from her debut album resulted in Yearwood's winning the new artist awards from the Academy of Country Music and the American Music Awards. Her debut album also earned two Grammy Award nominations.

Album number two, *Hearts in Armor*, in 1992, earned a platinum certificate. Four more singles from this effort were hits, with "Wrong Side of Memphis" and "Walkaway Joe," a duet with former Eagles member Don Henley, both making the Top 5. Her third album, *The Song Remembers When*, was released in 1993. The album also reached platinum sales status and the title cut became her

Trisha Yearwood (MCA/Randee St. Nicholas)

second number 1 hit on the country chart and entered *Billboard*'s Hot 100, the pop chart. The Disney Channel produced a special program, "The Song Remembers When," which focused on Yearwood, her career, and specifically, this album.

Her next recording effort was a Christmas album, *The Sweetest Gift* (1994), with her sister Beth singing harmony on the title cut. Her duet with Aaron Neville on Patsy Cline's "I Fall to Pieces," from the *Rhythm, Country and Blues* album (1994), won a Grammy Award in 1994. She contributed her rendition of "New Kid in Town" to the *Common Thread: Songs of the Eagles* album (1993) that won a Country Music Association Award in 1994.

Yearwood and her first husband, Chris, divorced in 1991. In 1994 she married Robert Reynolds, the bass player for MCA recording artists the Mavericks. They were married in the newly-renovated "cathedral of country music," the Ryman Auditorium in Nashville. They made their new home in Hendersonville, just north of Nashville.

Yearwood's next recording effort, the album *Thinkin' About You*, released on Valentine's Day, 1995, also went platinum. That album produced two number 1 hits: the title cut and "XXX's & OOO's," which was featured in the made-for-television film *An American Girl*.

The fifth album, *Everybody Knows*, released in August, 1996, earned several Grammy nominations. The single "Believe Me Baby (I Lied)" became another number 1 hit, remaining in that position for two weeks. "Everybody Knows" also reached the number 1 position. Yearwood performed during the closing ceremonies of the 1996 Centennial Olympics held in Atlanta. Shortly before the Olympic flame was extinguished, she sang "The Flame" from the torch's tower, high above Olympic Stadium.

Her sixth album, *Songbook—A Collection of Hits*, released in 1997, went platinum in five weeks, and her single "How Do I Live" zoomed to number 1. The song had been featured in the Touchstone motion picture *Con Air*. *Songbook* is a collection of seven previous chart toppers and three previously unreleased tracks: "How Do I Live"; "In Another's Eyes," a duet with Garth Brooks; and "Perfect Love."

Versatile Artist. Although Yearwood is not yet well known as a songwriter, artists such as Kenny Rogers and Michelle Wright have recorded some of her songs. She has had qualms about recording her own material. When questioned about that by interviewer Glenn Danforth, she responded: "I think, because of my background as a session singer . . . I have a great respect for a truly good song and I don't believe that I would be selling so many records and be this successful if I hadn't chosen the right songs. . . . I think I have potential as a writer, but I'm not ready yet to show these songs to the world."

Yearwood has toured the world, performed for U.S. presidents, appeared in director Peter Bogdanovich's film *The Thing Called Love* (1993), and sung with orchestras such as the London Symphony Orchestra. She has also been the focus of a one-hour Disney television special; appeared on hit television shows, including *Dr. Quinn, Medicine Woman*, starring Jane Seymour, and *Ellen*, starring Ellen Degeneres; performed the national anthem for Game Two of the 1995 World Series; and performed before a worldwide television audience during the Summer Olympics in Atlanta in 1996. —*Don Tyler*

SELECT DISCOGRAPHY
■ ALBUMS
Trisha Yearwood, 1991
Hearts in Armor, 1992
The Song Remembers When, 1993
The Sweetest Gift, 1994
Thinkin' About You, 1995
Everybody Knows, 1996
Songbook—A Collection of Hits, 1997
Where Your Road Leads, 1998

SELECT AWARDS
Academy of Country Music New Female Artist of the Year Award, 1992
American Music Award for Favorite New Artist, Country, 1992
Grammy Award for Best Country Vocal Collaboration for "I Fall to Pieces," 1995 (with Aaron Neville)
Grammy Award for Best Country Vocal Performance, Female, for "How Do I Live" and Best Country Collaboration with Vocals for "In Another's Eyes" (with Garth Brooks), 1997
Country Music Association Female Vocalist of the Year Award, 1997
Country Music Association Female Vocalist of the Year Award, 1998

SEE ALSO: Brooks, Garth; Cline, Patsy; Eagles, The; Henley, Don; Presley, Elvis; Ronstadt, Linda.

Yes

ORIGINAL MEMBERS: Jon Anderson (b. 1944), Peter Banks (b. 1947), Chris Squire (b. 1948), Bill Bruford (b. 1949), Tony Kaye (b. 1946)
OTHER MEMBERS: Steve Howe (b. 1947), Rick Wakeman (b. 1949), Alan White (b. 1949), Patrick Moraz (b. 1948), Trevor Rabin (b. 1954)
FIRST ALBUM RELEASE: *Yes*, 1969
MUSICAL STYLES: Progressive rock, pop

One of the most celebrated English progressive rock bands of the early 1970's, Yes developed an unmistakable ensemble sound that was equally successful on albums and in live concerts. While Yes continued as an entity into the 1990's, their heyday fell two decades earlier, when an international audience was drawn to that special alchemy of dazzling instrumental virtuosity, vocal harmonies, and ethereal lyrics.

Beginnings. The group came together in 1968 when twenty-four-year-old singer Jon Anderson returned home from performing in Germany with the desire to form his own band and met bassist Chris Squire. The original quintet consisted of Anderson on vocals, Squire, Peter Banks on guitar, Tony Kaye on keyboards, and Bill Bruford on drums. With this combination of well-experienced performers, they were able to explore various flavors of late 1960's rock. The group gained exposure by opening English concerts for more established performers of the time, such as Sly and the Family Stone and Janis Joplin. Yes also was chosen to open for Cream at their historic final concert at London's Royal Albert Hall (November 26, 1968).

Their first album, *Yes*, released in 1969, was not particularly successful; their second did somewhat better. Their first albums were learning experiences; bit by bit the band was improving and discovering the direction they wanted to take. Yet Yes had begun to attract its own fans, drawn to a sound that had become quite different from those of the top-billed groups for whom they were opening.

Yes Breaks Through. With its next three albums, each an impressive step beyond its predecessor, Yes hit its stride. After the second album, Banks left and was replaced by the remarkable and unique guitarist Steve Howe. *The Yes Album* (1971) showcased his abilities on both acoustic and electric guitars. The album rose to number 7 in Britain and made a fair showing in the United States. Three long tracks from it, "Yours Is No Disgrace," "Starship Trooper," and "I've Seen All Good People" were destined to become Yes standards, demanded by fans at concerts and re-released on several later compilations. "Starship Trooper" was typical of the Yes song suites of the time, subdivided into three parts, each composed by a different member of the group and playing to his particular musical abilities. The first section of "I've Seen All Good People" was released as the single "Your Move," which broke into the U.S. singles charts, reaching number 40.

Classically trained multi-keyboardist Rick Wakeman replaced Kaye in 1971 for that year's *Fragile* album. Wakeman expanded the group's sound, both on record and in concert, by playing Moog synthesizers, electric harpsichord, and Mellotron (a keyboard that reproduces violin and flute sounds) in addition to organ and piano. The single "Roundabout," destined to become another Yes mainstay, peaked at number 13. A sense of Yes's newfound breadth of inspiration emerges when one compares "Roundabout" first with "Cans and Brahms, " which incorporates music from nineteenth century German composer Johannes Brahms, and then with the many tempo jolts and sudden contrasts of "Heart of the Sunrise." *Fragile* was also the first album to feature the trademark Yes logo hovering above a surrealistic landscape, both of which were created by artist Roger Dean. Dean's phantasmagorical artwork became closely identified with the band.

Close to the Edge (1972), containing "And You and I," was a further move in the direction of "album-oriented rock" (AOR), for it consisted of only three extended tracks. *Close to the Edge* is arguably the band's peak achievement in the smoothness with which the instrumental sections flow and the effectiveness with which the pieces interweave accessible vocal sections with the instrumentals. In 1973 the three-record *Yessongs* offered live versions of previously released material, thus presenting something of the Yes concert experience.

With these albums the group had created a distinctive sound. Yes developed an ability to combine dissimilar basic musical components into a unified whole. The end result differed considerably from the typically structured pop song, in effect amounting to a rock composition, meticulously crafted from a number of contrasting musical ideas—some complementary, some contrasting. Yes went beyond standard rock chord progressions, meters, and bass and guitar parts. Jon Anderson's lyrics and, more so, his distinctive tenor voice, high but not abrasive, were important to nearly every Yes song. Yet much of their material was more instrumentally than vocally conceived, and the vocals had to find their place within the overall sound. Squire, for example, was among a handful of bassists who experimented successfully with expanding the instrument's roll in rock. (Among the others, who played very different styles of music, were English players John Entwistle, Jack Bruce, and Noel Redding and American Jack Casady of Jefferson Airplane.) Howe's parts on various guitars and other stringed instruments, Wakeman's classically influenced extroverted playing on synthesizer and organ, and the inspired and precise drumming of Bruford (later Alan White), all demanded attention as well.

For many fans the next studio release, the double album *Tales from Topographic Oceans* (1973), was disappointing. All the expected ingredients were present: the Roger Dean artwork, the long pieces with instrumental passages showcasing individual members, and the opaque, quasi-

Yes on the 1991 Union tour: Tony Kaye, Trevor Rabin, Rick Wakeman, Alan White, Bill Bruford, Chris Squire, Jon Anderson, Steve Howe (Lissa Wales)

mystical poetry of Jon Anderson, here inspired by Shastric scriptures. However, the album included only four pieces, each so long it covered an entire album side. Most listeners—and virtually all critics—found the album self-indulgent and incomprehensible. Nonetheless, it had many fine moments, and it subtly and effectively used repeated instrumental and vocal motifs throughout. This album was drummer Alan White's first with the band (Bruford left to join King Crimson). Wakeman, unhappy with the band's direction, departed to record solo albums. New keyboardist Patrick Moraz joined for *Relayer* (1974), after which the band took time off and released\ solo albums. Eventually they reunited with Wakeman for the albums *Going for the One* (1977) and *Tormato* (1978). These albums of the later 1970's marked a move toward the sound and shorter

tracks of mainstream rock.

The public's musical tastes had been changing since the mid-1970's, however, and, like other bands in the progressive rock genre, Yes found its popularity dwindling. In 1974 the Canadian hard-rock band Bachman-Turner Overdrive had forced the issue when it released an album entitled *Not Fragile* with a picture of a packing crate on the cover. The second half of the 1970's was the time of disco, then stripped-down punk and new wave bands. After *Tormato* both Wakeman and Anderson left the band; Yes put out *Drama* with singer Trevor Horn and keyboardist Geoff Downes in 1980, then disbanded.

The 1980's and 1990's. Downes and Steve Howe went on to form Asia, quite successful for a few years in the early 1980's. Meanwhile, Squire, White, former Yes keyboardist Tony Kaye, and new guitarist Trevor Rabin formed a new group to be called Cinema. However, once they brought in Anderson to do some singing, they decided simply to call the band Yes. This lineup had the most successful Yes single, the danceable, pop-oriented "Owner of a Lonely Heart." It spent two weeks at number 1. The 1983 album on which it appears, *90125*, was effectively produced by Trevor Horn and was also quite successful. This lineup's eventual follow-up release, *Big Generator* (1987), did not fare as well. Soon a different collection of Yes musicians—Anderson, original drummer Bruford, Wakeman, and Howe (who had left Asia in 1985)—began working together. Chris Squire, however, insisted that he had legal rights to the name "Yes" and went to court to keep them from using it. Released as *Anderson Bruford Wakeman Howe* in 1989, their record sold respectably, as did their concert tour.

Various members of Yes had long considered the idea of doing a reunion show featuring past and present members of the band, and in 1991 the concept became a reality. The album *Union* and the major tour that followed featured an astounding cast that somehow managed to work together: Howe and Rabin on guitar, Kaye and Wakeman on keyboards, Bruford and White on drums and percussion, Squire on bass, and Anderson on vocals. In the late 1990's Yes was still an active recording and touring band. The old and the new Yes coexisted, as new compilations of the old "classic" Yes sound of the 1970's sat side-by-side on the shelves with new albums such as *Talk* (1994) and *Open Your Eyes* (1997). Several members had also amassed catalogs of solo works, with Anderson in particular having releasing a number of solo albums and collaborations with Greek keyboardist and composer Vangelis. —*David Haas*

For the Record

The 1973 Yes album *Tales from Topographic Oceans* was the first album ever to be certified gold on its initial shipping.

SELECT DISCOGRAPHY
■ ALBUMS
Yes, 1969
Time and a Word, 1970
The Yes Album, 1971
Fragile, 1971
Close to the Edge, 1972
Yessongs, 1973
Tales from Topographic Oceans, 1973
Relayer, 1974
Going for the One, 1977
Tormato, 1978
Drama, 1980
90125, 1983
Anderson Bruford Wakeman Howe, 1989
Union, 1991
Talk, 1994
Open Your Eyes, 1997

SELECT AWARDS
Grammy Award for Best Rock Instrumental Performance for "Cinema," 1984

SEE ALSO: Asia; Emerson, Lake, and Palmer; Genesis; King Crimson; Vangelis.

Dwight Yoakam

BORN: Pikesville, Kentucky; October 23, 1956
FIRST ALBUM RELEASE: *A Town South of Bakersfield*, 1984 (extended-play single)
MUSICAL STYLES: Country, country rock

Dwight Yoakam, one of the most successful country artists of the 1980's and 1990's, worked out of Los Angeles instead of Nashville, Tennessee, the capital of country music. When he released his first album in 1986, he reminded audiences and record executives of the rich but neglected honky-tonk tradition of country music.

Roots. The grandson of a Kentucky coal miner, Yoakam was exposed to the music of country greats such as Hank Williams, Patsy Cline, and Johnny Cash when he was a child. However, country was not his only musical influence. He later recalled singing hymns with his family around the kitchen table. In addition, he enjoyed Elvis

Presley, and, like many of his generation, was impressed by the Beatles' 1964 appearance on *The Ed Sullivan Show*. Traditional country and early rock and roll would both have a great influence on Yoakam's music in later years.

Yoakam showed a talent for music and received a guitar as a gift when he was quite young. He spent his school years practicing guitar and headed a rockabilly band while in high school. He studied drama briefly at Ohio University, but in 1977 headed for California in hopes of starting a career in acting or music. Within months of arriving in Los Angeles, Yoakam was cast as a lead in a play. Despite this initial success as an actor, he remained focused on his music. He formed a band and played at local clubs, earning very little money.

At this point in his career, Yoakam met guitarist Pete Anderson, who was then working as a musician for hire. Anderson had experience as a producer and arranger, two skills which Yoakam lacked, and the two artists developed a strong working relationship. Anderson joined Yoakam's band, and the two shared a tiny apartment as they refined their music. The traditional honky-tonk

Dwight Yoakam (Reprise/Randee St. Nicholas)

style of country which they played was not in vogue, and the band was often fired from shows. Nonetheless, in 1984 Yoakam borrowed five thousand dollars from a friend to record some songs. The resulting extended-play single caught the attention of Reprise Records, which, after the addition of several songs, released the material under the title of *Guitars, Cadillacs, Etc., Etc.* in 1986.

A Nashville outsider, Yoakam shook up the country music world with this album, which soon went gold and later went platinum. It opened with the Johnny Horton classic "Honky-Tonk Man," the perfect way for Yoakam to declare his allegiance to an older style of country far removed from the "urban-cowboy" music that Nashville was churning out. Released as a single, "Honky-Tonk Man" reached number 3 on the country charts. One song which Yoakam wrote, "Guitars, Cadillacs," contained the word "hillbilly." The record company had asked to delete the word from the lyrics on the grounds that it was offensive; Yoakam refused and was proved correct in his instincts when the single reached the top 5.

New Traditionalism. Critics struggled to pigeonhole Yoakam's style, which harked back to the rough honky-tonk music of the 1950's, wrapping the traditional country themes of drinking, dancing, and heartbreak with elements of rock and roll. Labels such as hard country and neo-honky-tonk finally gave way to the title new traditionalism. Yoakam certainly showed his respect for the older statesmen of country. His early albums were usually a mix of new songs and old standards, often from the 1950's. Yoakam brought Buck Owens out of virtual retirement, performing a duet on the "Streets of Bakersfield," which was Yoakam's first number 1 single.

His second album, *Hillbilly Deluxe* (1987) went gold, as did the 1988 release *Buenas Noches from a Lonely Room*. A compilation of previously released material, *Just Lookin' for a Hit* (1989), reached number 3 on the country charts and appeared on the lower regions of the pop charts. The 1990 *If There Was a Way* went platinum and yielded several hits, including "It Only Hurts When I Cry," which he cowrote with the legendary Roger Miller.

For the Record

As a teenager, Yoakam kept his acting ambitions a secret from his family, not telling them that he was in school plays until opening night. His first lead role came at age fourteen, when he was cast as Charlie Brown in the play *You're a Good Man, Charlie Brown.*

Yoakam, a thin man who dressed in skintight jeans ripped at the knees, became something of a sex symbol. Album covers always depicted him wearing a cowboy hat, a Yoakam trademark which both symbolized his affinity for country music and covered his increasing hair loss. His videos were popular, and his concerts drew thousands of fans, which meant that he was booked in large arenas. However, critics complained that his live performances were uneven and lackluster, and the 1995 album *Dwight Live* received poor reviews and did not sell well (which did not prevent it from receiving a Grammy Award nomination).

His 1993 album *This Time*, which eventually sold more than three million copies, marked a departure in that it contained only new songs, no standards, most of them written by Yoakam. He continued in that vein with *Gone* (1995). However, Yoakam had not abandoned his love for cover tunes, as was revealed in 1997 when he released *Under the Covers* (1997), an assortment of songs by artists ranging from Jimmie Rodgers to the Beatles to Sonny and Cher. Yoakam also experimented on the album, successfully offering a big-band version of the Kinks' "Tired of Waiting for You." The album received favorable reviews and garnered a Grammy Award nomination. Yoakam's release for 1998, *A Long Way Home*, promised another departure, which one critic called "lush and languid, more introspective."

During the 1990's, Yoakam revived his interest in acting. He obtained a small part in the film *Red Rock West* (1994), and the lead in a play which Peter Fonda produced in Los Angeles in 1993. His performances as the abusive Doyle in *Sling Blade* (1996), and as the nitroglycerine expert Brentwood Glasscock in *The Newton Boys* (1998) both won positive reviews from film critics.

Despite these successes, music remained at the center of his career. Dwight Yoakam owed his popularity and success to his devotion to the traditional aspects of country, a legacy that Nashville record executives forgot as they expanded the audience for country music during the 1970's and 1980's. However, Yoakam did not allow his fidelity to great country performers and artists to limit his music; he was always willing to throw hillbilly and rock and roll into the mix. His partnership with Pete Anderson allowed him to release well-produced albums that did not sound overly polished, retaining some of the authenticity of the roadhouse jukebox and the oldtime honky-tonks.

—*Thomas Clarkin*

SELECT DISCOGRAPHY
■ ALBUMS
Guitars, Cadillacs, Etc., Etc., 1986
Hillbilly Deluxe, 1987
Buenas Noches from a Lonely Room, 1988
Just Lookin' for a Hit, 1989 (compilation)
If There Was a Way, 1990
This Time, 1993
Dwight Live!, 1995 (compilation)
Gone, 1995
Under the Covers, 1997

SELECT AWARDS
Academy of Country Music New Male Vocalist of the Year Award, 1986
Grammy Award for Best Country Vocal Performance, Male, for "Ain't That Lonely Yet," 1993

SEE ALSO: Cash, Johnny; Cline, Patsy; Owens, Buck; Williams, Hank.

Neil Young

BORN: Toronto, Canada; November 12, 1945
FIRST ALBUM RELEASE: *Neil Young*, 1969
MUSICAL STYLES: Rock and roll, country rock, folk, grunge

Neil Young (Reprise/Mike Hashimoto)

An enigmatic, inventive, and distinctive singer, songwriter, and guitarist, Neil Young maintained one of the longest-running, continually successful careers in rock and roll. Young was first encouraged to learn to play music when his father, a sportswriter for the *Toronto Sun*, gave him a ukulele for Christmas in 1958. Young's parents separated soon after, and, in 1960, he moved with his mother to Winnipeg, Canada. After learning to play banjo and guitar, Young dropped out of school to concentrate on his first band, Neil Young and the Squires. With Young's mother as their booking agent, the band moved from instrumental imitators of guitar-based bands such as the Ventures and the Shadows into a folk rock band with respectable regional notoriety.

From 1963 to the summer of 1965, the band played clubs until Young disbanded the Squires and recorded solo demos for Elektra Entertainment. Failing to secure a contract, Young continued to perform solo and with local coffeehouse bands. He worked with future soul singer Rick James and met folk artist Joni Mitchell. He also met guitarist Richie Furay and future partner Stephen Stills, who was leading the folk band the Company.

After one record with a band called the Mynah Birds, Young and Mynah Birds bassist Bruce Palmer moved to Los Angeles, California. There, they joined Stills, Furay, and drummer Dewey Martin in the seminal band Buffalo Springfield. Young attracted considerable attention for his idiosyncratic songwriting and performing style, his high voice and high-energy guitar playing, and his on- and offstage interplay with Stills. Young's major compositions foreshadowed his future solo works, notably "Broken Arrow," an inventive collage; "I Am a Child," a confessional, personal ballad; and "Mr. Soul," a precursor to Young's best hard-driving guitar work. "Broken Arrow," an ambitious fusion of styles and musical forms, took one hundred takes to perfect in the studio.

Superstar in Black Limousines. In 1968, Buffalo Springfield disbanded. After signing as a solo artist with Reprise Records, Young released *Neil Young*, an album created while he lived in Topanga Canyon, California. "The Loner" was the album's standout song, being one of several Young compositions chosen for the soundtrack of the 1970 film *The Strawberry Statement*. (Young songs would also be included in the 1980 sound track to *Where the Buffalo Roam*.)

Young then met guitarist Danny Whitten, bassist Billy Talbot, drummer Ralph Molina, and pianist, producer, and arranger Jack Nitzsche, all of whom formed the original lineup of Crazy Horse, the backup band Young would use most frequently in his subsequent career. In July, 1969, Neil Young and Crazy Horse issued *Everybody Knows This Is Nowhere*, an album recorded in Young's home studio. The album had broad appeal, showing the band played country and rock with equal, if rough-edged, verve. The opening

track, "Cinnamon Girl," became an instant standard and was quickly covered by the Gentrys. The
lengthy jams between Young and Whitten, "Cow-
girl in the Sand" and "Down by the River," were
widely popular on album-oriented radio stations
and were also covered by other musicians, notably
the Byrds and Buddy Miles.

The album also received special interest when
Young provisionally joined Crosby, Stills, and Nash
in June, 1969, just in time to appear with the super-
group at Woodstock. Despite only playing on one
studio album (*Déjà Vu*, 1970) and one live set (*Four
Way Street*, 1971), Young quickly became an integral member of the collective, contributing "Help-
less," "Country Girl," and "Ohio" to their repertoire. "Ohio" was a quickly written response to the
deaths of four Kent State University students at
the hands of the U.S. National Guard in May, 1970.
Young later rejoined his bandmates for 1988's
American Dream and 1991's *Crosby, Stills, and Nash*.

Young's success continued into the fall of 1970
with his third solo album, *After the Gold Rush*,
backed by Nils Lofgren and Crazy Horse. Its fol-
lowup, *Harvest* (1972), recorded in Nashville, Tennessee, included guest artists James Taylor and
Linda Ronstadt, who subsequently covered
Young's "Love Is a Rose." The album reached the
Top 10, and the cut "Heart of Gold" became
Young's best-selling single. "Sugar Mountain," an
acoustic ballad Young played on a home tape
recorder, became a staple in folk coffeehouses,
and the songs "Southern Man" and "Alabama"
prompted southern band Lynyrd Skynyrd to respond with "Sweet Home Alabama," in which the
band refers to Young's unfavorable comments
about the American South.

Less successful was the 1972 film and sound
track *Journey Through the Past*, which seemed premature for a retrospective. The ego-absorbed film
had little to recommend it other than a short
appearance by Buffalo Springfield. Another dis-
appointment was *Long May You Run*, a 1976 collaboration with Steven Stills.

Young's 1972 song "The Needle and the Damage Done" reflected his pain when his friends
Danny Whitten and Bruce Berry died of drug
overdoses. Young next released the dark *Tonight's

the Night album (1975), followed by *Zuma* (1975),
a rock album with a reorganized Crazy Horse.
Another important release was Young's *Decade*
(1977). More than a best-of retrospective, it included rarities such as "Burned," Young's first
recorded vocal in a Hollywood studio, and unreleased Buffalo Springfield material.

Young finished the 1970's with the acoustic
album *Comes a Time* (1978) and another hard-rock
effort, *Rust Never Sleeps* (1979), considered by
many to be Young's best album. The latter, named
by rock band Devo after a commercial for Rus-
toleum paint, led to *Live Rust* (1979), a film and
album based on the tour supporting the studio
album. Both "rust" albums featured various versions of "Hey Hey My My," a hard rocker praising
the Sex Pistols' Johnny Rotten with the refrain,
"Rock and Roll will never die."

The Restless Decade. In the 1980's, Young
proved to be both confusing and eclectic, jump-
ing from acoustic, country sounds (*American Stars
'n Bars*, 1977; *Hawks and Doves*, 1980; and *Old Ways*,
1985) to rock and roll (*Re-ac-tor*, 1981; *Life*, 1987;
and *Everybody's Rockin'*, 1983) to experimental
electronic music (*Trans*, 1982). While *Trans* was a
critical and commercial failure, the odd sounds
had special meaning for Young. Having two sons
with cerebral palsy, Young had become interested
in adaptive technology for the disabled, and *Trans*
was an outgrowth of his studies in electronic communications. This interest also resulted in
Young's design and manufacture of a special
wheelchair. With wife Peggy, Young cofounded
the Bridge School for Handicapped Children
near San Francisco, California, and highlights
from his annual benefit concerts for the school

 For the Record

When Nirvana singer Kurt Cobain committed suicide in 1994, he left a note quot-
ing lyrics from Neil Young's song "Hey Hey,
My My (Out of the Blue)." Afterward Young
said he would never sing the song again.

have been issued featuring performances by Young and all-star friends. Young also founded a company that makes high-tech toys and devices for the disabled.

Less esoteric but still heavily electronic was 1986's *Landing on Water*, which employed percussive synthesizers alongside the San Francisco Boys Choir. "Hippie Dream" was the first of Young's many eulogies to the ideals of the 1960's; other such songs included "Mansion on the Hill" from *Weld* (1991) and "Peace and Love" from *Mirror Ball* (1995). In 1988, turning in yet another direction, Young employed a horn section, the Bluenotes, on *This Note's for You*. The title track won MTV's Video of the Year award despite its clear attack against commercialism in popular music. However, the confusion over Young's unpredictability led Young's label, Geffen Records, to sue Young for his shifting artistic guises.

Renewal. The singer returned to his former company, Reprise, and then released his important comeback album, *Freedom* (1989), which included the rock anthem "Rockin' in the Free World" in two versions, one acoustic and one with a full band. With renewed energy, Young and Crazy Horse made the platinum-selling *Ragged Glory* (1990), followed by the 1991 trilogy *Arc*, *Weld*, and *Arc-Weld*. Among the live reworkings on *Weld* was Young's interpretation of Bob Dylan's "Blowin' in the Wind," complete with military sound effects and long, intense guitar solos. During the 1990's, Young was both an influence on and influenced by younger bands, notably Sonic Youth, Wilco, and Nirvana, who dubbed Young "the Godfather of grunge." As if to prove the point, Young recorded *Mirror Ball* with grunge hitmakers Pearl Jam and toured with them in 1995.

During this period, Young enjoyed both critical and popular acclaim for a series of albums, including *Sleeps With Angels* (1994), on which Young and Crazy Horse successfully recaptured the sounds of their *Everybody Knows This Is Nowhere* period, notably on "Change Your Mind." The album, built on Western saloon piano melodies, intrigued critics for its unusual production. Two lighter albums, *Harvest Moon* (1992; with the country band the Stray Gators) and *Unplugged* (1993) also kept fans

of Young's softer sounds interested.

Young received special attention for his performance of Jimi Hendrix's "All Along the Watchtower" for the Bob Dylan 30th Anniversary Concert Celebration in 1993, but his contribution to the sound track for the 1993 film *Philadelphia* was less well received. He also wrote the music to Jim Jarmusch's 1996 film *Dead Man*.

Broken Arrow, a 1996 studio outing with Crazy Horse, garnered a Grammy nomination for Best Rock Album. Jarmusch filmed the following summer's tour supporting the album, which resulted in 1997's documentary and two-compact-disc set *Year of the Horse*. While the film received largely unfavorable reviews, the audio recordings were perhaps Young's and Crazy Horse's finest live efforts.
—Wesley Britton

SELECT DISCOGRAPHY
■ ALBUMS
Everybody Knows This Is Nowhere, 1969
After the Gold Rush, 1970
Harvest, 1972
On the Beach, 1974
Tonight's the Night, 1975
Zuma, 1975
Decade, 1977 (previously released material)
Comes a Time, 1978
Rust Never Sleeps, 1979
Hawks and Doves, 1980
Re-ac-tor, 1981
Trans, 1982
Old Ways, 1985
Life, 1987
Freedom, 1989
Ragged Glory, 1990
Harvest Moon, 1992
Unplugged, 1993 (live)
Sleeps with Angels, 1994
Mirror Ball, 1995
Broken Arrow, 1996

SELECT AWARDS
Rolling Stone Artist of the Decade (1970's), 1979
MTV Video of the Year Award, 1988

SEE ALSO: Buffalo Springfield; Crosby, Stills, Nash, and Young; Dylan, Bob; Pearl Jam.

Z

Frank Zappa / The Mothers of Invention

Frank Zappa

BORN: Baltimore, Maryland; December 21, 1940
DIED: Los Angeles, California; December 4, 1993
FIRST ALBUM RELEASE: *Hot Rats*, 1969

The Mothers of Invention

ORIGINAL MEMBERS: Ray Collins; Roy Estrada; Jimmy Carl Black; Elliot Ingber

OTHER MEMBERS: Bunk Gardner; Jim "Motorhead" Sherwood; Don Preston (1932); Billy Mundi; Lowell George (1945-1979); Art Tripp III; Ian Underwood; Howard Kaylan (1945); Mark Volman (1944); Jim Pons (1943); George Duke (1946); Aynsley Dunbar (1946); Jean-Luc Ponty (1942, Zappa sideman); Adrian Belew (1949, Zappa sideman); Steve Vai (1960, Zappa sideman); Terry Bozzio (1950, Zappa sideman); others

FIRST ALBUM RELEASE: *Freak Out!* 1966

MUSICAL STYLES: Satirical rock and roll, classical, jazz, fusion, doo-wop

Frank Zappa was a unique figure in the history of popular and avant-garde music. Acclaimed as a brilliant composer and musician and a proficient guitarist, Zappa also was a satirist who provided scathing commentary on both the establishment and the counterculture during the tumultuous 1960's. Unlike many of his colleagues on the cutting edge of popular music, Zappa was able to outlive the 1960's, forging a prolific and far-ranging musical career until his death in 1993.

The Beginnings. Frank Zappa was brought up in a stable but eccentric household. His father was a free-spirited government scientist who played guitar for fun. Zappa inherited his father's love of music, playing in various school bands and settling on the electric guitar as his instrument of choice. When Zappa was ten, his family moved to the Los Angeles area, a hotbed of experiments in pop music. Zappa became an aficionado of rhythm and blues as well as rock and roll. He also listened avidly to modern classical music, particularly the works of avant-garde composer Edgard Varèse. In high school, Zappa started a band called the Black-Outs and became a fan of country blues. Zappa studied music theory at Chaffey College in 1959, but he seemed ill suited for formal education. He dropped out of the program after six months. From this point on, Zappa's musical education would take place in the school of hard knocks.

Zappa and the 1960's. The early 1960's found Zappa making a number of false starts in the music business as well as getting into minor trouble with the law. His forays into music included playing with lounge bands, composing scores for low-budget films, and songwriting. His trouble with the law was a symptom of his penchant for defying convention and, correspondingly, his dedication to free expression. In 1963, Zappa was accused of conspiracy to make a pornographic sound recording. The evidence was flimsy, and the actual crime (if any) inconsequential, but Zappa did serve a brief jail sentence. (In his autobiography, Zappa states that an undercover policeman came to him and asked him to make the recording, then arrested him for it.)

In 1964, Zappa joined the Soul Giants, which, under his demanding tutelage, would ultimately become the Muthers, then the Mothers, and finally—at the insistence of the band's first label, MGM/Verve—the Mothers of Invention. The band's first album, *Freak Out!*, was released in 1966. A double album, *Freak Out!* parodied pop music of the 1950's and 1960's with such tunes as "Go Cry on Somebody Else's Shoulder," "You Didn't Try to Call Me," and, in a different vein, the absurdist "Help, I'm a Rock." It also included politically oriented fare such as "Who Are the Brain Police" and "Trouble Every Day," a song about racial unrest inspired largely by the 1965

Watts riots. Though musically impeccable, the album emphasized off-center humor and social commentary. As such, it was not commercially successful, though it did win the band a small national following.

The band's next album, *Absolutely Free* (1967), included a song entitled "Plastic People," which well illustrates Zappa's philosophical perspective. The song makes it clear that plasticity (or phoniness) is a universal human quality. It applies to dominant social institutions (the establishment), so-called revolutionaries (the counterculture), and average record and radio listeners. Zappa by no means excluded himself. He, too, was capable of plasticity.

Lumpy Gravy, Zappa's first major experiment with orchestral arrangements, was released in 1967. The Mothers of Invention released *We're Only in It for the Money* in 1968. Widely recognized as a masterpiece, the album lampooned police, flower children, science-fiction author Robert Heinlein, and the Beatles. That year, the band also released *Cruisin' with Ruben and the Jets*, a full-scale tribute to, and takeoff on, doo-wop music. In 1969, the band released three more albums, including *Uncle Meat*. This two-album set featured fragments of dialogue from a film Zappa wished to produce (about the rigors of life in a commercially unsuccessful rock band) as well as strikingly original instrumental passages. By this time the band had moved to New York, where they played a lengthy engagement in Greenwich Village at the Garrick Theater, earning a reputation for unpredictable antics on stage. New York City, the Village in particular, was a center for radical experiments in rock music, featuring such non-mainstream groups as the Velvet Underground and the Fugs. Zappa and the Mothers of Invention more than held their own in this highly charged music scene. This fact, in addition to their albums, had made the Mothers of Invention, with Zappa clearly the driving force, one of the best-known and most respected "underground" bands in the United States. It was not long before Zappa moved the band back to Los Angeles.

In 1968 Zappa decided to form his own record labels, Straight and Bizarre, distributed by Warner

Frank Zappa (Popperfoto/Archive Photos)

Bros. He signed and produced the recordings of a number of other artists, including longtime friend Captain Beefheart (Don Van Vliet)—Zappa produced Beefheart's remarkable first record, *Trout Mask Replica*. He also released the first two (unsuccessful) albums by the young Alice Cooper as well as albums by such eccentric artists as Wild Man Fischer and the GTO's.

Admired both for his musicianship and for his unsparing irreverence, Zappa did not become very prosperous in the 1960's, but he did become a notable cultural figure. Posters of Zappa adorned many walls (one pictured him sitting on a toilet and was captioned "Phi Zappa Krappa"), his image symbolizing free-spiritedness and a willingness to question authority—key thematic anthems of the era.

The 1970's. Zappa disbanded the original Mothers of Invention band in the late 1960's but soon formed a new version. The 1971 album *Mothers Live at the Fillmore East* featured vocalists Howard Kaylan and Mark Volman (formerly of the Turtles) and emphasized extremely bawdy comedy dialogues. The "Uncle Meat" movie project may have failed, but Zappa did complete and release a film in 1971, *200 Motels*. It was an indescribably weird, hallucinogenic vision of performing and traveling on the road, with appearances by Theodore Bikel, Ringo Starr, and Keith Moon, and with Kaylan and Volman performing such antics as leading a torchlight parade while singing about "penis dimension." The 1973 release *Overnite Sensation* found Kaylan and Volman gone and Zappa himself doing most of the lead vocals. It was the Mothers' best-selling album to date, containing relatively normally-structured, accessible songs. Zappa humor abounded, from "Montana," to "Dinah-Moe Humm," about a woman who wagers that the singer will not be able to make her achieve a sexual climax, to "I'm the Slime," a whimsical protest about the "slime oozing out from your TV set." Zappa's next release, the solo album *Apostrophe* (1974), contained a song that actually entered the *Billboard* Hot 100 singles chart, "Don't Eat the Yellow Snow" (with its refrain "Watch out where the huskies go/ Don't you eat that yellow snow").

In 1975 Zappa and Captain Beefheart teamed up to release the live album *Bongo Fury*. Zappa made waves in 1979 with the satirical song "Jewish Princess," which was attacked by the B'nai B'rith Anti-defamation League. Zappa responded with the song "Catholic Girls," from *Joe's Garage (Act I)* (1979), to prove that his satire knew no ethnic or religious bounds. Zappa also skewered the disco era with "Disco Boy" (1976) and "Dancin' Fool" (1979); "Dancin' Fool" managed to rise to number 45 on the singles charts. Also in 1979 Zappa released another film, *Baby Snakes*.

The 1980's and 1990's. Zappa was most widely known in the 1980's for two things: the song "Valley Girl" and his (voluntary) appearance before a U.S. Senate Committee to testify regarding censorship of music. In 1982, with "Valley Girl," from *Ship Arriving Too Late to Save a Drowning Witch*, Zappa finally placed a song in the Top 40—

not that this had ever particularly been one of his goals. The song, which went to number 32, featured verses in which his young-teenage daughter, Moon (short for Moon Unit), lampooned the way her affluent schoolmates in the San Fernando Valley talked ("Barf me out . . . Gag me with a spoon . . . I am *sher*").

On a more serious note, the elder Zappa went to Washington in 1985, and in dead earnest argued strongly against proposals to censor music releases. In particular, he was opposing a group called the Parents' Music Resource Center, which managed to persuade the music industry to agree to put parental advisory labels on releases with particularly graphic sexual or violent content. Throughout his life Zappa stood out as an unwavering proponent of free expression, opposing censorship in any form—and himself managing to offend most identifiable groups in American society at one time or another. Zappa later served Czech president (and noted playwright) Václav Havel as an adviser on liberalization of the arts, after the Czech Republic was freed from Soviet domination.

Zappa might correctly be described as a workaholic. He continued to produce distinctive music until his death. From 1966 to the 1990's, either with the Mothers of Invention or solo, Zappa was responsible for more than sixty albums and countless live performances. He saw his serious compositions played and recorded by world-renowned orchestras, had his live guitar solos collected on a series of recordings, and won a Grammy Award for Best Rock Instrumental Album for *Jazz from Hell* (1986). Other notable recordings during these years include *Shut Up 'n Play Yer Guitar* (1981) and the *You Can't Do That on Stage Anymore* series of live recordings (beginning in 1988). In 1981, after yet

For the Record

"Rock journalism is people who can't write interviewing people who can't talk for people who can't read." —*Frank Zappa*

another dispute with a record company, Zappa had started his own Barking Pumpkin label. He also gained the rights to his older recordings. In the 1980's he also began remastering and re-releasing his old material through an arrangement with Rykodisc.

Zappa reportedly planned on running for president of the United States in the 1992 election. Undoubtedly, he would have found unique ways to propel his candidacy, holding the U.S. political system up to unprecedented scrutiny along the way. Unfortunately, he fell ill before his campaign could get under way. It was announced in 1991 that he was suffering from prostate cancer. He continued working on his music at his home studio until he was physically unable to do so. Zappa died in his Los Angeles home on the evening of December 4, 1993, at the age of fifty-two.

Impact and Legacy. Zappa's impact was felt in a number of ways. Along with artists such as Bob Dylan, Jimi Hendrix, the Doors' Jim Morrison, Lou Reed, Eric Clapton, and the Who's Pete Townshend, Zappa expanded the technical, intellectual, and aesthetic limits of rock music, purposefully mixing high and low (sometimes very low) culture in a highly expressive and innovative way. Zappa also helped to break down the barriers between musical forms, easily navigating the boundaries between rock, classical music, and jazz. In doing so, he enabled a generation of fans and some free-spirited musicians (John Zorn, for example) to follow in his footsteps.

Zappa also had two kinds of political impact. His music and lyrics foster a healthy skepticism about political motives and machinations regarding all wings of the ideological spectrum. It is important to note, however, that Zappa avoided the trap of mere negativism. His unconditional defense of free expression shows that, despite his deep skepticism, there are still principles and causes worth following.

Finally, along with figures such as comedian and social critic Lenny Bruce, Zappa himself exercised free expression in a way that was purposefully outrageous. He regularly challenged authority; he routinely stretched the parameters of acceptable topics for public discussion and com-

mentary. In this sense, Zappa can be seen as a pioneer of alternative music (before it, too, became commercialized). Zappa's willingness to go at least one step beyond normal expectations also helped to lay the groundwork for some of the more freewheeling experimentation in film and television which emerged during his lifetime.

—*Ira Smolensky*

SELECT DISCOGRAPHY
■ ALBUMS
The Mothers of Invention
Freak Out! 1966
Absolutely Free, 1967
Lumpy Gravy, 1967
We're Only in It for the Money, 1968
Cruisin' with Ruben and the Jets, 1968
Uncle Meat, 1969
Over-nite Sensation, 1973
Frank Zappa
Hot Rats, 1969
200 Motels, 1971
Apostrophe, 1974
Joe's Garage (Act I), 1979
Shut Up 'n Play Yer Guitar, 1981
London Symphony Orchestra, 1983
Jazz from Hell, 1986
You Can't Do That on Stage Anymore, Volume 1, 1988

SELECT AWARDS
Grammy Award for Best Rock Instrumental Performance (Orchestra, Group, or Soloist) for *Jazz from Hell,* 1987 (Zappa)
Grammy Award for Best Rock Instrumental Performance for "Sofa," 1993 (Zappa's Universe Rock Group Featuring Steve Vai)
Rock and Roll Hall of Fame, inducted 1995

SEE ALSO: Captain Beefheart and the Magic Band; Cooper, Alice; Dylan, Bob; Hendrix, Jimi; Reed, Lou.

Warren Zevon

BORN: Chicago, Illinois; January 24, 1947
FIRST ALBUM RELEASE: *Wanted Dead or Alive,* 1969
MUSICAL STYLE: Rock and roll

Though a product of the Southern California rock-and-roll scene of the 1970's, Warren Zevon stood apart from contemporaries such as the Eagles, Linda Ronstadt, and Jackson Browne in his darkly ironic vision of human nature.

Background. Zevon's early life was as colorful as anything in his songs. The son of a professional gambler, Warren spent most of his youth in Southern California where he studied classical music and once even met famed composer Igor Stravinsky. At sixteen, though, he abandoned his classical training for a career in popular music, heading to New York City in a Corvette which his father had won playing poker. Zevon eventually returned to the West Coast and released his first album, *Wanted Dead or Alive* (1969), on the Imperial label. This inferior collection of bluesy material attracted little attention, and he turned to session work, most notably serving as musical director to the Everly Brothers in the early 1970's. Zevon recruited guitarist and future collaborator Waddy Wachtel into the Everlys' band and honed his recording skills, alternately producing records for the feuding brothers. When the Everlys broke up for good, Zevon moved to Spain and supported himself by playing piano in tourist bars. He also used the time to work on a backlog of unconventional pop songs that would define his style and win him the label of alternative artist.

The friendship of Jackson Browne—and the success of Linda Ronstadt's 1976 recording of the Zevon-penned "Hasten Down the Wind"—helped Zevon secure a record deal with David Geffen's innovative Asylum label. Browne produced *Warren Zevon* (1976), a collection of musical vignettes about the California dream turned nightmare. In the tradition of literary satirist Nathanael West, Zevon used Hollywood as a metaphor for the materialism and self-absorption of American culture. The album is suffused with violence and disillusionment: the opening track, "Frank and Jesse James," provides a candid account of the outlaws' bloody exploits; "Carmelita" twists a mariachi love song into a pathetic self-portrait of an addict "all strung out on heroin on the outskirts of town." Boosted by Wachtel's powerful guitar work, Zevon's "Poor Poor Pitiful Me" is a

For the Record

Jackson Browne once summed up Zevon's songwriting: "He's the first and foremost proponent of song noir."

darkly comic vision of sexual excess—a far cry from Linda Ronstadt's sanitized single released in 1978. Yet the album's climax is "Desperadoes Under the Eaves," in which the Hollywood Hawaiian Hotel prefigures the Eagles' "Hotel California" as symbolic landscape of the damned. Unlike the Eagles, however, Zevon lightened his apocalyptic vision with his signature irony: "And if California slides into the ocean/ Like the mystics and statistics say it will/ I predict this motel will be standing until I pay my bill."

The follow-up album, *Excitable Boy* (1978), brought Zevon a mass audience, thanks largely to the quirky hit "Werewolves of London" (number 21). Zevon, collaborating with Jorge Calderon, LeRoy Marinell, and Waddy Wachtel, more fully developed the unusual personae of his songs. This flair for creating characters, as well as a revisionist's interest in history, drew Zevon inevitable comparisons with Randy Newman as he stripped the away layers of cultural myth to reveal the past as violent prologue to the present. "Roland the Headless Thompson Gunner" (cowritten with a former mercenary) combines a horror-story plot with a deft critique of Western adventurism in Africa while "Veracruz" takes aim at "Woodrow Wilson's guns" and U.S. interference in the Mexican Revolution of the 1910's.

Zevon was not as successful with *Bad Luck Streak in Dancing School* (1980). The album art indicated it was short on new ideas: where the inside jacket of *Excitable Boy* had featured a picture of a Colt .45 revolver laid across a home-cooked meal, the rear cover of *Bad Luck Streak in Dancing School* made a similar point with an Uzi semi-automatic weapon and a pair of dancing slippers. The title song was an interesting rocker with opaque lyrics that suggested a narrative that its author could not fully reveal. Similarly, "Bill Lee," based on the career of the odd professional athlete, seemed like a good idea only half developed. However, the album's best moment, "Jeannie Needs a Shooter," showed that Zevon was still capable of spinning a fine dark tale. Cowritten with Bruce Springsteen, the song is pure Zevon in its nihilistic take on the Springsteen's "Born to Run" heroes: the song's outlaw protagonist seeks to deliver Jeannie from her lawman father only to be gunned down by him at the end of the song, with Jeannie's acquiescence, if not complicity. The album was quickly followed with *Stand in the Fire* (1980), a live album of Zevon hits with a few new songs included. A fine band led by Wachtel revealed Zevon to be an energetic rocker; live versions of "Poor Poor Pitiful Me" and "I'll Sleep When I'm Dead" easily surpassed their original studio recordings. However, the performance was marred by Zevon's drunken caterwauling on "Jeannie Needs a Shooter" and "Lawyers, Guns and Money." Zevon made one more album with Asylum before being dropped by the label. *The Envoy* (1982) featured a rock-and-roll first: a title song about a career diplomat. Needless to say, the underrated album attracted little attention from an audience expecting sex and drugs and Zevon's typical mayhem. Yet album tracks such as "Charlie's Medicine" and "Hula Hula Boys" were a return to Zevon's finest songwriting form.

Attempts at a Comeback. In the mid-1980's Zevon took a five-year hiatus from recording. After completing a drug and alcohol rehabilitation program (documented against his will by *Rolling Stone* magazine), he resumed his recording career on the Virgin label. *Sentimental Hygiene* (1987) paired him with Peter Buck, Mike Mills, and Bill Berry of R.E.M. and included a bevy of guest artists ranging from Bob Dylan to Neil Young. The album showed Zevon's irony to be intact with songs such as "Bad Karma" (featuring Buck on electric sitar) and "Even the Dog Can Shake Hands," an unpretentious rocker about the pitfalls of the music industry. The album sold well enough to permit a follow-up, the cyberpunk concept album *Transverse City* (1989), a commercial and critical failure. Dropped by Virgin, Zevon banked on R.E.M.'s popularity to secure a record deal with Giant, which released outtakes of the *Sentimental Hygiene* sessions as *Hindu Love Gods* (1990). However, this mediocre blend of folk and blues standards did little to arrest his career free fall and only estranged him from Buck, Mills, and Berry. Zevon's next Giant release, *Mr. Bad Example* (1991), yielded little except the song "Things to Do in Denver When You're Dead," whose title was borrowed for a motion picture in 1995. His last album for Giant was the ballad-heavy *Mutineer* (1995), whose lack of success Zevon took in characteristic stride: "I intended this song as a gesture of appreciation and affection to my fans, none of whom bought the record."   —*Luke A. Powers*

SELECT DISCOGRAPHY
■ SINGLES
"She's Not There," 1965
"Tell Her No," 1965
"Time of the Season," 1969
■ ALBUMS
Warren Zevon, 1976
Excitable Boy, 1978
The Envoy, 1982
Sentimental Hygiene, 1987

SEE ALSO: Browne, Jackson; Everly Brothers, The; R.E.M.; Ronstadt, Linda.

The Zombies

ORIGINAL MEMBERS: Colin Blunstone (b. 1945), Paul Atkinson (b. 1946), Rod Argent (b. 1945), Hugh Grundy (b. 1945), Paul Arnold
OTHER MEMBERS: Chris White (b. 1943)
FIRST ALBUM RELEASE: *Begins Here*, 1965
MUSICAL STYLES: Rock and roll, pop

Guitarist Paul Atkinson, keyboardist Rod Argent, and drummer Hugh Grundy all met at St. Albans school in Hertfordshire, England, forming their group in 1962. In 1963 they were joined by vocalist Colin Blunstone and bassist Chris White (with original bassist Paul Arnold leaving). Together they won a local rock band contest with an arrangement of George Gershwin's "Summertime," and with it came an audition for British Decca Records.

The Band's Releases. Propelled by Blunstone's striking tenor vocals, their first single for Decca, Argent's "She's Not There," became a worldwide hit and went to number 2 on the U.S. pop charts in 1964. When the second single, "Leave Me Be," failed, the album *Begins Here* (1965) was rushed through production in order to capitalize on the popularity of "She's Not There." Though uneven, *Begins Here* produced the plaintive "Tell Her No," which peaked at number 6 in the United States (number 42 in the United Kingdom). With frequent touring and a brief spot performing in the 1965 film *Bunny Lake Is Missing*, the Zombies remained more popular in the United States than in Great Britain.

Their follow-up album, *Odyssey and Oracle*, was recorded late in 1967, just two weeks before the group broke up. It took Columbia producer Al Kooper one year to get the album released, and though it failed to hit the Top 40, the single "Time of the Season" went to number 3 on the U.S. charts. All offers to reform the group in the wake of this success were rejected, as Argent was already forming his own band called Argent.

Careers After the Zombies. Argent released six albums between 1970 and 1976, though only *All Together Now* (1972), featuring "Hold Your Head Up" (number 5), reached the Top 40. After Argent folded in 1976, Rod Argent continued to play, write, and produce for a number of projects through the 1990's. His musical *Masquerade* (1982) was staged in London, and he played keyboards for the London productions of Andrew Lloyd Webber's *Cats* and *Starlight Express*. Argent also scored music for British Broadcasting Corporation (BBC) television, released several solo albums, and played keyboards on the Who's 1978 album *Who Are You*. Blunstone released four albums between 1971 and 1978 and had several minor U.K. hits, including a cover of Denny Laine's "Say You Don't Mind," which broke into the Top 20. He went on to form the band Keats and to lend vocals to albums by the Alan Parsons Project. Blunstone, White, and Grundy reformed in the late 1980's, rerecording "Time of the Season" as a film track and recording the album *New World* (1991).

—*John Powell*

SELECT DISCOGRAPHY
■ SINGLES
"She's Not There," 1965
"Tell Her No," 1965
"Time of the Season," 1969
■ ALBUMS
Begins Here, 1965
Odyssey and Oracle, 1968
Time of the Zombies, 1973
Live on the BBC: 1965-1967, 1985
The Best and the Rest of the Zombies, 1986 (compilation)
Singles A's & B's, 1990 (compilation)
Greatest Hits, 1990 (compilation)

SEE ALSO: Parsons, Alan, Project; Who, The.

ZZ Top

ORIGINAL MEMBERS: Frank Beard (b. 1949), Billy Gibbons (b. 1949), Dusty Hill (b. 1949)
FIRST ALBUM RELEASE: *ZZ Top's First Album*, 1970
MUSICAL STYLES: Blues, rock and roll

ZZ Top has been making their singular brand of bluesy roots rock and roll since 1969. The undisputed kings of blues-based, tongue-in-cheek innuendo are almost as famous for their beards as they are for their music. The series of videos they made for MTV in the mid-1980's singing about blues, women, and cars has forever cemented them in U.S. pop culture.

The Beginnings. Though he came from a classical background (his father belonged to the Houston Philharmonic), guitarist Billy Gibbons discovered blues at an early age. While other teenagers were listening to the Beatles and the Rolling Stones, Gibbons was discovering artists such as Jimmy Reed, Little Richard, and Bobby "Blue" Bland. Before he was out of high school, he had joined a series of local bands, the most notable of which was Moving Sidewalks.

Dusty Hill had been playing in clubs since age thirteen, and with his brother Rocky he played in a band called the Warlocks, which would later become known as the American Blues. Their gim-

Popular Musicians

Time Line of First Releases

Year	Artist	Title
1923	Louis Armstrong (as sideman with Joe "King" Oliver)	"Just Gone" and "Canal Street Blues"
1927	Jimmie Rodgers	"The Soldier's Sweetheart"/"Sleep, Baby Sleep"
1933	Leadbelly	"Honey Take a Whiff on Me"
1934	Mahalia Jackson	"God's Gonna Separate the Wheat from the Tares"
1935	Ella Fitzgerald	"Love and Kisses"
1936	Bill Monroe and the Blue Grass Boys	"What Would You Give in Exchange (for Your Soul)"
	Les Paul	"Just Because"/"Deep Elm Blues"
	Ernest Tubb	"The Passing of Jimmie Rodgers"
	Bob Wills and His Texas Playboys	"Right or Wrong"/"Steel Guitar Rag"
1939	Frank Sinatra	"From the Bottom of My Heart"
1940	Willie Dixon (with the Five Breezes)	"Sweet Louise"
	Woody Guthrie	*Dust Bowl Ballads*
1941	Charlie Parker (with the Jay McShann Band)	"Swingmatism" and "Hootie Blues"
	Pete Seeger	*Songs for John Doe*
1943	Nat "King" Cole	"Straighten Up and Fly Right"
1944	Thelonious Monk	*Bean and the Boys*
1945	Eddy Arnold	"Each Minute Seems a Million Years"
1947	Hank Williams	"Move It on Over"
1949	Ray Charles	"St. Pete's Blues"
	Kitty Wells	"Death at the Bar"/ "Gathering Flowers for the Master's Bouquet"
1950	Tony Bennett	"Boulevard of Broken Dreams"
	Miles Davis	*Birth of the Cool*
	Fats Domino	"The Fat Man"
	Lefty Frizzell	"If You've Got the Money, I've Got the Time"/ "I Love You a Thousand Ways"
	Muddy Waters	"Rollin' Stone"
1951	Chet Atkins	*Chet Atkins Plays Guitar*
	Dave Brubeck	*Distinctive Rhythm Instrumentals*
	John Coltrane	*Dee Gee Days*

Year	Artist	Title
1951 cont'd	Howlin' Wolf	"Moanin' at Midnight"
	B. B. King	"Three O'Clock Blues"
1952	Marty Robbins	"Love Me or Leave Me Alone"
1953	The Drifters	"Money Honey"
	Charles Mingus	*Jazz at Massey Hall*
	The Staple Singers	"These Are They"
1954	Sammy Davis, Jr.	*Starring Sammy Davis Jr.*
	Bill Haley	*Rock with Bill Haley and the Comets*
	George Jones	"No Money in This Deal"
	Elvis Presley	"That's All Right"/"Blue Moon of Kentucky"
1955	Julian "Cannonball" Adderley	*Presenting Cannonball Adderley*
	Harry Belafonte	*Mark Twain and Other Folk Songs*
	Chuck Berry	"Maybellene"
	Johnny Cash (with the Tennessee Two)	"Cry, Cry, Cry"/"Hey Porter"
	Patsy Cline	"A Church, a Courtroom, and Then Goodbye"/"Honky Tonk Merry-Go-Round"
	Bo Diddley	"Bo Diddley"/"I'm a Man"
	The Everly Brothers	"The Sun Keeps Shining"/"Keep a-Lovin' Me"
	Little Richard	"Tutti Frutti"
	Carl Perkins	"Movie Magg"/"Turn Around"
1956	James Brown (with the Flames)	"Please, Please, Please"
	The Coasters	"Down in Mexico"
	Buddy Holly (with the Crickets)	"Blue Days, Black Nights"
	Rahsaan Roland Kirk	*Triple Threat*
	Jerry Lee Lewis	"Crazy Arms"
	Johnny Mathis	"When Sunny Gets Blue"
	Willie Nelson	"No Place for Me"/"Lumberjack"
	Roy Orbison	"Ooby Dooby"
	Buck Owens	"Down on the Corner"
	The Platters	*The Platters*
1957	Eddie Cochran	"Sittin' in the Balcony"
	Sam Cooke (as Dale Cook)	"Lovable"
	Dion and the Belmonts	"We Went Away"
	Gladys Knight and the Pips	"Whistle My Love"
	Rick Nelson	*Ricky*

Year	Artist	Title
1957 cont'd	Lou Reed (with the Shades)	"So Blue"
	Jackie Wilson	"Reet Petite (the Finest Girl You Ever Want to Meet)"
1958	Bobby "Blue" Bland	*Blues Consolidated*
	Dick Dale	"Ooh-Whee-Marie"
	Duane Eddy	*Have "Twangy" Guitar—Will Travel*
	Buddy Guy	"Sit and Cry (the Blues)"
	Waylon Jennings	"Jolé Blon"
	The Kingston Trio	"Tom Dooley"
	Curtis Mayfield	"Listen to Me"/"Shorty's Got to Go"
	Charlie Rich	"Whirlwind"
	Neil Sedaka	"The Diary"
1959	John Lee Hooker	*I'm John Lee Hooker*
	The Isley Brothers	"Shout"
	Jan and Dean	"Baby Talk"
	Conway Twitty	*Conway Twitty Sings*
	Ritchie Valens	*Ritchie Valens*
1960	Joan Baez	*Joan Baez*
	Dion (solo)	"Lonely Teenager"
	Aretha Franklin	"Today I Sing the Blues"
	Loretta Lynn	"I'm a Honky Tonk Girl"
	Chuck Mangione	*The Jazz Brothers*
	Dolly Parton	"Puppy Love"/"Girl Left Alone"
	The Ventures	*Walk, Don't Run*
1961	Glen Campbell	"Turn Around, Look at Me"
	Judy Collins	*A Maid of Constant Sorrow*
	The Crusaders	*Freedom Sound*
	Marvin Gaye	*The Soulful Moods of Marvin Gaye*
	Etta James	*At Last*
	Robert Johnson	*King of the Delta Blues Singers*
	Smokey Robinson	*Hi . . . We're the Miracles*
	Mel Tillis	*Walk on By*
	Ike and Tina Turner	*The Soul of Ike and Tina Turner*
1962	Herb Alpert	*The Lonely Bull*
	The Beach Boys	*Surfin' Safari*

Year	Artist	Title
1962 cont'd	The Beatles	"Love Me Do"
	Booker T. and the MG's	*Green Onions*
	Roy Clark	*The Lightning Fingers of Roy Clark*
	Jimmy Cliff	"Daisy Got Me Crazy"
	Bob Dylan	*Bob Dylan*
	The Four Seasons	*Sherry and 11 Others*
	Merle Haggard	"Singin' My Heart Out"
	Herbie Hancock	*Takin' Off*
	Albert King	*The Big Blues*
	Bob Marley	"Judge Not"
	Peter, Paul, and Mary	*Peter, Paul, and Mary*
	Lou Rawls (with Sam Cooke)	"Bring It On Home to Me"
	Otis Redding	"These Arms of Mine"
	Sam and Dave	"I Need Love"/"Keep Walkin' "
	Dionne Warwick	"Don't Make Me Over"
	Bobby Womack (with the Valentinos)	"Looking for a Love"
	Stevie Wonder	*Tribute to Uncle Ray*
1963	The Bee Gees	"The Battle of the Blue and the Grey"
	The Chieftains	*The Chieftains*
	Sergio Mendes	*Cannonball's Bossa Nova*
	Martha Reeves and the Vandellas	"I'll Have to Let Him Go"
	The Righteous Brothers	"Little Latin Lupe Lu"/"I'm So Lonely"
	Rolling Stones	"Come On"
	The Spinners	*Party: My Pad! After Surfin*
	Barbra Streisand	*The Barbra Streisand Album*
	The Supremes	*Meet the Supremes*
	Doc Watson	*Doc Watson and His Family*
1964	The Animals	"House of the Rising Sun"
	George Benson	*The New Boss Guitar of George Benson with the Brother Jack McDuff Quartet*
	José Feliciano	*The Voice and Guitar of José Feliciano*
	Tom Jones	"Chills and Fever"
	The Kinks	*The Kinks*
	The Ronettes	Presenting the Fabulous Ronettes Featuring Veronica
	Simon and Garfunkel	*Wednesday Morning, 3 A.M.*

Year	Artist	Title
1964 cont'd	The Temptations	*Meet the Temptations*
	Peter Tosh (with the Wailers)	"Simmer Down"
	Hank Williams, Jr.	"Long Gone Lonesome Blues"
	The Yardbirds	*Five Live Yardbirds*
1965	The Association	"Babe I'm Gonna Leave You"
	The Byrds	*Mr. Tambourine Man*
	The Chambers Brothers	*People Get Ready*
	Cher (solo)	*All I Really Want to Do*
	Donovan	"Catch the Wind"
	The Four Tops	*Four Tops*
	The Guess Who	"Shakin' All Over"
	The Hollies	*Here I Go Again*
	The Lovin' Spoonful	*Do You Believe in Magic*
	The Moody Blues	*Go Now: Moody Blues #1*
	Van Morrison	*Them*
	The O'Jays	*Comin' Through*
	Wilson Pickett	*In the Midnight Hour*
	The Rascals	"I Ain't Gonna Eat Out My Heart Anymore"/ "Slow Down"
	Boz Scaggs	*Boz*
	Paul Simon (solo)	*The Paul Simon Songbook*
	Sonny and Cher	"I Got You Babe"
	The Turtles	*It Ain't Me Babe*
	The Who	*The Who Sings My Generation*
	The Zombies	*Begins Here*
1966	Buffalo Springfield	*Buffalo Springfield*
	Cream	*Fresh Cream*
	Neil Diamond	*The Feel of Neil Diamond*
	The Fifth Dimension	"I'll Be Loving You Forever"
	Jefferson Airplane	*Jefferson Airplane Takes Off*
	Gordon Lightfoot	*Lightfoot*
	The Mamas and the Papas	*If You Can Believe Your Eyes and Ears*
	The Monkees	*The Monkees*
	The Mothers of Invention	*Freak Out*
	Olivia Newton-John	"Till You Say You'll Be Mine"

Year	Artist	Title
1966 cont'd	Charley Pride	*Country Charley Pride*
	Kenny Rogers	*New Kick!*
	Tammy Wynette	"Apartment #9"
1967	David Bowie	*The World of David Bowie*
	Captain Beefheart and the Magic Band	*Safe as Milk*
	The Doors	*The Doors*
	The Grateful Dead	*The Grateful Dead*
	Al Green	"Back Up Train"
	Isaac Hayes	*Presenting Isaac Hayes*
	Jimi Hendrix	*Are You Experienced?*
	Janis Joplin	*Big Brother and the Holding Company*
	Patti LaBelle	*Dreamer*
	Ted Nugent	*The Amboy Dukes*
	Pink Floyd	*The Piper at the Gates of Dawn*
	Procol Harum	*Procol Harum*
	Sly and the Family Stone	*A Whole New Thing*
	Cat Stevens	*Matthew & Son*
	Taj Mahal	*Taj Mahal*
	Traffic	*Mr. Fantasy*
	Velvet Underground	*The Velvet Underground and Nico*
	Jerry Jeff Walker	*Circus Maximus*
1968	The Band	*Music from Big Pink*
	Blood, Sweat, and Tears	*Child Is Father to the Man*
	Leonard Cohen	*Songs of Leonard Cohen*
	Creedence Clearwater Revival	*Creedence Clearwater Revival*
	Deep Purple	*Shades of Deep Purple*
	Dr. John	*Gris-Gris*
	Fleetwood Mac	*Peter Green's Fleetwood Mac*
	George Harrison	*Wonderwall Music*
	The Jackson 5	"Big Boy"/"You've Changed"
	Lynyrd Skynyrd (as Lynard Skynard)	"Need All My Friends"
	Steve Miller	*Children of the Future*
	Joni Mitchell	*Joni Mitchell*
	Anne Murray	*What About Me*

Year	Artist	Title
1968 cont'd	Randy Newman	*Randy Newman*
	The Ohio Players	*First Impressions*
	Bob Seger	*Ramblin' Gamblin' Man*
	Steppenwolf	*Steppenwolf*
	Rod Stewart	*Truth*
	James Taylor	*James Taylor*
	Richard Thompson	*Fairport Convention*
	Jethro Tull	*This Was*
1969	The Allman Brothers Band	*The Allman Brothers Band*
	Bread	*Bread*
	The Carpenters	*Ticket to Ride*
	Chicago	*Chicago Transit Authority*
	Joe Cocker	*With a Little Help from My Friends*
	Alice Cooper	*Pretties for You*
	Jim Croce	*Croce*
	Crosby, Stills, and Nash	*Crosby, Stills, & Nash*
	John Denver	*Rhymes and Reasons*
	Genesis	*From Genesis to Revelation*
	Julio Iglesias	*Yo Canto*
	Elton John	*Empty Sky*
	King Crimson	*In the Court of the Crimson King*
	Led Zeppelin	*Led Zeppelin*
	John Lennon (solo)	"Give Peace a Chance"
	John McLaughlin	*Extrapolation*
	Barbara Mandrell	"I've Been Loving You Too Long"
	Linda Ronstadt	*Hand Sown . . . Home Grown*
	Carlos Santana	*Santana*
	Three Dog Night	*Three Dog Night*
	Yes	*Yes*
	Neil Young	*Neil Young*
	Frank Zappa	*Hot Rats*
	Warren Zevon	*Wanted Dead or Alive*
1970	Jimmy Buffett	*Down to Earth*
	Eric Clapton (solo)	*Eric Clapton*

Year	Artist	Title
1970 cont'd	Crosby, Stills, Nash, and Young	*Déjà vu*
	Charlie Daniels	*Charlie Daniels*
	Emerson, Lake, and Palmer	*Emerson, Lake, and Palmer*
	Funkadelic	*Funkadelic*
	Crystal Gayle	"I've Cried (the Blue Right out of My Eyes)"
	J. Geils Band	*The J. Geils Band*
	Emmylou Harris	*Gliding Bird*
	Carole King	*Writer*
	Kris Kristofferson	*Kristofferson*
	Paul McCartney (solo)	*McCartney*
	Dave Mason (solo)	*Alone Together*
	Tony Orlando and Dawn	*Candida*
	Diana Ross	*Diana Ross*
	Todd Rundgren	*Runt*
	Black Sabbath	*Black Sabbath*
	Seals and Crofts	*Seals and Crofts*
	Supertramp	*Supertramp*
	War	*Eric Burdon Declares "War"*
	ZZ Top	*ZZ Top's First Album*
1971	Mac Davis	*Song Painter*
	The Doobie Brothers	*The Doobie Brothers*
	Michael Jackson (solo)	"Got to Be There"
	Kool and the Gang	*Live at the Sex Machine*
	Little Feat	*Little Feat*
	Loggins and Messina	*Kenny Loggins with Jim Messina Sittin' In*
	Manhattan Transfer	*Jukin'*
	Meat Loaf	*Stoney and Meat Loaf*
	The Osmonds	*The Osmonds*
	John Prine	*John Prine*
	Bonnie Raitt	*Bonnie Raitt*
	Helen Reddy	*I Don't Know How to Love Him*
	REO Speedwagon	*REO Speedwagon*
	Carly Simon	*Carly Simon*
	Pete Townshend (solo)	*Who Came First*

1216 — Time Line of First Releases

Year	Artist	Title
1971 cont'd	Vangelis	*The Dragon*
	Weather Report	*Weather Report*
1972	America	*America*
	Jackson Browne	*Jackson Browne*
	Harry Chapin	*Heads and Tales*
	The Eagles	*The Eagles*
	Earth, Wind, and Fire	*Earth, Wind, and Fire*
	Electric Light Orchestra	*No Answer*
	Peter Frampton	*Wind of Change*
	Hall and Oates	*Whole Oates*
	Billy Joel	*Cold Spring Harbor*
	Bette Midler	*The Divine Miss M*
	Roxy Music	*Roxy Music*
	Steely Dan	*Can't Buy a Thrill*
	Styx	*Styx*
	Tanya Tucker	"Delta Dawn"
1973	Abba	*Ring Ring*
	Aerosmith	*Aerosmith*
	Average White Band	*Show Your Hand*
	Brian Eno	*Here Come the Warm Jets*
	Bryan Ferry	*These Foolish Things*
	John Fogerty (solo)	*The Blue Ridge Rangers*
	Chaka Khan	*Rufus*
	Barry Manilow	*Barry Manilow*
	Gram Parsons	*GP*
	The Pointer Sisters	*The Pointer Sisters*
	Queen	*Queen*
	Bruce Springsteen	*Greetings from Asbury Park, N.J.*
	Tom Waits	*Closing Time*
	Barry White	*I've Got So Much to Give*
1974	Bad Company	*Bad Company*
	Bachman-Turner Overdrive	"You Ain't Seen Nothing Yet"
	The Commodores	*Machine Gun*
	John Hiatt	*Hangin' Around the Observatory*

Year	Artist	Title
1974 cont'd	Jefferson Starship	*Dragon Fly*
	Kansas	*Kansas*
	KC and the Sunshine Band	*Do It Good*
	Kiss	*Kiss*
	Robert Palmer	*Sneakin' Sally Through the Alley*
	Rush	*Rush*
1975	AC/DC	*High Voltage*
	Michael Bolton	*Michael Bolotin*
	Captain and Tennille	*Love Will Keep Us Together*
	Natalie Cole	*Inseparable*
	Journey	*Journey*
	Patti Smith	*Horses*
	Donna Summer	*Love to Love You*
	Tina Turner (solo)	*Acid Queen*
	Frankie Valli (solo)	*Inside You*
1976	Air Supply	*Air Supply*
	Blondie	*Blondie*
	Boston	*Boston*
	Heart	*Dreamboat Annie*
	John Mellencamp	*Chestnut Street Incident*
	The Neville Brothers	*Wild Tchoupitoulas*
	Graham Parker	*Howlin' Wind*
	The Alan Parsons Project	*Tales of Mystery and Imagination*
	Tom Petty and the Heartbreakers	*Tom Petty and the Heartbreakers*
	The Ramones	*Ramones*
	The Runaways	*The Runaways*
	The Sex Pistols	"Anarchy in the U.K."/"I Wanna Be Me"
1977	Laurie Anderson	"It's Not the Bullet That Kills You—It's the Hole"
	Cheap Trick	*Cheap Trick*
	Chic	*Chic*
	The Clash	*The Clash*
	Elvis Costello	*My Aim Is True*
	Foreigner	*Foreigner*
	Peter Gabriel (solo)	*Peter Gabriel*

Year	Artist	Title
1977 cont'd	Amy Grant	*Amy Grant*
	Kenny Loggins (solo)	*Celebrate Me Home*
	Reba McEntire	*Reba McEntire*
	Miami Sound Machine	*Live Again/Renacer*
	Steve Morse	*Free Fall*
	Teddy Pendergrass	*Teddy Pendergrass*
	The Police	*Outlandos d'Amour*
	Squeeze	*Packet of Three*
	Talking Heads	*Talking Heads: 77*
	George Thorogood and the Destroyers	*George Thorogood and the Destroyers*
	The Village People	*Village People*
	Steve Winwood (solo)	*Steve Winwood*
1978	Black Flag	*Nervous Breakdown*
	The Cars	*The Cars*
	Rosanne Cash	*Rosanne Cash*
	Devo	*Q: Are We Not Men? A: We Are Devo!*
	Dire Straits	"Sultans of Swing"
	Nanci Griffith	*There's a Light Beyond These Woods*
	Billy Idol	*Generation X*
	Rick James	*Come Get It*
	Los Lobos	*Los Lobos del Este Los Angeles: Just Another Band from East L.A.*
	Midnight Oil	*Midnight Oil*
	Prince	*For You*
	Toto	*Toto*
	Randy Travis	"She's My Woman"
	Van Halen	*Van Halen*
	XTC	*White Music*
1979	The B-52's	*The B-52's*
	Pat Benatar	*In the Heat of the Night*
	The Cure	*Three Imaginary Boys*
	Vince Gill	*Can't Hold Back*
	Joe Jackson	*Look Sharp*
	Rickie Lee Jones	*Rickie Lee Jones*

Year	Artist	Title
1979 cont'd	Sandi Patti	*Sandi's Song*
	Ricky Skaggs	*Sweet Temptation*
	The Specials	*The Specials*
1980	Bryan Adams	*Bryan Adams*
	Alabama	*My Home's in Alabama*
	Robert Cray	*Who's Been Talkin'*
	The Dead Kennedys	*Fresh Fruit for Rotting Vegetables*
	Def Leppard	*On Through the Night*
	Echo and the Bunnymen	*Crocodiles*
	The English Beat	*I Just Can't Stop It*
	INXS	*INXS*
	Iron Maiden	*Iron Maiden*
	Huey Lewis and the News	*Huey Lewis and the News*
	Oingo Boingo	*Oingo Boingo*
	Ozzy Osbourne (solo)	*Blizzard of Ozz*
	The Pretenders	*Pretenders*
	The Psychedelic Furs	*The Psychedelic Furs*
	The Smithereens	*Girls About Town*
	U2	*Boy*
	X	*Los Angeles*
1981	David Byrne (solo)	*My Life in the Bush of Ghosts*
	Phil Collins (solo)	*Face Value*
	Depeche Mode	*Speak and Spell*
	Duran Duran	*Duran Duran*
	Sheena Easton	*Take My Time*
	The Eurythmics	*In the Garden*
	The Go-Go's	*Beauty and the Beat*
	Ministry	*Cold Life*
	Mötley Crüe	*Too Fast for Love*
	George Strait	*Strait Country*
	The Stray Cats	*Stray Cats*
	Luther Vandross	*Never Too Much*
	The Winans	*Introducing the Winans*
1982	Asia	*Asia*

Year	Artist	Title
1982 cont'd	The Beastie Boys	*Polly Wog Stew*
	George Clinton (solo)	*Computer Games*
	Culture Club	*Kissing to Be Clever*
	The Dream Syndicate	*The Dream Syndicate*
	Kenny G	*Kenny G*
	Grandmaster Flash	*The Message*
	Don Henley	*I Can't Stand Still*
	Janet Jackson	*Janet Jackson*
	Michael McDonald (solo)	*If That's What It Takes*
	Bobby McFerrin	*Bobby McFerrin*
	Luis Miguel	*1+1=2 Enamorados*
	Lionel Richie	*Lionel Richie*
	Sonic Youth	*Sonic Youth*
	10,000 Maniacs	*Human Conflict Number Five*
1983	Anita Baker	*The Songstress*
	Gipsy Kings	*Allegria*
	James Ingram	*It's Your Night*
	The Judds	"Had a Dream (for the Heart)"
	Mark Knopfler (solo)	*Local Hero*
	Cyndi Lauper	*She's So Unusual*
	Madonna	*Madonna*
	Metallica	*Kill 'Em All*
	New Edition	*Candy Girl*
	R.E.M.	*Murmur*
	Tears for Fears	*The Hurting*
	Stevie Ray Vaughan	*Texas Flood*
	The Violent Femmes	*Violent Femmes*
	Wham!	*Fantastic*
1984	Rubén Blades	*Buscando América*
	Bon Jovi	*Bon Jovi*
	Sheila E.	*The Glamorous Life*
	k. d. lang	*A Truly Western Experience*
	Kathy Mattea	*Kathy Mattea*
	The Red Hot Chili Peppers	*The Red Hot Chili Peppers*

Year	Artist	Title
1984 cont'd	Run-D.M.C.	*Run-D.M.C.*
	Sade	*Diamond Life*
	Selena	*Selena y los Dinos*
	The Smiths	*The Smiths*
	Dwight Yoakam	*A Town South of Bakersfield*
1985	Whitney Houston	*Whitney Houston*
	Chris Isaak	*Silvertone*
	L. L. Cool J	*Radio*
	Loreena McKennitt	*Elemental*
	Sting (solo)	*The Dream of the Blue Turtles*
	Suzanne Vega	*Suzanne Vega*
1986	The Cowboy Junkies	*Whites off Earth Now!*
	Steve Earle	*Guitar Town*
	Enya	*Enya*
	Kool Moe Dee	*Kool Moe Dee*
	Lyle Lovett	*Lyle Lovett*
	New Kids on the Block	*New Kids on the Block*
	Salt-n-Pepa	*Hot, Cool and Vicious*
	Schoolly D	*Schoolly D*
	Brian Setzer (solo)	*The Knife Feels Like Justice*
	2 Live Crew	*The 2 Live Crew Is What We Are*
	Yanni	*Keys to Imagination*
1987	Babyface	*Lovers*
	Boy George (solo)	*Sold*
	Mary Chapin Carpenter	*Hometown Girl*
	Harry Connick, Jr.	*Harry Connick, Jr.*
	DJ Jazzy Jeff and the Fresh Prince	*Rock the House*
	Guns n' Roses	*Appetite for Destruction*
	Ice-T	*Rhyme Pays*
	Indigo Girls	*Strange Fire*
	Jane's Addiction	*XXX* (also known as *Jane's Addiction*)
	Alison Krauss	*Too Late to Cry*
	George Michael (solo)	*Faith*
	N.W.A.	*N.W.A. and the Posse*

Year	Artist	Title
1987 cont'd	Sinéad O'Connor	*The Lion and the Cobra*
	Public Enemy	*Yo! Bum Rush the Show*
	Henry Rollins (solo)	*Hot Animal Machine*
	Soundgarden	*Screaming Life*
	Keith Sweat	*Make It Last Forever*
1988	Bobby Brown (solo)	*Don't Be Cruel*
	Tracy Chapman	*Tracy Chapman*
	Melissa Etheridge	*Melissa Etheridge*
	Ana Gabriel	*Tierra de Nadie*
	Hammer	*Feel My Power*
	Sarah McLachlan	*Touch*
	Milli Vanilli	*All or Nothing*
	Morrissey (solo)	*Viva Hate*
	The Sugarcubes	*Life's Too Good*
	John Tesh	*Tour de France*
	Vanessa Williams	*The Right Stuff*
1989	Clint Black	*Killin' Time*
	Garth Brooks	"Much Too Young (to Feel This Damn Old)"
	Shawn Colvin	*Steady On*
	De La Soul	*3 Feet High and Rising*
	Ani DiFranco	*Ani DiFranco*
	Gloria Estefan (solo)	*Cuts Both Ways*
	The Gin Blossoms	*Dusted*
	Green Day	*1000 Hours*
	Nine Inch Nails	*Pretty Hate Machine*
	Nirvana	*Bleach*
	Phish	*Junta*
	Queen Latifah	*All Hail the Queen*
1990	Alice in Chains	*Facelift*
	Blues Traveler	*Blues Traveler*
	Brooks and Dunn	"Brand New Man"
	Mariah Carey	"Vision of Love"
	Celine Dion	*Unison*
	En Vogue	*Born to Sing*

Year	Artist	Title
1990 cont'd	Ice Cube	*AmeriKKKa's Most Wanted*
	Alan Jackson	"Here in the Real World"
	Travis Tritt	*Country Club*
1991	Blur	*Leisure*
	Boyz II Men	*Cooleyhighharmony*
	Cypress Hill	*Cypress Hill*
	Hole	*Pretty on the Inside*
	R. Kelly	*Born into the '90's*
	Alanis Morissette	*Alanis*
	The Orb	*The Orb's Adventures Beyond the Ultraworld*
	Pearl Jam	"Alive"/"Once"
	Seal	*Seal*
	Tupac Shakur	*2Pacalypse Now*
	Smashing Pumpkins	*Gish*
	Trisha Yearwood	*Trisha Yearwood*
1992	Tori Amos	*Little Earthquakes*
	Arrested Development	*3 Years, 5 Months & 2 Days in the Life of . . .*
	Mary J. Blige	*What's the 411?*
	Dr. Dre	*The Chronic*
	P. J. Harvey	*Dry*
	Wynonna Judd	"She Is His Only Need"
	Annie Lennox (solo)	*Diva*
	Brian McKnight	*Brian McKnight*
	No Doubt	*No Doubt*
	The Prodigy	*Experience*
	Rage Against the Machine	*Rage Against the Machine*
	Jon Secada	*Jon Secada*
	The Stone Temple Pilots	*Core*
	Sublime	*40 oz. to Freedom*
	TLC	*Oooooohhh . . . On the TLC Tip*
	The Wallflowers	*The Wallflowers*
1993	Beck	*Golden Feelings*
	Björk (solo)	*Debut*
	Toni Braxton	*Toni Braxton*

Year	Artist	Title
1993 cont'd	Counting Crows	*August and Everything After*
	The Cranberries	*Everybody Else Is Doing It, So Why Can't We?*
	Sheryl Crow	*Tuesday Night Music Club*
	The Dave Matthews Band	*Remember Two Things*
	Porno for Pyros	*Porno for Pyros*
	Radiohead	*Pablo Honey*
	Snoop Doggy Dogg	*Doggystyle*
	Shania Twain	*Shania Twain*
1994	Bush	*Sixteen Stone*
	Paula Cole	*Harbinger*
	Coolio	*It Takes a Thief*
	The Fugees	*Blunted on Reality*
	Hootie and the Blowfish	*Cracked Rear View*
	Marilyn Manson	*Portrait of an American Family*
	The Notorius	*Ready to Die*
	Oasis	*Definitely Maybe*
1995	The Chemical Brothers	*Exit Planet Dust*
	The Foo Fighters	*Foo Fighters*
	Jewel	*Pieces of You*
	Natalie Merchant (solo)	*Tigerlily*
1996	Fiona Apple	*Tidal*
	LeAnn Rimes	"Blue"
	The Spice Girls	*Spice*
1997	Erykah Badu	*Baduizm*
	Hanson	*Middle of Nowhere*
	Puff Daddy	*No Way Out*

Glossary

A cappella: A vocal performance by a soloist or group without instrumental accompaniment (literally, Italian for "in the manner of the chapel").

A side: The side of a single (a 45-rpm record, a cassette, or a CD single) containing the song that is intended to be promoted and played on the radio. *See also* Forty-five

Accompaniment: The background vocal or instrumental harmony and rhythm that supports and complements the melody.

Acoustic: Generally used to mean "non-amplified" or "non-electric." Originally used to refer to instruments that produce sound without electronic modification ("acoustic guitar") but expanded to include performances played on non-electric instruments. In actuality, most "acoustic" performances rely on amplification through microphones and electronic "pickups" on acoustic instruments.

Adult contemporary (AC): A term for a radio format that is similar to the older term "easy listening." Aimed at an older and more conservative audience than the rock-and-roll audience, it includes artists whose work is pleasant and nonthreatening. It contains overlap with Top 40 and light rock. The music of the Carpenters, Anne Murray, and Peter Cetera could be termed adult contemporary.

Advance: Money paid to a recording artist or songwriter at the beginning of a contract or project, to be deducted from future royalties. Beginning or little-known artists generally receive modest advances; advances for major stars can be in the millions.

Agent: The organization or person who negotiates contracts for booking an artist's live performances. The agent receives a percentage of the profits (usually 10 to 15 percent).

Album: A vinyl record or CD containing a collection of songs. The term began before the development of the LP (the 12" vinyl disk, introduced in the late 1940's), when multiple records were needed to reproduce a song collection or a long work. Although vinyl disks and CDs are actually single discs, rather than albums, the name "album" has stuck. *See also* Long-playing record (LP)

Album cut: A song (or track) recorded to be part of an album, not intended for release as a single.

Alternative: A term that began to be used in the early 1990's for an approach to rock music that avoided mainstream rock's commercialism and show-business aspects. The term has been applied to a wide range of styles and artists, from R.E.M. to the Replacements, Jane's Addiction, Nirvana, and Nine Inch Nails. Many so-called alternative artists experienced mass success, so the line dividing alternative and mainstream artists has become somewhat blurred.

AM radio: "AM" stands for "amplitude modulation," a technical term for a type of radio transmission. The first commercial AM radio station, KDKA in Pittsburgh, began broadcasting in 1920. AM radio was the standard type of radio transmission until the late 1960's, when FM began to be widely used for rock music programming. The Top-40 radio format developed as an AM format. *See also* FM radio; Top 40

Amplifier: "Amp" for short, an electrical device that makes an audio signal louder. Guitar amplifiers color the sound of the electric guitar in distinctive ways, whereas the amplifiers used in sound reinforcement ("PA systems," short for "public-address systems") are intended to reproduce sound as accurately as possible.

Anthem: Originally a hymn of praise or loyalty, as in "The Star Spangled Banner," the U.S. national anthem. The term "rock anthem" has been applied to rock songs that have inspirational and, usually, sing-along qualities. For example, Queen's "We Will Rock You" and "We Are the Champions" are frequently heard at sporting events.

Arrangement: The way a song is structured or orchestrated. "Arranging" a song involves deciding such things as what instruments will be included, whether there will be an instrumental solo, whether there will be harmonies, and how many sections the song will have.

Art rock. *See* Progressive rock

Artists and repertoire (A&R): The department of a record company in charge of artists and material. The A&R person may discover new artists, guide artists' careers, influence album content, and approve single releases.

B side: The side of a single that contains a song not intended for single release; also called the "flip side." Sometimes the B side is a track that is not available elsewhere, intended to encourage purchase by fans that already have the album.

Ballad: A slow, melodic song of a romantic or sentimental nature. An example is the Carpenters' hit "We've Only Just Begun," which has become a staple at weddings.

Billboard: A weekly music industry publication that contains information about record contracts and new releases and that maintains a series of charts reflecting sales and airplay for single and album releases.

Billboard "Hot 100": The chart in *Billboard* magazine, listing the week's one hundred most popular mainstream single recordings based on retail sales. The *Billboard* 200 lists the top two hundred albums.

Blue-eyed soul: Bluesy or soulful material performed by artists of European descent. The term has been applied to the music of the Righteous Brothers, the Rascals, Mitch Ryder, Hall and Oates, and others.

Bluegrass: A country music subgenre featuring unamplified stringed instruments, close-pitched harmonies, and rapid improvisation. The violin ("fiddle") and mandolin are generally featured instruments. Bill Monroe (of Bill Monroe and the Blue Grass Boys) is considered the father—in fact, the inventor—of bluegrass music.

Blues: A form of African-American folk music that evolved in the late nineteenth century.

Blues songs are usually songs of lamentation. The blues refers to both a feeling and a specific song structure. The verse of a blues song generally sings the same phrase twice, then adds a third phrase to complete or answer the thought. Musically, the blues verse is usually a set length (twelve measures, or bars) and has particular chord changes. The blues is central to both rock and roll and jazz.

Blues rock: A style of music of that emerged in the late 1960's as artists reconnected rock and roll with its rhythm-and-blues roots. Influential artists include Eric Clapton, Stevie Ray Vaughan, and the Allman Brothers.

Bootleg: An unauthorized recording of a concert or studio performance that is copied and distributed without the artist's or record company's approval. The recordings may be made by fans smuggling tape recorders into concerts, from stolen demo or studio tapes, or by the illegal copying of legitimate releases, with no revenues going to the artist. Bootlegs are often sold and traded among fans. Some artists hate the practice, whereas others, most notably the Grateful Dead, encourage it.

Boxed set: A collection of two or more vinyl discs, cassettes, or—most commonly—compact discs, intended to provide an overview of an artist's or group's recording career. Boxed sets may include demos, live recordings, alternate versions of songs, and sound-track material not otherwise readily available. They generally include a booklet discussing the music.

British invasion: A nickname for the wave of British bands that became hugely popular in the United States in the mid-1960's. The invasion began with the Beatles' arrival on the U.S. music scene in January, 1964. Many of these British bands were heavily influenced by American rhythm-and-blues. They adapted it to their own style, evolving partly from British "skiffle" music. The new British style—and the long-haired look and snappy clothes of the bands—had an immense influence on American popular music. British invasion bands other than the Beatles included the Rolling Stones, the Animals, the Dave Clark Five, the

Yardbirds, Chad and Jeremy, Herman's Hermits, the Kinks, Manfred Mann, and the Who.

Bubblegum: A simple, prepackaged form of music that appeared in the late 1960's, aimed at young teens and subteens—bubble-gum chewers. Artists included the Ohio Express ("Yummy Yummy Yummy"), the 1910 Fruitgum Co., and the Archies.

Cassette: A self-contained plastic cartridge containing magnetic recording tape that passes from one reel to another, introduced in 1965. (Previously, anyone wanting to play or record music on tape had to use individual reels of tape.) Prerecorded cassettes were a less expensive, more portable alternative to the vinyl record. Cassettes declined somewhat in popularity with the advent of compact discs and easily portable compact-disc players.

Charts: Regularly published rankings of single and album releases, generally based on sales, radio airplay, or a combination. See also *Billboard*; *Billboard* "Hot 100"; SoundScan.

Chord: Three or more musical notes played simultaneously.

Chorus: A stanza repeated throughout the course of a song. Many pop and rock songs have an alternating verse-chorus structure: The words of each verse are different, but the words of the chorus are repeated identically each time.

Classic rock: A nostalgia-based radio format that relies heavily on the same kind of rock and roll music that its listeners, in the thirty-to-fifty age group, listened to when they were teenagers. Among the bands that fit into the classic rock format are Led Zeppelin, the Doors, the Rolling Stones, and the Who.

Compact disc (CD): Introduced in 1982, the CD is a plastic-coated disc on which sound (and, increasingly, visual images) is digitally recorded, to be read and reproduced by a laser. CDs revolutionized the recording industry because they offer better sound reproduction, are more durable, and can hold more music than vinyl LPs or cassettes. The rapid acceptance of CDs in the 1980's and early 1990's surprised even the music industry itself.

Concept album: An album in which the songs are linked by a common theme. The Beatles' *Sgt. Pepper's Lonely Hearts Club Band* and the Who's *Tommy* (a "rock opera") were early concept albums.

Country: A broad musical genre that evolved from music descended from the folk songs of the southern and western United States. This folk music ultimately came from the musical traditions of America's early English and Scottish settlers. Around the 1930's, country began to evolve from string-band and "hillbilly" music. It was generally called "country and western" from the 1940's to the mid-1960's. Influential figures include Jimmie Rodgers, Roy Acuff, Hank Williams, Chet Atkins, and Marty Robbins. Country went through various evolutions in the 1970's and 1980's, including "outlaw country" and the arrival of the "new traditionalists." By the 1990's, country, rock and roll, and pop had strongly influenced each other, yet major artists such as Garth Brooks and Reba McEntire were still clearly, instantly identifiable as country artists.

Country rock: A style of music that combines elements of country with rock and roll. The term came into use in the late 1960's, when rock artists began to retreat from psychedelic music to a basic, more roots-oriented sound. Influential artists include the Byrds, Gram Parsons, Linda Ronstadt, and the Eagles.

Cover: The recording by one artist of a song already recorded by another artist. The term was first used when white performers in the 1950's "covered" songs of black artists, making them more acceptable to white audiences of the time. (Pat Boone's bland cover version of Little Richard's "Tutti' Frutti" is often cited.) The term is now widely applied to any artist's re-recording of an old song, either to interpret it differently or simply to capitalize on the song's familiarity.

Crossover: A "crossover" hit is a song that transcends its original genre, reaching new listeners for an artist. It has been most often used to describe songs or artists that are successful on the pop charts in addition to the soul chart or the country chart. For example, many Motown artists had crossover hits on the pop charts during the late 1960's and early 1970's. Country artists such as Kenny Rogers and Dolly Parton have also appeared on the pop charts.

Demo: Abbreviation of "demonstration." A demo recording, or demo tape, is made by an artist or group to demonstrate its songs and performing style. The goal is usually to catch the attention of a recording company or producer in the hopes of signing a recording contract.

Disc jockey (DJ): A person who introduces and plays recordings on the radio or in nightclubs. The term came into use in the 1940's. Originally, radio disc jockeys had considerable influence as to what records they played. By the mid-1980's, however, such "playlist" decisions were often being made by professional programming consultants hired by corporations. Club DJs, particularly those in New York City, were instrumental in the development of rap, hip-hop, and various types of electronic music.

Disco: Originally a shortened form of the word "discotheque." Disco refers both to a type of dance club and to a style of dance music that became tremendously popular in the second half of the 1970's. A disco is a nightclub where people dance to recorded music, often accompanied by elaborate, computer-controlled lighting effects. The musical genre emerged from these clubs, as did a showy style of dancing, epitomized in the film *Saturday Night Fever*.

Dixieland: An early style of jazz developed in New Orleans and featuring the combination of trombone, clarinet, and trumpet. A Dixieland band also has a drummer and often a piano player. Dixieland was named for the Original Dixieland Jazz Band, founded in 1912.

DJ. *See* Disc jockey (DJ)

Doo-wop: A rhythm-and-blues style popular in the 1950's and early 1960's. Doo-wop features male harmonies and nonsense sounds (such as "doo-wop," "sh-boom, sh-boom") sung in the background vocals. Influential doo-wop artists include Frankie Lymon and the Teenagers, Dion and the Belmonts, and the Marcels.

Down Beat: An influential monthly jazz publication that contains artist interviews and profiles, music reviews, and information for aspiring musicians. *Down Beat* is known for its annual polls naming the top jazz players of the year.

Drum machine: A type of synthesizer that produces and repeats drum sounds and patterns. Drum machines were crucial to the development of rap and hip-hop, and they have become widely used in nearly all types of recordings. They are also used in live performances.

Electronica: Most often used as a collective term for a variety of electronic-based styles, including house, ambient house, techno, and even industrial. Electronica is derived from dance-music forms, with their heavy use of sampling and computerized rhythm and sound-texture tracks.

Engineer: The engineer is responsible for the technical aspects of a recording session and works under the supervision of the producer. The engineer places microphones properly, adjusts sound levels and effects, interconnects electronic devices, and troubleshoots problems. Many producers (and some musicians) are also engineers, but some are not. *See also* Mixing; Producer

Extended-play single (EP): An EP contains more songs than a standard two-song single but fewer songs than an album—usually between three and six. Sometimes an EP includes an extended remix, or dance mix, of a song on one side. Other EP's are essentially mini-albums; new groups sometimes release an EP independently, since this is much less expensive and time-consuming than recording an album.

Flip side. *See* B side

FM radio: "FM" stands for "frequency modulation," a technical term for a type of radio transmission. AM ("amplitude modulation") radio was the standard type of radio transmission until the late 1960's. The earliest FM stations were classical stations taking advantage of the greater sound quality of FM. Pop music began to be broadcast on FM radio in the late 1960's, when "underground" rock stations emerged.

Because of the clearer sound of FM, and the fact that FM signals could easily be broadcast in stereo, by the mid-1970's FM had taken over as the standard pop-music broadcast media. *See also* AM radio

Folk music: Folk music is traditionally sung and played in a simple, direct style and performed on acoustic instruments—primarily guitar, but also violin, banjo, and other instruments. The style descended from European and southern U.S. story songs, or ballads. Woody Guthrie, in the 1930's and 1940's, was one of the first American folk artists to compose his own songs containing social and political commentary. Other influential folk artists include Pete Seeger, Bob Dylan, and Joan Baez. Since the 1960's, the term folk music has sometimes been used in a broader sense that includes the use of electric instruments and the work of singer-songwriters such as Joni Mitchell and Jackson Browne.

Folk rock: Music that combines folk-oriented lyrics with rock accompaniment. Bob Dylan's switch from acoustic to electric accompaniment in 1965 horrified folk traditionalists but also defined the folk-rock genre. Other early influential folk-rock artists include the Byrds, Simon and Garfunkel, and the Mamas and the Papas.

Forty-five (45): A 7-inch vinyl phonograph record. It is called a 45 because it plays at a speed of 45 revolutions per minute (rpm). In the 1950's and 1960's, the terms "single" and "45" were used interchangeably; a single was simply a 45-rpm record containing two songs, the A side and the B (or flip) side. In the 1970's, cassette singles began replacing vinyl singles; in the 1980's, CD singles came on the market.

Funk: Urban music characterized by strong, percussive rhythm and particularly by an emphasis on the bass. Funk combines elements of African music, jazz, rhythm and blues, and rock. Influential funk artists include James Brown, Sly and the Family Stone, and George Clinton.

Fusion. *See* Jazz fusion

Genre: A category of music characterized by a particular style, form, or content. Rock and roll, country, soul, rap, folk, and blues are all musical genres. Smaller genres, or subgenres, include such styles as trip-hop and grunge.

Gig: Slang for a musical performance, originally used by jazz musicians in the 1930's. Roughly synonymous with "show" or "concert."

Girl group: A pop act composed of female vocalists, usually a lead and two background singers. These groups were often assembled by record companies or producers in the early 1960's to fit a certain sound. Influential girl groups include the Ronettes, the Shangri-Las, the Chiffons, and the Shirelles.

Glam rock: Also known as "glitter rock," glam is a rock-and-roll subgenre that emerged in the 1970's. The artists, both male and female, wore striking makeup and colorful clothes. David Bowie's look for *The Rise and Fall of Ziggy Stardust* is sometimes considered the epitome of glam rock. A new generation of glam rockers, such as Poison, appeared in the 1980's; they were nicknamed the "hair bands."

Gold record: An album or single certified by the Recording Industry Association of America (RIAA) as having sold more than 500,000 units.

Golden oldie; oldie: The term originated in the 1960's when Top-40 stations would sometimes play an old song—a golden oldie—among current hits. Oldies radio is a radio format that plays songs from the 1950's and 1960's.

Gospel: An African American form of religious choral music. Gospel celebrates the joy of spiritual devotion and is believed to have evolve from the call-and-response speaking and singing between the pastor and the congregation in southern black churches. Many great soul singers began their careers as gospel singers, including Wilson Pickett and Aretha Franklin. Mahalia Jackson is often cited as one of the greatest gospel singers of all time.

Grammy Awards: The annual awards presented by the National Academy of Recording Arts and Sciences (NARAS) for particular achievements in the recording industry. Awards are given in a wide array of categories. Major awards include record of the year, album of the year, and song of the year. Winners receive a gold-plated replica of a gramophone.

Grand Ole Opry: The "Grand Ole Opry" was originally a weekly Nashville, Tennessee, radio program. It began in 1925. From 1941 to 1974 it was broadcast from the Ryman Auditorium; then it moved to the new Opryland entertainment complex. Appearing on the Grand Ole Opry was, and is, the sign that a country artist has "made it."

Grunge: An "alternative" subgenre that emerged from the Seattle, Washington, music scene, a fusion of punk and metal made popular by bands such as Nirvana and Soundgarden. *See also* Alternative

Heavy metal: A form of rock music popular during the 1970's and 1980's, basic in form and characterized by fast, distorted guitar solos, repetitive rhythms, and high volume levels. Influential artists include Led Zeppelin, Deep Purple, Black Sabbath, and Blue Cheer. Later metal bands include Mötley Crüe, AC/DC, and Metallica.

Hillbilly: The term "hillbilly music" dates back to the 1920's. Hillbilly music, which indeed emerged from the mountain regions of the American South, was the primary ancestor of country music. *See also* Country

Hip-hop: Hip-hop is practically synonymous with "rap." The term is applied to the music that provides the background for rapping, with much digital "sampling" and reuse of existing sounds and music. Hip-hop, used in a wider sense, refers to the urban culture that rap reflects. *See also* Rap; Sample, sampling

Hit: A successful single or album—one that many people buy, which usually means that it is widely played on the radio. In addition, since the mid-1980's, this typically means that videos of the song are shown on television. The definition of "hit" varies from artist to artist; for someone just starting out, reaching the *Billboard* Top 40 is an accomplishment. For an established artist, anything less than a Top-10 song might be considered unsuccessful.

Honky-tonk: A honky-tonk is a disreputable nightclub or other place of cheap entertainment. As a country-music subgenre, honky-tonk music was very popular in the 1950's and 1960's (Lefty Frizzell, Loretta Lynn, George Jones, Merle Haggard).

Hook: A brief but memorable portion of a song, either lyric or instrumental. It is supposed to grab or "hook" the listener into liking and remembering a song.

House band: A band with a steady engagement playing at a particular nightclub. The Doors were the house band at the Whisky-a-Go-Go in Hollywood before beginning their recording career.

House music: A style of dance music that became popular in the late 1980's, named for the Warehouse Club in Chicago, where the style originated. The sound is heavily electronic and repetitive, with heavy, deep bass and drums.

Improvisation: Deviation from the standard performance of a particular composition. When an artist improvises, he or she "makes something up" while playing it. An instrumental solo is one type of improvisation; spontaneous rapping is another. Bebop jazz groups and rock groups such as the Grateful Dead and Phish are noted for collective improvisation.

Independent label: A record company not affiliated with a major corporation. Since they are generally more concerned with making music than satisfying stockholders, "indie" labels tend to be more innovative and accessible to new artists than large companies are. If an independent-label artist strikes it big, a major label often signs the artist.

Industrial: A variation of house music, dubbed "industrial" because of its machine-like rhythms, use of sounds such as clanking metal pipes, and distorted "metal" guitar.

Intro: Short for "introduction." A section of music, usually brief, before the main body of the song begins.

Jam; jam session: Slang for an improvised music session, originally referring to jazz rehearsals. "Jam" is also used as a verb, meaning to play hard, often improvising.

Jazz: A type of popular music originating in New Orleans from the African American folk music prevalent in that area. Heavily influenced by blues, the main characteristics of jazz are syncopation, a strong rhythmic beat, and improvisation. Early jazz emphasized melodic improvisation by trumpet, clarinet, and trombone. By the 1950's the saxophone had largely replaced the clarinet, and the roles of the drummer, bassist, and pianist had all expanded. The history of jazz goes back to the early years of the twentieth century, and Dixieland, big-band swing music, bebop, cool jazz, hard bop, and free jazz are among its many subgenres.

Jazz fusion: Jazz fusion, or simply "fusion," includes characteristics of both jazz and rock. The term came into use in the late 1960's and early 1970's. Fusion employs some of the instruments and techniques (particularly improvisation) associated with jazz while retaining the heavy beat, rhythm, and volume of rock. Influential artists include Miles Davis, Weather Report, John McLaughlin's Mahavishnu Orchestra, Herbie Hancock, and Frank Zappa.

Label: Usually used to mean "record company," as in signing a recording contract with a label. Most labels are parts of huge corporations, but there are also small independent labels. Large record companies often have different labels for different genres, and some highly successful artists establish their own labels, as the Beatles did with Apple Records and Prince did with Paisley Park.

Lead guitarist: The guitarist providing the guitar melodies and solos for a recording session or live performance. The term came into use to distinguish the lead player from the rhythm guitarist. The term is now sometimes used even if there is only one guitarist in the band. It is sometimes shortened to "playing lead."

Liner notes: The descriptions of the music or recording process that sometimes appear on the back or inside cover of an album or in a CD booklet.

Live recording: A recording made while an artist is performing in front of an audience at a club or concert hall.

Long-playing record (LP): The 12-inch vinyl phonograph record, introduced in the late 1940's and designed to be played at a speed of $33\frac{1}{3}$ revolutions per minute (rpm). Until the advent of compact discs in 1982, LPs were the medium of choice for album releases. *See also* Album

LP. *See* Long-playing record (LP)

Lyrics: The words of a song.

Master: The finished tape from a studio session from which albums are made.

Middle of the road (MOR): Mellow pop music that appeals to a broad audience. *See also* Adult contemporary (AC)

Mixing: The process of combining all the instruments and singing produced during recording sessions into the final version of the song. In the recording process, twenty-four or more tracks of playing and singing are usually recorded. At its simplest, mixing involves setting all the sounds at the right volume levels, adjusting tone, and adding appropriate effects (such as reverb and delay). Mixing is supervised by the record's producer; engineers do much of the hands-on work.

Motown: A record label founded in Detroit by Barry Gordy, Jr., in 1959. Motown is credited with revitalizing (even reinventing) rhythm and blues in the 1960's and early 1970's. Once the largest African American-owned business in the United States, Motown Records was home to such artists as the Supremes, the Four Tops, Smokey Robinson, Marvin Gaye, and the Jackson 5.

MTV: Cable television network that began broadcasting in 1981, featuring youth-oriented music videos, news, and other specialty programming. MTV (Music Television) revolutionized the music industry by adding a visual element to what had been almost exclusively an audio art form. The first video broadcast on MTV was "Video Killed the Radio Star," by the Buggles. MTV was early accused of racism for showing hardly any videos of black artists; that situation changed when Michael Jackson's videos from *Thriller* were shown extensively.

Multiplatinum: Slang for an album that has sold two million or more copies. (A platinum record has sold one million copies.)

New Wave: A late 1970's term for new rock music that was different from 1970's mainstream rock but was not punk, generally being more melodic and less angry. The term was used so vaguely and widely that it had little real meaning. Artists sometime called new wave include Elvis Costello, Talking Heads, Blondie, and the Pretenders.

Platinum record: An album or single certified by the Recording Industry Association of America (RIAA) as having sold more than one million copies.

Playlist: The list of songs to be played by a radio station. Station managers or consultants hired by the station's owners generally determine the playlist, which is tailored to the station's format (country, classic rock, and so on) and audience.

Pop: Derived from the word "popular," the phrase "pop music" originally referred to any style of music popular with a variety of listeners. It also separated "popular" music from serious classical music. As the term evolved, "pop music" has come to mean music intended for mass consumption, with inoffensive, easy-to-remember melodies and lyrics. A Top-40 radio station generally plays pop music. "Pop" is also used to differentiate this type of music from genres such as country, rap, rock and roll, and soul— although they are certainly popular, they are usually differentiated from mainstream pop. *See also* Crossover

Producer: The producer (record producer) is generally charged with creating the sound of an album or single. The producer's duties vary depending on the artist. Producers review the material and suggest modifications, make budget decisions, select session musicians, and generally determine the best way to realize the artist's vision. Among the many well-known producers who have contributed immensely to the sounds of recordings are Phil Spector (who created the "wall of sound") and George Martin (who produced the Beatles). *See also* Engineer; Mixing

Progressive rock: A style of rock music that was particularly popular in the early 1970's. Progressive rock bands wrote long, complex songs— sometimes entire album sides—that drew on both psychedelic rock and classical music for inspiration. The most successful progressive bands were British, and they included King Crimson; Yes; Genesis; Emerson, Lake, and Palmer; and Gentle Giant. Some recordings by Jethro Tull, the Moody Blues, and Pink Floyd have also been called progressive. The term "art rock" is also sometimes used, but its meaning is somewhat less focused—art rock includes artists such as Roxy Music and Brian Eno.

Promotional record: A record that a record company distributes free to radio stations and reviewers, hoping to generate advance publicity and favorable reviews. Some "promos" contain interviews and nonalbum material and are widely sought after by collectors.

Psychedelic rock: A style of rock music popular in the mid-to-late 1960's that was intended to be "mind-expanding" and to emulate the effects of hallucinogenic drugs. It used feedback, distortion, unusual instrumentation such as Middle Eastern instruments, and sound effects. Among influential psychedelic bands were the Jefferson Airplane, the Grateful Dead, the Jimi Hendrix Experience, and early Pink Floyd. The Beatles' *Sgt. Pepper's Lonely Hearts Club Band* and *Magical Mystery Tour* also include psychedelic effects and arrangements.

Punk rock: Marked by extreme expressions of anger and social discontent, punk originated in New York, then evolved in working-class London in the mid-to-late 1970's. Punk rock was loud, fast, and generally so untrained as to sound sloppy. Punk is credited with reinvigorating rock and roll in the time of disco and heavily produced but bland rock records. Influential artists include the Sex Pistols, the Clash, and the Ramones. Other punk acts included the Germs, the Slits, and Siouxsie and the Banshees.

Race music: A name for African American popular music—blues and rhythm and blues—that was in use from the 1920's to the early 1950's. The name implied that only African Americans, not white audiences, would be interested in it. Gradually, beginning in the 1950's, white audiences began to hear and enjoy "black music," and the term rhythm and blues (soon supplemented by rock and roll) replaced race music.

Rap: A genre in which the vocalists are talkers and rhymers—"rappers"—rather than singers. Rap originated in New York in the 1970's. It was heard in nightclubs long before it found its way onto widely distributed recordings. Club disc jockeys, "spinners," teamed up with rappers to develop the genre. The Sugarhill Gang's novelty track "Rapper's Delight" is sometimes cited as the first widely popular rap song. Other influential early performers include Grandmaster Flash, then Run-DMC and LL Cool J. By the 1980's rap had become widely popular, and the 1980's and 1990's saw dozens of major rap stars.

Recording Industry Association of America (RIAA): The main trade association of the recording industry. The RIAA sets the standard for gold and platinum records and serves as a lobbying body for the interests of the industry.

Refrain. *See* Chorus

Reggae: A Jamaican music form based on repetitive bass, drum, and percussion patterns. Tempos are slow to midtempo, and reggae has a hypnotic effect because of its simple, interlocking instrumental parts. In Jamaica it is culturally intertwined with the Rastafarian religion. By the 1970's reggae was popular worldwide but never achieved major success in the United States. Major artists include Bob Marley, Jimmy Cliff, Peter Tosh, and Burning Spear.

Rhythm and blues (R&B): A style of African American popular music of the 1940's and 1950's with roots in jazz, blues, and big-band

music. R&B was an important precursor to rock and rock. Early R&B artists include the Orioles, Hank Ballard and the Midnighters, Louis Jordan, and Fats Domino. The term R&B came into vogue again in the 1980's and 1990's; this music is a smooth blend of pop, urban contemporary, and soul, and it generally emphasizes elaborate, skillful singing.

Rhythm guitarist: The guitarist providing the rhythmic accompaniment, rather than solo parts, for a recording or performance.

Riff: A repeated musical phrase. A riff can serve as the rhythmic basis for a song or can support or play against the melody.

Rock: The terms "rock music" and "rock and roll" are often used interchangeably. However, "rock" sometimes is used to separate the early rock and roll of the 1950's and early 1960's from the evolving "rock" music of the late 1960's and after.

Rock and roll: A style of music that evolved from rhythm and blues, mixed with country and, to a lesser degree, gospel, big-band, jazz, and even Afro-Cuban music. As big bands went out of style in the late 1940's, smaller groups filled the void with amplified guitars, shouted vocals, and a rapid beat. The music called "rock and roll" (or "rock 'n' roll") began developing clearly in the early 1950's, but the term itself was a sexual slang term in use among African Americans for many years. Among the characteristics of early rock and roll were driving drumming, saxophone solos, electric guitars, and intense, sometimes shouted or screamed, vocals. Early influential artists include Muddy Waters, Chuck Berry, Little Richard, Bo Diddley, Elvis Presley, and Jerry Lee Lewis. *See also* Rhythm and blues; Rockabilly

Rockabilly: A link between country and western (or "hillbilly") music and rock and roll. Rockabilly was the first form of rock performed by white musicians. Influential artists include Elvis Presley, Bill Haley and His Comets, Carl Perkins, and Buddy Holly.

***Rolling Stone*:** An entertainment magazine founded by Jann Wenner in 1967. It was originally a weekly on newsprint paper that focused on rock music. For a few years it was very important to rock recording artists and record companies because it was the only mass-market publication that took late-1960's music and the counterculture seriously. *Rolling Stone* has since branched out to include all forms of entertainment, fashion, and social commentary.

Royalties: Payments to an artist, group, or composer that represent a percentage of record sales. Artists must pay back their "advance" to the recording company before beginning to collect royalties. Royalties from a major hit record can be substantial. *See also* Advance

Sample; sampling: Sampling is an electronic process in which a sound or piece of music is digitally recorded. A sample is a sound or bit of music so recorded. Sampling has produced numerous lawsuits by artists whose work has been sampled and reused without their permission—and without their receiving any royalties on the new record sales. Sampling was first widely heard on rap and hip-hop recordings, and it has spread to nearly all genres of pop music.

Scat singing: Jazz singing that uses nonsense syllables. In scat singing the voice is treated purely as an instrument. Influential artists include Ella Fitzgerald and Louis Armstrong.

Session: Also "recording session." The gathering of musicians and usually a producer and engineer in a recording studio to record songs or tracks. A session may involve the recording of an entire song or only the recording of particular parts, such as drums and bass, guitar parts, or vocals. *See also* Session musician, Producer, Tracks

Session musician; session player: An individual musician hired to play at a recording session. Session, or "studio," musicians are most often hired to back up a solo artist, but they may also augment the sound of a band. Well-respected studio or session musicians can make a good living playing on other people's recordings. Session players may also record film sound tracks as well as music for television shows and commercials.

Seventy-eight (78): A 10-inch phonographic record designed to be played at a speed of 78 revolutions per minute (rpm), the standard speed for gramophones. These records were brittle and broke easily, but they were the only medium widely available until LPs were introduced in the mid-1940's.

Singer-songwriter: An artist who writes and performs his or her own music. Before the mid-1950's, it was virtually unheard of for a songwriter to publicly perform his or her compositions: Songwriters wrote songs, and singers sang them. Some early rock and rollers began to write their own songs, however, as did the bands of the 1960's, led by the Beatles and other "British invasion" bands. Bob Dylan, with his intense, lyric-driven folk rock, is probably the archetypal singer-songwriter. The label was widely applied in the early 1970's to such artists as Joni Mitchell, James Taylor, and Jackson Browne.

Single: A song intended for radio airplay and for individual sale, as opposed to an album cut. A single was originally a forty-five (45) vinyl record, but the term was subsequently applied to cassette singles and CD singles. Having a "hit single" is still the measure of success for many recording artists, but it was most important in the 1950's and 1960's, before albums and album sales became more profitable. *See also* A side; Album; Album cut; Hit; Forty-five (45)

Soul music: A gospel-influenced genre that evolved from 1950's rhythm-and-blues artists such as Ray Charles and Sam Cooke. James Brown, "soul brother number one," was an early star, and Aretha Franklin, the "queen of soul," and Otis Redding popularized the style in the 1960's. *See also* Funk

SoundScan: Established in 1991, the computerized method used by record companies and magazines (such as *Billboard*) to determine record sales, using weekly tallies of actual retail sales. Previously, sales and chart positions were determined by less exact record-company counts of volume orders. The results were often skewed toward pop and rock and roll. With the advent of SoundScan, other genres—most notably rap and country—assumed higher positions on the mainstream charts, more accurately reflecting the public's listening and buying habits.

Southern rock: A country-tinged version of blues rock, more metal. Influential artists include the Allman Brothers and Lynyrd Skynard.

Studio musician. *See* Session musician; session player

Stylist: Also "song stylist." A singer or artist noted primarily for performing in a particular style.

Techno: A dance-music genre that relies on computerized rhythms and sampled sounds ranging from music to noise, said to have originated in Detroit with Derrick May. Originally relatively anonymous dance-club music, techno was eventually popularized by groups such as the Orb.

Teen idol: A young, handsome male artist whose loyal fan base is composed mainly of legions of swooning teen-aged girls. Early teen idols included Elvis Presley, Paul Anka, Ricky Nelson, and Dion. The Beatles were also teen idols.

Top 10: The top ten records or songs on a sales chart or playlist, as on *Billboard* magazine's Hot 100 chart. A Top 10 record is a hit.

Top 40: The top forty records or songs on a sales chart or playlist, as on *Billboard* magazine's Hot 100 chart. A Top 40 record is successful, but it may or may not be considered a true hit.

Tour: A series of concerts by an artist or group, usually corresponding to the release of a new album. A tour may consist of a few weeks of performances or, in some cases, many grueling months. For example, an artist might play a "North American tour," a "European tour," or a "world tour." Being "on tour" is the same as "touring" or being "on the road." Being on tour is tiring and involves complex logistics, but it can also generate a lot of money.

Track: "Track" has two distinct meanings. First, it may simply mean a single song, as in "album track" or "the first track on the CD." Second, in a different context, a track is a single part of the recording process. That is, on a 24-track recording, there may be many tracks, or separate parts—guitar tracks, drum tracks, keyboard tracks, singing tracks—that are blended, or mixed, to produce the final sound of the record. *See also* Mixing

Twelve-inch single: Roughly, another name for an EP or extended-play single. A 12-inch single is generally intended for play at dance clubs. It most often contains a "dance mix" or a "remix" of a song, specifically arranged for dancing. *See also* Extended-play single

VH-1: A cable music channel introduced in 1985 by the same company that owns MTV. Aimed at the adult market (as opposed to MTV's primarily teenage audience), VH-1 features music videos, news, and specialty programming.

Vocals: Singing. A vocalist is a singer; "lead vocals" refers to the melody singing; "backing vocals" are the harmony singing parts.

Yodeling: A type of singing characterized by changing back and forth from a natural voice to a falsetto.

Bibliography

General Studies

Carlin, Richard. *The Big Book of Country Music: A Biographical Encyclopedia*. New York: Penguin, 1995.

Case, Brian, Stan Britt, Chrissie Murray, and John Woddward. *The Illustrated Encyclopedia of Jazz*. London: Tiger Books International, 1991.

Clifford, Mike, ed. *The Harmony Illustrated Encyclopedia of Rock*. 7th ed. New York: Harmony Books, 1992.

The Comprehensive Country Music Encyclopedia. New York: Times Books, 1994.

Contemporary Musicians: Profiles of the People in Music. 21 vols. Detroit: Gale Research.

Ewen, David. *American Songwriters: An H. W. Wilson Biographical Dictionary*. New York: H. W. Wilson, 1987.

Gregory, Hugh. *Soul Music A-Z*. Rev. ed. New York: Da Capo Press, 1995.

Hager, Andrew G. *Southern Fried Rock*. New York: Friedman/Fairfax, 1995.

_____. *Women of Country*. New York: Friedman/Fairfax, 1994.

Harris, Sheldon. *Blues Who's Who: A Biographical Dictionary of Blues Singers*. New York: Da Capo Press, 1993.

Heatley, Michael, ed. *The Encyclopedia of Rock: The World's Most Comprehensive Illustrated Rock Reference*. Rev. ed. London: Grange Books, 1997.

Helander, Brock. The *Rock Who's Who*. 2d ed. New York: Schirmer Books, 1996.

Herbst, Peter, ed. *The Rolling Stone Interviews 1967-1980: Talking with the Legends of Rock and Roll*. New York: St Martin's Press, 1981.

Herzhaft, Gerard, Paul Harris, Jerry Haussler, and Anton J. Mikofsky. *Encyclopedia of the Blues*. 2d ed. Fayetteville: University of Arkansas Press, 1997.

Jackson, Rick. *Encyclopedia of Canadian Rock, Pop, and Folk Music*. Kingston, Ontario: Quarry Press, 1994.

Jasper, Tony, and Derek Oliver. *The International Encyclopedia of Hard Rock and Heavy Metal*. Rev. ed. London: Sidgwick & Jackson, 1991.

Knapp, Ron. *American Legends of Rock*. Springfield, N.J.: Enslow, 1996.

Larkin, Colin, ed. *The Guinness Encyclopedia of Popular Music*. 6 vols. 2d ed. Enfield, England: Guinness Publishing, 1995.

_____. *The Guinness Who's Who of Heavy Metal*. Enfield, England: Guinness Publishing, 1992.

_____. *The Guinness Who's Who of Rap, Dance, and Techno*. Enfield, England: Guinness Publishing, 1994.

_____. *The Guinness Who's Who of Reggae*. Enfield, England: Guinness Publishing, 1994.

_____. *The Guinness Who's Who of Seventies Music*. Enfield, England: Guinness Publishing, 1993.

_____. *The Guinness Who's Who of Soul Music*. Enfield, England: Guinness Publishing, 1993.

Marschall, Richard. *The Encyclopedia of Country and Western Music*. Rev. ed. Rocky Hill, Conn.: Great Pond, 1992.

_____. *The Encyclopedia of Country Music*. North Dighton, Mass.: JG Press, 1995.

Perry, David. *Jazz Greats*. London: Phaidon, 1996.

Richards, Tad, and Melvin Shestack. *The New Country Music Encyclopedia*. New York: Simon & Schuster, 1993.

Rolling Stone. The Interviews: A Twenty-fifth Anniversary Special. New York: Straight Arrow, 1992.

Romanowski, Patricia, and Holly George-Warren, eds. *The New Rolling Stone Encyclopedia of Rock and Roll*. Rev. ed. New York: Fireside, 1995.

Russell, Tony. *The Blues: From Robert Johnson to Robert Cray*. London: Aurum Press, 1997.

Sansevere, John R., and Erica Farber. *Bad Boyz of Rap*. Racine, Wisconsin: Western, 1993.

Santelli, Robert. *The Big Book of Blues: A Biographical Encyclopedia*. London: Pavillion, 1994.

Stambler, Irwin. *Country Music: The Encyclopedia*. New York: St. Martin's Press, 1997.

_____. *The Encyclopedia of Pop, Rock, and Soul*. Rev.

ed. New York: St. Martin's Press, 1990.

Stambler, Irwin, and Grelun Landon. *Country Music: The Encyclopedia.* New York: St. Martin's Press, 1997.

Stancell, Steven. *Rap Whoz Who: The World of Rap Music.* New York: Schirmer Books, 1996.

Tee, Ralph. *Who's Who in Soul Music.* London: Weidenfeld & Nicolson, 1991.

_____. *Soul Music: Who's Who.* Rocklin, Calif.: Prima, 1992.

Tobler, John, ed. *Who's Who in Rock and Roll.* London: Hamlyn, 1991.

Vincent, Rickey. *Funk: The Music, the People, and the Rhythm of the One.* New York: St. Martin's Griffin, 1996.

Whitall, Susan, and Dave Marsh. *Women of Motown: An Oral History.* New York: Avon Books, 1998.

Profiles of Artists and Bands

Blues

Dixon, Willie, and Don Snowden. *I Am the Blues: The Willie Dixon Story.* London: Quartet, 1989.

Greenberg, Alan. *Love in Vain: A Vision of Robert Johnson.* New York: Da Capo Press, 1994.

Guralnick, Peter. *Searching for Robert Johnson.* London: Secker & Warburg, 1990.

King, B. B., and David Ritz. *Blues All Around Me: The Autobiography of B. B. King.* New York: Avon Books, 1996.

Tooze, Sandra B. *Muddy Waters: The Mojo Man.* Toronto: ECW Press, 1997.

Wilcock, Donald E., Buddy Guy, and Rick Siciliano. *Damn Right I've Got the Blues: Buddy Guy and the Blues Roots of Rock-and-Roll.* San Francisco: Woodford Press, 1993.

Wolfe, Charles K., and Kip Lornell. *The Life and Legend of Leadbelly.* New York: HarperPerennial, 1992.

Country

Allen, Bob. *George Jones: The Life and Times of a Honky Tonk Legend.* New York: St. Martin's Press, 1994.

Bego, Mark. *Alan Jackson: Gone Country.* Dallas: Taylor, 1996.

_____. *George Strait: The Story of Country's Living Legend.* New York: Kensington Books, 1997.

_____. *I Fall to Pieces: The Music and the Life of Patsy Cline.* Holbrook, Mass.: Adams, 1995.

Bennahum, David. *K. D. Lang.* London: Omnibus Press, 1993.

Brown, R. D. *Clint Black: A Better Man.* New York: Fireside, 1993.

Brown, Stuart E. *Patsy Cline: Singing Girl from the Shenandoah Valley.* Berryville, Va.: Virginia Book Company, 1996.

Campbell, Glen, and Tom Carter. *Rhinestone Cowboy: An Autobiography.* New York: Villard Books, 1994.

Cantwell, David, and Dave Marsh. *George Strait.* New York: Boulevard Books, 1996.

Caress, Jay. *Hank Williams: Country Music's Tragic King.* New York: Stein and Day, 1981.

Cash, Johnny, and Patrick Carr. *Cash: The Autobiography.* Thorndike, Maine: G. K. Hall, 1997.

Clark, Roy, and Marc Eliot. *My Life—In Spite of Myself!* New York: Pocket Books, 1994.

Conn, Charles Paul. *The Barbara Mandrell Story.* New York: Berkley, 1988.

Cooper, Daniel. *Lefty Frizzell: The Honky-Tonk Life of Country Music's Greatest Singer.* Boston: Little, Brown, 1995.

Cross, Wilbur, and Michael Kosser. *The Conway Twitty Story: An Authorized Biography.* New York: PaperJacks, 1986.

Cusic, Don. *Eddy Arnold: I'll Hold You in My Heart.* Nashville, Tenn.: Rutledge Hill Press, 1997.

_____. *Randy Travis: King of the New Country Traditionalists.* New York: St. Martin's Press, 1990.

_____. *Reba McIntyre: Country Music's Queen.* New York: St. Martin's Press, 1991.

Dolan, Sean. *Johnny Cash.* New York: Chelsea House, 1995.

Escott, Colin, George Merritt, and William MacEwen. *Hank Williams: The Biography.* Boston: Little, Brown, 1995.

Flippo, Chet. *Your Cheatin' Heart: A Biography of Hank Williams.* New York: St. Martin's Press, 1981.

Haggard, Merle, and P. J. Russel. *Sing Me Back Home: My Story.* New York: Pocket Books,1981.

Jones, George, and Tom Carter. *I Lived to Tell It All.* New York: Dell, 1996.

Jones, Margaret. *Patsy: The Life and Times of Patsy Cline.* New York: HarperPerennial, 1994.

Judd, Naomi. *Love Can Build a Bridge.* New York: Ballantine, 1993.

McCall, Michael. *Garth Brooks: A Biography.* New York: Bantam Books, 1991.

McEntire, Reba, and Tom Carter. *Reba: My Story.* New York: Bantam Books, 1994.

Mandrell, Barbara. *Get to the Heart: My Story.* New York: Bantam Books, 1990.

Millard, Bob. *The Judds.* New York: St. Martin's Press, 1988.

Mitchell, Rick. *Garth Brooks: One of a Kind, Workin' on a Full House.* New York: Simon & Schuster, 1993.

Nassour, Ellis. *Patsy Cline.* New York: Leisure Books, 1985.

Nelson, Willie, and Edwin Shrake. *Willie: An Autobiography.* New York: Pocket Books, 1988.

O'Meilia, Matt. *Garth Brooks: The Road out of Santa Fe.* Norman: University of Oklahoma Press, 1997.

Parton, Dolly. *Dolly: My Life and Other Unfinished Business.* New York: HarperCollins, 1994.

Pasternak, Judith Mahoney. *Dolly.* New York: MetroBooks, 1998.

Pride, Charley, and Jim Henderson. *Pride: The Charley Pride Story.* New York: W. Morrow, 1994.

Pugh, Ronnie. *Ernest Tubb: The Texas Troubadour.* Durham: Duke University Press, 1996.

Robertson, William. *K. D. Lang: Carrying the Torch.* Toronto: ECW Press, 1993.

Sgammato, Jo. *Dream Come True: The LeAnn Rimes Story.* New York: Ballantine Books, 1997.

———. *Keepin' It Country: The George Strait Story.* New York: Ballantine Books, 1998.

Starr, Victoria. *K. D. Lang: All You Get Is Me.* London: HarperCollins, 1994.

Streissguth, Michael. *Eddy Arnold, Pioneer of the Nashville Sound.* New York: Schirmer Books, 1997.

Tillis, Mel, and Walter H. Wager. *Stutterin' Boy.* New York: Dell, 1984.

Tritt, Travis, and Michael Bane. *Ten Feet Tall and Bulletproof.* New York: Warner Books, 1994.

Tucker, Tanya, and Patsi Bale Cox. *Nickel Dreams: My Life.* New York: Hyperion, 1997.

Williams, Dallas. *Shania Twain: On My Way.* Toronto: ECW Press, 1997.

Wills, Rosetta. *The King of Western Swing: Bob Wills Remembered.* New York: Billboard Books, 1998.

Wynette, Tammy, and Joan Dew. *Stand by Your Man: An Autobiography.* New York: Pocket Books, 1979.

Folk and Singer-Songwriters

Baez, Joan. *And a Voice to Sing With: A Memoir.* New York: Summit Books, 1987.

Charlesworth, Chris. *Cat Stevens.* New York: Proteus, 1984.

Coan, Peter M. *Taxi: The Harry Chapin Story.* New York: Carol Publishing Group, 1990.

Collins, Judy. *Voices.* New York: Clarkson Potter, 1995.

Collis, John. *Van Morrison: Inarticulate Speech of the Heart.* New York: Da Capo Press, 1996.

Denver, John, and Arthur Tobier. *Take Me Home: An Autobiography.* London: Headline, 1994.

Dunaway, David King. *How Can I Keep from Singing: Pete Seeger.* New York: Da Capo Press, 1990.

Glatt, John. *The Chieftains: The Authorized Biography.* London: Century, 1997.

Guthrie, Woody, Dave Marsh, and Harold Leventhal. *Pastures of Plenty: A Self-Portrait.* New York: HarperCollins, 1992.

Himes, Roger. *John Denver's Legacy: A Fire in His Heart and a Light in His Eyes.* Denver: Lamplighter Books of Colorado, 1998.

Hinton, Brian. *Celtic Crossroads: The Art of Van Morrison.* London: Sanctuary, 1997.

———. *Joni Mitchell: Both Sides Now.* London: Sanctuary, 1996.

Humphries, Patrick. *Bookends: The Simon and Garfunkel Story.* London: Proteus, 1982.

———. *Small Change: A Life of Tom Waits.* London: Omnibus Press, 1989.

Kingston, Victoria. *Simon and Garfunkel: The Biography.* New York: Fromm International, 1996.

Klein, Joe. *Woody Guthrie: A Life.* London: Faber, 1981.

Matteo, Stephen. *Dylan.* New York: Metro Books, 1998.

Meek, Bill. *Paddy Moloney and the Chieftains.* London: Sidgwick & Jackson, 1987.

Morella, Joe, and Patricia Barey. *Simon and Garfunkel: Old Friends.* New York: Carol, 1991.

Nadel, Ira Bruce. *Leonard Cohen: A Life in Art.* London: Robson, 1994.

Rogan, Johnny. *Van Morrison: A Portrait of the Artist.* London: Proteus Books, 1984.

Seeger, Pete, and Peter Blood. *Where Have All the Flowers Gone: A Musical Autobiography.* Bethlehem, Pa.: Sing Out, 1997.

Shelton, Robert. *No Direction Home: The Life and Music of Bob Dylan.* New York: Da Capo Press, 1997.

Spitz, Bob. *Dylan: A Biography.* New York ; London: Norton, 1989.

Turner, Steve. *Van Morrison: Too Late to Stop Now.* London: Bloomsbury, 1993.

Wiseman, Rich. *Jackson Browne: The Story of a Hold Out.* Garden City, N.Y.: Doubleday, 1982.

Jazz

Chambers, Jack. *Milestones: The Music and Times of Miles Davis.* New York: Da Capo Press, 1983.

Crisp, George. *Miles Davis.* New York: Franklin Watts, 1997.

Davis, Miles, and Quincy Troupe. *Miles: The Autobiography.* New York: Simon and Schuster, 1990.

Fraim, John. *Spirit Catcher: The Life and Art of John Coltrane.* West Liberty, Ohio: GreatHouse, 1996.

Giddins, Gary. *Celebrating Bird: The Triumph of Charlie Parker.* New York: Da Capo Press, 1987.

Haskins, James. *Ella Fitzgerald: A Life Through Jazz.* London: New English Library, 1991.

Long, Daryl N. *Miles Davis for Beginners.* New York: Writers and Readers, 1992.

Nicholson, Stuart. *Ella Fitzgerald: A Biography of the First Lady of Jazz.* New York: Da Capo Press, 1994.

Nisenson, Eric. *Ascension: John Coltrane and His Quest.* New York: St. Martin's Press, 1993.

_____. *'Round About Midnight: A Portrait of Miles Davis.* New York: Da Capo Press, 1982.

Porter, Lewis. *John Coltrane: His Life and Music.* Ann Arbor: University of Michigan Press, 1997.

Woideck, Carl. *Charlie Parker: His Music and Life.* Ann Arbor: University of Michigan Press, 1996.

Wyman, Carolyn. *Ella Fitzgerald: Jazz Singer Supreme.* New York: F. Watts, 1993.

Pop

Ammons, Kevin, and Nancy Bacon. *Good Girl, Bad Girl: An Insider's Biography of Whitney Houston.* Secaucus, N.J.: Carol, 1996.

Bowman, Jeffery, and John Niendorff. *Diva: The Totally Unauthorized Biography of Whitney Houston.* London: Headline, 1994.

Carrick, Peter. *Barbra Streisand: A Biography.* Robert Hale, 1991.

Clarke, Donald. *All or Nothing at All: A Life of Frank Sinatra.* London: Pan, 1998.

DeStefano, Anthony M. *Gloria Estefan: The Pop Superstar from Tragedy to Triumph.* New York: Signet, 1997.

Eng, Steve. *Jimmy Buffett: The Man from Margaritaville Revealed.* New York: St. Martin's Griffin, 1996.

Fidelman, Geoffrey Mark. *First Lady of Song: Ella Fitzgerald for the Record.* Secaucus, N.J.: Carol, 1994.

Fitzgerald, Judith. *Building a Mystery: The Story of Sarah McLachlan and Lilith Fair.* Kingston, Ontario: Quarry Music Books, 1997.

Fogelson, Genia. *Belafonte.* Los Angeles: Holloway House, 1980.

Freedland, Michael. *All the Way: A Biography of Frank Sinatra.* New York: St. Martin's Press, 1997.

Guterman, Jimmy. *Sinéad: Her Life and Music.* Harmondsworth, England: Penguin, 1991.

Harvey, Diana Karanikas, and Jackson Harvey. *I'm Gonna Make You Love Me: The Story of Diana Ross.* New York: Dell, 1980.

_____. *Neil Diamond.* New York: MetroBooks, 1996.

Hayes, Dermott. *Sinéad O'Connor: So Different.* London: Omnibus Press, 1991.

Heath, Chris. *Pet Shop Boys Versus America.* London: Penguin, 1993.

Holder, Deborah. *Completely Frank: The Life of Frank Sinatra.* London: Bloomsbury, 1995.

Lulow, Kalia. *Barry Manilow.* New York: Ballatine Books, 1985.

Manilow, Barry. *Sweet Life: Adventures on the Way to Paradise.* New York: McGraw-Hill, 1987.

Matthew-Walker, Robert. *Madonna: The Biography.* Rev. ed. London: Pan, 1991.

Norman, Philip. *Elton.* New York: Harmony Books, 1991.

Oldham, Andrew, Tony Calder, and Colin Irwin. *Abba: The Name of the Game.* London: Pan, 1995.

Plutzik, Roberta. *Lionel Richie.* New York: Dell, 1985.

Randall, Lucian. *Annie Lennox.* London: Orion, 1994.

Ryan, Thomas. *The Parrot Head Companion: The Insider's Guide to Jimmy Buffett.* Secaucus, N.J.: Carol, 1998.

St. Michael, Mick. *Madonna: In Her Own Words.* London ; New York: Omnibus Press, 1990.

Savage, Jeff. *Whitney Houston.* Parsippany, N.J.: Dillon Press, 1998.

Snaith, Paul. *Abba: The Music Still Goes On, the Complete Story.* Chessington, England: Castle Communications, 1994.

Taraborrelli, J. Randy. *Call Her Miss Ross: The Unauthorized Biography of Diana Ross.* Secaucus, N.J.: Carol, 1989.

_____. *Sinatra: A Complete Life.* Seacaucus, N.J.: Carol, 1997.

_____. *Sinatra: The Man Behind the Myth.* Sydney: Pan Macmillan, 1998.

Rap and Hip-hop

D., Chuck. *Public Enemy.* New York: Thunder's Mouth Press, 1994.

Eichhorn, Dennis P. *Hammer.* Seattle: Turman Publishing, 1993.

Hildebrand, Lee. *Hammertime.* New York: Avon Books, 1992.

L. L. Cool J and Karen Hunter. *I Make My Own Rules.* New York: St. Martin's Press, 1997.

Washington, Bobby. *Queen Latifah.* New York: Dell, 1992.

White, Armond. *Rebel for the Hell of It: The Life of Tupac Shakur: An Interpretation.* London: Quartet Books, 1997.

Reggae

Davis, Stephen. *Bob Marley: Conquering Lion of Reggae.* London: Plexus, 1994.

Talamon, Bruce, and Roger Steffens. *Bob Marley: Spirit Dancer.* New York: W. W. Norton, 1994.

White, Timothy. *Catch a Fire: The Life of Bob Marley.* Rev. ed. New York: H. Holt, 1998

Rock

Alexander, Danny, and Dave Marsh. *Soul Asylum.* New York: Boulevard Books, 1996.

Amburn, Ellis. *Buddy Holly: A Biography.* New York: St. Martin's Press, 1995.

_____. *Pearl: The Obsessions and Passions of Janis Joplin: A Biography.* London: Warner, 1992.

Assayas, Michka, and Claude Meunier. *The Beatles and the Sixties.* New York: Henry Holt, 1996.

Bateson, Keith, and Alan Parker. *Sid's Way: The Life and Death of Sid Vicious.* London: Omnibus Press, 1991.

Berry, Chuck. *Chuck Berry: The Autobiography.* London: Faber, 1987.

Bockris, Victor. *Lou Reed: The Biography.* Rev. ed. London: Vintage, 1995.

_____. *Transformer: The Lou Reed Story.* New York: Simon & Schuster, 1994.

Bono and Susan Black. *Bono: In His Own Words.* London: Omnibus Press, 1997.

Booth, Stanley. *Keith: Standing in the Shadows.* New York: St. Martin's Griffin, 1996.

Bowler, Dave, and Bryan Dray. *U2: A Conspiracy of Hope.* London: Pan, 1994.

Bruce Springsteen: The Rolling Stone Files: The Ultimate Compendium of Interviews, Articles, Facts, and Opinions from the Files of Rolling Stone. New York: Hyperion, 1996.

Budnick, Dean. The *Phishing Manual: A Compendium to the Music of Phish.* New York: Hyperion, 1996.

Clapton, Eric. *Eric Clapton: In His Own Words.* London: Omnibus Press, 1993.

Clarkson, Wensley. *Sting: The Secret Life of Gordon Sumner.* London: Blake, 1995.

Coleman, Ray. *Rod Stewart: The Biography.* London: Pavilion, 1994.

Cruikshank, Ben. *Frank Zappa: A Strictly Genteel Genius.* Andover, Mass.: Agenda, 1996.

Daily, Robert. *Elvis Presley: The King of Rock 'n' Roll.* New York: F. Watts, 1996.

Dallas, Karl. *Bricks in the Wall.* New York: S.P.I./ Shapolsky, 1994.

Dalton, David. *El Sid: Saint Vicious.* New York: St. Martin's Griffin, 1998.

_____. *Piece of My Heart: A Portrait of Janis Joplin.* Da Capo Press, 1991.

Davies, Dave. *Kink: An Autobiography.* New York: Hyperion, 1996.

Davies, Hunter. *The Beatles.* Rev. ed. New York: W. W. Norton, 1996.

Davis, Stephen. *Hammer of the Gods.* New York: Boulevard Books, 1997.

DeWitt, Howard A. *Chuck Berry, Rock 'n' Roll Music.* Ann Arbor, Mich.: Pierian Press, 1985.

Eliot, Marc, and Mike Appel. *Down Thunder Road: The Making of Bruce Springsteen.* London: Plexus, 1992.

Eno, Brian. *A Year with Swollen Appendices.* London: Faber and Faber, 1996.

Farren, Mick. *Rolling Stones: In Their Own Words.* London: Omnibus Press, 1994.

Fleetwood, Mick. *My Twenty-five Years in Fleetwood Mac.* London: Weidenfeld and Nicolson, 1993.

Friedman, Myra. *Buried Alive: The Biography of Janis Joplin.* New York: Harmony Books, 1992.

Gaines, Steven S. *Heroes and Villains: The True Story of the Beach Boys.* New York: Da Capo Press, 1995.

Garodkin, John. *Little Richard Special.* Denmark: Mjoelner Edition, 1984.

Giuliano, Geoffrey. *Behind Blue Eyes: A Life of Pete Townshend.* London: Hodder and Stoughton, 1996.

———. *Rod Stewart: Vagabond Heart.* London: Coronet Books, 1993.

Goldrosen, John, and John Beecher. *Remembering Buddy: The Definitive Biography.* New York: Da Capo Press, 1996.

Gray, Marcus. *Last Gang in Town: The Story and Myth of the Clash.* London: Fourth Estate, 1995.

Greenfield, Robert. *Dark Star: An Oral Biography of Jerry Garcia.* New York: W. Morrow, 1996.

Gruen, Bob. *Chaos: The Sex Pistols.* London: Omnibus Press, 1990.

Harvey, Spike. *Red Hot Chili Peppers.* London: Omnibus Press, 1995.

Heatley, Michael. *Neil Young: In His Own Words.* London: Omnibus Press, 1997.

Henderson, David. *'Scuse Me While I Kiss the Sky: The Life of Jimi Hendrix.* Rev. ed. New York: Bantam Books, 1996

Huxley, Martin. *Nine Inch Nails: Self Destruct.* New York: St. Martin's Griffin, 1997.

Keizer, Brian, and Dave Marsh. *Neil Young.* New York: Boulevard Books, 1996.

Lydon, John, and Keith Zimmerman. *Rotten: No Irish, No Blacks, No Dogs, the Authorised Autobiography, Johnny Rotten of the Sex Pistols.* London: Coronet, 1994.

Marsh, Dave. *Glory Days: The Bruce Springsteen Story.* 3d ed. New York: Thunder's Mouth Press, 1996.

Morrell, Brad, and Chris Charlesworth. *Nirvana and the Sound of Seattle.* London: Omnibus Press, 1996.

Neil Young: The Ultimate Compendium of Interviews, Articles, Facts and Opinions from the Files of the Rolling Stone. New York: Hyperion, 1994.

Nickson, Chris. *Soundgarden: New Metal Crown.* New York: St. Martin's Griffin, 1995.

Nikart, Ray. *Sting and the Police.* New York: Ballantine Books, 1984.

O'Regan, Denis. *Queen: The Full Picture.* London: Bloomsbury, 1995.

Presley, Elvis, Mick Farren, and Pearce Marchbank. *Elvis: In His Own Words.* London: Omnibus Press, 1994.

Roberts, Chris. *Fugees: The Unofficial Book.* London: Virgin, 1997.

Robertson, John. *Lennon: A Journey Through John Lennon's Life and Times in Words and Pictures.* London: Omnibus Press, 1995.

Rossi, Melissa. *Courtney Love: Queen of Noise: A Most Unauthorized Biography.* New York: Pocket Books, 1996.

Saidman, Sorelle. *Bryan Adams: Everything He Does.* London: Sidgwick & Jackson, 1993.

Sandford, Christopher. *Clapton: Edge of Darkness.* London: V. Gollancz, 1994.

———. *Kurt Cobain.* London: Gollancz, 1995.

Schaffner, Nicholas. *Pink Floyd.* London: Sidgwick & Jackson, 1991.

Sellers, Robert. *Sting: A Biography.* London: Omnibus Press 1989.

Shapiro, Marc. *The Story of the Eagles: The Long Run.* London: Omnibus Press, 1995.

Simmons, Sylvie, and Malcolm Dome. *Lude, Crude, and Rude: The Story of Mötley Crüe.* Chessington, England: Castle Communications, 1994.

Thompson, Dave. *Never Fade Away: The Kurt Cobain Story.* London: Pan, 1994.

Troy, Sandy. *Captain Trips: A Biography of Jerry Garcia.* New York: Thunder's Mouth Press, 1995.

Twelker, Uli, and Roland Schmitt. *Happy Boys Happy! A Rock History of the Small Faces and Humble Pie.* London: Sanctuary, 1997.

U2: The Ultimate Compendium of Interviews, Articles, Facts, and Opinions from the Files of the Rolling Stone. London: Sidgwick & Jackson, 1994.

Wall, Mick, and Malcolm Dome. *Stone Temple Pilots.* London: Omnibus Press, 1995.

Walley, David. *No Commercial Potential: The Saga of Frank Zappa.* New York: Da Capo Press, 1996.

Watson, Ben. *Frank Zappa: The Negative Dialectics of Poodle Play.* Rev. ed. London: Quartet Books, 1996.

Watts, Chris. *Red Hot Chili Peppers: Sugar and Spice.* Chessington, England: Castle Communications, 1994.

Welch, Chris. *Hendrix: A Biography.* London: Omnibus Press, 1982.

_____. *Pink Floyd: Learning to Fly.* Chessington, England: Castle Communications, 1994.

White, Charles. *The Life and Times of Little Richard: The Quasar of Rock.* New York: Da Capo, 1984.

White, George R. *Bo Diddley, Living Legend.* Chessington, England: Castle Communications, 1995.

Williams, Paul. *Neil Young: Love to Burn, Thirty Years of Speaking Out, 1966-1996.* London: Omnibus Press, 1997.

Wilson, Brian, and Todd Gold. *Wouldn't It Be Nice: My Own Story.* New York: HarperCollins, 1991.

Wincentsen, Edward. *Good Vibrations: The Encyclopedia of the Beach Boys.* Westport, Conn.: Greenwood Press, 1998.

Wise, Nick. *Courtney Love.* London: Omnibus Press, 1995.

_____. *Omnibus Press Presents the Story of the Smashing Pumpkins.* London: Omnibus Press, 1996.

Zappa, Frank. *The Real Frank Zappa Book.* New York: Poseidon Press, 1989.

Soul, Motown, and Disco

Brown, Geoff, and Chris Charlesworth. *James Brown: Doin' It to Death.* London: Omnibus Press, 1996.

Brown, James, and Bruce Tucker. *James Brown: The Godfather of Soul.* New York: Thunder's Mouth Press, 1986.

Charles, Ray, and David Ritz. *Brother Ray: Ray Charles' Own Story.* New York: Da Capo Press, 1992.

Davis, Sharon. *I Heard It Through the Grapevine: Marvin Gaye, the Biography.* Edinburgh: Mainstream, 1991.

Douglas, Tony. *Lonely Teardrops: The Jackie Wilson Story.* London: Sanctuary Publishing, 1997.

Gordy, Berry. *To Be Loved: The Music, the Magic, the Memories of Motown, an Autobiography.* New York: Warner Books, 1995.

Gourse, Leslie. *Aretha Franklin: Lady Soul.* New York: F. Watts, 1995.

Knight, Gladys. *Between Each Line of Pain and Glory: My Life Story.* New York: Hyperion, 1997.

Leigh, Keri. *Stevie Ray: Soul to Soul.* Dallas: Taylor, 1993.

Lewis, Jerry Lee, and Charles White. *Killer!* London: Arrow, 1993.

Mills, David, and Dave Marsh. *George Clinton and P-Funk: An Oral History.* New York: Avon Books, 1998.

Moore, Sam, and Dave Marsh. *Sam and Dave: An Oral History.* New York: Avon Books, 1998.

Peisch, Jeffrey. *Stevie Wonder.* New York: Ballantine Books, 1984.

Rego, Mark. *Aretha Franklin: The Queen of Soul.* London: Hale, 1989.

Ritz, David. *Divided Soul: The Life of Marvin Gaye.* London: Omnibus Press, 1985.

Robinson, Smokey, and David Ritz. *Smokey: Inside My Life.* New York: Jove Books, 1989.

Rose, Cynthia. *Living in America: The Soul Saga of James Brown.* London: Serpent's Tail, 1990.

Ross, Diana. *Secrets of a Sparrow: Memoirs.* London: Headline, 1993.

Selvin, Joel, and Dave Marsh. *Sly and the Family Stone: An Oral History.* New York: Avon Books, 1998.

Sheafer, Silvia Anne. *Aretha Franklin: Motown Superstar.* Springfield, N.J.: Enslow, 1996.

Swenson, John. *Stevie Wonder.* London: Plexus, 1986.

Taylor, Rick. *Stevie Wonder.* London: Omnibus Press, 1985.

Turner, Tina, and Kurt Loder. *I, Tina: My Life Story.* New York: Avon Books, 1986.

Welch, Chris. *The Tina Turner Experience.* Rev. ed. London: Virgin, 1994.

Williams, Otis. *Temptations.* New York: Simon & Schuster, 1989.

List of Artists by Musical Styles

NOTE: Many artists are listed in multiple categories.

ADULT CONTEMPORARY and SOFT ROCK (*see also* **POP**)
Herb Alpert
The Association
The Bee Gees
The Carpenters
Phil Collins
José Feliciano
Kenny G
Hootie and the Blowfish
Tom Jones
Loggins and Messina /
    Kenny Loggins
Barry Manilow
The Righteous Brothers
Linda Ronstadt
Sade
Seals and Crofts
Barbra Streisand

ALTERNATIVE ROCK
Alice in Chains
Tori Amos
Beck
Björk / The Sugarcubes
Black Flag / Henry Rollins
Blur
Counting Crows
The Cure
Depeche Mode
The Dream Syndicate
The Foo Fighters
The Gin Blossoms
John Hiatt
Hole
Julio Iglesias
Jane's Addiction /
    Porno for Pyros
Sarah McLachlan
The Dave Matthews Band

Nirvana
No Doubt
Pearl Jam
Radiohead
The Red Hot Chili Peppers
R.E.M.
Smashing Pumpkins
Patti Smith
The Smiths / Morrissey
Sonic Youth
Soundgarden
Sublime
Tears for Fears
Suzanne Vega
The Violent Femmes
Tom Waits
The Wallflowers
XTC

AMBIENT, NEW AGE, and INSTRUMENTAL
Brian Eno
Enya
Loreena McKennitt
The Orb
John Tesh
Vangelis
Yanni

ART ROCK and PROGRESSIVE ROCK
Emerson, Lake, and Palmer
Brian Eno
Genesis
Jethro Tull
Kansas
King Crimson
The Moody Blues
The Alan Parsons Project
Roxy Music / Bryan Ferry

Rush
Supertramp
Traffic / Steve Winwood /
    Dave Mason
Yes

BIG BAND and SWING
Harry Connick, Jr.
Ella Fitzgerald
Joe Jackson
Manhattan Transfer
Linda Ronstadt
Frank Sinatra
The Stray Cats / Brian Setzer

BLUEGRASS
Charlie Daniels
Vince Gill
Alison Krauss
Kathy Mattea
Bill Monroe and the
    Blue Grass Boys
Ricky Skaggs

BLUES
The Allman Brothers Band
The Animals
Louis Armstrong
Harry Belafonte
Bobby "Blue" Bland
Blues Traveler
Booker T. and the MG's
Captain Beefheart and the
    Magic Band
Tracy Chapman
Ray Charles
Eric Clapton
Harry Connick, Jr.
Robert Cray
Cream

Miles Davis
Willie Dixon
The Doors
Bob Dylan
Fleetwood Mac
Aretha Franklin
The Grateful Dead
Woody Guthrie
Buddy Guy
Jimi Hendrix
John Lee Hooker
Howlin' Wolf
Etta James
Robert Johnson
Janis Joplin
Albert King
B. B. King
k. d. lang
Leadbelly
Lyle Lovett
John McLaughlin
Steve Miller
Van Morrison
The Neville Brothers /
    Aaron Neville
Bonnie Raitt
Jimmie Rodgers
The Rolling Stones
Carlos Santana
Rod Stewart
Taj Mahal
George Thorogood and the
    Destroyers
Stevie Ray Vaughan
Tom Waits
Muddy Waters
Hank Williams
ZZ Top

BOLERO
Luis Miguel

CALYPSO
Harry Belafonte

CELTIC and IRISH TRADITIONAL
The Chieftains
Enya
Loreena McKennitt
Van Morrison

CLASSICAL and CLASSICAL CROSSOVER
Dave Brubeck
Elvis Costello
Paul McCartney
Bobby McFerrin
Frank Zappa / The Mothers
    of Invention

COUNTRY
Alabama
Eddy Arnold
Chet Atkins
Clint Black
Garth Brooks
Brooks and Dunn
The Byrds
Glen Campbell
Mary Chapin Carpenter
Johnny Cash
Rosanne Cash
Ray Charles
Roy Clark
Patsy Cline
Eddie Cochran
Elvis Costello
Charlie Daniels
Mac Davis
John Denver
Bob Dylan
Steve Earle
Duane Eddy
Lefty Frizzell
Crystal Gayle
Vince Gill
Nanci Griffith
Woody Guthrie
Merle Haggard
Emmylou Harris
Don Henley

Buddy Holly / The Crickets
Alan Jackson
Waylon Jennings
George Jones
Tom Jones
The Judds / Wynonna Judd
The Kingston Trio
Kris Kristofferson
k. d. lang
Jerry Lee Lewis
Gordon Lightfoot
Lyle Lovett
The Lovin' Spoonful
Loretta Lynn
Reba McEntire
Barbara Mandrell
Manhattan Transfer
Kathy Mattea
Bill Monroe and the
    Blue Grass Boys
Anne Murray
Willie Nelson
Olivia Newton-John
Roy Orbison
The Osmonds
Buck Owens
Dolly Parton
Les Paul
Carl Perkins
The Pointer Sisters
Elvis Presley
Charley Pride
John Prine
Bonnie Raitt
Helen Reddy
Charlie Rich
LeAnn Rimes
Marty Robbins
Jimmie Rodgers
Kenny Rogers
The Rolling Stones
Seals and Crofts
Selena
Ricky Skaggs
George Strait
Talking Heads / David Byrne
Mel Tillis

Randy Travis
Travis Tritt
Ernest Tubb
Tanya Tucker
Shania Twain
Conway Twitty
Jerry Jeff Walker
Doc Watson
Kitty Wells
Hank Williams
Hank Williams, Jr.
Bob Wills and His Texas
	Playboys
Tammy Wynette
Trisha Yearwood
Dwight Yoakam

COUNTRY ROCK
The Band
Garth Brooks
Brooks and Dunn
Buffalo Springfield
Jimmy Buffett
The Byrds
Glen Campbell
Rosanne Cash
The Cowboy Junkies
Creedence Clearwater Revival
	/ John Fogerty
Jim Croce
Sheryl Crow
Charlie Daniels
Mac Davis
Dire Straits / Mark Knopfler
The Doobie Brothers /
	Michael McDonald
The Dream Syndicate
Bob Dylan
The Eagles
Steve Earle
The Everly Brothers
The Gin Blossoms
Emmylou Harris
Buddy Holly / The Crickets
Waylon Jennings
Janis Joplin
k. d. lang

Little Feat
Loggins and Messina /
	Kenny Loggins
Los Lobos
Lyle Lovett
Lynyrd Skynyrd
Steve Morse
Rick Nelson
Gram Parsons
Kenny Rogers
Linda Ronstadt
Travis Tritt
Tanya Tucker
Shania Twain
Jerry Jeff Walker
Hank Williams, Jr.
Trisha Yearwood
Dwight Yoakam
Neil Young

DISCO
Abba
Average White Band
The Bee Gees
Blondie
James Brown
Chic
Electric Light Orchestra /
	Jeff Lynne
Michael Jackson
The Jackson 5
KC and the Sunshine Band
R. Kelly
Patti LaBelle
Queen
The Rolling Stones
Roxy Music / Bryan Ferry
Boz Scaggs
Donna Summer
Talking Heads / David Byrne
The Village People

DOO-WOP
Dion and the Belmonts /
	Dion
The Drifters
Jan and Dean

Frank Zappa / The Mothers
	of Invention

ELECTRONICA See
INDUSTRIAL and
ELECTRONICA

FOLK
Joan Baez
Harry Belafonte
Jackson Browne
Jimmy Buffett
Mary Chapin Carpenter
Rosanne Cash
Tracy Chapman
The Chieftains
Leonard Cohen
Judy Collins
Shawn Colvin
The Cowboy Junkies
Jim Croce
Sheryl Crow
John Denver
Dion and the Belmonts / Dion
Donovan
Bob Dylan
The Fugees
Amy Grant
The Grateful Dead
Nanci Griffith
Woody Guthrie
Emmylou Harris
John Lee Hooker
Janis Joplin
The Kingston Trio
Leadbelly
Gordon Lightfoot
Lyle Lovett
The Lovin' Spoonful
Sarah McLachlan
Kathy Mattea
Joni Mitchell
Peter, Paul, and Mary
John Prine
Bonnie Raitt
Kenny Rogers
Linda Ronstadt

Seals and Crofts
Pete Seeger
Carly Simon
Paul Simon
Simon and Garfunkel
Bruce Springsteen
The Staple Singers
Taj Mahal
James Taylor
The Turtles
Suzanne Vega
Tom Waits
Jerry Jeff Walker
Doc Watson
Neil Young

FOLK ROCK
The Association
Buffalo Springfield
The Byrds
Harry Chapin
Leonard Cohen
Judy Collins
Crosby, Stills, Nash, and Young
Ani DiFranco
Donovan
Bob Dylan
The Eagles
José Feliciano
Julio Iglesias
Jefferson Airplane /
    Jefferson Starship
Jethro Tull
Jewel
Gordon Lightfoot
Los Lobos
Sarah McLachlan
The Mamas and the Papas
Joni Mitchell
Linda Ronstadt
Cat Stevens
Rod Stewart
Richard Thompson

FUNK
Average White Band
David Bowie

James Brown
George Clinton / Parliament
    / Funkadelic
The Commodores
Dr. John
Sheila E.
Earth, Wind, and Fire
The Fugees
Rick James
R. Kelly
Kool and the Gang
Little Feat
Curtis Mayfield
The Neville Brothers /
    Aaron Neville
The Ohio Players
Prince
The Red Hot Chili Peppers
Lionel Richie
Seal
Sly and the Family Stone
Talking Heads / David Byrne
War
Weather Report

FUSION
Blood, Sweat, and Tears
Miles Davis
Herbie Hancock
John McLaughlin
Steve Morse
Carlos Santana
Sting
Weather Report
Frank Zappa / The Mothers
    of Invention

**GLITTER ROCK and GLAM
  ROCK**
Blondie
David Bowie
Roxy Music / Bryan Ferry

GOSPEL and SPIRITUALS
Mary J. Blige
Ray Charles
Roy Clark

Sam Cooke
Charlie Daniels
The Drifters
Aretha Franklin
Amy Grant
Al Green
Whitney Houston
Mahalia Jackson
Little Richard
Barbara Mandrell
Manhattan Transfer
Kathy Mattea
Sandi Patti
Charley Pride
The Staple Singers
Taj Mahal
Dionne Warwick
The Winans

GRUNGE
Alice in Chains
Tori Amos
The Cure
Depeche Mode
The Foo Fighters
Hole
Jane's Addiction /
    Porno for Pyros
Nirvana
Pearl Jam
Neil Young

HARD ROCK
AC/DC
Aerosmith
Alice in Chains
Black Sabbath / Ozzy Osbourne
Bon Jovi
Alice Cooper
Def Leppard
The Foo Fighters
Led Zeppelin
Nirvana
Ted Nugent
Pearl Jam
Queen
Rush

HEAVY METAL

Alice in Chains
Black Flag / Henry Rollins
Black Sabbath / Ozzy Osbourne
Bon Jovi
Bush
Def Leppard
Guns n' Roses
Ice-T
Iron Maiden
Metallica
Mötley Crüe
Rage Against the Machine
The Red Hot Chili Peppers
The Runaways
Rush
Soundgarden

HIP-HOP and RAP

Arrested Development
Erykah Badu
The Beastie Boys
Mary J. Blige
James Brown
The Chemical Brothers
The Clash
Coolio
Cypress Hill
De La Soul
DJ Jazzy Jeff and the
    Fresh Prince
Dr. Dre
En Vogue
The Fugees
Grandmaster Flash
Hammer
Ice Cube
Ice-T
Kool Moe Dee
L. L. Cool J
Milli Vanilli
New Kids on the Block
The Notorious B.I.G.
N.W.A.
Public Enemy
Puff Daddy
Queen Latifah

Rage Against the Machine
Run-D.M.C.
Salt-n-Pepa
Schoolly D
Tupac Shakur
Snoop Doggy Dogg
Sublime
TLC
2 Live Crew

HOUSE See TECHNO and HOUSE

INDUSTRIAL and ELECTRONICA

Ministry
Nine Inch Nails
The Prodigy

JAZZ and JAZZ POP

Julian "Cannonball" Adderley
Herb Alpert
Louis Armstrong
Erykah Badu
Harry Belafonte
Tony Bennett
George Benson
Blood, Sweat, and Tears
Dave Brubeck
Ray Charles
Nat "King" Cole
Natalie Cole
John Coltrane
Harry Connick, Jr.
The Crusaders
Miles Davis
Dr. John
The Fifth Dimension
Ella Fitzgerald
Kenny G
Herbie Hancock
Rickie Lee Jones
Rahsaan Roland Kirk
Bobby McFerrin
John McLaughlin
Chuck Mangione
Manhattan Transfer

Sergio Mendes
Charles Mingus
Joni Mitchell
Thelonious Monk
Charlie Parker
Les Paul
Frank Sinatra
Steely Dan
Taj Mahal
Tom Waits
Dionne Warwick
Bobby Womack
Frank Zappa / The Mothers
    of Invention

LATIN

Herb Alpert
Rubén Blades
Sheila E.
Gloria Estefan
José Feliciano
Ana Gabriel
Gipsy Kings
Sergio Mendes
Linda Ronstadt
Jon Secada
Selena

MEXICAN FOLK

Los Lobos
Linda Ronstadt
Ritchie Valens

MUSICA ROMANTICA

Luis Miguel

MUSICAL THEATER and LIGHT OPERA

Louis Armstrong
Rubén Blades
Judy Collins
Linda Ronstadt
Barbra Streisand

NEW WAVE

The B-52's
Blondie

The Cars
Elvis Costello
Devo
Joe Jackson
Oingo Boingo
Graham Parker
The Police
The Psychedelic Furs
Squeeze
Talking Heads / David Byrne

PERFORMANCE ART
Laurie Anderson
Bobby McFerrin

POP
Abba
Bryan Adams
Air Supply
Alabama
America
Tori Amos
Fiona Apple
Louis Armstrong
Eddy Arnold
Asia
Babyface
Anita Baker
The Beach Boys
The Beatles
The Bee Gees
Harry Belafonte
Tony Bennett
George Benson
Björk / The Sugarcubes
Rubén Blades
Mary J. Blige
Blondie
Blood, Sweat, and Tears
Blur
Michael Bolton
Boston
David Bowie
Boyz II Men
Toni Braxton
Bread
Garth Brooks

Buffalo Springfield
The Byrds
Glen Campbell
Captain and Tennille
Mariah Carey
The Carpenters
The Cars
Rosanne Cash
Cheap Trick
The Chemical Brothers
Chicago
Roy Clark
The Clash
Patsy Cline
Leonard Cohen
Nat "King" Cole
Natalie Cole
Paula Cole
Judy Collins
Phil Collins
Shawn Colvin
The Commodores
Elvis Costello
Counting Crows
The Cowboy Junkies
The Cranberries
Jim Croce
Sheryl Crow
Culture Club / Boy George
The Cure
Sammy Davis, Jr.
John Denver
Depeche Mode
Devo
Neil Diamond
Bo Diddley
Celine Dion
The Doobie Brothers /
     Michael McDonald
Duran Duran
Sheila E.
Sheena Easton
Echo and the Bunnymen
Duane Eddy
Electric Light Orchestra /
     Jeff Lynne
En Vogue

The English Beat
Gloria Estefan
José Feliciano
The Fifth Dimension
Ella Fitzgerald
Fleetwood Mac
Foreigner
The Four Seasons / Frankie Valli
The Four Tops
Peter Frampton
Aretha Franklin
Kenny G
Ana Gabriel
Peter Gabriel
Marvin Gaye
Crystal Gayle
Genesis
The Go-Go's
Amy Grant
Hanson
George Harrison
P. J. Harvey
Heart
Don Henley
The Hollies
Hootie and the Blowfish
Whitney Houston
James Ingram
INXS
Janet Jackson
Michael Jackson
The Jackson 5
Etta James
Billy Joel
Elton John
Rickie Lee Jones
Tom Jones
KC and the Sunshine Band
R. Kelly
Carole King
The Kingston Trio
The Kinks
Kool and the Gang
Patti LaBelle
k. d. lang
Cyndi Lauper
John Lennon

Huey Lewis and the News
Loggins and Messina /
    Kenny Loggins
Los Lobos
Lyle Lovett
Paul McCartney
Bobby McFerrin
Brian McKnight
Sarah McLachlan
Madonna
Barbara Mandrell
Chuck Mangione
Manhattan Transfer
Barry Manilow
Johnny Mathis
Meat Loaf
Sergio Mendes
George Michael / Wham!
Bette Midler
Luis Miguel
Milli Vanilli
Joni Mitchell
The Monkees
Alanis Morissette
Van Morrison
Anne Murray
Rick Nelson
Willie Nelson
New Edition / Bobby Brown
New Kids on the Block
Randy Newman
Olivia Newton-John
Oasis
Sinéad O'Connor
Oingo Boingo
The O'Jays
Tony Orlando and Dawn
The Osmonds
Robert Palmer
The Alan Parsons Project
Dolly Parton
Sandi Patti
Les Paul
Tom Petty and the
    Heartbreakers
The Platters
The Pointer Sisters

The Police
Elvis Presley
Charley Pride
Prince
John Prine
The Psychedelic Furs
Bonnie Raitt
Lou Rawls
Helen Reddy
Martha Reeves and the
    Vandellas
R.E.M.
REO Speedwagon
Charlie Rich
Lionel Richie
LeAnn Rimes
Marty Robbins
Smokey Robinson
Kenny Rogers
The Ronettes
Linda Ronstadt
Diana Ross
Roxy Music / Bryan Ferry
Todd Rundgren
Sade
Salt-n-Pepa
Boz Scaggs
Seal
Seals and Crofts
Jon Secada
Neil Sedaka
Bob Seger
Carly Simon
Paul Simon
Simon and Garfunkel
Frank Sinatra
The Smithereens
The Smiths / Morrissey
Sonny and Cher / Cher
The Spice Girls
The Spinners
Bruce Springsteen
Squeeze
Cat Stevens
Rod Stewart
Sting
Barbra Streisand

Donna Summer
Supertramp
The Supremes
Keith Sweat
James Taylor
The Temptations
10,000 Maniacs /
    Natalie Merchant
Three Dog Night
Toto
Traffic / Steve Winwood /
    Dave Mason
Tanya Tucker
Ike and Tina Turner /
    Tina Turner
The Turtles
Shania Twain
Conway Twitty
Ritchie Valens
Luther Vandross
Vangelis
Van Halen
The Ventures
The Village People
The Wallflowers
Dionne Warwick
Vanessa Williams
Jackie Wilson
XTC
The Yardbirds
Yes
The Zombies

PROGRESSIVE ROCK *See*
ART ROCK and
PROGRESSIVE ROCK

PSYCHEDELIC ROCK
The Animals
The Beatles
Black Sabbath /
    Ozzy Osbourne
The Byrds
The Chambers Brothers
The Chemical Brothers
Cream
The Doors

The Grateful Dead
Jefferson Airplane /
    Jefferson Starship
Pink Floyd
The Rolling Stones
Carlos Santana
Sublime
Traffic / Steve Winwood /
    Dave Mason
The Yardbirds

PUNK ROCK
The Beastie Boys
Björk / The Sugarcubes
Black Flag / Henry Rollins
Blondie
The Clash
The Dead Kennedys
Green Day
Billy Idol
Jane's Addiction /
    Porno for Pyros
No Doubt
Graham Parker
The Pretenders
Rage Against the Machine
The Ramones
The Red Hot Chili Peppers
The Runaways
The Sex Pistols
Patti Smith
Sonic Youth
Soundgarden
Squeeze
Sublime
Talking Heads / David Byrne
X

RAP *See* **HIP-HOP and RAP**

REGGAE
The Clash
Jimmy Cliff
Bob Marley
Robert Palmer
The Police
Queen Latifah

The Rolling Stones
Sting
Sublime
Peter Tosh

RHYTHM AND BLUES
Aerosmith
The Animals
Erykah Badu
George Benson
Chuck Berry
Mary J. Blige
Toni Braxton
James Brown
Mariah Carey
The Chambers Brothers
Ray Charles
George Clinton / Parliament
    / Funkadelic
The Coasters
Nat "King" Cole
Natalie Cole
Phil Collins
Robert Cray
Bo Diddley
Willie Dixon
Dr. John
Fats Domino
The Doobie Brothers /
    Michael McDonald
The Drifters
Earth, Wind, and Fire
En Vogue
The Eurythmics /
    Annie Lennox
The Fifth Dimension
The Four Tops
Aretha Franklin
The Fugees
Kenny G
J. Geils Band
The Guess Who /
    Bachman-Turner Overdrive
Buddy Guy
Bill Haley
Hall and Oates
Isaac Hayes

Jimi Hendrix
John Hiatt
Whitney Houston
Howlin' Wolf
Chris Isaak
The Isley Brothers
Janet Jackson
Michael Jackson
The Jackson 5
Etta James
Rick James
Janis Joplin
R. Kelly
Albert King
B. B. King
Rahsaan Roland Kirk
Patti LaBelle
Huey Lewis and the News
Little Feat
Loggins and Messina /
    Kenny Loggins
Los Lobos
The Lovin' Spoonful
Brian McKnight
Barbara Mandrell
Manhattan Transfer
Johnny Mathis
Curtis Mayfield
Van Morrison
The Neville Brothers /
    Aaron Neville
New Edition / Bobby Brown
Graham Parker
Wilson Pickett
The Platters
The Pointer Sisters
Prince
Queen Latifah
Bonnie Raitt
Lou Rawls
Martha Reeves and the
    Vandellas
Charlie Rich
Smokey Robinson
The Rolling Stones
Diana Ross
Sade

Boz Scaggs
Selena
Tupac Shakur
Sly and the Family Stone
The Spinners
Donna Summer
The Supremes
Keith Sweat
The Temptations
George Thorogood and the
    Destroyers
Ike and Tina Turner /
    Tina Turner
Ritchie Valens
Luther Vandross
Tom Waits
Dionne Warwick
Barry White
Vanessa Williams
Jackie Wilson
The Winans
Bobby Womack
Stevie Wonder
The Yardbirds

ROCK and ROCK AND ROLL
Bryan Adams
Air Supply
The Allman Brothers Band
America
The Animals
Fiona Apple
Asia
The B-52's
Bad Company
The Band
The Beach Boys
The Beatles
Beck
Pat Benatar
Chuck Berry
Blues Traveler
Blur
Boston
David Bowie
James Brown
Jackson Browne

Buffalo Springfield
Bush
The Byrds
Captain Beefheart and the
    Magic Band
Mary Chapin Carpenter
The Cars
Johnny Cash
Rosanne Cash
The Chambers Brothers
Cheap Trick
Chicago
Eric Clapton
The Clash
The Coasters
Eddie Cochran
Joe Cocker
Paula Cole
Phil Collins
Elvis Costello
Counting Crows
The Cranberries
Robert Cray
Cream
Creedence Clearwater Revival
    / John Fogerty
Crosby, Stills, Nash, and Young
Sheryl Crow
The Cure
Dick Dale
Deep Purple
Def Leppard
Neil Diamond
Bo Diddley
Ani DiFranco
Dion and the Belmonts / Dion
Dire Straits / Mark Knopfler
Dr. John
Fats Domino
The Doobie Brothers /
    Michael McDonald
The Doors
The Dream Syndicate
Duran Duran
Bob Dylan
Sheila E.
The Eagles

Steve Earle
Sheena Easton
Echo and the Bunnymen
Duane Eddy
Electric Light Orchestra /
    Jeff Lynne
Melissa Etheridge
The Eurythmics /
    Annie Lennox
The Everly Brothers
Fleetwood Mac
Foreigner
The Four Seasons / Frankie Valli
Peter Frampton
Aretha Franklin
Peter Gabriel
J. Geils Band
The Gin Blossoms
The Go-Go's
Green Day
The Guess Who /
    Bachman-Turner Overdrive
Guns n' Roses
Woody Guthrie
Buddy Guy
Bill Haley
Hall and Oates
George Harrison
P. J. Harvey
Heart
Jimi Hendrix
Don Henley
Buddy Holly / The Crickets
Hootie and the Blowfish
Billy Idol
INXS
Chris Isaak
The Isley Brothers
Joe Jackson
Etta James
Rick James
Jan and Dean
Jane's Addiction /
    Porno for Pyros
Jefferson Airplane /
    Jefferson Starship
Jethro Tull

Billy Joel
Elton John
Rickie Lee Jones
Janis Joplin
Journey
Carole King
The Kinks
Kiss
Gladys Knight and the Pips
Led Zeppelin
John Lennon
Huey Lewis and the News
Jerry Lee Lewis
Little Richard
Los Lobos
The Lovin' Spoonful
Lynyrd Skynyrd
Paul McCartney
The Mamas and the Papas
Manhattan Transfer
Marilyn Manson
Johnny Mathis
The Dave Matthews Band
Meat Loaf
John Mellencamp
George Michael / Wham!
Midnight Oil
Steve Miller
The Monkees
Alanis Morissette
Van Morrison
Steve Morse
Mötley Crüe
Randy Newman
Olivia Newton-John
Ted Nugent
Oasis
Sinéad O'Connor
Oingo Boingo
Roy Orbison
Tony Orlando and Dawn
The Osmonds
Robert Palmer
The Alan Parsons Project
Carl Perkins
Tom Petty and the
    Heartbreakers

Phish
Pink Floyd
The Platters
The Pointer Sisters
The Police
Elvis Presley
The Pretenders
Prince
John Prine
Bonnie Raitt
The Rascals
The Red Hot Chili Peppers
Lou Reed
R.E.M.
REO Speedwagon
The Righteous Brothers
The Rolling Stones
The Ronettes
Linda Ronstadt
The Runaways
Todd Rundgren
Neil Sedaka
Bob Seger
Selena
Carly Simon
The Smiths / Morrissey
Sonny and Cher / Cher
The Specials
Bruce Springsteen
Steely Dan
Steppenwolf
Rod Stewart
Sting
The Stone Temple Pilots
The Stray Cats / Brian Setzer
Styx
Taj Mahal
James Taylor
Tears for Fears
10,000 Maniacs /
    Natalie Merchant
Richard Thompson
George Thorogood and the
    Destroyers
Three Dog Night
Traffic / Steve Winwood /
    Dave Mason

Ike and Tina Turner /
    Tina Turner
The Turtles
U2
Ritchie Valens
Van Halen
Velvet Underground
The Ventures
Tom Waits
The Wallflowers
The Who / Pete Townshend
Hank Williams
Bobby Womack
X
XTC
The Yardbirds
Neil Young
Warren Zevon
The Zombies
ZZ Top

ROCKABILLY

Johnny Cash
Eddie Cochran
Duane Eddy
Bill Haley
Buddy Holly / The Crickets
Chris Isaak
Jerry Lee Lewis
Roy Orbison
Carl Perkins
Elvis Presley
Charlie Rich
Marty Robbins
The Stray Cats / Brian Setzer
Conway Twitty
Hank Williams

SKA

The English Beat
Bob Marley
No Doubt
Oingo Boingo
The Specials
Sublime

SOFT ROCK *See* **ADULT CONTEMPORARY and SOFT ROCK**

SOUL
Average White Band
Babyface
Anita Baker
Bobby "Blue" Bland
Michael Bolton
Booker T. and the MG's
Boyz II Men
James Brown
Mariah Carey
Ray Charles
Natalie Cole
The Commodores
Sam Cooke
Earth, Wind, and Fire
The Fifth Dimension
The Four Tops
Aretha Franklin
Marvin Gaye
Al Green
Hall and Oates
James Ingram
Janet Jackson
Michael Jackson
The Jackson 5
Etta James

Tom Jones
Janis Joplin
R. Kelly
Albert King
Gladys Knight and the Pips
Patti LaBelle
Brian McKnight
Curtis Mayfield
The Neville Brothers /
    Aaron Neville
New Edition / Bobby Brown
The Ohio Players
The O'Jays
Teddy Pendergrass
Wilson Pickett
The Rascals
Lou Rawls
Otis Redding
Charlie Rich
The Righteous Brothers
Smokey Robinson
Diana Ross
Sam and Dave
Carlos Santana
Boz Scaggs
Sly and the Family Stone
The Staple Singers
Rod Stewart
Donna Summer
The Supremes

The Temptations
TLC
Luther Vandross
Barry White
Bobby Womack
Stevie Wonder

SOUTHERN ROCK
The Allman Brothers Band
Little Feat
Lynyrd Skynyrd

SPOKEN WORD
Laurie Anderson
Black Flag / Henry Rollins
Captain Beefheart and the
    Magic Band

TECHNO and HOUSE
The Chemical Brothers
The Orb
The Prodigy

WESTERN SWING
Bill Haley
George Strait
Bob Wills and His Texas
    Playboys

Popular Musicians

Index of Song and Album Titles

Popular Musicians

Index of Song and Album Titles

Ba-Dop-Boom-Bang, 436

Baba O'Riley, 1156

Babe, 1043

Babe I'm Gonna Leave You, 43, 631

Baby Baby, 438

Baby-Baby-Baby, 1076

Baby Blue, 1036

Baby Come Close, 915

Baby, Come to Me, 518

Baby Don't Forget My Number, 727

Baby, Don't Get Hooked on Me, 284-285

Baby Don't Go, 1003, 1005

Baby I Love You, 925, 927

Baby I Love Your Way, 403

Baby I Need Your Loving, 401

Baby I'm-a Want You, 130-131

Baby, Let's Play House, 848

Baby Love, 1051

Baby, Now That I've Found You, 615

Baby Please Don't Go, 781

Baby Talk, 546

Baby Workout, 1168

Babylon and On, 1018

Babylon Sisters, 1023

Baby's Gotten Good at Goodbye, 1036

Bachman-Turner Overdrive, 451

Back, 789

Back at Your Ass for the Nine-4, 1103

Back from Hell, 936

Back Here on Earth, 642

Back Home Again, 299

Back in Black, 5, 67

Back in My Arms Again, 1051

Back in the High Life, 1085

Back in the U.S.A., 94

Back in the U.S.S.R, 77

Back N Tha Day, 323

Back on the Bus Y'All, 516-517

Back on the Chain Gang, 852

Back Stabbers, 792

Back to Avalon, 649

Back 2 the Base, 1180

Back to the Egg, 666

Back Up Train, 444

Backstage, 1005

Bad, 265, 538, 1105

Bad Animals, 482

Bad, Bad Leroy Brown, 264

Bad Blood, 214, 960

Bad Boy/Having a Party, 1112

Bad Boys, 715

Bad Case of Loving You (Doctor, Doctor), 803

Bad Company, 55

Bad Girl, 915, 960

Bad Girls, 1047

Bad Goodbyc, A, 98

Bad Influence, 256

Bad Karma, 1204

Bad Liver and a Broken Heart, 1132

Bad Luck Blues, 589

Bad Luck Streak in Dancing School, 1203

Bad Medicine, 119

Bad Moon Rising, 261, 1001-1002

Bad to the Bone, 1072-1073

Bad Wisdom, 1122

Badge, 259

Badmotorfinger, 1007

Baduizm, 56-57

Baggy Pants, 546

Baile Esta Cumbia, 967

Balance, 1117

Balance of Power, 364

Ball and Chain, 575

Ball of Confusion (That's What the World Is Today), 1065, 1094

Ballad of a Teenage Queen, 172

Ballad of Easy Rider, 155

Ballad of Jed Clampett, The, 742

Ballad of Peter Pumpkinhead, The, 1183

Ballad of Sally Rose, The, 474

Ballads, 887

Ballads, Blues, and Boasters, 85

Ballbreaker, 5

Bamba, La, 651-652, 1109, 1111

Bamboleo, 432

Banana Boat Song, 84-85

Banana Wind, 151

Band, The, 62, 63, 345

Band of Gypsys, 486

Band on the Run, 665, 666

Bang Bang Bang, 183

Bang Bang (My Baby Shot Me Down), 1003, 1005

Bang the Drum All Day, 940

Banned in the U.S.A., 1103

Banquet, 734

Barabajagal, 330

Barbra Joan Streisand, 1042

Barbra Streisand Album, The, 1042

Barbra: The Concert, 1042

Bare Trees, 395

Bargain, 1156

Bark, 553

Bark at the Moon, 103

Barrel of a Gun, 302

Barry, 694

Barry and Glodean, 1154

Barry Lyndon, 197

Barry Manilow II, 694

Barry White Sings for Someone You Love, 1154

Barry White's Greatest Hits, 1154

Barry White's Greatest Hits, Vol. 2, 1154

Barrytown, 1022

Bartender's Blues, 569

Basement Tapes, The, 61, 64, 348

Basie Swings, Bennett Sings, 89

Basket Case, 446

Bat out of Hell, 708-709, 941

Bat out of Hell II: Back into Hell, 708, 709

Battle of Epping Forest, The, 425

Battle of the Blue and the Grey, The, 81

Battle Rages On, The, 295

Bayou Country, 260, 263

B.B.D. (I Thought It Was Me), 765

Be-Bop Baby, 757, 758

Be for Real, 219

Be Here Now, 785

Be My Baby, 925, 927

Be on Your Merry Way, 589

Be Yourself Tonight, 381

Beach Boys Concert, 67

Beach Boys' Party, The, 67

Beach Boys Today, The, 67

Beaches, 719

Beaches of Cheyenne, The, 134

Beacon Street Collection, The, 779

Beat, 599

Index of Song and Album Titles

Index of Song and Album Titles

Popular Musicians

Index of Song and Album Titles

Index of Song and Album Titles

Index of Song and Album Titles

Index of Song and Album Titles

Index of Song and Album Titles

Index of Song and Album Titles

Index of Song and Album Titles

Index of Song and Album Titles

Popular Musicians

Index of Song and Album Titles

Index of Song and Album Titles

Index of Song and Album Titles

Index of Song and Album Titles

Index of Song and Album Titles

Index of Song and Album Titles

Popular Musicians

Index of Song and Album Titles

Index of Song and Album Titles

Index of Song and Album Titles

Index of Song and Album Titles

Index of Song and Album Titles

Index of Song and Album Titles

Popular Musicians

Index of Song and Album Titles

Popular Musicians

Index of Song and Album Titles

Popular Musicians

Index of Song and Album Titles

Index of Song and Album Titles

Popular Musicians

Index of Song and Album Titles

Popular Musicians

Index of Song and Album Titles

Index of Song and Album Titles

Popular Musicians

World Outside, 865
Worried Man, A, 600
Would I Lie to You, 380
Would You Lay with Me, 1091, 1093
Wouldn't It Be Good, 1074
Wouldn't It Be Nice, 64, 67
WPA Blues, 1158
Wrap Around Joy, 597
Wrapped Around Your Finger, 845
Wrath of My Madness, 874
Wreck of the Edmund Fitzgerald, The, 642
Wreck of the Hesperus, 862
Wreck on the Highway, 1014
Wrecking Ball, 474
Writer, 597
Wrong, 555
Wrong Side of Memphis, 1189
Wurlitzer Prize, The, 554
Wynonna, 581

X, 520
X Factor, The, 521
X-Static, 467
Xanadu, 771
XXX, 549
XXX's & OOO's, 1189

Y Kant Tori Read, 28
Ya Lo Se Que Tu Te Vas, 966
Ya Se Va, 966
Yah Mo B There, 518
Yakety Yak, 212, 214
Ye Yo, 56
Year of Sunday, 957
Year 2000, The, 793
Years, 686
Yellow Bird, 1125
Yellow Moon, 764
Yellow Rose of Texas, The, 1090
Yellow Submarine, 74, 78
Yentl, 1042
Yes, 1193
Yes Album, The, 1193
Yes I Am, 379
Yes, I'm Ready, 584
Yes We Can Can, 840
YesIThinkTheyOughtaNameADrink AfterYou, 859

Yessongs, 1193
Yesterday, 73, 78, 118, 185
Yesterday . . . and Today, 74, 78
Yesterday Once More, 168
Yesterday, Today and Tomorrow, 1012
Yesterday When I Was Young, 200, 202
Yesterday's Wine, 761
Yield, 821
Y.M.C.A., 1128
Yo! Bum Rush the Show, 868
You Ain't Seen Nothing Yet, 450
You Ain't Woman Enough (to Take My Man), 658
You and I, 544
You and Me, 1152
You and Me Against the World, 893
You Are So Beautiful, 217
You Are the Sunshine of My Life, 1174, 1176
You Baby, 1097
You Beat Me to the Punch, 914
You Belong to Me, 332, 974
You Better Run, 885
You Better Sit Down Kids, 1005
You Came, You Saw, You Conquered, 926
You Can All Join In, 1083
You Can Dance, 682
You Can Do Magic, 24
You Can Get It If You Really Want, 206
You Can Have Her, 554
You Can Tune a Piano, but You Can't Tuna Fish, 903
You Can't Always Get What You Want, 922
You Can't Do That on Stage Anymore, Volume 1, 1202
You Can't Hurry Love, 1051
You Could Have Been with Me, 358
You Didn't Have to Be So Nice, 656
You Don't Bring Me Flowers, 306-307, 1041-1042
You Don't Know Like I Know, 948
You Don't Know Me at All, 488
You Don't Mess Around with Jim, 263, 265
You Don't Stand Another Chance, 529

You Get Me Hummin', 948
You Get What You Play For, 903
You Give Good Love, 504-505
You Give Love a Bad Name, 119
You Got Gold, 860
You Got It, 796
You Got Lucky, 829
You Got That Right, 662
(You Gotta) Fight for Your Right (to Party), 68
You Have Placed a Chill, 381
You Haven't Done Nothin, 1176
You Keep Me Hangin' On, 833, 1051
You Keep Running Away, 402
You Know I Love You, 593
You Know What I Mean, 1096
(You Lift Me) Up to Heaven, 668
You Light Up My Life, 911
You Light Up My Life: Inspirational Songs, 911
You Make Lovin' Fun, 393
(You Make Me Feel Like) A Natural Woman, 405, 595
You? Me? Us?, 1071
You Mean the World to Me, 128
You Might Think, 171
You Must Love Me, 682
You Need Love, 319, 631
You Needed Me, 755
You Never Been So Good up to Now, 654
You Oughta Know, 745
You Really Got Me, 601, 604, 629, 1115
You Remind Me, 107
You Remind Me of Somethin', 586
You Send Me, 118, 242
You Shook Me, 630-631, 1028
You Shook Me All Night Long, 3
You Should Be Dancing, 82-83
You Should Be Mine (Don't Waste Your Time), 674
You Showed Me, 291, 1097
You Smile—The Song Begins, 24
You Took the Words Right out of My Mouth, 708
You Turn Me On (I'm a Radio), 734

Index of Song and Album Titles

Name and Subject Index

Popular Musicians

Popular Musicians

Name and Subject Index

Popular Musicians

Franklin, Aretha, 380, 403-407
Franklin, Melvin, 1062
Frantz, Chris, 803, 1056
Fraser, Andy, 54
Free, 54
Freed, Alan, 92, 339, 465, 1109
Freedman, Max, 464
Frehley, Ace, 607
Freiberg, David, 549
Fresh Kid Ice, 1102
Frey, Glenn, 350, 487
Friends of Distinction, The, 387
Fripp, Robert, 372, 416, 597, 845, 1057
Frizzell, Lefty, 407-409, 461
Froom, Mitchell, 1122
Frusciante, John, 888
Fugees, The, 409-411
Fugs, The, 1200
Full Tilt Boogie, 576
Funkadelic, 209-212
Fuqua, Harvey, 418
Furay, Richie, 147, 648

G, Kenny, 412-414
Gabriel, Ana, 414
Gabriel, Peter, 229, 415-417, 424
Gahan, David, 299
Gallagher, Liam, 784
Gallagher, Noel, 190, 784
Gamble, Kenny, and Leon Huff, 821, 833
Gano, Gordon, 1129
Garcia, Jerry, 439
Gardner, Carl, 212
Garfunkel, Art, 514, 978
Garrett, Peter, 720
Gates, David, 129
Gaudio, Bob, 398
Gaugh, Floyd "Bud," 1043
Gaye, Marvin, 417-420, 914
Gayle, Crystal, 420-422
Geffen, David, 142, 351, 487
Geldof, Bob, 342
General Public, 370
Generation X, 512
Genesis, 229, 415, 424-426
Gentry, Teddy, 16
George, Lowell, 643
Gerde's Folk City, 343, 1121

Germs, The, 396
Gibb, Barry, 81, 1041
Gibb, Maurice, 81
Gibb, Robin, 81
Gibbons, Billy, 1205
Gibson, Don, 46
Giger, H. R., 293
Gilbert, Ronnie, 961
Gilder, Nick, 6
Giles, Michael, 597
Gill, Vince, 427-429, 669
Gillan, Ian, 101, 293
Gillespie, Dizzy, 232, 286, 390, 736, 805
Gilmour, David, 834
Gimme Shelter (film), 922
Gin Blossoms, The, 429-431
Ginestera, Alberto, 367
Ginger Baker's Air Force, 1083
Ginsberg, Allen, 347
Gipsy Kings, 431-432
Giraldo, Neil, 86
Glaser, Tompall, 760
Glass, Philip, 30, 336
Glover, Roger, 293
Go-Go's, The, 432-435
Godchaux, Donna, 439
Godchaux, Keith, 439
Godfather of Grunge, 1198
"Godfather of Soul," 137
Goffin, Gerry, and Carole King, 32, 154, 405
Gold, Andrew, 928
Gold, Julie, 448
Golliwogs, The, 260
Gooden, Sam, 706
Goodridge, Robin, 151
Gordon, Florence LaRue, 387
Gordon, Jim, 1082
Gordon, Kim, 1000
Gordon, Mike, 830
Gordy, Berry, Jr., 419, 539, 897-898, 1049, 1167, 1172. *See also* Motown Records
Gore, Martin, 299
Gorgeous George, 139
Gossard, Stone, 818
Goudreau, Barry, 121
Graham, David, 113
Graham, Larry, Jr., 988, 990

Graham Bond Organisation, 257
Gramm, Lou, 396
Grand Funk Railroad, 32, 595
Grandmaster Flash, 435-436
Grant, Amy, 436-438
Grant, Peter, 631, 1187
Granz, Norman, 390
Grateful Dead, The, 439-443
Gravenites, Nick, 576
Grease (film), 771
Grech, Rick, 198, 259, 812, 1082
Green, Al, 443-445, 1167
Green, Peter, 392
Green Day, 445-447
Green on Red, 337
Greenberg, Steve, 472
Greene, Pamela, 945
Greenfield, Howie, 595
Greenfield, Manny, 57
Greenwood, Colin, 876
Greenwood, Jonathan, 876
Grey, Nigel, 842
Griffin, James, 129
Griffith, Nanci, 447-449
Grohl, Dave, 395, 775
Grossman, Albert, 343, 575, 973
Gruska, Jay, 1073
GTO's, The, 1200
Guard, Dave, 599
Guercio, James, 194
Guess Who, The /
    Bachman-Turner Overdrive, 449-451
Guitar Slim, 185
Guns n' Roses, 451-453
Gurtu, Trilok, 678
Guthrie, Arlo, 456
Guthrie, Woody, 343, 453-457, 961
Gutterball, 338
Guy, Billy, 212
Guy, Buddy, 457-460

Hackett, Steve, 424
Haden, Charlie, 677
Hagar, Sammy, 1115
Haggard, Merle, 409, 461-463, 1166
Hail! Hail! Rock 'n' Roll (film), 256
Hair (musical), 388
Hakim, Omar, 1146

Name and Subject Index

Name and Subject Index

Popular Musicians

Name and Subject Index

Name and Subject Index

Name and Subject Index

Popular Musicians